WORKPLACE EQUALITY

Library of Public Policy and Public Administration

Volume 7

General Editor:

DICK W.P. RUITER

Faculty of Public Administration and Public Policy,
University of Twente,
Enschede, The Netherlands

The titles published in this series are listed at the end of this volume.

WORKPLACE EQUALITY

International Perspectives on Legislation, Policy and Practice

edited by

Carol Agocs

Social Science Centre,
The University of Western Ontario,
London, Ontario, Canada

KLUWER LAW INTERNATIONAL

THE HAGUE / LONDON / NEW YORK

A C.I.P. Catalogue record for this book is available from the Library of Congress.

ISBN 90-411-1843-8

Published by Kluwer Law International,
P.O. Box 85889, 2508 CN The Hague, The Netherlands.

Sold and distributed in North, Central and South America
by Kluwer Law International,
101 Philip Drive, Norwell, MA 02061, U.S.A.
kluwerlaw@wkap.com

In all other countries, sold and distributed
by Kluwer Law International, Distribution Centre,
P.O. Box 322, 3300 AH Dordrecht, The Netherlands.

Printed on acid-free paper

To
my father,
John Gordon Wills, Jr.,

and to the memory of
my mother,
Elizabeth Larson Wills

WORKPLACE EQUALITY: INTERNATIONAL PERSPECTIVES ON LEGISLATION, POLICY AND PRACTICE

TABLE OF CONTENTS

WORKPLACE EQUALITY: INTERNATIONAL PERSPECTIVES ON LEGISLATION, POLICY AND PRACTICE

PREFACE

A survey and comparison of workplace equality policies in various parts of the world is long overdue in this era of globalization. While "globalization" has an imprecise meaning, it clearly connotes a trend toward diversity in the populations and labour markets of countries across the world. The growing representation of women in paid employment is a global trend, and in Europe and North America, new sources of immigration as well as an aging population have contributed significantly to the diversity of the labour market. Despite the clear benefits of diversity to the economic, social and cultural life of many nations, what is troubling is that globalization has also brought new forms of oppression and discrimination for working people.

From another perspective, little has changed: both diversity and inequality have been defining characteristics of societies formed by immigration, colonialism and conquest. Discrimination in employment on the basis of gender, race and disability is a persisting reality, and there is nothing new about the oppression of indigenous peoples and their exclusion from employment opportunities. What is new is the development of a global concern about inequality, social justice and human rights, including the rights to employment, fair compensation and opportunities for development on the job. The progressive face of globalization is a growing worldwide consciousness that we are all connected as part of one human family, and that we share the responsibility to develop the human potential of all its members.

The impetus to develop effective policy responses to discrimination in employment has come from several sources. These include principles established in international and national human rights legislation and case law, political advocacy by those who experience discrimination and their allies, and economic pressures to connect with a diverse marketplace and to maximize the productivity of human resources. Several countries have responded to persisting patterns of workplace discrimination by developing and implementing affirmative action or employment equity policies. These proactive approaches seek to end and prevent discriminatory employment practices and to work toward a workplace that is representative of the diversity of the labour market.

This book examines equality policy approaches that eight countries have established in response to systemic discrimination in employment on the basis of gender, race, religion, ethnicity or culture, disability, aboriginal status or immigrant status. The first and last chapters provide theoretical perspectives on the problem of systemic discrimination in employment and an overview of alternative policy and institutional responses. The remaining chapters survey various aspects of equality policy and its implementation in Australia, Canada, India, Malaysia, the Netherlands, Northern Ireland, South Africa and the United States.

The development and completion of this project during 2000 – 2001 was made possible by a research grant from the Social Sciences and Humanities Research Council of Canada and a sabbatical from the University of Western Ontario. Harish C. Jain's encouragement and collaboration throughout the project has been instrumental and is greatly appreciated. The authors who contributed chapters to *Workplace Equality* are dispersed across five continents and seven countries. Their expertise and commitment has made this project possible. Penny Abel's formatting skills were indispensable.

Employment equity and affirmative action are poorly understood by many, and in some settings they have faced misinformed and damaging opposition and recent retreats from earlier policy commitments. Yet discrimination in employment remains an intractable problem that will have to be addressed in the interest of productivity as well as social justice. *Workplace Equality* represents the authors' joint effort to initiate the comparative study of policy responses to systemic discrimination in the workplace, and to stimulate the sharing of knowledge and experience that may lead to the development of more effective approaches to equality policy and practice across the world.

CHAPTER 1

CAROL AGOCS

SYSTEMIC DISCRIMINATION IN EMPLOYMENT: MAPPING THE ISSUE AND THE POLICY RESPONSES

Inequality is a world-wide reality for women, indigenous peoples, persons with disabilities, and peoples who are racial or ethnic minorities – in the sense that they lack access to the power and opportunity available to dominant groups in their societies (on women see Anker, 1997; Neft and Levine, 1997; Roos, 1985). Available data suggest that levels of ethnic or racial discrimination against immigrants in employment are similar in Australia, Canada and the United States (Reitz, 1998: 39). A research program sponsored by the International Labour Organisation, using a standardised research approach involving testing, has found pervasive and widespread discrimination in hiring against workers who are ethnic minorities and/or immigrants in industrialised countries (Zegers de Beijl, 1997). In Britain, Black, Indian, Pakistani and Bangladeshi men and women face disadvantage in the labour market that is partly due to discrimination by employers (Carmichael and Woods, 2000). In Canada, Christofides and Swidinsky (1994) found significant wage differentials on the basis of race and gender that are not explained by productivity-related factors. While the impacts of employment discrimination take varied forms for different groups across the world and their manifestations have changed over time, there are some consistent patterns. These include discrimination in hiring, harassment in the workplace, wage and salary disadvantage, higher incidence of unemployment and underemployment, concentration in a restricted range of occupations, exclusion from management positions where power is concentrated, and limited access to career advancement and benefits such as pensions. In India, women and other disadvantaged segments of the population (scheduled castes and scheduled tribes) work mostly within the informal, unorganised sector and are unprotected by employment standards legislation, unions and social security benefits (Jain, 2001; Jain and Ratnam, 2001; Hodges-Aeberhard and Raskin, 1997: 43). In many countries exploitation of undocumented migrants is a matter of concern. These manifestations of discrimination are institutionalised as typical and persisting patterns, not unusual events. Legislated positive action programs that are effectively enforced have been recommended by the ILO as an approach to combating employment discrimination (Zegers de Beijl, 1997).

This chapter provides an overview of the concept of systemic discrimination in employment with illustrative examples from the research literature and selected court decisions. Next, it surveys affirmative action and employment equity policies in seven countries and assesses these approaches as strategic responses to the problem of systemic discrimination. In the discussion of systemic discrimination the majority of sources and examples cited relate to Canada and the United States, but it is suggested that the conceptual frameworks proposed here have broad applicability. The remaining chapters in this book present specific discussions of policy responses to discrimination, in most cases affirmative action policies, that are found in eight countries including Australia,

C. Agocs (ed.), Workplace Equality, 1–33.

Canada, India, Malaysia, the Netherlands, Northern Ireland, South Africa and the United States.

SYSTEMIC DISCRIMINATION IN THE WORKPLACE: MAPPING THE ISSUE

The concept of systemic discrimination is discussed here in relation to the behaviour of individuals and groups within the workplace: the organisation or work setting is taken as the unit of analysis. Of interest are the patterns of organisational behaviour that create disadvantage for people who identify themselves, or who are identified, in terms of gender, race, ethnic background, culture, religion, ability/disability status, or combinations of these categories. Organisational behaviours that have been shown to have discriminatory impacts in some circumstances include policies, practices and decision-making surrounding jobs and careers, as well as norms, values, attitudes, and informal social behaviour and communication patterns. Discriminatory impacts can occur across a spectrum of employment decisions including access to employment, terms and conditions of employment, access to training and development, promotion, evaluation of performance, task and work assignment, compensation, opportunity to participate in decision-making, and termination of employment. The quality of work life, including informal social interaction on the job, a sense of belonging, job satisfaction and personal identity may also be significantly damaged by workplace discrimination. Employment discrimination shapes the economic circumstances of the employee who experiences it and of dependent family members through the life course, from children's well-being and access to opportunity, to economic status during the years following retirement from paid work. These impacts on individuals manifest themselves at an aggregate level. For example, as a group, women and their children in single parent families tend to live in poverty, and women on their own are likely to live out their retirement years in poverty. These realities are partly due to systemic discrimination that creates inequality in career development, wages and benefits for women in the labour market (Phillips and Phillips, 1993). The link between socio-economic disadvantage and inequality in the labour market is also well documented for aboriginal people, immigrants, and persons with disabilities (Jenson, 2000).

Systemic discrimination may be defined as patterns of behaviour that are part of the social and administrative structures of the workplace, and that create or perpetuate a position of relative disadvantage for some groups, and privilege for other groups, or for individuals on account of their group identity. The analysis or diagnosis of systemic discrimination means adopting a structural perspective on the workplace and recognising the recurrent, patterned nature of some discriminatory behaviours and the processes through which they become institutionalised. Attention is centred on the "institutional arrangements" (Alvarez, 1979:ix) that present barriers or blockages, or that impose extra burdens, in ways that impede the full and equal participation of people with disabilities, women, aboriginal peoples, racial minorities, or others who may experience discrimination. Other terms used in the literature as synonyms for systemic discrimination include "institutional discrimination," "structural discrimination," "constructive discrimination," and "oppression" (e.g. Young, 1990, ch. 2). The terms "racism" and "sexism", when used to refer to behaviours embedded in social structures and reinforced in ideologies, may also connote systemic discrimination (e.g. Essed, 1990).

An analytical focus on the social and administrative structures of the workplace is not meant to suggest that individuals are not responsible for discriminatory behaviour. Patterns of organisational behaviour are clearly enacted through the behaviours of individuals that over time create, reinforce, perpetuate and change organisational structures and cultures. Individuals in positions of authority have legal and ethical responsibility for the kinds of organisational policies and practices they help to create and condone. However, organisational behaviours embedded in policies, practices and organisational culture persist as individuals come and go. These institutionalised patterns shape the behaviour of individuals who enter the organisation through processes of socialisation as well as formal and informal rewards and sanctions that serve to reinforce and perpetuate patterns of discrimination, even if this effect is not intended. In the words of Iris Marion Young, "the conscious actions of many individuals daily contribute to maintaining and reproducing oppression, but those people are usually simply doing their jobs or living their lives, and do not understand themselves as agents of oppression" (Young, 1990: 32). Identifying and changing discriminatory patterns of organisational behaviour requires a structural perspective, a stakeholder-based analysis, a collective learning process, and a sharing of responsibility for changing institutionalised patterns of discrimination. What is needed is not a determination of guilt, but a rigorous analysis of the processes through which systemic discrimination is created and perpetuated, in order to eliminate and prevent the occurrence of discriminatory behaviours and provide appropriate and fair remedies and future opportunities for those who have been disadvantaged.

It is also important to emphasise that categories and labels such as "women", "aboriginal peoples", "racial minorities" and "people with disabilities" are gross, imprecise, socially constructed, and subject to manipulation for a variety of ends (Bacchi, 1996). Individuals may fit uneasily into such categories, which clearly do not do justice to the complexities of personal identity and experience, particularly when identity spans these categories. For example, women who are members of racial minority or aboriginal populations, or who are disabled, often find that their experiences are not addressed by analyses of barriers faced by "women", or "racial minorities", or "persons with disabilities", and that they face additional and unique forms of discrimination (Bell, Denton and Nkomo, 1992; Boyd, 1992; Duclos, 1993; Epstein, 1997; Karambayya, 1997; Doren and Benz, 1998). An analysis of systemic discrimination in a workplace can and should be a diagnostic and problem-solving exercise that enquires into the distinctive situations and experiences of individuals, using what is known about group patterns as a guide.

Kanter (1979: 54) suggests that "the structure of opportunity, the structure of power, and relative numbers (proportions and social composition) form the central explanatory dimensions of an integrated structural model of human behaviour in organisations." In her view, "it is the relationship between opportunity, power and relative numbers that indicates the presence of institutional racism/sexism." The distribution of women and men, and of persons with disabilities and members of racial and ethnic minorities, within the organisation's structures of power and opportunity is often the starting point for an analysis of systemic discrimination in the workplace. The analysis continues with an examination of the specific employment policies and practices that, singly and as an inter-connected system, create barriers, blockages or burdens for members of marginalised groups.

In human rights law as it evolved in the United States, Canada, the United Kingdom and Australia in the 1960s and 1970s, employment discrimination was (and still is) generally viewed as an idiosyncratic incident or series of related incidents, and as an interaction between individuals. Diagnosis and remedy require the victim of discrimination to complain against an identified perpetrator. The complaint triggers a process of gathering and weighing the evidence and making a decision as to whether a specific allegation of illegal discrimination occurred against the complainant. This complaint-based individualistic paradigm in which discrimination consists of unequal treatment of specific individuals by other individuals remains the dominant model for understanding and responding to discrimination. In practice, most such complaints are dealt with informally through mediation or conciliation, or withdrawn because of delays, or dismissed for administrative reasons or for lack of evidence acceptable in legal proceedings; it is particularly difficult to amass evidence of discrimination in hiring (Murdrick, 1997). In rare cases courts or tribunals may render decisions substantiating the complaint and may order some form of compensation for victims and/or penalty for perpetrators. In Canada only one to two percent of discrimination complaints to the Canadian Human Rights Commission in a year are referred to a tribunal (Birenbaum and Porter, 2000). Rarely does the human rights process lead to an acknowledgement that the workplace environment and its practices have caused, permitted, condoned or legitimated the illegal behaviour. Hence, an analysis of discrimination from the perspective of the individualistic complaint-based model has a limited capacity to lead to organisational change that will prevent discrimination from occurring in the future. Nor is there any way to know on the basis of the small number of complaints filed and evaluated how widespread discrimination in employment is, or what specific forms it takes – a benefit to those who would deny the significance of discrimination as an issue of concern.

In the 1970s, scholars and human rights legal experts as well as equality seekers made a significant theoretical advance in recognising the role of adverse impact discrimination in perpetuating workplace inequality. Adverse impact discrimination occurs through the application of a policy or practice that may appear neutral, but when it is applied to all employees in the same way it may produce unequal results – and disadvantage—for those who are different from the population for which that rule was designed. For example, if a police force uses a height requirement in hiring, this would create an unfair disadvantage for women as a group, as well as for people of Asian or aboriginal ancestry, for a reason that has no proven relationship to job performance. If a practice that has adverse impact is not demonstrably necessary for the operation of the organisation's business, and if its purpose can be served by an alternative practice that has less (or no) discriminatory impact, then the continued use of the discriminatory practice cannot be justified.

Adverse impact discrimination may occur even if there is no evidence of intent or motive to discriminate. Behaviour and its results are what matters in identifying discrimination, a principle established in the United States Supreme Court case of Griggs v. Duke Power Company (1971). In Canada, a landmark decision of the Supreme Court defined systemic discrimination as "discrimination that results from the simple operation of established procedures of recruitment, hiring and promotion, none of which is necessarily designed to promote discrimination" (Action travail des femmes v. Canadian National Railway, 1987: 1139).

Understanding of the systemic nature of workplace discrimination evolved still further during the 1970s and 1980s with the realisation that practices having adverse impact, like instances of unequal treatment, might not be isolated events. Discrimination may be systemic in the sense that there are mutually reinforcing behaviours that perpetuate traditional structures of power and opportunity, and exclude or create disadvantage for outsiders to those structures. An example is the historical and continuing pattern in many workplaces of women's concentration in clerical and administrative occupations with low pay, no union protection, and truncated career ladders providing no possibility of advancement to positions of decision-making power. These occupations have been especially vulnerable during the wave of downsizing and creation of contingent jobs that is sweeping over organisations, particularly in the public sector. On the other hand, women who challenge workplace norms by venturing out of the pink collar ghetto into the better paid traditionally male occupations, such as the skilled trades or engineering, may be "punished" by being targeted for more harassment than they would experience in traditionally women's work. These interlocking patterns of gender segregation in turn reinforce traditional stereotypes and hiring decisions regarding women and the jobs they "prefer" and are "best suited" for, and discourage women from considering non-traditional work. In addition to facing all of these issues, racial minority and aboriginal women may confront racial harassment and inequality in pay and promotion that exceeds that experienced by white women. The job ghettos, glass ceilings, wage discrimination, under-employment and harassment that continue to characterise the position of marginalised groups in the power and opportunity structures of organisations form mutually reinforcing elements of a system that perpetuates inequality.

The systemic nature of inequality in employment extends beyond the workplace, whose social relations reflect the structure of the surrounding society. For example in Northern Ireland, a persisting pattern of educational and residential segregation on the basis of religion reinforces the segregation and stratification of Catholics and Protestants in employment (Heaton and Teague, 1997). Segregated educational and residential patterns, and institutionalised inequality in education, also form interlocking parts of the system of inequality in employment on the basis of race in the United States and South Africa.

Many of the customary practices as well as policies that prevail in the workplace were designed to fit the traditionally dominant group in the labour market – white able-bodied males of European cultural heritage, in the North American context. Privileges and penalties based on race and gender were explicit in the establishment of structures of hiring, job assignment, pay and promotion that survive today and tend to persist unless pressure for change is intense (Baron, 1994: 73-75). Policies and practices designed by and for the dominant white male able-bodied employee population, when applied to employees who are different from this norm, create unfair discrimination.

During the 1980s and 1990s, human rights decisions and experts in the field of employment discrimination called attention to employers' failure to accommodate diversity within their workforce as a form of adverse impact discrimination. For example an employee who has a disability that impairs mobility cannot work in a facility that is not accessible, even if she is qualified and able to perform. In this instance the employer has a duty to accommodate the employee or applicant with a disability, short of undue hardship for the employer, by making the workplace accessible. Not to do so creates a form of systemic discrimination in that treating people who are not alike in identical ways produces unequal results: people who are "different" suffer disadvantage or exclusion for arbitrary reasons that are unrelated to their ability to do the job. According to this analysis, employers have a duty to accommodate those who are "different" by creating exceptions for them to a rule that generally applies to the majority of employees, if that rule results in discrimination, and if the job can be done without the rule. In the case of an employee with a disability, the employer is obligated to "make some investment to enable" the employee's work performance (Mudrick, 1997:55). However, dealing with "difference" by means of accommodation on a case-by-case basis fails to challenge the norms and patterns in the workplace that construct customary practice as normative, and what is "different" as aberrant. For example, the presence of a person with a disability in the workplace remains exceptional, and the person remains marginal to the life of the organisation.

In Canada, a 1999 decision of the Supreme Court established a unified approach to dealing with both forms of adverse impact discrimination, as well as with direct discrimination that occurs when an employer adopts a standard for the purpose of discriminating (British Columbia v. BCGSEU, 1999). The unanimous decision dealt specifically with the employer's duty to change an employment standard in order to avoid adverse impact. The employer, the government of British Columbia, had adopted a set of minimum fitness standards for all its forest fire fighters that included an aerobic test involving running. Tawney Meiorin, a woman who had performed successfully as a fire fighter for three years prior to the adoption of this standard, passed three of the fitness tests but failed to pass the running test after four tries, and was dismissed from her job. She filed a grievance alleging that the aerobic standard discriminated against women. Evidence demonstrated that women have a lower aerobic capacity than men do, on average, and that most women would not be able to increase their aerobic capacity enough to pass the test even with training. The Court held that a fitness test for fire fighters based on a standard that most women are physiologically incapable of achieving discriminates against women. The B.C. human rights code states that an employer can impose a standard that is a bona fide occupational requirement even if it results in discrimination. However the Court found that the particular aerobic test used by the employer could not be justified as a requirement for the safe and efficient performance of the job of fire fighter by either men or women. The test had been standardised on existing (male) fire fighters and did not establish the minimum aerobic capacity that men or women must have to perform as fire fighters. Meiorin was reinstated to her position with compensation for lost wages and benefits.

In this case the Court set out a practical three-step test for determining whether an employer has a valid claim that an occupational requirement that discriminates against women or any other group protected under human rights codes is bona fide, or necessary to the performance of a job. First, the purpose of the standard must be rationally connected to the requirements of the job. Second, the standard or requirement must have been adopted by the employer in good faith, in an honest belief that it is necessary to the fulfilment of the work-related purpose, and not with the intention of discriminating. Third, the employer must show that the specific requirement is necessary to job performance and cannot be replaced by an alternative requirement that would serve the purpose without discriminating, and without creating undue hardship for the employer.

In other words, a job standard or requirement that has adverse effects on members of a group can remain in place only if it is necessary for the performance of the work, and if there are no reasonable alternatives to using this standard. It is not acceptable for the employer to keep the discriminatory standard for which a non-discriminatory alternative is available, and provide an accommodation or exceptional arrangement for individuals who are "different" from the mainstream employee. Speaking for the Court, Chief Justice Beverly McLaughlin explained the reasoning for this as follows:

> The difficulty with this [accommodation] paradigm is that it does not challenge the imbalances of power, or the discourses of dominance, such as racism, ablebodyism and sexism, which result in a society being designed well for some and not for others. It allows those who consider themselves 'normal' to continue to construct institutions and relations in their image, as long as others, when they challenge this construction are 'accommodated'... Accommodation does not go to the heart of the equality question, to the goal of transformation, to an examination of the way institutions and relations must be changed in order to make them available, accessible, meaningful and rewarding for the many diverse groups of which our society is composed (British Columbia v. BCGSEU, 1999: 12).

The remedy for systemic discrimination, in other words, is to change the organisation so that authentic equality is possible in a diverse society. It is not enough to "allow" groups who have been excluded from the workplace to enter if they can conform to the way things have always been done there. Their entry and full participation is a human right, the realisation of which may require the workplace to change its customary practices. To paraphrase Justice McLachlin, it is not enough to "make some concessions to individuals who are 'different'". Substantive equality means "abandoning the idea of 'normal' and working for genuine inclusiveness", rather than seeking assimilation of persons who are "different" by trying to make them "fit into existing systems" (British Columbia v. BCGSEU, 1999:12). Reducing the impacts of systemic discrimination in the workplace requires measures to identify and remove discriminatory policies and practices and replace them with others that accomplish the organisation's purpose without discriminating.

Traditional structures of power and privilege are increasingly questioned and challenged in the contemporary workplace. Yet in many organisations they have not been subjected to critical assessment and revision as the population of the workplace and the nature of work have changed and become more diverse. In the Meiorin decision the Supreme Court of Canada provided practical guidance both for identifying illegal discrimination in policies and practices and for remedying such discrimination, thereby bringing about appropriate changes in the workplace. The Court also extended our understanding of systemic discrimination in employment and clarified the necessity of addressing it by transforming organisations so as to remove the causes of adverse impact against groups.

A significant step has been taken beyond the traditional assumption that equality means assimilation of people who are different into organisations as they are, toward a transformative standard of equity in employment. It acknowledges that workplace equality in a diverse society requires not assimilation, but organisational transformation.

DIAGNOSING SYSTEMIC DISCRIMINATION: SYSTEMS, CULTURE, NUMBERS

Like societies, organisations vary as to the degree of inequality and disadvantage they create for women, aboriginal people, racial or ethnic minorities and people with disabilities. The extent to which discrimination is institutionalised within an organisation, then, is an empirical question – a matter for diagnosis, with reference to symptoms or indicators of discriminatory impacts associated with the policies, practices and culture of organisations.

A large research and theoretical literature, as well as the case law, contains examples of specific ways in which human resource management policies and practices may create barriers or adverse impacts that limit the entry and full participation of some groups, while at the same time preserving privilege for those whom the practices have benefited in the past. Most of this literature addresses inequality and discrimination affecting women and racial minorities, Blacks in particular; there is little published research on specific forms of workplace discrimination confronted by persons with disabilities and by persons of aboriginal ancestry. Research findings document discrimination in organisational decision-making concerning recruitment and selection, job assignment, compensation, terms and conditions of employment, training and development, promotion, performance evaluation, and termination, among other kinds of career-related decisions. Agocs, Burr and Somerset (1992) suggest that when analysing organisational practices to identify potential sources of systemic discrimination it is useful to consider three categories of organisational characteristics: employment systems, organisational culture, and numerical representation and distribution.

Employment Systems

Organisational policies and practices governing human resource management are known collectively as "employment systems". The categories of policies and practices of particular concern are recruitment and selection, training and development, promotion, compensation, retention and termination. Other areas of importance include job assignment, terms and conditions of employment, performance appraisal and feedback from supervisors, and discipline. Employment systems may be formal or informal, and they may be organisation-wide or specific to a work unit.

Some common forms of unequal treatment are obviously motivated by intent to discriminate and are clearly illegal, yet they continue to be used in employment-related decisions. For example, women, but not men, may be asked questions in selection interviews about their family situation and plans for having children. Or a qualified job applicant who does not have a familiar European name, or who speaks with an accent, or has dark skin, may be refused employment (e.g. Brown and Gay, 1994; Billingsley and Muszynski, 1985; Henry and Ginzberg, 1985).

Adverse impact discrimination can be identified in many conventional employment practices. For example, word-of-mouth recruitment through informal networks tends to perpetuate the existing social composition of a workplace (Reskin, McBrier and Kmec, 1999). Use of unstructured employment interviews as an important component of the hiring process may contribute to discriminatory and invalid hiring decisions (e.g. Arvey and Campion, 1982; Graves and Powell, 1988). Hiring decisions that use tests, educational credentials or physical standards that do not provide valid and reliable indicators of required job-related abilities may unfairly screen out aboriginal people, people with disabilities, women or minorities (Hogan and Quigley, 1986). A significant barrier to access to employment for immigrants is employers' failure to accept qualifications and credentials earned in other countries (Calleja, 2000; Kunz, Milan and Schetagne, 2000). Ironically this defeats the purpose of immigration policies which favour immigrants whose education was acquired at the expense of their home countries, yet its potential benefits to the economy of the receiving society are not realised (Calleja, 2000; Reitz, 1998:240).

Sex-typed job assignment based on stereotypes about women's capabilities and interests continues to perpetuate gender segregation (e.g. Bielby and Baron, 1984 and 1986; Collinson, Knights and Collinson, 1990). Channelling Black women and men into racialised managerial jobs whose mandate is to mediate between the organisation and the Black community, customers or employees restricts their career development opportunities while reserving non-racialised management jobs for whites (Collins, 1997).

In a longitudinal study of a large and representative sample of American employees, Maume (1999) found a glass ceiling effect -- Black men, Black women and white women waited longer for promotions to management than white men did. Racial and gender segregation and discrimination in promotion contribute significantly to disadvantage in pay for white and Black women as well as Black men, as compared with white men (Baron and Newman, 1990; Halaby, 1979; Reskin and Ross, 1995). In an analysis of U.S. survey data covering 1972 through 1994, Smith (1997) found a persisting and substantial race-based income gap favouring white men over Black men in positions at the highest level of authority when occupational position, place of residence and human capital attributes were taken into account.

The low representation of women, racial minorities, persons with disabilities and persons of aboriginal ancestry in positions of power is a widespread pattern. A tendency toward "cloning" in decisions about promotion to senior levels of management, such that preference is given to those who are members of the same informal social networks as current managers, is a mechanism for exclusion of women and racial minorities (Brass, 1985; Ibarra, 1993; Kanter, 1978). On the other hand, white and Black men working in occupations in which women are concentrated are highly likely to be promoted out of those occupations into management positions, while both white and Black women in those occupations are much less likely to be promoted (Maume, 1999). This illustrates the importance of attention to overlapping impacts of sexism and racism. Gender and/or race bias has been shown to affect performance appraisal (Mobley, 1982; Dorfman and Loveland, 1986; Simpson, McCarrey and Edwards, 1987), resulting in negative impacts on salary and promotion. Both Steinbeg (1990) and Quaid (1993) demonstrated the adverse impact of "gender neutral" job evaluation schemes in which fewer points are awarded for the skills women use in their jobs than for the skills in men's jobs.

The examples listed above are primarily taken from the research literature, and refer both to studies based on representative samples of the workforce and to case studies in particular organisations. The practices and impacts mentioned may be considered conventional and commonly occurring behaviours. In addition, the extensive documentation available to readers of the case law on employment discrimination provides many detailed examples of systemic discrimination in employment systems (e.g. Action travail des femmes v. Canadian National Railway, 1987).

Organisational Culture

Workplace culture includes organisational behaviours surrounding communication, informal inter-personal interaction and socialising, decision-making practices, expressions of values and attitudes, and norms about behaviour. The culture of the workplace influences the degree to which racial or ethnic minorities, aboriginal people, persons with disabilities and women are accepted, included, valued and rewarded as equal participants in work activities, information networks, and informal social situations involving co-workers. A significant example of the impact of workplace culture is the extent to which harassment on the basis of gender and race occurs and is accepted within an organisation or work unit (Aggarwal, 1987; Cockburn, 1991; Sheppard, 1995/96; Thacker and Ferris, 1991).

A workplace culture that creates adverse impact or a poisoned environment may be permitted or encouraged as a result of decision makers' racist or sexist attitudes and inclinations to engage in stereotyping (Gutek, 1982). The employer may condone behaviours by co-workers, clients, suppliers, subordinates or supervisors that reflect negative or stereotypical attitudes about women, racial minorities or other groups (Larwood et al, 1988; Pettigrew and Martin, 1987). Racial minority men and women report experiences of "subtle" racism in applying for jobs and promotions (Kunz, Milan and Schetagne, 2000). An expectation that women, minorities, aboriginal peoples or persons with disabilities who are hired will change themselves to resemble the dominant white able-bodied male majority also contributes to systemic discrimination within an organisation's culture (Feagin, 1987; Morrison, van Velsor and White, 1987).

Discrimination is perpetuated by an employer's failure to take steps to stop harassment or to improve a discriminatory environment, or failure to express and demonstrate support for equity-oriented organisational change. An organisation's culture is difficult to change. It is unlikely to become more inclusive in the absence of senior management commitment to principles of equity and fairness as demonstrated by public actions to encourage full participation of traditionally under-represented groups (Jacobson, 1985).

Numerical Representation and Distribution

The most obvious indication that systemic discrimination may be a factor in an organisation's systems or culture is the absence or marked under-representation of members of racial minorities, women, persons with disabilities or aboriginal people in a workforce, in comparison with their representation in relevant labour markets. High rates of unemployment, lack of access to employment, and lack of reliable data on employment are realities for persons with disabilities. For example in the European Union, where an estimated 12 percent of the population are disabled, their employment rate is 20 to 30 percent below that for able-bodied people. People with disabilities are over-represented in unskilled or low-skilled jobs and are consequently poorly paid, and at higher risk of termination (European Foundation, 2001).

In addition to lack of access to employment, uneven distribution across the horizontal and vertical dimensions of the organisation are also indicators of a need to scrutinise employment systems and the culture of the workplace to identify barriers to entry, development and promotion. Concentration of women, minorities, persons with disabilities and aboriginal people in a narrow range of jobs, in lower ranks within the organisation, and in part time or temporary positions – and their absence from higher levels of management – is a typical pattern.

A continuing pattern of under-representation despite hiring of members of these groups is symptomatic of a retention problem which often results from harassment, lack of supportive supervision or mentoring, racism or sexism in the organisational climate, or inequity in compensation or promotion (Braddock and McPartland, 1987; Jacobs, 1989). Recent surveys in the United States found that 42 percent of women of colour working in Fortune 1000 companies were looking for new jobs, as were 71 percent of responding members of the Society for Black Engineers (Gilbert and Ivancevich, 2000: footnote 5). During the 1980s and 1990s many women left management positions in large Canadian organisations because of career blockages or harassment (Orser, 2001; Griffin, 1997). Many of these women opted for self-employment, contributing to the leading role of women in job creation during the 1990s. Canadian data also show that members of racial minorities who hold managerial positions are much more likely than white managers to be self-employed (Kunz, Milan and Schetagne, 2000).

Numerical under-representation and imbalance may also influence an organisation's employment systems and culture. For example, absence or near absence of women and minorities from senior management perpetuates a homogeneous culture that tends to exclude those who are not white and male from entry to positions of power. Admitting a single member or a couple of members of a previously excluded group is unlikely to lead to change, since such individuals are highly visible and vulnerable to discrimination and strong pressures to conform to traditional practices (Kanter, 1979; South et al, 1982). A homogeneous leadership group also models a lack of openness to diversity to all within the organisation as well as to the community and prospective job applicants (Kanter, 1978 and 1979; Morrison, van Velsor and White, 1987).

From the perspective of an analysis of systemic discrimination, a lack of representativeness at all levels of a workforce is the most significant evidence of the need for change in an organisation's employment systems and culture. Thus a confidential survey of the workforce using voluntary self-identification in order to determine the numbers and distribution of traditionally marginalised or under-represented groups is often the first step in the diagnosis of systemic discrimination in a workplace. The results of the census provide an indication of where to direct attention in a subsequent diagnosis of employment systems and organisational culture in order to identify and remove discriminatory barriers.

Diagnosing Sources of Systemic Discrimination: The Employment Systems Review

An employment systems review is an analysis of the employment systems used by an employer in order to identify whether they create unequal treatment or adverse impact, and whether they entail requirements or standards that have a rational and valid connection to the requirements of the job. An employment systems review is one of the cornerstones of an affirmative action or employment equity program. It represents a systematic empirical approach to the identification of barriers that may impede the full and equal participation of women, persons with disabilities, aboriginal persons, members of racial or ethnic minorities or other groups that may be disadvantaged in employment. It is important to consider the impact of organisational culture as part of such a review in order to identify discriminatory informal practices such as harassment, marginalisation, exclusion from social or communication networks, or stereotyped patterns of decision-making about promotion or career development.

The participation in an employment systems review of members of groups who may be adversely affected by organisational policies and practices provides an essential source of knowledge about the possible existence of discriminatory barriers. The participation of line and human resource management as well as union representatives brings needed expertise to the process and helps to ensure that the barriers identified will be appropriately addressed as part of an employment equity change process (Agocs, Burr and Somerset, 1992).

ORGANIZATIONAL RESPONSES TO SYSTEMIC DISCRIMINATION

The foregoing analysis suggests a number of considerations involved in a diagnosis of potential sources and types of systemic discrimination in a workplace. Appropriate organisational responses will depend on the specific issues identified in the workforce census and the employment systems review, and on the organisational setting involved. In order to provide effective responses to systemic discrimination an employer's process of organisational change might, in general, consist of the following elements:

1) management commitment, demonstrated in word and deed, to making the organisation a leader in attaining equality of results for all groups, and measures to ensure accountability for progress toward this goal;
2) diagnosis of the current composition of the workforce and of barriers in employment systems and workplace culture that may impede the full and equal participation of members of under-represented and disadvantaged groups;
3) development of goals and timetables for improving their representation in hiring, promotion, and training and development opportunities, and of plans for retention of under-represented groups in a context of restructuring;
4) development of a plan for eliminating sources of adverse impact and unequal treatment in employment systems and organisational culture, and for developing alternative approaches wherever this is possible;
5) development of new measures to attract, retain and develop members of under-represented groups; and

6) development of arrangements to monitor these organisational change activities on an on-going basis, and to make appropriate revisions in organisational policies and practices in order to ensure results, as evidenced by improvements in the representation of members of previously under-represented groups at all levels of the organisation.

These are the elements of an employment equity or affirmative action change process that would contribute to transformative organisational change in persisting patterns of systemic discrimination.

POLICY RESPONSES TO SYSTEMIC DISCRIMINATION

Several countries have adopted policy responses, variously called employment equity, affirmative action or positive action, that recognise systemic discrimination as an issue that must be dealt with in the public interest, and that require employers to take action at the level of the workplace. Such policies are distinguished by being proactive rather than reactive in addressing discrimination: their primary objectives are to remove, prevent and remedy discrimination without requiring its victims to complain or litigate. Hence the purposes of affirmative action or employment equity are not served by individualistic complaint-based processes under human rights statutes. Affirmative action or employment equity policies require action and change on the part of employers, who alone have the power to eliminate discriminatory employment practices within their organisations (Reskin, 1998).

Misinformation and inaccurate assumptions about what is involved in affirmative action or employment equity are pervasive. Leonard (1990:49) notes, "In the heated political arguments over whether and what affirmative action should be, mythic visions have come to overwhelm any clear conception of what affirmative action actually is." The discussion that follows surveys legislative or policy frameworks that are not limited to making voluntary affirmative action permissible, but that make affirmative action or employment equity mandatory in at least some contexts.

Where they exist, mandatory affirmative action requirements are usually applicable to a subset of employers rather than to all employers. For example, mandatory affirmative action requirements may apply to public sector employers, firms that benefit from government contracts, employers of a certain size, or employers subject to federal jurisdiction for purposes of employment. Countries differ as to the populations that are the focus of such equality policies, the content and requirements of their policies, and the instruments used to influence employers to counteract systemic discrimination and ameliorate its effects. In all countries, social and economic values and political and ideological contexts shape the nature and effectiveness of equality policies. Related policy contexts concerning human rights, immigration or migration, education and training, child care, income support, and employment standards also have a significant influence on inequality in employment. Some government entities have adopted pay equity policies that seek to realise the principle of equal pay for work of equal value, a proactive approach with a much narrower focus than that of employment equity or affirmative action policies.

It is also important to acknowledge the significance of voluntary self-help and advocacy initiatives undertaken by marginalised groups and communities themselves in the struggle against systemic discrimination and its impacts. For example, organising unions and seeking change through collective bargaining, job creation through entrepreneurship, and community organisations that help job seekers and those victimised by discrimination in employment are essential actions in response to systemic discrimination. An effort to understand what constitutes an effective institutional response to discrimination is incomplete unless such initiatives are considered.

The discussion that follows attempts a preliminary and limited mapping of some features of governmental equality policy, taking related policy frameworks and political context into account only in passing. Table 1 (page 14) summarises some characteristics of equality policies in seven countries that are described in some detail in the remaining chapters in this book.

Coverage of disadvantaged groups

Table 1 (page 14) indicates that coverage varies among countries. Australia, Canada, South Africa and the United States provide some employment equity or affirmative action initiatives for women's employment. Blacks and people of Asian and South Asian ancestry are covered by pro-active policies in Canada under the term "visible minorities", and in the United States, as well as in South Africa where they constitute over four fifths of the population. Women and racial and ethnic minorities are also covered in Northern Ireland by legislation that has some pro-active features (Rogers, 2001). Immigrants and their children who are members of disadvantaged ethnic minorities are covered in the Netherlands (Glastra, Schedler and Kats, 2001), and Hispanics are covered in the United States. In Northern Ireland, Roman Catholics, who comprise about 40 percent of the labour force, are disadvantaged in that they are over-represented among the unemployed and in unskilled and semi-skilled jobs, and they are covered by both affirmative action and contract compliance (Burke, 1994; Heaton and Teague, 1997; Rogers, 2001). India has quotas for disadvantaged segments of the population ("scheduled castes and tribes" and "backward classes") as well as women and persons with disabilities in higher education and public sector employment (Hodges-Aeberhard and Raskin, 1997). India's constitution also provides for quotas for women's representation in political office at local, state and central levels (Ratnam and Chandra, 1996:86; Jain and Ratnam, 2001). Australia has a form of affirmative action for women in private and public sector employment as well as for Aborigines and Torres Strait Islanders, migrants from non-English speaking backgrounds and people with disabilities (Strachan and Burgess, 2001). Proactive legislation that covers private and public sector employment of people with disabilities is in force in Canada and the Netherlands (Thornton and Lunt, 1997).

The designation of groups that are disadvantaged is a critical component of an equality policy. This usually occurs as a result of such influences as:

(a) research evidence of a group's persisting disadvantage in employment, perhaps involving an accumulation of evidence from the case law as well as academic and government research;

(b) political mobilisation and advocacy by disadvantaged groups that convinces a government in power that it will receive political support in return for its support for employment equity, or suffer the withdrawal of electoral support if it does not support equality policy (Tummala, 1999);

(c) court and tribunal decisions that point to a need for new legislation or for the expanded application of existing legislation pertaining to human rights and/or discrimination in employment, and that create a legal dilemma that government must address;

Table 1. Countries, Groups and Employers Covered, and Policy Mechanisms

COUNTRIES:	**Australia**	**Canada**	**India**	**Netherlands**	**Northern Ireland**	**South Africa**	**USA**
GROUPS COVERED:							
WOMEN	X	X	X		X	X	X
RACIAL/ETHNIC GROUPS		Visible Minorities			Religion Race	X	X
ABORIGINAL PEOPLE	X	X					X
PEOPLE WITH DISABILITIES	X	X		X		X	X
IMMIGRANTS	X			X			
SCHEDULED CASTES AND TRIBES AND BACKWARD CLASSES			X				
EMPLOYERS COVERED:							
PUBLIC SECTOR	X	X	X	X	X	X	X
PRIVATE SECTOR	X (women)	Federal jurisdiction		X	X (religion)	X	
CONTRACTORS	X	X	X	X	X	X	X
PROACTIVE POLICIES:							
EE/AA	X	X	X	X	X	X	X
PAY EQUITY	X	Provinces		X		X	States
EE POLICY MECHANISMS							
LEGISLATION	AA 1986 (women) PE 1996	EE 1987	Disability 1996	EE 1994 PE 1975	Sex 1976 Religion 1989 Race 1997	EE PE 1998	Disability 1990
REGULATION		EE 1987	SC 1947 ST 1950 BC 1990				X 1965
GOVERNMENT CONTRACTS	X	X	X	X	X	X	X
COURT OR TRIBUNAL DECISIONS	X	X	X	X	X	X	X
CENTRALIZED COLLECTIVE BARGAINING	X			X			
CONSTITUTIONAL PROVISIONS		X 1982	X 1947	X		X 1996	
POLICY/PROGRAM CHARACTERISTICS:							
RATIONALE	+	+	+	+	+	+	+
CLEAR REQUIREMENTS	+	+	+	+	+	+	+
GOALS	+	+	+	+	+	+	+
ENFORCEMENT	-	+	-	-	+	+	-
SANCTIONS	-	-	+SC	-	+	-	-
WEAKENING OR REPEAL OF AA?	2000	Ontario 1995	No	1997	No	No	1980s – 1990s

EE Employment equity
AA Affirmative action
PE Pay equity

SC Scheduled castes
ST Scheduled tribes
BC Backward classes

(d) external legal or quasi-legal influences such as United Nations Conventions, directives of the European Council (such as Council Directive 2000/78/, establishing a general framework for equal treatment in employment), or decisions of the European Court of Justice, or a felt need to conform to human rights or employment standards exemplified in the policy frameworks of present or potential trading partner nations or international organisations.

Of course the reverse of the above series of points is also true. Equality policies themselves, as well as coverage of specific disadvantaged groups, have been threatened and undermined by political mobilisation against them and by court decisions that weaken their legal foundations. External pressures such as international economic competition and trade agreements that threaten national employment standards are currently raising concerns for equality-seekers. As will be discussed later in this chapter, in several countries the neo-liberal political climate of the 1990s has brought a reversal of earlier political commitments to employment equity or affirmative action policies, despite the continuing need for them.

Coverage of employers

All countries included in Table 1 (page 14) require public sector employers to implement equality policies. Private sector employers are covered in Australia, Northern Ireland, South Africa and the Netherlands, and larger private firms that are federally regulated are covered in Canada. Canada, Northern Ireland, South Africa and the USA require firms that sell goods or services under contract to the government to implement equality programs for some disadvantaged groups.

Policy mechanisms

Countries differ as to the policy mechanisms they utilise in instituting mandatory employment equity or affirmative action; some countries employ more than one of the mechanisms listed in Table 1 (page 14). The most frequently used vehicles are:

1. Constitutional provisions

Only in India is there a constitutional provision making affirmative action mandatory. The constitutions of Canada (the Charter of Rights and Freedoms), the Netherlands and South Africa permit the implementation of programs to redress and prevent disadvantage in employment. Such permissive constitutional provisions provide legal protection against charges of "reverse discrimination" and largely prevent the kinds of protracted legal struggles over the rights of employers to engage in voluntary affirmative action that have occurred in the United States.

2. Legislation

All seven countries have employment equity or affirmative action legislation applying to one or more disadvantaged groups. Most of this legislation was passed during the 1980s and 1990s. The Canadian Employment Equity Act, 1987, was an influential example for employment equity legislation subsequently enacted in the Netherlands (Glastra, Schedler and Kats, 2001), South Africa, and Northern Ireland (Osborne, 1992). In several countries there is separate legislation covering persons with disabilities, racial or ethnic minorities and women, rather than omnibus legislation.

3. Regulation

In India, regulations to give effect to constitutionally mandated quotas for the scheduled castes were enacted in 1947 following independence, followed by regulations covering the scheduled tribes in 1950, and the backward classes in 1990. India thus has the longest history of mandatory affirmative action of any of the seven countries.

4. Orders or agreements made under the auspices of courts, tribunals, or human rights commissions

In some countries in legal cases where allegations of discrimination are substantiated, an employment equity, affirmative action or pay equity requirement may be ordered or agreed to in order to remedy past discrimination and prevent future discrimination. In other instances courts decide the legal status of voluntary affirmative action programs undertaken by employers (Hodges-Aeberhard, 1999). Court decisions are significant in clarifying grounds for affirmative action or employment equity approaches, or in ordering or making agreements for such approaches explicitly to address systemic discrimination in the United States and Canada as well as in India, South Africa and the European Union.

For example in the United States, a settlement between Coca-Cola and Black employees who filed a class action suit alleging discrimination in pay, promotion and performance evaluation includes monetary awards to 2,000 employees and external oversight and enforcement powers over corporate employment practices (Associated Press, Atlanta, November 16, 2000). The U.S. court orders and agreements take place in a complaint-based statutory regime under which victims of discrimination, and/or federal or state enforcement agencies acting on their behalf, must initiate an investigation by filing a complaint. Settlements or orders that benefit complainants such as in the Coca-Cola case are extremely rare (Leonard, 1990: 59-61; Mudrick, 1997). Furthermore, decisions of the U.S. Supreme Court dominated by Republican appointees have severely restricted the possibilities for race-conscious initiatives since the 1980s. It has become difficult or impossible for U. S. employers, particularly in the public sector, to mount a legal defence of race-conscious programs whose purpose is to assist persons who have not themselves been victims of discrimination by that organisation (Gullett, 2000).

5. Requirements applicable to employers that benefit from government contracts and/or grants

Affirmative action using contract compliance as a mechanism was introduced by executive order in the United States in the early 1960s and extended in 1974, and was introduced by regulation in Canada in 1986 and in the province of Quebec in 1987. In the United States and Canada federal contractors are required to develop affirmative action plans including goals and timetables. Australia, India, the Netherlands, Northern Ireland and South Africa also have contract compliance requirements under which employers must implement equity programs in some form, in several instances for persons with disabilities.

6. Decisions arising from the collective bargaining process

Provisions of collective agreements (Weiler, 2000) and reinforcement of such provisions by decisions of arbitrators or labour relations tribunals have been vehicles for the implementation of affirmative action, employment equity and pay equity as well as protection against sexual harassment. In Australia under a centralised system of collective bargaining, decisions by industrial relations tribunals were an important source of pay equity gains for women during the 1960s, 1970s and 1980s (Strachan and Burgess, 2001). In the Netherlands some collective agreements provide for quotas or other measures to assist persons with disabilities (European Foundation, 2001), and equality bargaining on gender issues such as affirmative action, parental leave, child care and sexual harassment is "well developed" (European Foundation, 1997).

Characteristics of effective policy frameworks

Countries also vary in the degree to which their policy frameworks include features that are essential to ensuring that the policy is implemented and its objectives are attained. The following characteristics might be considered necessary conditions for the effective implementation of an equality policy, or perhaps any policy:

(a) It is based on a rational analysis and theory concerning the causes of the issue the policy is designed to address, in this case systemic discrimination in the workplace. The theory provides a rationale for the specific requirements contained in the policy.
(b) The policy states clear goals and standards to be used in assessing compliance.
(c) The policy sets out practical requirements and procedures and communicates them clearly to employers, and to stakeholders interested in holding employers accountable for results.

All seven countries' policies appear to demonstrate characteristics (a), (b) and (c) to at least some degree. Requirements that employers report data on the composition of their workforce so that their progress can be monitored are included in the policies of Australia, Northern Ireland, Canada, the Netherlands, South Africa, and the United States. However requirements for reporting, in the absence of requirements to demonstrate equity results, are not directly and rationally linked to the goal of reducing inequality and increasing representation of disadvantaged groups. Burke (1994) criticises Northern Ireland's affirmative action legislation for not being clear as to the actions and outcomes that are required of employers. In particular, he notes that the goal of a more representative distribution of Protestants and Catholics in the workforce is not embraced, and there is no legislative protection against charges of reverse discrimination for voluntary affirmative action programs. In contrast, employment quotas are required of public sector employers in India with respect to scheduled castes and tribes and backward classes, and in the Netherlands for people with disabilities in both public and private sectors (Thornton and Lunt, 1997). In the United States where there has been long experience with affirmative action, policy approaches have not reflected a consistent rationale but have evolved in a piecemeal fashion, changing as political support ebbs and flows and as court decisions expand and contract the scope of affirmative action.

(d) Appropriate expertise and resources are allocated to enforcement by an agency that has authority to review compliance and to monitor implementation and results, with clear determinations as to whether compliance has been attained.

It is difficult to obtain specific information on enforcement arrangements and results (e.g. Murdrick, 1997). Enforcement of affirmative action for Catholics is taken seriously in Northern Ireland, where the Fair Employment Commission is regarded by employers as being thorough in conducting investigations, with a focus on compliance with reporting requirements (Burke, 1994: 35; Heaton and Teague, 1997). In the United States under the federal contractors regulations enforcement was quite active between 1972, when enforcement powers under the Civil Rights Act were strengthened, and the beginning of the Reagan presidency in 1981, when enforcement activity and resources were nearly extinguished (Donohue and Heckman, 1994; Rose, 1994). In Canada the situation is mixed: while enforcement arrangements were strengthened under revised employment equity legislation in 1995, some enforcement powers were weakened (Agocs, 2001). Enforcement of equity provisions appears to be weak in the Netherlands and Australia.

(e) The policy provides meaningful consequences linked to implementation, which may include sanctions for failure to implement, rewards for implementing, or a combination of these.

Sanctions are minimal in Australia, where an employer who does not file the required report can be named in Parliament (Strachan and Burgess, 2001). In the Netherlands, the Equity Act allows lawsuits against employers who are not in compliance, but this has not occurred (Glastra, Schedler and Kats, 2001). Sanctions can be substantial in the United States in cases under Title VII of the Civil Rights Act when courts find discrimination and order remedies for lost pay and injury. However sanctions are rare under the contractors regulations: debarment was used less than 30 times prior to 1990 (Leonard, 1990: 49). In Canada and South Africa there are sanctions for failure to file required reports. Sanctions for employers' failure to make good faith effort are also possible but there is as yet little experience with enforcement. India provides for sanctions in relation to quota requirements for scheduled castes in public organisations. In Northern Ireland, Fair Employment Tribunals have awarded compensation when complaints of religious discrimination are substantiated and ordered actions to prevent future discrimination (Heaton and Teague, 1997).

Equality policies vary widely among countries on the dimensions mentioned above and comparison among them requires specialised expertise on each government's policy and its results, a need that the subsequent chapters in this book begin to meet. Furthermore, there are frequent changes in policies arising from new or amended legislation, regulatory changes and court decisions. Hence an inventory such as that presented in Table 1 (page 14) is soon out of date, and observers may not agree on some specifics. There is clearly a need for comparative research in order to move beyond description of policies to an analysis of contents of policies and their institutional context in order to identify features that contribute to effectiveness in counteracting the impacts of systemic discrimination. There is also a need for adequate data to enable comparative research and development of indicators and benchmarks in order to assess outcomes of policies for marginalised groups (Plantenga and Hansen, 1999).

DO AFFIRMATIVE ACTION AND EMPLOYMENT EQUITY PRODUCE MORE EQUALITY?

Comparative research by Reitz (1998) on Australia, Canada and the United States demonstrated that initial employment earnings of immigrants from the same countries of origin are substantially lower in the United States than in the other two destination countries, suggesting the critical influence of policy frameworks in the receiving society on outcomes for immigrants. In the absence of comparative research on specific impacts of affirmative action or employment equity policies on disadvantaged groups, it is necessary to rely upon within-country studies for analyses of their success in bringing about greater equality. Generally, such research uses as indicators of progress data on improvement in the representation of designated groups in workplaces covered by equality policy, improvement in their representation in management and among those hired and/or promoted, and relative wage or salary gains.

Research in several countries demonstrates the positive impact of the implementation of equality policy in reducing inequality for women, religious minorities and racial minorities. Evidence of these kinds of gains for aboriginal peoples and persons with disabilities is difficult to find, and there is a pressing need for research to identify generalised and specific impacts for these groups (Murdrick, 1997). India's quota policy has produced "a small and growing middle class of untouchables and tribals" – although the primary beneficiaries have been the better-off segments of these populations (Jain and Ratnam, 2001). However available Canadian data and research show little benefit of employment equity policy for aboriginal people to date, and the same appears to be true in Australia (Agocs, 2001; Strachan and Burgess, 2001). In Canada the representation of persons with disabilities in organisations covered by employment equity legislation has actually declined (Agocs, 2001).

In Canada, summaries of employers' annual reports over the twelve years for which data are available show a small increase in women's representation among employees hired and promoted in companies under federal jurisdiction, and an increase of nearly ten percent in the federal public service. However women remain clustered in traditionally women's occupations and at low salary levels and markedly under-represented in senior management and at the high end of the salary range. Gains in representation were somewhat greater for visible minorities in the private sector, but for them too, traditional occupational concentrations and the glass ceiling pattern persisted. Gains for visible minorities in public sector employment were negligible (Agocs, 2001). These disappointing results are not surprising in that few employers appear to have undertaken special measures for the purpose of attaining their equity goals, evidently because the threat of enforcement and sanctions has not been sufficient to motivate them.

However, Canadian research shows that implementation of equity requirements makes a difference. Research by Leck and Saunders (1992) found that firms that implemented the most formalised and complete equity programs made the most progress toward improving the representation of women and visible minorities and reducing their salary disadvantage in lower and middle level occupations compared to white men (also see Marino, 1982). Employers whose efforts exceeded minimal compliance requirements of equity legislation obtained better results. Agocs (1990) also found that federal contractors that had done most to implement equity requirements also had the most progressive overall human resource management practices for all employees.

In Northern Ireland, data reported by employers "suggest a pattern of progressive improvement in Catholic employment opportunities" from the first reports in 1990 through 1993 and on to 2000, with increases for both women and men in every occupational group, a result that may be attributable to vigorous enforcement of equality legislation (Heaton and Teague, 1997; Rogers, 2001). However Burke (1994) argues for stronger legislation, pointing out that nearly five years after the passage of the Fair Employment (Northern Ireland) Act, Catholics were still over-represented among the unemployed. Furthermore, while the enforcement process is considered effective, employers generally have not acted unless they are targeted by a discrimination complaint or a compliance review (Burke, 1994: 41).

In the Netherlands, where the Equity Act as revised in 1997 has been in force only a short time, there has been a slightly greater increase in the representation of ethnic minorities in firms covered by the act than in those not covered, and there has been some decrease in minority unemployment (Glastra, Schedler and Kats, 2001).

Research assessing the impact of affirmative action in the United States demonstrates significant employment gains for Black men and women and negligible improvements for white women (Leonard, 1989). Federal contractors were required to implement affirmative action for Blacks as early as 1961, but women were not covered until 1972. Litigation under Title VII of the Civil Rights Act of 1964 has been effective in bringing about significant improvements in the employment of Black men and even more, for Black women, particularly in professional and management positions (Leonard, 1990:60). A recent overview of available research evidence from the standpoint of economic performance concludes that "affirmative action offers significant redistribution toward women and minorities, with relatively small efficiency consequences" (Holzer and Neumark, 2000: 483).

In one of many published analyses of affirmative action outcomes for women and racial minorities, Leonard (1990) reported results of a comparison of federal contractor and non-contractor firms in the United States between 1974 and 1980, when affirmative action was most vigorously enforced. Employment shares of Black men and women increased significantly faster in contractor than in non-contractor firms when establishment size, region, industry and occupational structure were taken into account. In contrast, after 1980 enforcement budgets and staff were severely reduced and activities were curtailed; consequently, representation of Black women and men grew more slowly in contractor than in non-contractor firms between 1980 and 1984 (Leonard, 1990:58). Consistent with these results, Rodgers and Spriggs (1996) found an improvement in the representation of non-white workers, both men and women, in contractor firms in the years following the Reagan administration. Rodgers and Spriggs (1996) also reported a significant positive impact of the contractors program on the representation of workers of Asian as well as African-American descent, but a negative effect for Hispanics at the level of the firm.

Leonard found that compliance reviews have an additional significant effect that reinforces the impact of coverage by the contractors program: for Black men the impact of a compliance review was about twice the effect of coverage alone, and the effect for Black women was more than twice as great. Leonard's research also demonstrates the importance of goal setting to employers' affirmative action results. The goals set by employers were the best predictor of improved representation of Blacks and women in those firms a year later, even though employers tended to set low goals and most did not actually attain their goals (Leonard, 1990: 55-56).

Leonard also assessed impacts of affirmative action on wage levels by statistically controlling for productivity factors, and taking the remaining systematic variations in wages by race, sex and ethnicity as evidence of discrimination (Leonard, 1996: 285). Leonard found that white women's wage disadvantage relative to men's pay decreased substantially in the 1980s, while wage disadvantage increased for Blacks, Native Americans, Hispanics and Asians during the same decade.

Hence there was not a uniform pattern of improvement under affirmative action in the United States. Moreover, affirmative action was not the most important direct influence on changes in the wage gap (Leonard, 1996) or on representation of designated groups in firms (Rodgers and Spriggs , 1996). More important were the macro-level impacts of geographic location, occupational structure of the employer's firm, and changes in the workforce linked to cutbacks in industries covered by the federal contractor's regulations. Furthermore, there is no evidence that affirmative action has brought a marked improvement in the unemployment rates of Blacks compared to whites in the United States (Leonard, 1990: 53).

In South Africa in the brief time since the introduction of employment equity there has been a large and rapid increase in the representation of Blacks, mostly men, in management and skilled occupations. Progress in the largest firms is notable (Horwitz and Jain, 2001). However the degree to which employment conditions will improve for the vast majority of Black employees in post-apartheid South Africa remains to be seen.

In Australia, mandatory pay equity in the form of awards by labour tribunals resulted in gains in compensation for women. Indeed the gender-based pay gap is less in Australia than in any of the other countries. As of 1997-98, Australian women earned 91 percent of men's wages, as compared with 72 percent in Canada, 77 percent in the Netherlands, 73 percent in South Africa and 75 percent in the United States (O'Connor, Orloff and Shaver, 1999). However the establishment of decentralised collective bargaining in the early 1990s restructured the earlier arrangements through which pay equity gains for women were achieved. Furthermore, increasing numbers of women are working in part time and casual jobs that are not covered by affirmative action (Strachan and Burgess, 2001). Australia's affirmative action legislation, with its minimal requirements and sanctions and low level of employer compliance, has not produced clear gains for women or aboriginal people in employment.

These findings point to the gains that are possible when affirmative action is implemented and enforced, but they also caution us to maintain realistic expectations about what can be accomplished through affirmative action or employment equity policy. It is not a panacea for all forms of inequality, but is a central component of a policy framework. The policy impacts occur at the level of the organisation, and in sectors directly covered by the policy, not for the economy as a whole, and results differ for the various disadvantaged groups. Hence there is a need for research directed toward assessing the specific effects for the various groups of equity interventions at the organisational level, in order to establish a profile of "best practices" in making gains for each group. Leonard's findings as well as those of Rodgers and Spriggs (1996) also point to the need to examine the specific effects of policy coverage and of enforcement activities of various kinds, as well as sanctions for non-compliance, at the level of the firm and industry. It is also important to examine policy impacts against the background of the contemporary restructuring of the labour market.

Several generalisations can be made about the results of research on impacts of equality policy on the representation and compensation of groups that have been disadvantaged by systemic discrimination. First and most important, a policy that is not implemented cannot be effective. There is clearly a relationship between the extent to which employers take action to implement the requirements of equality policies, and progress for marginalised groups.

Second, it is established that formalised equity programs with mandatory goal-setting and vigorous and continuous enforcement by government authorities make a significant difference in results. Being under the direct threat of a compliance review clearly stimulates employers to implement requirements, as does knowledge of the possibility of legal action or enforcement activity that could result in meaningful sanctions. Experience in the United States and Canada also demonstrates that the role of human rights complaints by employees who have experienced discrimination, and advocacy of their cause by organisations representing disadvantaged groups and by government enforcement agencies, has been critically important in forcing employers to recognise their obligations. Employment equity or affirmative action and human rights litigation work hand in hand in creating an environment in which progress toward workplace equality becomes a priority that must be addressed by employers.

Third, affirmative action or employment equity is only a part of a larger policy framework directed toward reducing social inequality for women and other disadvantaged groups (O'Connor, Orloff and Shaver, 1999). Legislation and programs to reduce the gender gap in pay, provide paid maternity and parental leave, provide public child care, stimulate employment growth, reduce income inequality, and enable disadvantaged groups to develop their educational and skill levels are necessary complements. There is evidence that pay equity in Canada, Australia and the United States has contributed to some reduction in the gender-based wage gap, but the additional wage gap due to race has not been addressed (Lapidus and Figart, 1998). Moreover, a comparative assessment of women's employment status in the countries of the European Union notes that

> gender equality in work and income can only be achieved if there is complementary policy on (unpaid) care. As long as care responsibilities continue to be seen primarily as a private concern, the unequal division of unpaid work will translate into an unequal position of women on the labour market (Plantegna and Hansen, 1999: 379).

Finally, it is of critical importance that equality policy be mandatory rather than voluntary for employers, as discussed in the paragraphs that follow.

MANAGING DIVERSITY: A DETOUR ON THE ROAD TO EQUALITY?

From a policy perspective a voluntary approach is much less effective than mandatory approaches in bringing about transformative change for marginalised groups. The primary difficulty with voluntary policy frameworks is that very few employers implement programs that could reasonably be expected to produce gains for designated groups. For example in Canada, employers were legally permitted to introduce voluntary equity programs from the enactment of the Canadian Human Rights Act in 1978 through 1987, when employment equity became mandatory for some federally regulated employers. Yet only a very small number of employers initiated such programs (Agocs, 1986). Even under mandatory employment equity, employers tend to implement requirements only when faced with compliance audits (Agocs, 2001).

Voluntary diversity management programs have become the preferred corporate response to the growing and future diversity of the workforce in many countries. Many corporate and academic advocates of diversity management programs position them as a preferable alternative to affirmative action (e.g. Gilbert, Stead and Ivancevich, 1999). There is no generally accepted definition or set of practices associated with "managing diversity", and there is wide variation among organisations as to what this term means in theory or in practice. Definitions in the literature are vague and usually do not refer to addressing discrimination: e.g. "diversity is defined as all the ways in which people differ, and it encompasses all the characteristics that make one individual or group different from another " (Wentling, 2000: 36), or, "diversity has been defined as inclusion of all groups at all levels in the company" (Gilbert and Ivancevich, 2000:2). Published research results indicate that in most organisations managing diversity means senior management statements about the importance of diversity as a business issue, and training for employees, usually of short duration and delivered by external consultants (Agocs and Burr, 1996; Wentling, 2000; Rynes and Rosen, 1995).

However a case study in the United States documented a diversity management program in a Fortune 500 manufacturing firm that goes far beyond perfunctory training. It includes hiring of women or racial minorities into half of all professional job vacancies, equalisation of pay among employees at the same level, child care and leave programs to assist working families, multi-faceted employee involvement to support change in organisational culture, and rewards to managers for diversity-related performance (Gilbert and Ivancevich, 2000). This organisation denies that it is implementing affirmative action, pointing out that its actions far exceed legal compliance. Yet it appears to have undertaken many of the program elements required or recommended by Canadian employment equity policy for women and racial minorities (although no measures for persons with disabilities or people of aboriginal ancestry were reported).

While there are instances of change-oriented diversity programs and the appeal of voluntary diversity management programs has grown rapidly, there has been "no systematic empirical research regarding the effectiveness of diversity programs" (Wentling, 2000) and no "rigorous evaluation of diversity training effectiveness" (Ivancevich and Gilbert, 2000). Hence it is not surprising that there has been no assessment of results of managing diversity for members of racial or ethnic minorities, women, people with disabilities or persons of aboriginal ancestry, although there have been efforts to measure outcomes for business (Wright et al, 1995). This reflects the fact that the objectives associated with diversity management are primarily business-oriented, including reducing turnover and retaining women and minorities who are hired, reputation as an employer of choice, service to a diverse clientele or customer base, or global competitiveness (Wentling, 2000).

An exception is the anti-discrimination training approach of the European Union in countries that receive immigrants, which attempts to create organisational change by targeting training to those gatekeepers who make decisions about access to employment and about treatment on the job (Wrench, 2000). This specific training focus on behaviour as well as attitudes, and its emphasis on anti-discrimination, promises to produce more effective outcomes in addressing systemic discrimination than the kind of vague and unfocussed training often implemented in the name of managing diversity.

In a voluntary policy context it is likely to be the most progressive firms, with respect to their broad approach to human resource management, that implement the most effective equity-related programs. In other words, the firms that already are leaders in their treatment of employees "volunteer" to do the most to move toward equity, while those that most need to change their policies and practices do the least. Diversity training may be undertaken by some firms as window-dressing that cannot reasonably be expected to lead to organisational transformation. Agocs and Burr (1996) argue that affirmative action, employment equity and managing diversity are three different approaches with varying goals. While diversity management may have a place as strategy to complement affirmative action or employment equity by contributing to change in organisational culture, it is not a replacement for these legislated approaches because it is not designed to remove and remedy systemic discrimination. For this reason, mandatory policy frameworks are needed.

THE FUTURE OF EMPLOYMENT EQUITY: CHALLENGES OF THE CHANGING NATURE OF WORK

The past decade has seen significant changes in the structure of the labour market and the nature of work, creating a changing context that demands adaptation by affirmative action and employment equity policies. Both private and public sectors have experienced a decade of restructuring and downsizing in countries where neo-liberal political ideology has had strong influence including the United States, the United Kingdom, Canada and Australia. Downsizing has brought large negative impacts for clerical occupations as well as the public sector where women are concentrated.

On the other hand, the strategy of downsizing middle management in the public and private sectors has resulted in job loss for large numbers of men over the age of 50. This in turn has tended to bring about some narrowing of the wage gap between men and women, and some increases in the proportion of supervisory and middle management positions held by women and younger racial minority men. However for the most part these ostensible improvements result less from employment equity efforts than from the statistical effects of the early "retirement" of a cohort of older white male workers as a corporate cost-cutting strategy.

The restructuring of the labour market in the nineties also brought a shift toward contingent work and away from the creation and maintenance of traditional long-term full time jobs with benefits, which has contributed to the growth of inequality in income on the basis of gender and race. An increasing proportion of jobs are part time, temporary or contract positions with limited or no benefits, no union protection, and limited coverage by employment equity, pay equity and other workplace legislation. The vast majority of part time jobs are held by women in most countries (Rossilli, 2000:9). Data for 1995 show the following proportions of employed women in part time work: Australia, 43 percent; Canada, 28 percent; Netherlands, 67 percent; United States, 27 percent (O'Connor, Orloff and Shaver, 1999:73). Of women workers employed part time in Australia, more than half are casual (temporary) employees who do not receive leave entitlements (Strachan and Burgess, 2001). In India, women are concentrated in the unorganised sector of the workforce. A study of the gender-based wage gap in Britain points out the limitations in what an equality policy agenda can accomplish "within a wider regime of burgeoning labor market inequalities" (Bruegel and Perrons, 1998: 103). For example, women who are part of the contingent workforce in the United States may not be protected by legislation against sexual harassment in the workplace (Espinosa, 1997), and affirmative action only applies to regular employees, not to temporary or contracted workers (Reskin, 1998: 95). The same is true in Australia (Strachan and Burgess, 2001).

Chicha (1999) has noted that current trends such as these are resulting in the deterioration of women's position in the labour market, and that employment equity policy as it is presently designed may not be effective in addressing some of these emerging realities. Employment equity policy assumes long-term jobs with somewhat specialised descriptions, not the fluid and contingent jobs favoured by many employers, or the very small businesses or self-employment arrangements that are becoming more common, particularly among women and immigrants. The corporate restructuring and "flexible" strategies pursued by many firms are likely to threaten benefits that are possible under employment equity policy, with negative impacts for women in particular. Indeed employment equity policy and its enforcement need to become stronger and more vigorous just to protect women's position in the labour market from further deterioration.

At present, about seventy percent of Canadian employment is concentrated in the service sector, and a growing proportion of jobs involve office work in technical, managerial and professional functions. A recent review of published tribunal and court decisions in racial harassment cases revealed that 47 percent of complaints arose in organisations in the public sector, and 76 percent came from white collar employees -- the majority in professional, managerial and technical jobs (Jain, Al-Waqfi and Agocs, 1999). As the structure of the labour market and work evolve toward an "information society" in which job descriptions are less specific and more flexible and standards for hiring and promotion may become less clear, greater emphasis may be placed on subjective criteria such as "fit" and "teamwork". Employment equity and affirmative action policies generally contain no provisions that directly address issues of workplace culture or climate, aside from the requirement to explain the purpose of employment equity to employees. The lack of specific provisions in employment equity policy to address systemic discrimination in the organisation's culture is a significant weakness, particularly as employment becomes increasingly concentrated in functions involving the communication and management of information.

THE IMPORTANCE OF POLITICAL WILL

"Policy-setting defines social visions, but is constrained by political imperatives" (Abella, 1989: 4). In all countries, the development and implementation of equality policy depends upon the prevailing political environment, including dominant ideologies and values, and upon the extent of public and governmental commitment to equality and to a role for government action in the advancement of marginalised segments of the population (Corby, 1994). The 1980s and 1990s saw a retreat from earlier commitments to affirmative action or employment equity implementation in several countries. Progressive employment equity legislation was repealed in the province of Ontario in Canada in 1995 after only a few months in force. In the Netherlands in 1997, equity legislation was revised and somewhat curtailed in response to employers' interests (Glastra, Schedler and Kats, 2001). In Australia where pay equity gains were made under centralised collective bargaining, legislation in 1993 and 1996 weakened the power of unions and created a fragmentation of the collective bargaining system. Furthermore in 2000, a review of Australia's affirmative action legislation resulted in a reduction of its requirements and a change of name to Equal Opportunity for Women in the Workplace Act 1999 (Strachan and Burgess, 2001). In Western Europe, a hardening of attitudes toward ex-colonial "guest workers", refugees and other immigrants took place in the late 1980s and right-wing political parties capitalised on this (Pettigrew, 1998).

In the United States the 2000 presidential election was won by an outspoken opponent of affirmative action, and two states have passed legislation prohibiting affirmative action by public employers. These events do not mark a new trend, however, since the attack on affirmative action has been going on for a generation in the United States. In Jonathan Leonard's words,

> The federal policy of affirmative action effectively passed away with the inauguration of the Reagan administration in 1981. The Supreme Court decisions in the summer of 1989 nailed down the coffin lid. But affirmative action has carried more symbolic than real weight, and symbols have ways of persisting even when the body of law and regulation lies six feet under (Leonard, 1990:47).

As Leonard suggests, the notion that affirmative action is needed as a transformative strategy is far from extinguished even though the current ideological climate is adverse.

The pressure for effective affirmative action legislation and enforcement is likely to grow in the future as women, immigrants, ethnic minorities and people with disabilities become larger and more politically mobilised segments of the workforce in many countries.

In recent years individualistic ideology and the dominance of market mechanisms have become dominant policy commitments in many countries and the role of government has been sharply curtailed, creating a negative environment for the kinds of policy approaches that are required to effectively counter systemic discrimination. Public opinion polls show that attitudes toward racial minorities in the United States and toward immigrants in Western Europe are related to levels of support for equality and immigration policies (Krysan, 2000; Pettigrew and Meertens, 1995). Resistance to government policies to assist Blacks is related to an individualistic analysis that attributes racial inequality to deficiencies in Black motivation or ability, rather than to systemic discrimination (Kluegel, 1994). In general, people who identify themselves as politically conservative and who favour limited government tend to oppose equality policies and racial preferences in hiring and promotion (Krysan, 2000).

Social policies such as affirmative action or employment equity, as well as complementary approaches such as pay equity, limitation of working hours or publicly subsidised child care, have not found a place on the currently ascendant agenda of corporate globalisation. There appears to be widespread denial that systemic discrimination on the basis of race or gender still exists, or that the trend toward greater inequality in the distribution of income is an issue that demands a policy response. Most countries of the European Union have given only weak support, at best, to positive action programs, and these have been fragmentary and concentrated in the public sector (Rossilli, 2000: 7-8). In some European countries there is resistance to the notion that immigrant populations should be included as full and equal participants in society, as citizens or potential citizens rather than "guest workers" (Pettigrew and Meertens, 1995). The United Nations High Commissioner for Human Rights has expressed concern about a "Fortress Europe" mentality and about widespread denial that racism and xenophobia exist (United Nations, October 2000).

Commenting on discriminatory barriers in employment faced by racial minorities, Reitz notes that

> governments have proven strangely reluctant to inquire more fully into these facts, using available methods. The opportunity to invest resources in a definitive and reliable empirical assessment of the extent of such discrimination is rarely taken...Perhaps there is a justifiable fear of the truth: that conclusive evidence of discrimination will generate pressure for decisive action (Reitz, 1998: 240).

There is evidence that the mis-education of public opinion about affirmative action by political discourse, the media and survey researchers has played a large role in perpetuating a cycle of politician's opposition and public resistance to affirmative action in the United States and Canada. There is public support in the United States for affirmative action programs when they are justified by providing evidence that they are needed (Kravitz et al, 1999). There is also support for specific elements of affirmative action policy when they are clearly explained (Steeh and Krysan, 1996). The specific requirements of the equality policy, and the manner in which it is communicated to the public, make a large difference both in what the policy can achieve in combating systemic discrimination, and in the level of public support for it (Kravitz et al, 1999; Steeh and Krysan, 1996). There is strong public support for outreach recruitment of women and minorities and posting of job vacancies, and for assistance to several minority groups rather than exclusively to Blacks in the United States, for example. Furthermore, because poll results show "extremely limited" personal or family experience of "reverse discrimination" in the United States, negative personal experience with affirmative action is not a basis for opposition to it by members of the majority population (Steeh and Krysan, 1996: 139). However survey researchers, the media and political discourse have taken a restricted and misleading view of affirmative action and employment equity, equating these policies with preferential hiring and ignoring the range of elements that characterise such policies (Steeh and Krysan, 1996). As a result, the public is misinformed and misled about what such policies actually involve and resistance to affirmative action is heightened for reasons that are generally without foundation. Hence there is a significant need for public information and education regarding what affirmative action and employment equity actually are, and why they are needed, in a time when the growing diversity of the labour market is accompanied by trends toward greater inequality in several countries.

A retreat from action against discrimination has occurred in the United States, the province of Ontario in Canada, Australia and the Netherlands. In contrast, the1990s were a time of progressive developments and substantial political support for affirmative action in India, South Africa and Northern Ireland – arguably the most challenging environments in which to take action to reduce inequality. In India and South Africa, the extent and nature of inequality not only in employment but also in basic infrastructure, housing, health care and education, as well as high unemployment, would seem so daunting as to make affirmative action a matter of low priority. However these countries have placed policy emphasis on creating opportunity for the large disadvantaged segments of their populations. Affirmative action has been adopted as a priority in order to put fundamental values of equality and social justice into practice, prevent social cleavage, ensure the legitimacy of political institutions, and make the highest and best use of valuable human resources on which their economies depend. Given the history of apartheid and the migrant labour system in South Africa, the caste system in India, and religious sectarianism in Northern Ireland, the reality of discrimination in employment in these countries cannot be denied. The need for policy and action, while opposed by some, has broad support and has engaged the co-operative efforts of government, business, unions and representatives of disadvantaged groups. However, South African employers are said to have given their support for employment equity legislation in return for amendments that made concessions, such as voluntary targets instead of quotas. Furthermore, employers expect that government will lack the resources for vigorous enforcement of compliance (Mittger, 1998).

Affirmative action is showing results in the form of a more representative workforce on the basis of religion in Northern Ireland, a growing middle class of untouchables and tribal people in India, and an emergent Black corporate, political and bureaucratic elite and middle class in South Africa. From 1995 to 1998, the representation of Blacks in senior management in South Africa increased from 4.8 percent to 11.5 percent, and from 9.7 percent to 21.3 percent in middle management (Mittger, 1998). Since the end of legal apartheid, South Africa has developed innovative institutional responses to the most challenging issues of inequality in a democratic multi-racial society (Seidman, 1999). These innovations include not only the constitutional and legislative foundations of employment equity, but also the Truth and Reconciliation Commission and the Gender Commission, which examines the gender-related implications of all new legislation. The rest of the world has much to learn from the South African policy framework, implementation and results.

WORKPLACE EQUALITY: AN AGENDA FOR COMPARATIVE RESEARCH

This chapter has argued that progress toward equality of results in employment in a diverse society begins with recognition that discrimination plays a part in the persistence of inequality. An appropriate response at the level of the workplace is to undertake a rigorous diagnosis of organisational behaviours that may contribute to systemic discrimination. Based upon such a diagnosis a program of organisational change can be undertaken that can lead to the removal of barriers and the implementation of measures that expand opportunity and inclusiveness. Processes of organisational diagnosis and change are most likely to occur and to be effective within the framework of a mandatory equality policy that is enforced to ensure accountability and compliance.

A state articulates its primary values through its policies. Hence it is appropriate that political communities that value the full expression of the human potential of all members, free from discrimination, implement effective affirmative action or employment equity policies.

The development of more effective equality policy will be advanced by comparative international research and by the communication of its findings to the public. Comparative research is needed at the level of the organisation, and also at the macro-scale, situating equity policy within a larger policy and institutional context. An agenda for such comparative research might include the following questions:

1) What are the most effective equality-oriented policies and practices at the level of the organisation? What indicators of success are most appropriate for comparative study? What are the characteristics of organisational change processes that produce the most effective results for each of the disadvantaged groups? Longitudinal studies are needed to identify the "best practices" in attaining results for each group.
2) Based on a comparison of governments' affirmative action or employment equity policies, implementation, and enforcement arrangements, what characteristics produce the most effective outcomes for racial minorities, people with disabilities, aboriginal people and women? How do these characteristics of effective policy frameworks relate to the interests of business, trade unions and governments?
3) In effective equity policy processes as measured by results for disadvantaged groups, what are the respective roles of:
   (a) equity legislation and regulation,
   (b) human rights legislation and adjudication,
   (c) enforcement of legislative, regulatory and legal requirements and orders,
   (d) collective bargaining,
   (e) advocacy by organisations representing disadvantaged groups,
   (f) public information and education about the impacts of discrimination and the policies to address it, and
   (g) voluntary market mechanisms?

How can these components complement and reinforce, rather than work against, each other?

4) What is the influence of contextual or environmental factors? These include demographic and economic trends, relative strength of trade unions, dominant political ideology and priorities, national cultural values, political activism by minorities and their advocates and allies, and the external environment shaped by

cross-national structures such as the European Union and international trade agreements.

5) How does the presence or absence of a system of supportive legal and policy measures influence the effectiveness of affirmative action or employment equity policy? Such measures include labour standards legislation regulating hours of work, minimum wage, etc.; pay equity; family supports such as caregivers' leave and public child care services; and legislation and programs that address immigration and immigrant settlement and integration.

The time has come for researchers, policy makers, legal experts and equality seekers to collaborate in clarifying the questions and the solutions needed to address discrimination and inequality in employment in the diverse communities of the present and future.

Carol Agocs is a Professor in the Department of Political Science at the University of Western Ontario, London, Ontario, Canada.

REFERENCES

Abella, Rosalie Silberman. "The Scholar and the Pragmatist." *Policy Options (* Sept. 1989): 3-6.

Act*ion travail des femmes v. Canadian National Railway,* Supreme Court of Canada [1987] 1 S.C.R. 1114.

Agocs, Carol. "Affirmative Action, Canadian Style: A Reconnaissance." *Canadian Public Policy* 12. 1 (1986): 148-162.

Agocs, Carol. "Canada's Employment Equity Legislation and Policy, 1986-2000: Unfulfilled Promises." Carol Agocs (ed.). *Workplace Equality: International Perspectives on Legislation, Policy and Practice*. Dordrecht: Kluwer Academic Publishers, 2001.

Agocs, Carol. "Employment Equity Activity Among Federal Contractors in Ontario." *Proceedings of the 26th Conference of the Canadian Industrial Relations Association*. 1990, 517-529.

Agocs, Carol and Catherine Burr. "Employment Equity, Affirmative Action and Managing Diversity: Assessing the Differences." *International Journal of Manpower* 17.4/5 (1996): 30-45.

Agocs, Carol, Catherine Burr and Felicity Somerset. *Employment Equity: Cooperative Strategies for Organizational Change*. Scarborough: Prentice Hall Canada, 1992.

Aggarwal, A. *Sexual Harassment in the Workplace*. Scarborough: Butterworths, 1987.

Alvarez, Rodolfo, K.G. Lutterman, et al. *Discrimination in Organizations*. San Francisco: Jossey Bass, 1979, ch. 1.

Anker, R. *Gender and Jobs: Sex Segregation of Occupations in the World*. Geneva: International Labour Office, 1997.

Arvey, Richard and James Campion. "The Employment Interview: A Summary and Review of Recent Research." *Personnel Psychology* 35 (1982): 281-322.

Associated Press. "Coca-Cola to Create Ombudsman as Part of Discrimination Settlement." Atlanta: November 16, 2000.

Bacchi, Carol. *The Politics of Affirmative Action: "Women", Equality and Category Politics*. London: Sage, 1996.

Baron, James. "Organizational Evidence of Ascription in Labor Markets." in Paul Burstein (ed.). *Equal Employment Opportunity: Labor Market Discrimination and Public Policy*. New York: Aldine De Gruyter, 1994, 71-84.

Baron, J. N. and A. E. Newman. "For What It's Worth: Organizations, Occupations and the Value of Work Done by Women and Nonwhites." *American Sociological Review* 55 (1990): 155-175.

Bell, E.L., T.C. Denton and S.M. Nkomo. "Women of Color in Management: Towards an Inclusive Analysis." in L. Larwood and B. Gutek (eds.). *Women in Management: Trends, Issues, Challenges*. Newbury Park: Sage, 1992.

Bielby, William and James Baron. "A Woman's Place is with Other Women: Sex Segregation within Organizations." in Barbara Reskin (ed.). *Sex Segregation in the Workplace*. Washington: National Academy Press, 1984, 27-55.

Bielby, William and James Baron. "Men and Women at Work: Sex Segregation and Statistical Discrimination," *American Journal of Sociology* 91 (1986): 759-99.

Billingsley, Brenda and Leon Muszynski. "No Discrimination Here? Toronto Employers and the Multi-Racial Workforce." Toronto: Urban Alliance on Race Relations and Social Planning Council of Metropolitan Toronto, 1985.

Birenbaum, Joanna and Bruce Porter. "Screening Rights: The Denial of the Right to Adjudication Under the Canadian Human Rights Act and How to Remedy It." report to the Canadian Human Rights Act Review Panel, 2000.

Boyd, Monica. "Gender, Visible Minority and Immigrant Earning Inequality: Reassessing an Employment Equity Premise." in Vic Satzewich (ed). *Deconstructing a Nation: Immigration, Multiculturalism and Racism in the 90s Canada.* Toronto: Garamond Press, 1992.

Braddock, J.M. and McPartland. "How Minorities Continue to be Excluded from Equal Employment Opportunities: Research on Labor Market and Institutional Barriers." *Journal of Social Issues* 43.1 (1987): 5-39.

Brass, Daniel. "Men's and Women's Networks: A Study of Interaction Patterns and Influence in an Organization." *Academy of Management Journal* 28.2 (1985): 327-43.

British Columbia Public Service Employee Relations Commission v. British Columbia Government and Service Employees' Union. Supreme Court of Canada [1999] 3 S.C.R..

Brown, Colin and Pat Gay. "Racial Discrimination: 17 Years After the Act." in in Paul Burstein (ed.). *Equal Employment Opportunity: Labor Market Discrimination and Public Policy.* New York: Aldine De Gruyter, 1994, 315-328.

Bruegel, I. And D. Perrons. "Deregulation and Women's Employment – the Diverse Experiences of Women in Britain." *Feminist Economics* 4.1 (1998) 103-125.

Calleja, Dawn. "Right Skills, Wrong Country." *Canadian Business* (June 26,2000): 35-39.

Canadian Human Rights Commission (CHRC). *Annual Report.* 2000.

Carmichael, F. and R. Woods. "Ethnic Penalties in Unemployment and Occupational Attainment: Evidence for Britain." *International Review of Applied Economics,*" 14.1 (2000): 71-98.

Chicha, Marie-Therese. "The Impact of Labour Market Transformations on the Effectiveness of Laws Promoting Workplace Gender Equality." in R. Chaykowski and L. Powell (eds.). *Women and Work*. Kingston: Mcgill-Queen's University Press, 1999, 283-304.

Christofides, L. N. and R. Swidinsky. "Wage Determination by Gender and Visible Minority Status: Evidence from the 1989 LMAS." *Canadian Public Policy* 20. 1 (1994): 34-51.

Cockburn, Cynthia. *In the Way of Women: Men's Resistance to Sex Equality in Organizations.* Ithaca: ILR Press, 1991.

Collins, Sharon. "Black Mobility in White Corporations: Up the Corporate Ladder but Out on a Limb." *Social Problems* 44 (1997): 55-67.

Collison, David, David Knights and Margaret Collison. *Managing to Discriminate.* London: Routledge, Chapman and Hall, 1990.

Corby, Susan. "The Rise and Fall of Equal Opportunities." *Personnel Management* 26. 13 (1994): 34 ff.

Donohue, John III and James Heckman. "Continuous versus Episodic Change: The Impact of Civil Rights Policy on the Economic Status of Blacks." in Paul Burstein (ed.). *Equal Employment Opportunity: Labor Market Discrimination and Public Policy.* New York: Aldine De Gruyter, 1994, 155-182.

Doren, Bonnie and Michael Benz. "Employment Inequality Revisited: Predictors of Better Employment Outcomes for Young Women with Disabilities in Transition." *Journal of Special Education* 31. 4 (1998) 425 ff.

Dorfman, Peter, Walter Stephan and John Loveland. "Performance Appraisal Behaviors: Superior Perceptions and Subordinate Reactions." *Personnel* 39.3 (1986): 579-97.

Duclos, Nitya. "Disappearing Women: Racial Minority Women in Human Rights Cases." *Canadian Journal of Women and the Law* 6 (1993): 25-51.

Epstein, S.. *We Can Make It: Stories of Disabled Women in Developing Countries.* Geneva: International Labour Office, 1997.

Espinosa, Dula. "Sexual Harassment Protection for Whom?" in Carol R. Ronai, Barbara Zsembik and Joe R. Feagin (eds.). *Everyday Sexism in the Third Millennium.* New York: Routledge, 1997.

Essed, Philomena. *Everyday Racism.* Alameda, California.: Hunter House, 1990.

European Foundation for the Improvement of Living and Working Conditions (EUROFOUND). "Equal Opportunities and Collective Bargaining in the EU." April 1997.

European Foundation for the Improvement of Living and Working Conditions (EUROFOUND). "Workers with Disabilities: Law, Bargaining and the Social Partners." Feb. 1. 2001.

Feagin. Joe R.. "Changing Black Americans to Fit a Racist System." *Journal of Social Issues* 43.1 (1987): 85-9.

Gilbert, Jacqueline and John Ivancevich. "Valuing Diversity: A Tale of Two Organizations." *Academy of Management Executive* 14.1 (2000): 93-105.

Gilbert, Jacqueline, Bette Ann Stead and John Ivancevich. "Diversity Management: A New Organizational Paradigm." *Journal of Business Ethics* 21.1 (1999): 61-76.

Glastra, Folke, Petra Schedler and Erik Kats. "Between Public Controversy and Market Initiative: The Politics of Employment Equity and Diversity in the Netherlands." in Carol Agocs (ed.). *Workplace Equality: International Perspectives on Legislation, Policy and Practice*. Dordrecht: Kluwer Academic Publishers, 2001.

Graves, L.M. and G.N. Powell. "An Investigation of Sex Discrimination in Recruiters' Evaluations of Actual Applicants." *Journal of Applied Psychology* 73 (1988): 20-29.

Griffin, Paulette. *Closing the Gap: Women's Advancement in Corporate and Professional Canada*. New York: Catalyst, 1997.

Gullett, Carlos. "Reverse Discrimination and Remedial Affirmative Action in Employment: Dealing with the Paradox of Nondiscrimination." *Public Personnel Management* 29.1 (2000): 107 ff.

Gutek, Barbara. *Sex Role Stereotyping and Affirmative Action Policy*. Los Angeles, University of California, Institute of Industrial Relations, 1982.

Halaby, Charles. "Sexual Inequality in the Workplace: An Employer-specific Analysis of Pay Differences." *Social Science Research* 8.1 (1979): 79-104.

Heaton, Norma and Paul Teague. "Towards Fair Employment in Northern Ireland?" *International Review of Applied Economics*. 11.2 (1997): 263-285.

Henry, Frances and Effie Ginzberg. *Who Gets the Work? A Test of Racial Discrimination in Employment*. Toronto: Social Planning Council of Metropolitan Toronto and Urban Alliance on Race Relations, 1985.

Hodges-Aeberhard, Jane. "Affirmative Action in Employment: Recent Court Approaches to a Difficult Concept." *International Labour Review* 138.3 (1999): 247-272.

Hodges-Aeberhard, Jane and Carl Raskin (eds). *Affirmative Action in the Employment of Ethnic Minorities and Persons with Disabilities*. Geneva: ILO, 1997.

Hogan, Joyce and Ann Quigley. "Physical Standards for Employment and the Courts." *American Psychologist* 41 (1986): 1193-12117.

Holzer, Harry and David Neumark. "Assessing Affirmative Action." *Journal of Economic Literature* 38..3 (2000): 438-568.

Horwitz, Frank and Harish Jain. "Employment Equity in South Africa: Overcoming the Apartheid Legacy." in Carol Agocs (ed.) *Workplace Equality: International Perspectives on Legislation, Policy and Practice*. Dordrecht: Kluwer Academic Publishers, 2001.

Ibarra, Herminia. "Personal Networks of Women and Minorities in Management: A Conceptual Framework." *Academy of Management Review* 18.1 (1993): 56-87.

Ivancevich, John and Jacqueline Gilbert. "Diversity Management: Time for a New Approach." *Public Personnel Management* 29.1 (2000): 75 ff.

Jacobs, J. A. *Revolving Doors: Sex Segregation and Women's Careers*. Stanford: Stanford University Press, 1989.

Jacobson, C. K.. "Resistance to Affirmative Action: Self Interest or Racism?" *Journal of Conflict Resolution* 29 (1985): 306-29.

Jain, Harish C.. "Employment Equity in Selected Counties: The Case of Racial and Ethnic Minorities." in Carol Agocs (ed.). *Workplace Equality: International Perspectives on Legislation. Policy and Practice*. Dordrecht: Kluwer Academic Publishers, 2001.

Jain, Harish C., Mohammed Al-Waqfi and Carol Agocs. "Racial Discrimination in Employment in Canada: An Analysis of Human Rights Cases." Canadian Race Relations Foundation. December 1999.

Jain, Harish C. and C. S. Venkata Ratnam. "Gender Equality in India." in Carol Agocs (ed.). *Workplace Equality: International Perspectives on Legislation, Policy and Practice*. Dordrecht: Kluwer Academic Publishers, 2001.

Jenson, Jane. "Thinking About Marginalisation: What, Who and Why?". Ottawa: Canadian Policy Research Networks, November 2000.

Kanter, Rosabeth Moss. "Differential Access to Opportunity and Power." in R. Alvarez and K. G. Lutterman et al (eds.) *Discrimination in Organizations*. Washington: Jossey Bass, 1979, 52-68.

Kanter, Rosabeth Moss. *Men and Women of the Corporation*. New York: Free Press, 1978.

Karambayya, Rekha. "In Shouts and Whispers: Paradoxes Facing Women of Colour in Organizations." *Journal of Business Ethics* 16.9 (1997): 891-897.

Kluegel, James. "Trends in Whites' Explanations of the Black-White Gap in Socioeconomic Status, 1977-89." in Paul Burstein (ed.). *Equal Employment Opportunity: Labor Market Discrimination and Public Policy*. New York: Aldine De Gruyter, 1994, 395-406.

Kravitz, David et al. "A Review of Psychological and Behavioral Research on Affirmative Action." The Society for Industrial and Organizational Psychology, American Psychological Society, 1999.

Krysan, Maria. "Prejudice. Politics and Public Opinion: Understanding the Sources of Racial Policy Attitudes." *Annual Review of Sociology* 26 (2000): 135-168.

Kunz, Jean Lock, Anne Milan and Sylvain Schetagne. *Unequal Access: A Canadian Profile of Racial Differences in Education, Employment and Income*. Toronto: Canadian Race Relations Foundation, 2000.

Lapidus, J. and D. Figart. "Remedying Unfair Acts – U.S. Pay Equity by Race and Gender." *Feminist Economics* 4.3 (1998): 7-28.

Larwood, L.E., E. Szwajkowski and S. Rose. "Sex and Race Discrimination Resulting from Manager-Client Relationships: Applying the Rational Bias Theory of Managerial Discrimination." *Sex Roles* 18 (1988): 9-29.

Leck, Joanne and David Saunders. "Hiring Women: The Effects of Canada's Employment Equity Act." *Canadian Public Policy* 18.2 (1992): 203-220.

Leonard, Jonathan. "The Impact of Affirmative Action Regulation and Equal Employment Law on Black Employment." *Journal of Economic Perspectives* 4.4 (1990): 47-63.

Leonard, Jonathan. "Wage Disparities and Affirmative Action in the 1980s." *American Economic Association Papers and Proceedings* 86.2 (1996): 285-93.

Leonard, Jonathan S.. "Women and Affirmative Action." *Journal of Economic Perspectives* 3.1 (1989): 61-75.

Marino, Kenneth. "Structural Correlates of Affirmative Action Compliance." *Journal of Management* 8.1 (1982): 75-93.

Maume, David. "Glass Ceilings and Glass Escalators." *Work and Occupations* 26.4 (1999): 483-509.

Mittger, Maarten. "Drawing the Teeth of the Equity Act." *Finance Week – South Africa*, Dec. 11, 1998, 12.

Mobley, William. "Supervisor and Employee Race and Sex Effects on Performance Appraisals: A Field Study of Adverse Impact and Generalizability." *Academy of Management Journal* 25 (1982): 586-97.

Morrison, Ann, Ellen van Velsor and Randall White. *Breaking the Glass Ceiling*. Reading, Mass.: Addison-Wesley, 1987.

Murdick, Nancy. "Employment Discrimination Laws for Disability: Utilization and Outcome." *Annals of the American Academy of Political and Social Science* 549 (Jan. 1997): 53-70.

Neft, Naomi and Ann Levine. *Where Women Stand: An International Report on the Status of Women in 140 Countries. 1997-1998*. New York: Random House, 1997.

O'Connor, Julia, Ann Shola Orloff and Sheila Shaver. *States, Markets, Families: Gender, Liberalism and Social Policy in Australia, Canada, Great Britain and the United States*. New York: Cambridge University Press, 1999.

Orser, Barbara. *Sexual Harassment is Still a Management Issue*. Toronto: Conference Board of Canada, 2001.

Osborne, Robert. "Fair Employment and Employment Equity: Policy Learning in a Comparative Context." *Public Money and Management* 12.4 (1992): 11-18.

Pettigrew, Thomas. "Reactions Toward the New Minorities of Western Europe." *Annual Review of Sociology* 24 (1998): 11-103.

Pettigrew, Thomas and Joanne Martin. "Shaping the Organizational Context for Black American Inclusion." *Journal of Social Issues* 43.1 (1987): 41-78.

Pettigrew, Thomas and R. W. Meertens. "Subtle and Blatant Prejudice in Western Europe." *European Journal of Social Psychology* 25 (1995): 57-75.

Phillips, Paul and Erin Phillips. *Women and Work: Inequality in the Canadian Labour Market*. Toronto: James Lorimer, 1993.

Plantegna, Janneke and Johan Hansen. "Assessing Equal Opportunities in the European Union." *International Labour Review* 138.4 (1999): 351-379.

Quaid, Maeve. *Job Evaluation: The Myth of Equitable Assessment*. Toronto: University of Toronto Press, 1993.

Radford, Mary F. . "Affirmative Action in American Employment Law: Past, Present, and Future." in Carol Agocs (ed.). *Workplace Equality: International Perspectives on Legislation, Policy and Practice*. Dordrecht: Kluwer Academic Publishers, 2001.

Ratnam, C.S. Venkata and V. Chandra. "Sources of Diversity and the Challenge Before Human Resource Management in India." *International Journal of Manpower* 17.45 (1996): 76-108.

Reitz, Jeffrey G.. *Warmth of the Welcome: The Social Causes of Economic Success for Immigrants in Different Nations and Cities*. Boulder: Westview Press, 1998.

Reskin, Barbara. *The Realities of Affirmative Action in Employment*. Washington: American Sociological Association, 1998.

Reskin, Barbara. Debra McBrier and Julie Kmec. "The Determinants and Consequences of Workplace Sex and Race Composition." *Annual Review of Sociology* 25 (1999): 335-361.

Reskin, R. and C. E. Ross. "Jobs, Authority and Earnings Among Managers: The Continuing Significance of Sex." in J. A. Jacobs (ed.). *Gender Inequality at Work*. Thousand Oaks, California: Sage, 1995.

Rogers, Sheila. "Northern Ireland – Gender, Race and the New Equality Agenda." in Carol Agocs (ed.). *Workplace Equality: International Perspectives on Legislation, Policy and Practice*. Dordrecht: Kluwer Academic Publishers. 2001.

Rogers. W. M. III and W. E. Spriggs 'The Effect of Federal Conractor Status on Racial Differences in Establishment-level Employment Shares: 1979-1992." *American Economic Association Papers and Proceedings* 86.2 (1996): 290-93.

Roos, Patricia. *Gender and Work: A Comparative Analysis of Industrial Societies*. SUNY Press, 1985.

Rose, David. "Twenty-five Years Later: Where Do We Stand on Equal Employment Opportunity Law Enforcement?" in Paul Burstein (ed.). *Equal Employment Opportunity: Labour Market Discrimination and Public Policy*. New York: Aldine De Gruyter, 1994, 39-58.

Rossilli, Mariagrazia (ed.). *Gender Policies in the European Union*. New York: Peter Lang, 2000.

Rynes, Sara and Benson Rosen. " A Field Survey of Factors Affecting the Adoption and Perceived Success of Diversity Training." *Personnel Psychology* 48.2 (1995): 247 ff.

Seidman, Gay. "Is South Africa Different? Sociological Comparisons and Theoretical Contributions from the Land of Apartheid." *Annual Review of Sociology* 25 (1999): 419-40.

Sheppard, Coleen. "Systemic Inequality and Workplace Culture: Challenging the Institutionalization of Sexual Harassment." *Canadian Labour and Employment Law* 3 (1995-96): 249-286.

Simpson, Suzanne, Michael McCarrey and Henry Edwards. "Relationship of Supervisors' Sex Role Stereotypes to Performance Evaluation of Male and Female Subordinates in Non-traditional Jobs." *Canadian Journal of Administrative Sciences* 4 (1987): 15-30.

Smith, Ryan A.. "Race, Income and Authority at Work: A Cross-temporal Analysis of Black and White Men (1972-1994)." *Social Problems* 44 (1997): 19-37.

South, Scott, Charles Bonjean, William Markham and Judy Corder. "Social Structure and Intergroup Interaction: Men and Women of the Federal Bureaucracy." *American Sociological Review* 47 (1982): 587-99.

Steeh, Charlotte and Maria Krysan. "The Polls – Trends. Affirmative Action and the Public, 1970-1995." *Public Opinion Quarterly* 60 (1996): 128-158.

Steinbeg, R. J. "The Social Construction of Skill." *Work and Occupations* 17 (1990): 449-82.

Strachan, Glenda and John Burgess. "Unfinished Business: Employment Equality in Australia." in Carol Agocs (ed.). *Workplace Equality: International Perspectives on Legislation, Policy and Practice*. Dordrecht: Kluwer Academic Publishers, 2001.

Thacker, Rebecca and Gerald Ferris. "Understanding Sexual Harassment in the Workplace." *Human Resource Management Review* 1.1 (1991): 23-37.

Thornton, Patricia and Neil Lunt. *Employment Policies for Disabled People in Eighteen Countries: A Review*. University of York: Social Policy Research Unit, 1997.

Tummala, Krishna. "Policy of Preference: Lessons from India, the United States, and South Africa." *Public Administration Review* 59.6 (1999): 495-508.

United Nations, Press Release HR/4497, RD/901. October 16, 2000.

Weiler, Anni. "Organizational Structures, Gender and Industrial Relations: Equal Opportunity Provisions in Collective Agreements in the EU." paper presented at the 12th World Congress of the International Industrial Relations Association, Tokyo, May 29-June 2, 2000.

Wentling, Rose Mary and Nilda Palma-Rivas "Current Status of Diversity Initiatives in Selected Multi-national Corporations." *Human Resource Development Quarterly* 11.1 (2000): 35-60.

Wrench, John. "Towards an International Typology of Anti-discrimination Training in Employment." paper presented at the Fifth International Metropolis Conference, Vancouver, November 2000.

Wright, P., S. Ferris, J. Hiller and M. Kroll. "Competitiveness Through Management of Diversity: Effects on Stock Price Valuation." *Academy of Management Journal* 38 (1995): 272-287.

Young, Iris Marion. *Justice and the Politics of Difference*. Princeton: Princeton University Press. 1990, ch. 2.

Zegers de Beijl, Roger. "Combating Discrimination Against Migrant Workers: International Standards, National Legislation and Voluntary Measures – the Need for a Multi-pronged Strategy." Geneva: International Labour Organization, 1997.

CHAPTER 2

HARISH C. JAIN

EMPLOYMENT EQUITY IN SELECTED COUNTRIES: THE CASE OF RACIAL AND ETHNIC MINORITIES[1]

INTRODUCTION

One of the challenges faced by policy makers at both macro and micro levels (government and firm level respectively) is the extent to which equality of opportunity is afforded to members of the increasingly diverse workforces in various nations around the world and in the global economy. A growing number of countries have gone beyond providing equality of opportunity by means of anti- discrimination laws, which are complaint based and passive, and have moved to pro-active policy initiatives such as employment equity/affirmative action (EE/AA) to improve the representation of racial and ethnic minorities or majorities in employers' workforces.

This chapter examines:

(a) the experiences of countries where equal employment and employment equity/affirmative action policies have been designed to assist the majority population, such as in Malaysia; and
(b) selected countries' experiences with quotas or reservations, legislated goals and timetables and positive action policies and programs. For example, India and Malaysia have affirmative action programs with constitutionally sanctioned mandatory programs. The United States has Presidential Executive Orders requiring AA with mandated goals and timetables for federal contractors and sub-contractors. Canada has legislated equal opportunity and EE/AA policies with goals and timetables. Britain has a policy of voluntary AA programs, while Northern Ireland has legislated goals and timetables and AA programs for Catholic minorities.

This chapter discusses these selected countries and lessons to be drawn from the successes and failures of these policies in the five countries, and hypothesises that such policies can be a source of competitive advantage in the global economy.

SELECTED COUNTRIES' POLICY RESPONSES TO SYSTEMIC DISCRIMINATION IN EMPLOYMENT

I have selected several countries to illustrate variations in EE/AA policy responses to discrimination in employment. These are: India, Malaysia, Canada, United States, Britain, and Northern Ireland. EE/AA policies of these countries will be examined in some detail.

In Malaysia, AA policies deal with the majority community -- the *Bumiputras* ("sons of the soil"), who comprise approximately 59 percent of the population.

C. Agocs (ed.), Workplace Equality, 35–46.

In India, the government's task is one of addressing inequalities for a significant number of minorities categorised as scheduled castes (SCs) and scheduled tribes (STs). Both groups together constitute 21 percent or more than 200 million of the 864 million population as of 1991 (Jain and Ratnam, 1994).

In Canada and the United States, EE target groups include racial minorities, women, aboriginal people and persons with disabilities. In both countries, close to 45 percent of the workforce consists of women; racial minorities constitute more than 21 percent in the United States and 10.3 percent of the labour force in Canada.

In Britain, racial minorities form only 5 percent of the working population but their visibility is increased by their concentration in large metropolitan areas. Women make up 43 percent of those at work. In Northern Ireland, ethnicity and religiosity are closely intertwined. For instance, a person's community of origin greatly affects their marriage partner, residential area, school to be attended by their children, choice of employers, etc. (Cormack and Osborne, 1991). The Catholic minority is sizeable and growing relative to the Protestant majority: 58 percent are Protestants vs. 42 percent Catholics. AA is the key mechanism, under the Fair Employment legislation, to affect the working environments inside companies.

The Indian Experience

Indian society has traditionally been based on a caste hierarchy, which places the priestly caste at the top and those doing manual labour at the bottom. One group of disadvantaged people are the so-called untouchables. They are generally known as the scheduled castes (SCs). The second group are the tribes who are disadvantaged because they are isolated in remote places. They are known as the scheduled tribes (STs). Members of the SCs and STs are predominantly in the unorganised, informal sector, and thus largely unprotected by employment standards and other labour legislation. A substantial majority are dependent on agriculture but do not own land, which leads to very low wages and bonded labour (Kaur, 1997).

When India became independent in 1947, the nationalist leadership was committed to removing job and other barriers faced by the two groups. They wrote into the Constitution provisions prohibiting discrimination on grounds of religion, race, caste, sex, descent, place of birth or residence. The purpose was to eliminate discrimination against the untouchables (SCs) and to facilitate spatial and social mobility for tribal people (STs).

The Indian Constitution came into effect in 1950. As a direct result of the constitutional provisions, a reservations or quota policy came into effect as noted earlier. Both SCs and STs were given seats in the parliament and in the state legislative assemblies in proportion to their population. Quotas or reservations provisions were also made for employment in government and public sector jobs (i.e., public enterprises), in the national and state governments, as well as for admissions into schools, colleges, medical and engineering schools (see the Constitution of India, articles 46, 15, 16 and 35 in Bakshi, 2000).

Thus, the Indian experience is one in which AA is defined quite rigidly in terms of reservations and quotas. The rationale for constitutional safeguards and AA programmes for the socially and economically depressed classes lies in the obnoxious practice of untouchability in respect of SCs and exploitive slavery in respect of both the SCs and STs.

In 1990, the Indian government announced that there would be additional quotas or reservations for "other backward classes" (OBCs). The OBCs are socially and educationally backward classes of citizens, comprising approximately 27 percent of India's population (See Bakshi, 2000: 28). The government adopted a quota of 27 percent for the OBCs on top of the 22 percent provided for the scheduled castes (SCs) and the tribals (STs). Thus, in all, 49 percent of government jobs and admissions into colleges, medical and engineering schools were put aside for approximately three-quarters of the population (Jain and Ratnam, 1994).

The Supreme Court of India was asked by several parties to stay the government's order of a quota of 27 percent for the OBCs. In its decision of November 16, 1992, the Supreme Court upheld the government's order (by a majority of 6 to 3) to provide job quotas for the OBCs. The Court decided that reservations for all three groups (SCs, STs and OBCs) should not ordinarily exceed 50 percent. As well, candidates selected for reserved positions must meet certain conditions of eligibility to satisfy the requirement of efficiency in administration. The judgement exempted from reservations appointments to certain positions, for example, defence personnel, research scientists, medical scientists, university professors, etc. (Indra Sawhney and others, Petitioners v. Union of India and others, Respondents, November 16, 1992).

The achievements of AA in India are significant even if they fall short of quotas -- that is, even if exact parity in representation according to their availability as per the 1991 Census was not achieved -- particularly with regard to securing proportional representation in professional and managerial positions (Jain and Ratnam, 1994). There is a small and growing middle class of untouchables and tribals.

AA in India has survived and strengthened because of popular and political support; more than one out of every five seats in the parliament are represented and filled by SC and ST candidates as guaranteed by the Constitution. Similar reservations exist with respect to state legislatures, as noted earlier. Continued political pressure from the elected representatives belonging to these communities, who account for 22.5 percent of parliamentarians and legislators, helps keep the governments and the public enterprise managers on their toes (Jain and Ratnam, 1994).[2] Despite these provisions, the progress has been slow on account of a low economic growth rate in the 1950-1990 period. Resources available for the expansion in education and other social services have remained scarce.

It has become increasingly apparent that the beneficiaries from the disadvantaged communities are likely to be the better-off and not the worst-off members of the communities to which they belong and in whose name quotas are made.[3] The Supreme Court of India, in its 1992 decision noted earlier, was concerned about the flow of benefits to what is called "creamy layers" among the disadvantaged and that no really effective way has been found for diverting the benefits of reservation from the better-off to the worst-off members of backward communities (Beteille, 1993).

Experience in Malaysia

The post-independence government in Malaysia was formed by a coalition of three ethnic groups: the Chinese, the Indians, and the Malays. Following independence in 1957, an accord was forged among the three ethnic groups: citizenship for the Chinese and Indians in return for the native Malays (that is, the indigenous people relative to Chinese and Indians) receiving preferential treatment under the constitution (Puthucheary, 1993; Weiner, n.d.). However, following the riots after the 1969 elections it was felt that the ethnic Malay community was economically disadvantaged and that this situation was not conducive to national stability and unity. A new economic policy (NEP) resulted in a fundamental restructuring of the Malaysian economy in order to correct economic imbalances. Several strategies were employed to increase the employment and earned income of *Bumiputras*. Quotas were introduced in various areas such as admission to university and equity ownership, that is, native Malays' ownership in firms that were not owned by them. Quotas were used extensively in the public sector where *Bumiputras* (meaning "sons of the soil") or Native Malays, especially those with educational qualifications, found ready employment. Appointments in the civil service were made at a ratio of four Malays to one non-Malay. While there was some resentment on the part of non-Malays, the Chinese leadership within the governing alliance was willing to go along. In fact, there was a political bargain struck between the Malays and the Chinese elites. The deal was that the Chinese could make money while the Malays could run an administration that pursued pro-growth policies (Emsley, 1992).

Substantial changes were made to the Constitution, which guaranteed the special position of Malays. These provisions could not be removed even by the normal two-thirds majority required for other constitutional amendments. Thus, future governments could not amend this section of the Constitution even if they had a two-thirds majority. In addition, amendments to the sedition laws were passed to make it illegal to question these rights in parliament or outside (Puthucheary, 1993).

In the post-NEP period, the government decided to continue the quota program (Mahathir, 1991). According to Professor Puthucheary (in Weiner, n.d.), the combination of economic growth and special benefits produced a Malay middle class.

In 1969, Malays had only 2 percent of equity in firms, and few Malays were in management. Arrangements were made to expand Malay equity capital, so that by 1990 it reached 22 percent, though much of it was in the hands of Malay institutions rather than individuals (Weiner, n.d.). For the past two decades, the economy of Malaysia grew at between 6 and 7 percent per year. In private sector employment, the Malays exceeded the fifty percent target set in the first Outline Prospective Plan (OPP1), reaching 61.8 percent by 1990 in the professional and technical categories. The Malays also improved their representation from 22.4 percent in 1970 to 31.3 percent in 1990 in the administrative and managerial occupational groups, even though their targeted representation level was 49.3 percent. This lower representation reflects low Malay representation at the managerial and supervisory levels in the manufacturing and service sectors (Hodges-Aberhard and Raskin, 1997).

Some negative consequences of AA in Malaysia have been that:

(a) it has been difficult for the civil service to maintain its image as impartial and politically neutral when it is constantly making political decisions based on ethnic considerations rather than on objective criteria of need and merit, according to Puthucheary (1993);
(b) AA can result in the perpetuation and even strengthening of ethnic cleavages;
(c) AA programs also tend to result in conflicts within the preferential groups themselves since the benefits of AA programs accrue disproportionately to better off than to poorer sections of these groups. This is especially the case between the dominant Malay group and the other indigenous sub-groups that together make up the *Bumiputra* category, such as Sarawak and Sabah groups;
(d) some critics have argued that once AA measures are introduced, they become permanently entrenched in the political system, serving the interests of a small minority.

Experience in the United States

In the United States, initially the country had to address the problem of a disadvantaged minority rather than a majority or large plurality. According to Farley (2000), the United States was essentially a Black-White country until 1960. Today, America -- like Canada -- is becoming a multi-cultural country having people from numerous nationalities and racial and ethnic backgrounds. This is because of slowing birth rates of Blacks and whites, and increasing immigration from Asian and Latin American countries; there were almost 13 million immigrants during the 1980s and early 1990s (Jackson ,2000; Farley, 2000). Farley suggests that the Spanish-origin population will numerically pass the Black population within ten years, due to their rapidly growing population relative to Blacks (Farley, 2000). This demographic diversity is to be found throughout the United States (Farley, 2000) and not just in big cities, as in Canada.

According to Farley (2000), 90 percent of Blacks lived in poverty at the beginning of World War II and while relative gains have occurred in the median income of Blacks in the 1990s, the Black-white earnings gap is likely to continue.

The term affirmative action first appeared in American law in the Civil Rights Act of 1964, title VII. This statute covers both private and public sector employers with 15 or more employees. All employers of 100 or more employees are required to submit employment statistics reporting employment by race and other protected categories in broad job classifications each year. Although not specifically required under Title VII, affirmative action may be required as part of a conciliated or court settlement between employers and the federal enforcement agencies. According to Leonard (1985), more than 1,700 class action suits were filed under this legislation. These suits have been among the most powerful prods to increasing minority and female employment because they affected the most people, resulted in large awards, and generated much publicity.

In 1965, President Lyndon Johnson issued an executive order requiring affirmative action in employment and promotion of all federal contractors, even if they had never discriminated. Presidential Executive Order 11246 requires affirmative action on the part of all federal contractors with 50 or more employees and a contract of $50,00 or more. A federal contractor's entire organization must abide by the terms of affirmative action; if just one facility in the company has a government contract, all of the facilities of that company are subject to the Executive Order. The federal contractors are required to submit a five-year affirmative action plan including goals and timetables and special measures to achieve the goals. Such goals must be significant, attainable and specific for planned results. Failure to develop and implement an acceptable AA program within a specified time could result in cancellation or termination of existing contracts, and disbarment from competing for future contracts (Jain, 1994). The United States contract compliance program covers employers employing an estimated 27 million workers and providing the federal government over 100 billion dollars in construction, goods, and services (Cascio, 1992).

Leonard (1985) has found that even though the goals may be inflated somewhat by a federal contractor and not usually attained, the contractor that promises to employ more minorities does actually employ more in subsequent years. Affirmative action plans by federal contractors have resulted in employment and occupational advances for minorities in the United States (Leonard, 1984b). This trend has continued (Leonard, 1990; Rodgers and Spriggs, 1996; Holzer and Neumark, 1999).

The third annual survey of "America's best 50 companies for minorities" on diversity conducted by the nonprofit Council on Economic Priorities on behalf of the Fortune Magazine found that members of ethnic minorities hold about 16 percent of the board seats, make up 22 percent of the officials and managers, and make 13 percent of the 50 largest pay checks (Mehta, July 10, 2000: 182). This year's survey was focussed on diversity in the upper ranks of each company. According to the magazine, these are key signs that a company has gone beyond political correctness. About 65 percent of the Fortune 1,000 companies have at least one member of an ethnic minority on their board of directors, up from 58 percent in 1998 (Mehta, July 10, 2000: 183).

Experience in Britain and Northern Ireland

There were more than 3 million ethnic minorities in Britain according to the 1991 Census; they constituted 5.5 percent of the total population. Britain has a separate statute to cover race discrimination -- the Race Relations Act of 1976. This legislation is administered by the Commission of Racial Equality Commission (CRE). The Commission has issued codes of practice for employers, trade unions, employment agencies and employees in order to provide guidance for eliminating discrimination and enhancing equality of opportunity. The provisions of the Codes are admissible in evidence in proceedings under the statutes before an industrial tribunal.

Britain became a member of the European Economic Community (EEC) in 1973 and thus subject to the EEC law. An important development since 1973 is the role of European community legislation, which takes precedence over United Kingdom law and has brought about changes in Britain's legislation, especially relating to women (Sloane and Mackay, 1997).

Although there is no general provision for affirmative action (AA) in the above mentioned legislation, AA is permissible in recruitment and training where there have been fewer or no members of one race or sex in particular work in the previous twelve months.

The Race Relations Act in Britain has had positive effects. It has helped to curb the worst kinds of discrimination in employment and has also had an impact on the general climate of opinion (Parekh, 2000). The weaknesses of the RRA include (a) failure to deal with institutional racism and organizational culture; (b) does not prohibit religious discrimination; and (c) is concerned with negative duties, that is avoidance of discrimination, rather than promoting diversity (Parekh, 2000).

In Northern Ireland the legislation covering racial discrimination was enacted recently (1996), and was to be administered by the Commission for Racial Equality. Religion, not covered by legislation in Britain, has the most extensive legislative coverage in Northern Ireland with provisions for both AA and contract compliance. Although legislation prohibiting discrimination on the basis of religion has existed in Northern Ireland since the partition of Ireland in 1920, it was not until the enactment of the Fair Employment Act (FEA) of 1976 that employment discrimination on the basis of religion and political opinion in both public and private employment was outlawed.

Due to the ineffectiveness of the first FEA, it was strengthened in 1989 and 1998 under the Fair Employment and Treatment Order. Fair employment legislation placed obligations on employers, such as the requirement to review employment practices, and mandatory monitoring of their workforces. These features have been absent from any other anti-discrimination legislation in Britain. The 1989 FEA provided for compulsory: (a) registration of employers of more than ten workers with the Fair Employment Commission (FEC); (b) annual monitoring of workforces and of applicants for employment; and (c) review every three years of recruitment, training and promotion practices. It also required affirmative action with goals and timetables and a new code of practice. Penalties under the

Act include criminal penalties, economic sanctions and exclusion from tendering for government contracts and denial of any government grants (Sloane and Mackay, 1997). There is clear evidence that the FEA has had a significant impact on reducing inequalities in the workplace in Northern Ireland (Rogers, 2000).

In April 1998 the Belfast Agreement was signed by the Irish and British Governments and ratified by a majority of people in Northern Ireland. Political power was devolved from the British Parliament to Northern Ireland. The equality dimension of this Agreement was translated into legislation in the form of Northern Ireland Act of 1998. The Act provided for the establishment of a new Commission called the Equality Commission. The Commission assumed the functions of the existing equality agencies in Northern Ireland: the Commission for Racial Equality, and the Fair Employment Commission, as well as the Northern Ireland Disability Council (Rogers, 2000). The new Equality Commission opened its doors to the public in October 1999.

In Northern Ireland the Race Relations Order (RRO) does not have any requirement for employers to monitor for ethnicity as there is in relation to religious discrimination in the Fair Employment legislation of 1998. The Equality Commission can issue Codes of Practice as in the case of CRE and tribunals will have to take these into account. There is no provision for contract compliance as there is in the case of the Fair Employment legislation. The RRO provisions do not appear to apply to all public bodies in Northern Ireland (Rogers, 2000).

The proposed amendments to the British RRA will include a positive duty on public employers to promote equality of opportunity and monitoring by the CRE. However, unlike the FEA, there are no such requirements in the case of the Race Relations Order in Northern Ireland. The positive action provisions in both the RRA and RROs are weak, as noted earlier; in addition, there is no contract compliance under these laws.

Experience in Canada

The Canadian response to improving the status of ethnic minorities has taken three forms. One category of response is in the form of prohibiting discrimination on enumerated grounds. All the provinces and territories as well as the federal government have human rights legislation prohibiting discriminatory treatment on several grounds including gender, race, ethnic, origin, religion, age, etc. The Constitution Act of 1982 contains the Canadian Charter of Rights and Freedoms. Section 15(2) of the Charter guarantees certain rights and freedoms without precluding employment equity programmes. This section applies to all government agencies across Canada (e.g. federal, provincial, territorial and municipal).

The second category of responses has been to enact specific legislation aimed at implementing employment equity programs. This has taken the form of the federal Employment Equity Act (EEA) of 1986, recently amended (October 1995) and strengthened to include federal government agencies for the first time.

To establish the context for policy formulation in this area, it is useful to review the latest census information regarding racial minorities or visible minorities (VMs), as they are called in official statistics in Canada. In 1996, VMs made up 11.2 percent of the Canadian population. They are a growing proportion of the population in Canada's principal cities. For instance, they made up 32 percent of the population of Toronto, 31 percent in Vancouver, as well as 16 percent in Calgary, 14 percent in Edmonton, 12 percent in Ottawa/Hull, and 11 percent in Winnipeg (Jain et. al., 2000:47).

Table 1 (page 42) shows the representation of racial minorities in the Canadian workforce from 1981 to 1996. Their proportion has more than doubled from 4.9 percent to 10.3 percent.

The Employment Equity Act (EEA) applies to employers in the private sector, as noted above and to federal government departments with 100 or more employees. The legislation requires these employers to file an annual report with Human Resources Development Canada (HRDC). Employers are required to provide annual information on the representation of four designated groups -- VMs, women, Aboriginal people and persons with disabilities -- by occupational groups and salary ranges, as well as hires, promotions and terminations. The public sector employers were required to provide similar information to the Treasury Board of Canada beginning in 1996 (Jain, November 1997).

Table 1. Percentage of Workforce Representation of Women and Racial Minorities in Canada (1981, 1986, 1991 and 1996)

	1981	1986	1991	1996
Females	42.1	44.0	45.9	46.4
Visible Minorities	4.9	6.3	9.1	10.3

Source: 1981, 1986, 1991, 1996 Census of Canada, Statistics Guide

Under the 1995 Act, in addition to this statistical information, employers are also required (as of October 1996) to include in their annual reports: (1) a description of the measures taken to implement EE and the results achieved; and (2) the consultations between the employer and its employee representatives concerning EE implementation.

Failure to comply with the filing requirements can result in an administrative penalty for three specific reporting violations (for private sector employers only): (a) failure to file an annual report; (b) failure to include the required information; and (c) knowingly filing a report containing false or misleading information. The amount of monetary penalty is $10,000 for a single violation and $50,000 for repeated and continued violations. All records used in the compilation of the annual reports must be retained by the employer for two years following the submission of the report. The annual reports are made publicly available and also given to the Canadian Human Rights Commission (CHRC) (Jain, November 1997).

The CHRC was given the authority to conduct on-site compliance reviews (i.e., audits) under the EEA to verify and ensure employer compliance as of October 24, 1997. The Act also provided for final enforcement, where necessary, by an EE Tribunal. The Tribunal was empowered to hear disputes and issue orders enforceable by courts.

The 1995 Act prescribed four factors to be taken into account in setting goals by an employer (Jain, November 1997). These were:

(1) the degree of under-representation of each designated group in each occupational category;
(2) availability of qualified persons in designated groups within the employer's workplace and the Canadian workforce;

(3) the anticipated growth or reduction of the employer's workforce during the period of numerical goals; and
(4) the anticipated turnover within the employer's workforce in respect of which the numerical goals apply.

In the private sector firms covered by the EEA since 1986, overall, the representation of members of VM groups more than doubled in the twelve years, 1987 to 1998, from 4.9 percent to 9.9 percent. However, it remained below the 10.3 percent availability rate established by the 1996 Census (Annual Report, 1999: 81). VMs remained concentrated in some occupational groups and under-represented in others, including senior management (Annual Report, 1999: 82).

Their representation varied considerably by industrial sector. In banking, their representation was 15.3 percent in 1998 relative to 9.5 percent in 1987. In communications, they made up 9.0 percent, more than double their 1987 representation rate of 4 percent (this rate was below availability). Progress was slowest in the transportation sector, where VMs' representation rate was 5.7 percent in 1998 relative to 2.8 percent in 1987 (Annual Report, 1999: 81-82).

As noted earlier, the EE Act did not apply to the public service (that is, federal government departments and agencies) until 1996; hence data are available since 1997. As of March 31, 1999, the representation of VMs in the federal public service was 5.9 percent relative to 5.1 percent in 1997.

In the first two years of audits since the 1995 EEA came into effect -- 1998 and 1999 -- the CHRC reports in its 1999 Annual Report that only four employers (of the 136 employers audited in the two years) were actually in compliance at the time of the initial compliance audit. However, many have given undertakings to bring themselves into compliance.

The CHRC reports that while there has been progress for some designated groups, "movement towards an equitable federal workplace continues at a snail's pace" (Annual Report, 1999: 86). Visible minorities in the public sector "are simply not making acceptable gains".

The third category of Canada's response to inequality in employment has been to use administrative policy (as opposed to legislation) to require implementation of employment equity programs. The best example here is the Federal Contractors Program (1986) which requires organizations with 100 or more employees bidding on federal government contracts of $200,000 or more to undertake employment equity programs. This program covers 1,286 employers with a workforce of more than a million (1,129,708) workers as of 31 March 1995 (Jain, 1995). Contractors are required to remove barriers faced by the four designated groups in selection, hiring, promoting and training; mount proactive positive measures; and come up with specific goals and timetables. There are no studies available to evaluate the results of the contract compliance program.

ORGANIZATIONAL LEVEL IMPLICATIONS

At a micro or organizational level, much of the success or failure of EE/AA programs can be attributed to whether employees believe that staffing processes for designated groups were procedurally fair, that is, perceived equity of the recruitment, selection, promotion processes used to make managerial decisions relating to the target groups. If the process appears unfair, designated groups may suffer negative self-perceptions of competence. Several studies support the notion that employees have higher perceptions of fairness when EE/AA is achieved through certain competitive advantage arguments (Greenberg, 1990; Heilman, McCullough, and Gilbert, 1996). Studies have also shown the relationship between procedural fairness and organizational outcomes such as trust in a decision-maker.

Similarly, micro-organizational determinants such as the status of the EE/AA officer can have an impact on the success or failure of such programs. Pfeffer, Davis-Blake, and Julius (1995) found that salary paid to the head of EE/AA was associated with the amount of change in racial and gender composition of senior positions. Officers with higher status, hence higher pay relative to other administrators in the same organization, were more likely to mobilize resources and have a higher proportion of women and other designated groups.

CONCLUSIONS AND IMPLICATIONS

We have reviewed the experiences of six countries with their equal opportunities, employment equity and affirmative action policies and programs. It is not possible to conclude that there is a universal panacea or prescription for removing the employment problems of disadvantaged groups in each of the countries. The only possible conclusion one can come to is that the cultural constraints, unique features of the policies and the groups covered have an impact on the success of such programs. For instance, the constitutional provisions resulting in quotas for the disadvantaged groups in India and Malaysia have achieved mixed success. In the United States and Canada, a great deal of progress has been achieved by minority groups and women but much remains to be done. In these two countries, the policies do not mandate quotas and yet, perhaps due to enforcement relative to India, some groups have seen their earnings and occupational status enhanced.

Harish C. Jain is Professor of Human Resources and Labour Relations at the Michael DeGroote School of Business, McMaster University, Hamilton, Ontario, Canada.

NOTES

[1] Adapted from a paper presented at the 12th World Congress of the International Industrial Relations Association in Tokyo, Japan, and published in the *Proceedings* of the Congress, entitled *Search for Flexibility, Fairness and Prosperity: Alternative Employment Policies in the Twenty-First Century,* International Industrial Relations Association, May 29-June 2, 2000, Tokyo, Japan, pages 70-81, and from an upcoming book by the author and others.

[2] Despite their minority status, SCs and STs are able to have considerable influence since the present federal government, as well as the last several governments, is a coalition of several parties and hence the balance of power can be tilted by minorities such as SCs and STs.

[3] The beneficiaries of the quotas are economically well-to-do people among the SCs and STs and not the poor SCs and STS, and that is the reasons that the Supreme Court labelled them as "creamy layers" among the disadvantaged.

REFERENCES

Bakshi, P.M. *The Constitution of India*. Delhi: Universal Books, 2000.

Beteille, A. "India: Equal Opportunities for All and Special Opportunities for Some." *Development and Democracy*. Johannesburg: The Urban Foundation, 1993, 3-20.

Britain 1996, An Official Handbook. London: HMSO, 1995.

Cascio, Wayne. *Managaing Human Resources: Productivity, Quality of Work Life, Profits*. New York: McGraw-Hill, Inc., 1992.

Cormack R.J. and Osborne, R.D. (eds). *Discrimination and Public Policy in Northern Ireland.*. Oxford: Clarendon Press, 1991.

Canadian Human Rights Commission (CHRC). *Annual Report 1999*. Ottawa: Minister of Public Works and Government Services, 2000.

Emsley, I. "Affirmative Action: The Malaysian Experience." *OPTIMA* November 1992.

Farley, Reynolds. "Demographic, Economic and Social Trends in a Multicultural America." in Jackson, James S.(ed). *New Directions: African Americans in a Diversifying Nation*. Washington, D.C.: National Policy Association, 2000.

Ganguly, S. "Ethnic Policies and Political Quiescence in Malaysia and Singapore." in Michael Brown and Sumit Ganguly (eds). *Government Policies and Ethnic Relations in Asia and the Pacific*. Cambridge, Mass.: MIT Press, 1997.

Greenberg, J. "Organizational Justice: Yesterday, Today and Tomorrow." *Journal of Management* 16 (1990).

Heilman, M.E., W. F..McCullough, and D. Gilbert. "The Other Side of Affirmative Action: Reactions of Nonbeneficiaries to Sex-based Preferential Selection." *Journal of Applied Psychology* 81 (1996).

Heritage Canada. *Annual Report 1994-1995 on the Operation of the Canadian Multi-Culturalism Act*. Ottawa: Heritage Canada, January 1996.

Hodges-Aberhard, J. and C. Raskin (eds). *Affirmative Action in the Employment of Ethnic Minorities and Persons with Disabilities*. Geneva: International Labour Office, 1997.

Holtzer, Harry and David Neumark. *What Does Affirmative Action Do?* Nber Working Paper No. 6605, 1998.

Jackson, James S. "Introduction and Overview." in Jackson, James (ed). *New Directions: African Americans in a Diversifying Nation*. Washington, D.C.: National Policy Association, 2000.

Jain, H.C. "Canadian Federal Employment Equity Policies" in David Saunders (ed.) *New Approaches to Employee Management*, Greenwich, Conn.: .JAI Press Inc., 1994.

Jain, H.C. "Employment Equity in Canada." *Human Resource Management in Canada*. Toronto: Prentice-Hall Canada, September 1995.

Jain, H.C. and A. Bowmaker-Falconer. *Employment Equity/Affirmative Action Codes of Practice and Best Practices in USA, Britain, Canada and Other Selected Countries*. Pretoria, South Africa: Department of Labour, 1998.

Jain, H.C. and C. S. V. Ratnam. "Affirmative Action in Employment for the Scheduled Castes and the Scheduled Tribes in India." *International Journal of Manpower* 15.7 (1994): 6-25.

Jain, H.C., Parbudyal Singh and Carol Agocs. "Recruitment, Selection and Promotion of Visible Minority and Aboriginal Officers in Selected Canadian Police Services." *Canadian Public Administration* 43.1 (2000): 46-74.

Jain, Harish C. "Employment Equity in Canada." *Human Resources Management in Canada,*. November 1997.

Jones, R.E. (Chair). *Task Force Report on "Best" Equal Employment Opportunity Policies, Programs, and Practices in the Private Sector*. Washington, DC: Equal Employment Opportunity Commission, December 1994.

Kaur, A. "India." in Jane Hodges-Aberhard and Carl Raskin (eds.) *Affirmative Action in the Employment of Ethnic Minorities and Persons with Disabilities*. Geneva: International Labour Office, 1997.

Leonard, J. "The Impact of Affirmative Action on Employment." *Journal of Labour Economics* 2 (1984a).

Leonard, J. "Employment and Occupational Advance Under Affirmative Action." *Review of Economics and Statistics* 66 (1984b).

Leonard, J. "What Promises Are Worth: The Impact of Affirmative Action Goals." *Journal of Human Resources* 20 (1985).

Leonard, J. "The Impact of Affirmative Action Regulation and Equal Employment Opportunity Law on Black Employment." *Journal of Economic Perspectives* 4. 4 (Fall 1990).

Mahathir, M. "Speech at Parliament." *New Straits Times*, June 18, 1991.

Northern Ireland. London: HMSO, 1995.

Mehta, Stephanie. " What Minority Employees Want." *Fortune (* July 10, 2000).

Pfeffer, J., A. Davis-Blake and D. Julius. "AA Officer Salaries and Managerial Diversity: Efficiency Wages or Status," *Industrial Relations* 34 (1995).

Parekh, B. *The Future of Multi-ethnic Britain*, London: Profile Books, 2000.

Puthucheary, M. "Malaysia: Safeguarding the Malays and the Interests of Other Communities." *Development and Democracy*. Johannesburg, The Urban Foundation, 1993: 23-40.

Rodgers, William and William Spriggs. "The Effect of Federal Contractor Status on Racial Differences in Establishment Level Employment Shares, 1979-1992." *American Economic Review* 86. 2 (May 1996).

Rogers, S. "Employment Equity: The View from Northern Ireland." paper presented at the Fifth International Metropolis Conference, Vancouver, November 2000.

Sloane, P. J., and D. Mackay. "Employment Equity and Minority Legislation in the UK After Two Decades: A Review." *International Journal of Manpower* 18 (1997).

Weiner, M. "Affirmative Action: The International Experience." *Democracy and Development.* Johannesburg: Urban Foundation, n.d.

CHAPTER 3

GLENDA STRACHAN AND JOHN BURGESS

UNFINISHED BUSINESS: EMPLOYMENT EQUALITY IN AUSTRALIA

Discrimination by race and gender has been a major feature of Australian history since European settlement in 1788. The period until the 1970s was characterised by overt discrimination on the grounds of gender and race with discriminatory policies affecting the employment of women, Aborigines and non-European migrants. Agitation for changes grew in the 1960s with lobbying from a variety of groups within the community including burgeoning women's groups, trade unions, and groups pursuing changes on racial issues. Changes in legislation and policies began to be achieved in the late 1960s, with equal pay awards on the basis of gender and race and the removal of some discriminatory employment practices such as the "marriage bar", which prevented married women from retaining permanent employment in public services and areas of private employment. Beginning in 1975, anti-discrimination legislation was introduced on the grounds of race and sex. In the following decade affirmative action legislation required large employers to take a more pro-active stance on examining discrimination against women within their organisation and instituting a program which would assist in the achievement of equal employment opportunity.

At the beginning of the twenty-first century in Australia there is public recognition of women's and all ethnic groups' rights to work and not be subjected to discriminatory practices. The outcomes from these policies, however, are not so clear cut. Women and Aborigines (1.5 per cent of the population) earn less than white men and Aborigines have a significantly higher unemployment rate. Women form the majority of temporary and part-time workers. In an increasingly decentralised industrial relations system that emphasises collective bargaining at the workplace, regulations for minimum working standards are being reduced. Thus, despite continuing anti-discrimination and affirmative action policies, the labour market is becoming increasingly insecure for more of the workforce. Yet security in employment and minimum standards are crucial for the achievement of employment equity. This chapter discusses the evolution of policies designed to achieve equal opportunity in employment. It concentrates on policies that affect women and Aborigines.

AUSTRALIAN SOCIETY AND DISCRIMINATION

The first European settlers arrived in 1788 to establish a British penal colony of convicts and jailers. Mass migration from Europe in the nineteenth century created the twentieth century nation of Australia. One and a half million immigrants arrived from Europe, principally from the United Kingdom, between 1821 and 1900 (Haines and Shlomowitz, 1992). Migration from 1879 to 1910 increased Australia's labour force by 42 percent,

C. Agocs (ed.), Workplace Equality, 47–64.

third in the New World behind Argentina (86 percent) and Canada (44 percent) (Hatton and Williamson, 1998: 208). In the twentieth century the largest wave of immigrants came from Europe after World War II until the 1960s. Immigration in Australia was closely tied to labour market needs with migrant men and women the major source of workforce growth in the post war period (Collins, 1991:12). Today 15 per cent of the population report that they speak a language other than English at home (ABS, 1996).

The overwhelming majority of immigrants have been British and Irish, followed by settlers from other European countries. This has been part of a deliberate policy, enshrined in legislation in the *Immigration Protection Act 1901* and known as the White Australia Policy (Collins, 1991: 204-207). This official racial discrimination was not removed until the 1970s when the policies of multiculturalism emerged: "Distinctive migrant cultural trappings...were to be celebrated and encouraged as multicultural enlightenment and diversity replaced assimilationist homogeneity" (Collins, 1991: 231). Today 25 per cent of the labour force was born outside Australia (ABS, 1999b).

In the 1990s the indigenous population of Australia numbered approximately 265,000 or 1.5 per cent of the total population of 19 million (ABS, 1997b: 125). Discrimination by race has been a major feature of Australian history since European settlement. The period until the 1970s was characterised by overt discrimination on the grounds of race against the Aboriginal population. In the nineteenth century there were acts of genocide against the Aboriginal population and periods of open conflict now referred to as "race wars" (Evans, 1975). At the time of European settlement the indigenous population practised a hunter gatherer economy (Dingle, 1988) and the Aboriginal people were judged by the British Government to have no prior claim on the land (Kociumbas, 1992: 135; McGrath and Stevenson, 1996: 41). No treaties were made with the Aborigines and the doctrine of *terra nullius* was maintained legally until 1992. Indeed, it was not until 1967 that a referendum enabled a change to the constitution that allowed full-blood Aborigines to be counted in the census.

Until the late 1960s Aborigines were the subject of unequal wage decisions. Aboriginal workers were left largely outside mainstream industrial relations, despite the fact that Aboriginal labour was significant in the pastoral industry in northern Australia. Unequal pay was a feature of the industry (see Table 1).

Table 1: Aboriginal wages compared to wages for white workers.

	Aboriginal General Station Hand weekly wages with keep	General Station Hand weekly wages with keep
1926	£2 (66%)	£3
1945	£1 10s (45%)	£3 7s
1964	£10 12s (70%)	£15 3s 6d

Source: Hagan, Castle and Clothier, 1998: 413.

In 1999 there were over 9 million people in the work force, 43 per cent female. Women's labour force participation rates increased from 22 per cent in 1947 to 37 per cent in 1967, to 44 per cent in 1983, and to 54 per cent in 1999. Since 1983 male participation rates have declined from 83 per cent to 73 per cent (ABS, 1999b; Department of Prime Minister and Cabinet, 1984: 18; Burgess and Strachan, 1998). Historically Australia's labour market was highly segregated by gender and characterised by overt discrimination policies such as the "marriage bar" which meant that women, once they married, could not retain their jobs in public services or with many private employers. For the first seventy years of the twentieth century between 55 per cent and 75 per cent of women were employed in occupations where more than half of the workers were women (Power, 1975). Although the most common women's occupations have changed, a high level of segregation remains. In May 1996, 56 percent of all women workers were employed in two occupational classifications: clerical, and salespersons and personal service workers (ABS, 1997a: 73).

Until the 1970s the dominant concept in wage fixation was the living or family wage, that is, a wage sufficient for a male worker to maintain himself, his wife and three children "as a human being living in a civilized society" (CCCA, 1907: 1-19; Hutson, 1971: 4). The consequence of this decision was to entrench a lower wage rate for the overwhelming majority of women workers (who were judged not to have responsibility for dependents) of approximately 54 per cent of the male wage. This remained until the labour market disruptions of the Second World War caused a revision of women's pay rates which were generally adjusted to 75 per cent of the male rate (Strachan, 1996; Ryan and Conlon, 1989).

These wage determinations occurred within the Australian industrial relations system which, for most of the twentieth century, can be characterised as a centralised system. While it has endured many changes, the essential framework of permanent tribunals setting industry wide awards of minimum conditions, which applied to all workers in the specified job category and industry, survived from 1904 until the early 1990s. Awards were comprehensive documents covering a wide range of employment matters including minimum rates of pay, leave entitlements, overtime and shift rates, hours of work, meal breaks, travelling allowances and much more, and stipulated whether employment was on a weekly, daily, permanent or casual basis (Deery, Plowman and Walsh, 1997: 9.23). Australian governments have been loath to legislate minimum labour standards and the award system has acted to establish a floor of minimum labour standards underpinning the conditions of employees. Therefore award regulation has acted as a system of protection for individual employees against the untrammelled operations of the free market, supplementing the much more partial protection offered by individual trade unions. This system changed in the 1990s to emphasise collective bargaining at the workplace and reduced protection for workers (Strachan and Burgess, 2000).

AN OVERVIEW OF LEGISLATION AND POLICIES WHICH PROMOTE EQUALITY

Major changes have occurred since the late 1960s that have resulted in successful equal pay cases, legislation and policies designed to promote equal employment opportunity (EEO). This has been tackled in several ways in Australia. An overt inequality was unequal pay that was explicitly offered to the majority of women workers and Aboriginal workers. From the late 1960s successful equal pay cases were processed through the industrial relations system. From the 1980s discussion about women's wages has widened to encompass a broader understanding of equal pay. Anti-discrimination legislation has been enacted at the federal level and in all states, beginning in 1975. This legislation seeks to redress essentially individual cases of discrimination after they have occurred and covers complaints on grounds such as sex, race, ethnicity, religion, family status, sexuality, and disability.

A second type of legislation has been labelled affirmative action in Australia. Australia has developed unique legislation using the term affirmative action but creating a system that is different to that in North America. The major piece of legislation, the

Affirmative Action (Equal Opportunity for Women) Act 1986, relates to women, however, three other groups have been added in some public sector legislation (Aborigines and Torres Strait Islanders, migrants from non-English speaking backgrounds, and people with disabilities). In Australia affirmative action was defined as "a systematic approach to the identification and elimination of the institutional barriers" faced by women in employment, and an affirmative action program was "a planned, results-oriented, management program designed to achieve Equal Employment Opportunity". EEO "rests on a commitment by an employer to ensure that all personnel activities are conducted in a manner which provides fair and equal treatment and equal opportunity for all people" (Public Service Board EEO Bureau, 1984: 5). Affirmative Action legislation also relies on the underlying principle of bringing women up to equality with men. This has been called an inclusionary or incorporation model, as affirmative action programs concentrate on training for women and the integration of women into non-traditional areas; indeed it treats women as the problem and endeavours to fix this (Bacchi, 1996: 84).

There are several philosophies that underlie policies and legislation designed to promote gender and race equity. In the majority of cases the underlying principle is to make women in the workforce equal to men (white European men) or Aborigines equal to Europeans, women's pay equal to men's, and so on. The legislation focuses on remedying discrimination on the basis that women have been discriminated against in relation to a comparator, that is men, and this applies to both equal pay decisions and anti-discrimination legislation. It also applies to Australia's notion of affirmative action.

A major criticism of this type of legislation has been that it tries to make women equal to men and Aborigines equal to white men. Indeed, affirmative action in Australia "is theoretically victim-centred rather than perpetrator-centred in that it is designed to take account of the structural factors which constitute barriers for women and minorities" (Thornton, 1990: 242). It does not try to change the *status quo* which is a European male working life pattern of the post World War II era. Under this model the world of work does not change. As Thornton (1995: 8) notes, "the legislative endeavours carefully cordon off the domestic sphere from scrutiny". More recent debate has questioned this public-private divide and noted the importance of altering the world of work to accommodate the demands of the home. In Australia in the 1990s a new raft of policies have been discussed under the term of work and family policies. This philosophy also extends to the change from maternity leave to parental leave. Yet there are two problems here: first, many workers cannot access these conditions, and secondly, they are used overwhelmingly by women and seen as policies for women. As discussed in a later section of this chapter, these policies have made little impact on conditions of work in the face of longer hours for full-time workers, increased use of temporary workers and extended working hours.

EQUAL PAY

In Australia, along with Canada and USA, equal pay laws preceded feminist mobilisation, suggesting that "the primary focus was on moving women into the labour force" as there was "a labour shortage which women were invited to end" (Bacchi, 1996: 80). Against the backdrop of increasing female labour market participation in the 1960s, plus the emerging recognition of race and sex discrimination, the peak trade union organisation, the Australian Council of Trade Unions (ACTU), initiated and led a successful equal pay case in the federal Conciliation and Arbitration Commission in 1969. Support came from organisations such as the Australian Federation of Business and Professional Women's

Clubs, the National Council of Women, the Australian Federation of Women Voters and the Union of Australian Women, who expressed their views at the hearings (Lake, 1999: 218).

The 1969 decision had limited coverage of women workers as it contained a provision that equal pay would not be awarded "where the work in question is essentially or usually performed by females but is work upon which male employees may also be employed". As a result of gender segregation a mere 18 per cent of female employees benefited from this decision (O'Donnell and Hall, 1988: 54). But through this decision, Lake (1999: 218) argues, "feminists secured, after decades of struggle, an important symbolic victory".

The equal pay case of December 1972 broadened the concept and removed the "essentially or usually performed" restriction and awarded female workers "equal pay for work of equal value". The potential coverage of this judgement was estimated to be one and a half million female workers (out of 1,795,000 women in the workforce) (Ryan and Conlon, 1989: 162). The cases set out principles that were to be followed by unions when applying to have equal pay implemented in their awards. Therefore after 1972 the pursuit of equal pay occurred on an *ad hoc* basis, relying on individual trade unions to institute cases on behalf of their membership. Generally, employers and unions merely agreed on the integration of male and female classifications without any quasi-scientific studies of work valuation and comparison, such as job evaluation (Short, 1986: 325). Despite the case-by-case implementation of equal pay, Australia's female to male earnings ratio increased faster in the 1970s than that of any other country, from around 0.60 to 0.80 in six years (Burgess et al, 1998).

Aboriginal Employment Conditions

By the late 1950s wages and working conditions of Aborigines were beginning to attract the attention of multinational bodies and organisations of Aboriginal and white people. Regulations fixing station hands' wages were of special interest to many non-Aboriginal groups. Towards the end of the decade the establishment of the Federal Council for Aboriginal Advancement (FCAA) provided unity and a national forum for state and other groups working for the integration of Aborigines into society, which also attracted the support of trade unions. FCAA affiliated unions were among those sponsoring motions for equal pay and removal of all forms of discrimination at the 1959 and 1961 ACTU Congresses. The 1963 ACTU Congress adopted a broad policy statement on Aborigines based on the view that there must be an end to wage discrimination (Markus, 1978: 155; Evans, 1966: 216-217).

In 1965 the ACTU took a more proactive role by supporting industrial action and giving assistance to trade union applications for the removal of discriminatory provisions from awards covering the pastoral industry. The result of this case was that in March 1966 the Commonwealth Arbitration Commission handed down a judgment establishing the principle of equality for Aboriginal workers (Kidd, 1997: 236; Markus, 1978: 155-156; Evans, 1966: 217-218).

Comparable Worth

In the 1980s, the women's movement and ACTU pushed for a case along comparable worth lines as such cases had been successful in some employment sectors in USA. In 1986 the ACTU submitted a claim in relation to nurses' salaries along comparable worth lines. The commission decided that acceptance of any version of comparable worth would "strike at the heart of long accepted methods of wage fixation in this country" (ACAC, 1986) and refused to accept the general nature of the claim for reviewing women's wages. The nurses' claim was processed as an individual case and the commission ensured that it had no ramifications for women's wages generally (Rafferty, 1994: 467). To this day there has been no definition of the terms, no agreed method of evaluation and any implementation must be on a case-by-case basis. The historical undervaluing of women's work (for example Strachan, 1996) that has been perpetrated largely because of the high level of gender segregation of jobs has not been adequately addressed. Indeed, "work value has been assessed for changes over time but never for comparative work value with men to see if the original rate was discriminatory" (Short, 1986: 329).

Equal Pay in the 1990s

In the 1990s requirements for equal pay for work of equal value have been inserted in the federal industrial relations acts. Section 170B of the *Workplace Relations Act 1996* allows the commission to make orders for equal remuneration for work of equal value between men and women, with the Act relying on the 1951 ILO Equal Remuneration Recommendation for any interpretation of equal value. Once again, however, in the most recent case, there has been no definition of the terms, no agreed method of evaluation and any implementation must be on a case-by-case basis (AIRC, 1998).

The last years of the twentieth century show some signs for concern over women's wages. Progress in women's wages is measured generally in comparison with men's wages, so changes in men's wages can have an impact on this comparative figure. Analysis of wage trends shows that relatively women do not appear to be doing worse under the increasingly decentralised industrial relations arrangements because lower paid men are doing worse (Whitehouse and Zetlin, 1999).

Yet there have been moves to examine the historical undervaluing of women's work. In one Australian state, New South Wales, a Labor Government was elected in 1995 with an expressed commitment to pay equity for women. It established a tripartite taskforce in 1996 to look at pay equity issues and the Pay Equity Inquiry began the following year. Comparisons were made between childcare workers and metal trades workers, hairdressers and beauty therapists and motor mechanics, and other occupational groups. The inquiry found that the work performed by women was undervalued historically and that new equal remuneration principles needed to be developed (New South Wales Pay Equity Taskforce, 1996). New wage fixing principles were adopted in June 2000 and the crux of these is that "the assessment of the work, skill and responsibility...is to be approached on a gender neutral basis and in the absence of assumptions based on gender" (NSWIRC, 2000). Other states are beginning to hold similar inquiries. While no wage rates have yet been adjusted, the prospect of change is there.

ANTI-DISCRIMINATION LEGISLATION

In 1973 the federal Labor Government ratified ILO Convention 111 that required a commitment to remove discrimination from employment on the basis of race, colour, sex, political opinion, national extraction or social origin. The Government believed this action testified to its determination to remove discrimination in employment, not just by removing cases of blatant discrimination, but also by taking positive action to promote real equality of opportunity in employment (Cameron, 1973:3). The Government's position was fully supported by business, the ACTU and the state governments. Subsequently, the first federal anti-discrimination law, the *Racial Discrimination Act 1975* (RDA) was enacted, making it "unlawful to take 'certain actions' by reason of race, colour or national or ethnic origin of a person or a relative or associate of that person" (Ronalds, 1987:194). The federal Government intended to use the framework of the RDA to make discrimination on the grounds of sex unlawful. However, before the Bill was introduced into Parliament the conservative Liberal/National Party Coalition Government came to power in November 1975. It took another nine years and a Labor Party victory before this legislation was passed. In this period the states that had Labor Party Governments enacted anti-discrimination legislation through which complaints could be taken on grounds such as sex, race, ethnic origin, religion and physical disability.

In the years between 1975 and 1984 there were ongoing activities by various parties towards the ultimate achievement of anti-discrimination legislation on the grounds of sex at a federal level. The 1977 Royal Commission on Human Relationships' review of the position of women in Australia found a need for comprehensive nation-wide legislation against discrimination on the grounds of sex and marital status in employment and other areas (Royal Commission on Human Relationships, 1977:60-61). As a result of an extensive review of its employment practices, the federal Public Service Board established an Equal Employment Opportunity Bureau in 1975. This unit was the first of its kind in Australia and was responsible for the implementation and co-ordination of a number of EEO programs for women, migrants, Aboriginals and disabled persons in the Commonwealth Public Service (Dredge and Conway, 1980:4). The ACTU established the Working Women's Centre in 1975 with staff devoted to securing the same rights, pay and working conditions for women as were enjoyed by men. In 1978 the Federal Government established the National Women's Advisory Council which offered advice to the Government on a range of policy matters of special importance to women (Ellicott, 1980) and set up employment discrimination committees, which operated in each State, although these had no power to enforce compliance with any recommendations (Gaudron, 1982:108). Outside the public sector, the Women's Electoral Lobby formulated its law reform agenda that had anti-discrimination measures as a high priority (Ryan, 1997:46).

While there was much support for these views, not all sections of society were in favour of the moves. Feelings towards women in the workplace, particularly married women, varied. Some newspaper articles suggested that women were taking the jobs of young people, leaving them unemployed. With the headline "If mum quit work, there'd be jobs for the boys (and girls)", one article commenced with the view that "The first reason why the school-leaver is unable to get a job is his teacher. The second is his mother – she has already taken the job" (Weekend Australian, 1978). Further arguments against women in the workplace were that the family unit would be affected with a rise in divorce rates due to inadequate child care facilities and inflexible work hours. Women also became less dependent on spouses and more independent which was said to increase the divorce rate (National Times, 1 September 1979; National Times, 25 August 1979). Despite these contrary views, by 1980 equal pay had been implemented for many women, and race and sex discrimination had been legislated against in a number of states.

In 1983 the newly elected federal Labor Government asserted that women were disadvantaged in the workplace compared to their male counterparts: women were concentrated in a relatively narrow range of occupations and industries, at the lower end of the hierarchy, in positions with lower status and lower pay and with limited career prospects. In addition, there were far more women than men in part-time employment and in less secure jobs (Department of Prime Minister and Cabinet, 1984: 10; Ronalds, 1987: 1-7). The Government moved swiftly to enact the *Sex Discrimination Act 1984*. The Act makes it unlawful to discriminate on the grounds of sex, marital status or pregnancy in the areas of employment, education, accommodation, the provision of goods, facilities and services, the disposal of land, the activities of clubs and the administration of Commonwealth laws and programs. The Act also makes unlawful discrimination involving sexual harassment in education and employment. Sex discrimination legislation provides an avenue for the redress of individual and group complaints of unlawful discrimination.

The *Sex Discrimination Act 1984* recognises structural or indirect discrimination which "arises from the fact that organisational norms, rules and procedures, used to determine the allocation of positions and benefits, have generally been designed...around the behaviour patterns of the historically dominant group in public life (Anglo-Australian, able-bodied, heterosexual males)" (Hunter 1992: 5; see also Department of the Prime Minister and Cabinet, 1984: 12-13). Groups of women have been able to pursue remedies after an alleged case of discrimination and a number of major cases have been conducted by trade unions. In the first instance, anti-discrimination board staff and the parties to the case attempt to reach a solution through conciliation. The overwhelming majority of cases are settled at this stage with a minority proceeding to a public legal hearing. While important in resolving some instances of discrimination, framing a case that meets the terms of the legislation can be difficult (Scutt, 1990: 76). Nevertheless the legislation marked government recognition of the equal rights of women in society and it established public acknowledgement that society would no longer accept women as second class citizens thereby denying them access to many benefits only available to men (Department of Prime Minister and Cabinet, 1984: 13).

Complaints are still being received under the various anti-discrimination acts. In 1998-99, 1780 complaints were received under Federal anti-discrimination legislation, an increase of 17 percent over the previous year.[1] Forty four percent of the complaints were on the basis of race, 29 percent on the basis of disability and 19 percent on the basis of sex. Four hundred and thirty four complaints were received under the *Sex Discrimination Act 1984*. Of these 39 percent were withdrawn. Of the remaining 266 cases, 61 percent were conciliated and 26 percent were referred for legal hearings (the remainder were terminated or transferred) (HREOC, 1999). While the emphasis is on conciliation, a substantial proportion cannot be resolved between the parties and must proceed through the courts.

One recent study of employment complaints concerning the banking industry provides evidence of the issues still causing concern. From 1987-97 a total of 74 complaints were made against 14 banks in the area of employment by individual complainants and by the Finance Sector Union. Three main grounds for complaint were sex discrimination (14 complaints), sexual harassment (31 complaints), and pregnancy or family responsibility related or "motherhood" complaints (29 complaints). "Motherhood" complaints included matters such as accessing maternity leave, treatment while pregnant, return after maternity leave to a "comparable position" or access to redundancy. In 1995 "motherhood" complaints accounted for well over half of all complaints lodged (Charlesworth, 1999).

AFFIRMATIVE ACTION

After the passage of the *Sex Discrimination Act 1984* the Labor Government continued with its policy development in relation to removal of employment disadvantage for women. The Government recognised that its anti-discrimination legislation alone could not address or correct several workplace obstacles faced by women. It could not improve women's position in the labour market, could not totally open up a greater range of jobs to women or ensure that women would be able to compete on equal terms with men for promotion (Department of Prime Minister and Cabinet, 1984: 1).

The *Affirmative Action (Equal Opportunity for Women) Act 1986* provided legislative remedies for discrimination that did not rely on individual grievance procedures. Affirmative action "is the pursuit of equal employment opportunity by means of legislative reform and management programs" (Ziller, 1983: 23). This required the barriers that restricted employment and promotion opportunities for women in the workplace to be systematically eliminated (Affirmative Action Agency, 1990: 1). The Act compelled organisations with more than one hundred employees to implement an affirmative action program. The legislation specified an eight step program in which companies were to undertake an analysis of the position of women in their organisation through an examination of employment statistics, personnel practices and by direct consultation with women employees and trade unions. From the resulting information the company was required to devise a program that directly addressed the identified problems and set targets for specific organisational activities (for example selection procedures, training, and policies on dealing with sexual harassment) against which future EEO progress could be evaluated (Strachan, 1987). The legislation preserved an individual rather than collectivist focus in its reliance on the merit principle as "competitive individualism is central to the process of appointment and promotion" (Thornton, 1990: 246).

The focus of the Act was towards individual enterprise responsibility in achieving the goals as opposed to legislative and economy wide standards (Strachan, 1987). The implementation of EEO principles presumed good corporate citizenship, the effective participation of women employees in the development and implementation of the agenda, and a process of shared goals and participation. There were no explicit national guidelines or standards as to the process or outcomes; instead an array of national prizes and case studies provided the benchmarks from which enterprises could establish their own progress and success in realising EEO objectives.

While the ACTU and many women's groups supported strict penalties for organisations which did not comply, the Business Council of Australia (representing big business) and the Confederation of Australian Industry wanted participation to be on a voluntary basis (Working Party on Affirmative Action Legislation, 1985: 24-28). The upshot was that the penalties for non-compliance were weak: a company that did not submit a report might be named in parliament that, as Thornton (1990:231) suggests, is no sanction at all. In 1992 the Government added the sanction that companies breaching the legislation were ineligible for Federal Government contracts or specified industry assistance, similar to the American approach. This sanction was never used and has been removed under the 1999 legislation.

As with the sex discrimination legislation, debate followed the tabling of affirmative action legislation. The affirmative action legislation was seen by many well organised right-wing groups, especially conservative women's groups, as being an insult to women. It was seen by many employer groups as being a "Stalinist plot to force otherwise profitable companies to sack their male employees and replace them with incompetent women" (Ryan, 1997:47).

The affirmative action legislation has been subject to criticism. Thornton (1990: 243) asserts that

> The legislation...operates to maintain the status quo by deferring to managerial prerogative. The distinction is largely one of form and substance. The form is victim–oriented; that is, it purports to be operating so as to secure justice and equity for women.... Indeed, the process may well make a difference for some individual women...who are most like their white, Anglo-Celtic, able-bodied male comparators in terms of education, experience and social class. This concentration on form occludes the substance of AA legislation which reveals that it is not directed towards outcome in the interests of women...but, in fact, can be manipulated by the perpetrator class who constitute the mangers in the workplace.

Thornton is correct in that the effectiveness of the legislation relies totally on what management wants to do about affirmative action.

The majority of the 2,500 organisations covered by the Act submit their reports on a regular basis. There is a small core of companies (approximately 3 per cent), however, who do not do this (Affirmative Action Agency, 1998: 13). Since 1993, 56 employers have not complied for three or more years (Affirmative Action Agency, 1994-98) so it is clear that a number of employers do not care if they suffer the penalty of being named in parliament for breaching the Act.

Since 1994 the Affirmative Action Agency has assessed reports and divided them into three categories. The distinguishing features of reports graded at the highest level is that they demonstrate careful planning including the setting and evaluation of their goals, objectives and evaluation mechanisms; include information on the results achieved; "show they are seeking to actively address the lingering effects of past discriminatory practices; recognise that workplaces need to adapt to the changing roles and aspirations of women" (Affirmative Action Agency, 1995: 7). Approximately ten percent of organisations, especially large organisations, submit reports graded at this level (Affirmative Action Agency, 1998: 27-34). The lowest grade signifies a minimum level of progress in developing and implementing an affirmative action program (Affirmative Action Agency, 1995: 9). Approximately one quarter of all reports is assessed at the lowest grade and organisations with high proportions of female employees are over-represented in this group. It seems that the more women employed the less likely organisations are to see the relevance of affirmative action. Issues like lack of career paths, undervaluing of women's work, high levels of casual employees and the disproportionate number of men in senior positions are major concerns in female dominated industries but are often not seen by employers as relevant to affirmative action (Affirmative Action Agency, 1995: 16).

It may be that a proportion of organisations, about one quarter, are satisfied to meet the letter of the law by supplying a report but in reality do little or nothing to advance equal employment opportunity. There has been no great movement for organisations to gain a higher rating, and the proportion of firms located within these three levels of assessment remains relatively stable.

Affirmative action legislation has been the most controversial of Australia's legislative attempts at equity and has been criticised particularly by employers. With the election of a conservative federal government in 1996 the legislation was reviewed and changes initiated on 1 January 2000. One of the most controversial features had been the term affirmative action and the name of the Act was changed to the *Equal Opportunity for Women in the Workplace Act 1999*. The guidance given to employers on how to implement a program has been reduced; indeed, the previous eight steps of an affirmative action program have been deleted, removing the emphasis on consultation with women and trade unions. To comply with the new Act, organisations only have to take actions on the priority issues identified when undertaking an organisational analysis. Reporting is still required on an annual basis (although this can be waived under certain circumstances) but the reporting form is no longer prescriptive (Affirmative Action

Agency, 1999b). In addition, since 1999 organisations are only assessed on the basis of whether the report meets the minimum requirements of the Act (Affirmative Action Agency, 1999: 40).

Not all women are included in affirmative action legislation. More than half (56 per cent) of private sector female employees were not covered by the *Affirmative Action Act 1986* in 1994/95 (ABS, 1999a) since they were employed in enterprises with less than 100 employees. The most vulnerable group of workers, casual (temporary) employees, account for approximately one third of all women workers and it is estimated that only a minority of these workers (approximately one third) were covered by the Act because of the concentration of casual employment in the small, private business sector (Campbell, 1996). In addition, other women workers are likely to be ignored and excluded from the operation of a company's affirmative action policies if they work in part-time, temporary or low paid positions. In effect there may be an affirmative action program that covers some women workers in an organisation and excludes others. In a study of clerical workers Strachan and Winter (1995) found that there could be different policies within an organisation for different groups of women workers, with professional women having greater access to training and policies designed to retain women after they have had children.

The assessment of the impact of any affirmative action program is complex. The success of an affirmative action program relies on its implementation rather than just reporting. For example, many banks have received the top assessment from the Affirmative Action Agency (Affirmative Action Agency, 1997) but the pattern of employment within banks includes ghettos of women in the lowest levels of their organisations. These women, many of whom are part-time or temporary, may not have access to maternity leave, have little access to training and are employed expressly as a pool of workers without a career path. These women form "a large group of unskilled or semi-skilled women employees who will have no career futures, only limited access to full-time employment, and ever-diminishing opportunities to earn a reasonable income unless they work several part-time jobs concurrently" (Still, 1997: 16). An analysis of reports to the Affirmative Action Agency shows that the second group is larger than the group with career prospects (Strachan and Winter, 1995). Employers are seeking cheap staffing solutions in the labour intensive industries where most women work. These strategies have been easier to pursue through the decentralised industrial relations system of recent years, which has removed (and continues to remove) barriers to the employment of part-time workers and increases the inter-temporal flexibility of all workers.

WORK AND FAMILY POLICIES

Some recent debates have criticised the approach of removing women's disadvantage to make them equal to men, particularly as the male norm is not challenged (see Webb, 1997). Writers such as Bacchi (1996) and Cockburn (1991) argue that this entrenches women's disadvantaged position in the labour market and argue that the model of work and caring patterns as shared between women and men must undergo profound changes. These questions have been debated in Australia. The term "work and family" is used to cover policies that assist male and female workers to combine their paid work with home and family duties. Gary Johns, as Assistant Minister for Industrial Relations in 1994, identified "policies such as flexible working arrangements, permanent part-time work, job-sharing, career break schemes, paid or unpaid family leave, and assistance with childcare and elder care responsibilities, can help workers balance their work and family responsibilities" ("Government Perspective", 1994). Frequently in the Australian context "work and family" is used to justify significant workplace changes that may or may not promote sharing of responsibilities or make the combination of responsibilities easier to bear.

In the 1990s in Australia the work and family rhetoric has been taken up by government, business and trade unions (Strachan and Burgess, 1998). The Minister for Industrial Relations, Peter Reith, asserted that the government had focused on work and family considerations in developing the 1996 Workplace Relations Bill because, "apart from a genuine concern for the family, by implementing initiatives to assist workers with family responsibilities you will get increased productivity" (The Workplace Relations Bill: Supporting Work and Family, 1996: 9).

There has been no detailed consideration of what constitutes policies which would assist adults in the community to combine paid work and caring for a family, a policy which would surely have to start with the provision of an adequate income (Strachan and Burgess, 1998). Instead, the "work and family" rhetoric talks frequently and uncritically about "flexible" or "new ways to work" which tend to encompass a range of flexible or "alternative" working time arrangements such as expanded ordinary hours, annualised hours, job sharing, career breaks, *and* part-time work. The most obvious manifestation has been the implementation of carer's leave in many awards and agreements. This generally means that an employee can use a few days of their sick leave a year to care for an ill dependent.

There are a number of difficulties with this overall approach in the Australian context. Although maternity leave has been widened to parental leave in many workplaces, paid maternity leave is more widely available than paid paternity leave (34 per cent of workplaces offered paid maternity leave in 1995 compared with 18 per cent paid paternity leave) (Morehead et al, 1997: 115-16). Although the trend in European laws is to offer longer periods of parental leave, the usage of this leave remains low, largely because of the reduced income or damage to careers that results and men "show little enthusiasm" for parental leave ("Perspectives: Parental Leave", 1997: 119,125). Indeed since the effectiveness of parental leave "depends on take-up rates and the conditions governing return to work, the increasingly precarious nature of employment must be seen as a threat" ("Perspectives: Parental Leave", 1997: 128). Similar conclusions can be reached for Australia.

ABORIGINAL EMPLOYMENT IN THE 1980S AND 1990S

By the 1970s there was a growing awareness of the vitality and complexity of traditional culture of Aborigines and the extent of the Aboriginal dispossession of lands was acknowledged by a wider group of the population. These developments led to increased government funding for Aboriginal projects and assistance. New opportunities opened up for Aborigines to obtain employment serving the diverse needs (legal aid, housing and education) of their people. In most cases it was women who were able to take advantage of these developments (Fox and Lake, 1995: 56). Community Development Employment Projects, established in 1976, attempted to provide people living in remote Aboriginal communities with the opportunity to overcome long-term unemployment (Whitehouse, 1994: 10).

Recognition of Aboriginal culture and traditions increased and in 1989 the Public Sector Union gained an award for their members employed at the Central Land Council, an Aboriginal organisation. In this award the Industrial Relations Commission gave important recognition to Aboriginal traditions by inserting clauses pertaining to ceremonial activities and bereavement leave (Domm, 1989: 4). In 1991-92 two organisations negotiated awards which contained self-determination clauses which involved traditional ways of settling disputes, as well as clauses pertaining to ceremonial leave and extended bereavement leave (Plater, 1995: 214).

The ACTU widened the scope of its approach to Aboriginal employment in the 1990s by supporting the Labor Government's commitment to improving the conditions of Aboriginal and Torres Strait Islander people, seen in 1991 as "still the most disadvantaged group in Australia today" (ACTU, 1991). In September 1991 the ACTU Congress resolved to continue the campaign to establish full award coverage and compliance for all Aboriginal workers and workers in Aboriginal communities. Affiliated unions were encouraged to intensify their pursuit of award coverage for all Aboriginal workers by allocating sufficient resources to adequately research the needs of such workers (ACTU, 1991). As well as looking at industrial areas as priorities for the future, the 1991 Congress also considered the union movement's role in reconciliation and justice, consultation, education, national land rights legislation and infrastructure (ACTU, 1991). The 1994 ACTU Aboriginal Affairs strategy aimed at ensuring that no Aboriginal or Torres Strait Islander worker, enterprise or organisation would be award free over the following twelve months (Whitehouse, 1994: 11).

Despite the changes within the trade union movement and the wider community, employment disadvantage remains. The 1994 National Aboriginal and Torres Strait Islander Survey (NATSIS) interviewed 15,700 Aboriginal and Torres Strait Islander people at a time when the Aboriginal population of Australia was 303,250 people, which comprised 1.7 per cent of the entire Australian population (ABS, 1996: 113). At this time 27 per cent of the population in the Northern Territory were Aborigines compared to only one or two percent in other states. The labour force participation rate for aboriginal workers in 1994 was 58 per cent over all of Australia with Victoria (64 per cent) and Tasmania (63 per cent) recording the highest participation rates (ABS, 1996: 119). The mean income for employed persons in Australia in June 1994 was $27,100; however, the NATSIS showed a mean income for employed Aboriginal and Torres Strait Islander people of $21,300. Even when people employed in CDEP schemes were excluded Aboriginal income was still 10 percent below that of other Australians (see Table 2).

Table 2: Employed persons - mean annual income, 1994.

	Income $ Employed Non-CDEP	Income $ Employed CDEP	Income $ Total Employed
Males	26,500	12,200	22,300
Females	21,200	13,800	19,600
Total	24,300	12,700	21,300

Source: ABS, 1996.

DECENTRALISED INDUSTRIAL RELATIONS SYSTEM

In the 1990s there are several competing forces that influence women's participation in the labour force. Anti-discrimination legislation continues to operate, as does Affirmative Action legislation, although this was modified in 1999. Work and family policies, which aim to enhance a worker's ability to combine paid work and private caring activities, have been promoted widely. The question of equal pay has been revived with inquiries into this issue being undertaken recently. On the other hand changes in the labour market and conditions of work may have made it harder for women to participate in the labour market or worsened their working conditions. The deregulation of the industrial relations system that has promoted workplace and individual bargaining has been influential in the growth of temporary workers and in the spread of anti-social working hours.

The 1990s have seen a change in industrial relations and wage determination in Australia towards a system of collective bargaining at the workplace known as enterprise bargaining. This is now the primary avenue for wage determination with adjustments made on an employer-by-employer basis, a situation that would require many more cases to achieve the same coverage. Moves towards a decentralised system of industrial relations began slowly in 1987 (Burgess and Macdonald, 1990) and culminated in the introduction of the *Industrial Relations Reform Act 1993* which initiated enterprise bargaining. Under this legislation the primary way to obtain a wage increase was through a collective agreement negotiated at an enterprise, either with or without trade union involvement. Workers without access to an enterprise agreement were reliant on a national wage case that provided minimal increases in wage rates.

The federal conservative (Liberal-National Party Coalition) government, elected in 1996, introduced industrial relations legislation whose major thrust is to deregulate employment arrangements and remove the potential intrusion over workplace arrangements provided by the award system and trade unions. The *Workplace Relations Act 1996* introduces the individualisation of workplace agreements and severely limits union powers. These changes are especially significant for many women workers who are dependent on the award system as the main source of employment protection, rights and wage increases.

A major feature of workforce change in the 1990s is the continued growth of insecure, temporary employment where workers do not receive leave entitlements. A large component of the growth in female employment is part-time work that has doubled since 1984 and now forms 39 per cent of all female employment. More than half of this part-time employment is undertaken on a temporary (the Australian term is casual) basis. Casual workers do not receive any leave entitlements. A mere 44 per cent of women workers work on a full-time permanent basis (Burgess and Strachan, 1998). This means that many of the measures designed to assist women workers such as parental leave and carer's leave are not usually available to this group of workers.

In the past decade flexible working hours arrangements have dominated the bargaining agenda (ACIRRT, 1998: 39). Over 70 per cent of agreements contain clauses that deal with changed working time arrangements - these include the introduction of annualised salaries, 12 hour shifts, time off in lieu arrangements and banking of hours provisions (ACIRRT, 1998: 40). The result is that many employees have a longer and less predictable working week than was the case a decade ago. Overtime and penalty rates are being absorbed into the base rate of pay, thus removing the economic disincentive for employers to utilise labour at anti-social times or in long shifts (ACIRRT, 1997: 29-30). Where women workers predominate, agreements are more likely to contain working hours and contract of employment provisions, and "while open-ended flexibility may be beneficial to the enterprise, they may prove onerous for workers with childcare arrangements that are often inflexible" (ACIRRT, 1997: 28). Indeed the unpredictability of hours makes it more difficult to integrate the needs of family life. Flexible working hour arrangements are not necessarily beneficial for women or men and some arrangements such as the increased span of hours and the increased uncertainty of working hours are detrimental (ACIRRT, 1999: 101-125).

The current bargaining climate emphasises wage increases in return for productivity improvements and trading off conditions for increases. Many groups of women workers are disadvantaged as they have fewer conditions to trade and are frequently working in publicly funded service delivery organisations where productivity issues are difficult to judge. The centralised industrial relations system in Australia provided "a reasonable degree of equity for women workers" when compared to less centralised systems (Hammond and Harbridge, 1995: 373). The ability of the centralised system to enable changes to flow from one sector to another was seen as a distinct advantage for women workers and one that is lacking in the changes to enterprise bargaining (Whitehouse, 1990; Bennett, 1994).

CONCLUSION

The picture of employment for women, Aborigines and non-English speaking migrants in Australia in 2000 is radically different from that in 1960. Overt discrimination policies have been removed and policies designed to achieve equal opportunity in employment have been put in place. Overwhelmingly, these policies have been designed to remove perceived barriers which these groups possess when competing for employment, that is, they seek to make women equal to men and so on. Few policies have sought to address the structure of work and the workplace. While "work and family" policies of the 1990s have received publicity, they have no legislative force and the impact of these policies is limited and may even be detrimental to women's equal participation in some cases. The implementation of equal opportunity policies in Australia has spanned several decades and in the 1990s it coincided with dramatic changes in the industrial relations system. This has brought profound changes in working conditions such as increased temporary work and altered working hours that may be detrimental to the achievement of equal employment opportunity.

At the beginning of the twenty-first century the picture of employment for women, Aborigines and other groups is complex. It is still possible to discuss women's employment as a distinct category as gender segregation of occupations remains a major feature of the labour market. Distinct features remain in the contours of Aboriginal employment. Overt discrimination against women and racial groups has lessened and there is legislation to remedy this. Yet the combination of paid employment and care of family is still a difficult one for many women who revert to part-time work or leave the workforce for a few years in order to accommodate these competing demands. Demands for equal employment opportunity, however, are ever-present so achieving equal participation in employment for women, Aborigines and non-English speaking migrants in Australia is still on the national agenda.

Glenda Strachan is Associate Professor at the School of Management, University of Newcastle, Newcastle, Australia. John Burgess is Associate Professor in the Department of Economics at the University of Newcastle.

ACKNOWLEDGEMENTS

The authors would like to thank Anne Sullivan for her diligent and perceptive assistance in preparing this paper. We would also thank Carol Agocs for her editorial comments.

NOTES

[1] These Acts are the Racial Discrimination Act 1975, Sex Discrimination Act 1984, Human Rights and Equal Opportunity Act 1986 and Disability Discrimination Act 1992. The total number of complaints alleging discrimination would increase if complaints lodged under state anti-discrimination legislation was included

REFERENCES

Australian Bureau of Statistics (ABS). *Year Book Australia 1996*. ABS Catalogue No 1301.0. 1996.

ABS. *Australian Women's Year Book 1997*. Catalogue No 4124.0. 1997a.

ABS. *Australian Demographic Trends 1997*. Catalogue No. 3102.0. 1997b.

ABS. *Small Business in Australia*. Catalogue 1321.0. 1999a.

ABS. *Labour Force – Australia*. Catalogue 6203.0. 1999b.

Australian Centre for Industrial Relations Research and Teaching (ACIRRT). *Agreements Database and Monitor (ADAM)*. ACIRRT: University of Sydney, 1999.

Australian Centre for Industrial Relations Research and Teaching (ACIRRT). *Agreements Database and Monitor (ADAM)*. ACIRRT: University of Sydney, March 1998.

Australian Centre for Industrial Relations Research and Teaching (ACIRRT). *Agreements Database and Monitor (ADAM)*. ACIRRT: University of Sydney, June 1997.

ACIRRT. *Australia at Work*. Sydney: Prentice Hall, 1999.

Australian Council of Trade Unions (ACTU). "Aboriginal and Torres Strait Islanders Affairs Strategy." ACTU Congress September. 1991. Internet address: http://www.actu.asn.au.

Affirmative Action Agency. 1990

Affirmative Action Agency. *Annual Reports*, Canberra: AGPS, 1994, 1995, 1996, 1997, 1998, 1999a.

Affirmative Action Agency. Action News (20 December) 1999b.

Australian Industrial Relations Commission (AIRC). Automotive, Food, Metals, Engineering, Printing and Kindred Industries Union and HPM Industries Case concerning equal remuneration for work of equal value, Decision, 4 Mar., print P9210. 1998.

Australian Conciliation and Arbitration Commission (ACAC) Private Hospitals' and Doctors' Nurses (ACT) Award variation (Comparable Worth), Decision, 18 Feb., print G2250. 1986.

Bacchi, C. *The Politics of Affirmative Action*. London: Sage, 1996.

Bennett, L. "Women and Enterprise Bargaining: The Legal and Institutional Framework." *Journal of Industrial Relations* 36.2 (1994): 191-212.

Burgess, John, Nic Croce, Richard Denniss, Roy Green, and Glenda Strachan. Statement by the Employment Studies Centre, University of Newcastle, to NSW Pay Equity Inquiry. 1998

Burgess, J., and D. Macdonald. "The Labour Flexibility Imperative." *Journal of Australian Political Economy* 27 1990: 15-35.

Burgess, J., and G. Strachan. "Winding Back the Clock: Equal Employment Opportunity in Australia into the 21st Century". Paper presented at 13th Annual Employment Research Unit Conference: Disadvantage and Discrimination in Employment: Equalising Opportunity in the 21st Century, Cardiff Business School, Wales. 1998.

Cameron, Clyde. Discrimination in Employment and Occupation. A statement of National Policy made by Minister for Labour in the House of Representatives, Canberra. (22 May) 1973.

Campbell, I. "Casual Employment, Labour Market Deregulation and Australian Trade Unions" in G. Griffin (ed.) *Contemporary Research on Unions: Theory, Membership, Organisation and Non-Standard Employment*, National Key Centre in Industrial Relations Monograph no. 7, Melbourne, 1996: 173-206.

Charlesworth, S. "Working Mums: The Construction of Women Workers in the Banking Industry. " *Journal of Interdisciplinary Gender Studies* 4.2 (December 1999): 12-28.

Cockburn, C. *In the Way of Women: Men's Resistance to Sex Equality in Organisations*. London: Macmillan, 1990.

Collins, Jock. *Migrant Hands in a Distant Lane. Australia's Post-war Immigration*. Marrickville: Southwood Press, 1991. Second Edition.

Commonwealth Court of Conciliation and Arbitration (CCCA). *Commonwealth Arbitration Reports* Vol. 2, 1907: 1-19.

Deery, S., D. Plowman, and J. Walsh. *Industrial Relations: A Contemporary Analysis*. Sydney: McGraw-Hill, 1997.

Department of Prime Minister and Cabinet. *Affirmative Action for Women*. Vol. 1, Canberra: AGPS, 1984a.

Department of Prime Minister and Cabinet. *Affirmative Action for Women*. Vol. 2, Canberra: AGPS, 1984b.

Dingle, Tony. *Aboriginal Economy*. Melbourne: McPhee Gribble, 1988.

Domm, Robert. "First Australians Achieve first Public Sector Union Award." *Our Voice*. PSU Report. September 1989.

Dredge, R. and L. Conway. "Aspects of Equal Employment Opportunity in Australia – Part 1". *Work and People* 6.3 (1980): 4.

Ellicott, Bob. "National Women's Advisory Council Strengthened." News Release by Minister for Home Affairs. No 66 (27 August) 1980.

Evans, Raymond "The Nigger Shall Disappear..." in Raymond Evans, Kay Saunders and Kathryn Cronin (eds) *Race Relations in Colonial Queensland*, Brisbane: University of Queensland Press, 1975: 25-145.

Evans, W. P. "A.C.T.U. Policy and the Pastoral Decision – A Trade Unionist's View" in Ian G. Sharp and Colin M Tatz (eds) *Aborigines in the Economy. Employment, Wages and Training*. Brisbane: Jacaranda Press, 1966.

Fox, Charles, and Marilyn Lake. (eds) *Australians at Work. Commentaries and Sources*. Ringwood Victoria: Penguin, 1990.

"Government Perspective." *Work & Family* 6 (June 1994): insert 2.

Gaudron, Mary. "Women in the Workforce and the Elimination of Discrimination – Whose Responsibility?" 42 (May 1982): 108.

Hagan, Jim, Rob Castle, and Craig Clothier. "Fixing Wages for Aborigines in the Queensland Cattle Industry 1901-1965." *Journal of Industrial Relations* 40.3 (1998): 409-421.

Haines, R., and R. Shlomowitz. "Immigration from the United Kingdom to Colonial Australia: A Statistical Analysis." *Journal of Australian Studies* 34 (1992): 43-52.

Hammond, S. and R. Harbridge. "Women and Enterprise Bargaining: The New Zealand Experience of Labour Market Deregulation." *Journal of Industrial Relations* 37.3 (1995): 359-376.

Hatton, T., and J. Williamson. *The Age of Mass Migration: Causes and Economic Impact*. New York: Oxford University, 1998.

Human Rights and Equal Opportunity Commission (HREOC). *Annual Report 1998-99*. Canberra: AGPS, 1999.

Hunter, R. *Indirect Discrimination in the Workplace*. Sydney: Federation, 1992.

Hutson, J. *Six Wage Concepts*. Sydney: Amalgamated Engineering Union, 1971.

Kidd, Rosalind. *The Way We Civilise. Aboriginal Affairs – the untold story*. St Lucia Queensland: Queensland University Press, 1997.

Kociumbas, J. *Oxford History of Australia: Volume 2: Possessions 1770-1860*. Melbourne: Oxford University Press, 1992.

Lake, M. *Getting Equal: The History of Australian Feminism*. Sydney: Allen and Unwin, 1999.

Markus, Andrew. "Talka Longa Mouth." In Ann Curthoys and Andrew Markus (eds) *Who are Our Enemies? Racism and the Working Class in Australia*. Neutral Bay: Hale and Iremonger (1978): 138-157.

McGrath, Ann and Winona Stevenson. "Gender, Race and Policy: Aboriginal Women and the State in Canada and Australia." *Labour History* 71 (November 1996): 37-53.

Morehead, A., M. Steele, M. Alexander, K. Stephen, and L. Duffin. 1997 *Changes at Work: The 1995 Australian Workplace Industrial Relations Survey*. Melbourne: Longman, 1997.

National Times. 25 August and 1 September, 1979.

New South Wales Industrial Relations Commission (NSWIRC). Equal Remuneration Principle [2000] NSWIR Commission 113

New South Wales Pay Equity Task Force. *Woman's Worth: Pay Equity and the Undervaluation of Women's Skills in NSW*. Sydney: Women's Equity Bureau, NSW Department of Industrial Relations, 1996.

O"Donnell, C., and P. Hall. *Getting Equal: Labour Market Regulation and Women's Work*. Sydney: Allen and Unwin, 1988.

"Perspectives: Parental Leave."" *International Labour Review* 136.1 (1997): 109-128.

Plater, Diane. "From Dreamtime to Overtime: Awards for Aboriginal Workers." *Labour History* 69 (1995): 213-216.

Power, M. "Women's Work is Never Done by Men: A Socio-economic Model of Sex Typing in Occupations." *Journal of Industrial Relations* 17.2 (1975): 225-239.

Public Service Board EEO Bureau. Affirmative Action Programs for Women in the Australian Public Service. Canberra: AGPS, 1984.

Rafferty, F. "Equal Pay: The Evolutionary Process 1984-1994." *Journal of Industrial Relations* 36.4 (1994): 451-467.

Ronalds, C. *Affirmative Action and Sex Discrimination*. Sydney: Pluto Press, 1987.

Royal Commission on Human Relationships. Final Report Volume 5. Canberra: Australian Government Publishing Service, 1977.

Ryan, E., and A. Conlon. *Gentle Invaders: Australian Women at Work*. Melbourne: Penguin, 1989. Revised edition.

Ryan, S. "In the Beginning was a Bill to Tackle Discrimination". In E. Davis and C. Harris (eds) (1997) *Making the Link 8: Affirmative Action and Industrial Relations*. Sydney: Affirmative Action Agency and Macquarie University, 1997: 46-48.

Scutt, J. *Women and the Law*. Sydney: Law Book, 1990.

Short, C. "Equal Pay - What Happened?" *Journal of Industrial Relations* 28.3 (1986): 315-335.

Still, L. "Brave New World? Women and Part-time Employment: The Impact on Career Prospects and Employment Progression." *International Journal of Employment Studies* 5.1 (1997): 1-22.

Strachan, G. "Equal Employment Opportunity and Industrial Relations: The Path to Equality." *Journal of Industrial Relations* 29.2 (1987): 190-206.

Strachan, G. *Labour of Love: The History of the Nurses' Association in Queensland 1860-1950.* Sydney: Allen and Unwin, 1996.

Strachan, G., and J. Burgess. "The Incompatibility of Decentralised Bargaining and Equal Employment Opportunity in Australia." *British Journal of Industrial Relations* 38.3 (September 2000): 361-381.

Strachan, G., and J. Burgess. "The "Family Friendly" Workplace: Origins, meaning and application at Australian workplaces." *International Journal of Manpower* 19.4 (1998): 250-265.

Strachan, G., and M. Winter. *Overcoming Barriers to Women's Employment and Advancement in the Information Technology Intensive Industries in Queensland.* Brisbane: Department of Business, Industry and Regional Development, 1995.

Thornton, M. "The Cartography of Public and Private." In Margaret Thornton (ed.) *Public and Private: Feminist Legal Debates.* Melbourne: Oxford University Press, 1995.

Thornton, M. *The Liberal Promise: Anti-Discrimination Legislation in Australia.* Melbourne: Oxford University Press, 1990.

Webb, J. "The Politics of Equal Opportunity." *Gender, Work and Organization* 4.3 (1997): 159-69.

Weekend Australian. January 14-15, 1978

Whitehouse, Allan. "Aboriginal Unemployment and Industrial Relations in the "90s." *Southland Magazine* 5 (Winter 1994).

Whitehouse, G. "Unequal Pay: A Comparative Study of Australia, Canada, Sweden and the UK." *Labour and Industry* 3.2&3 (1990): 354-371.

Whitehouse, G., and D. Zetlin. "Globalisation and the Pursuit of Pay Equity: Contradictory Trends in the Australian Case." In P. Edwards and J. Elger. (eds). *The Global Economy, National States and the Regulation of Labour*, London: Mansell, 1999.

Working Party on Affirmative Action Legislation. Report. Canberra: Australian Government Publishing Service, (September) 1985.

"The Workplace Relations Bill: Supporting Work and Family." *Work & Family* 12 (1996): 6-9.

Ziller, A. *Affirmative Action Handbook.* Sydney: Potstill Press, 1983. 2nd Edition.

CHAPTER 4

CAROL AGOCS

CANADA'S EMPLOYMENT EQUITY LEGISLATION AND POLICY, 1986-2000: UNFULFILLED PROMISES

Between the mid-seventies and the mid-eighties, the concept of systemic discrimination moved to the forefront of debates about the causes of and remedies for inequality in employment in Canada and provided a touchstone for legislative and judicial advancements in employment equity. The federal Employment Equity Act (1986) and Federal Contractors Program (1986), as well as important complementary sections of the Canadian Human Rights Act (1978) and the Charter of Rights and Freedoms of the Constitution Act (1982), were Canada's legislative and policy responses to systemic discrimination in the workplace. In 1986 the province of Quebec passed contract compliance regulations for the private sector and employment equity legislation for women in its public sector (Gagnon and Letourneau, 1996; Chicha, 2000), followed by stronger equity legislation for the broader public sector in 2000 (Quebec, 2000). In 1993 Ontario enacted what some would consider the world's most comprehensive employment equity legislation. A path-breaking 1987 Supreme Court decision in *Action Travail des Femmes and the Canadian Human Rights Commission v. Canadian National Railway Company* (CNR) found systemic discrimination against women at CNR. The Court ordered an employment equity program, including a hiring quota, to ensure that CNR's past pattern of discrimination would not continue in the future.

Pay equity complements employment equity by addressing wage discrimination that affects workers in predominantly female occupations (Weiner, 1993). The Canadian Human Rights Act (1978) includes complaint-based provisions for equal pay for work of equal value in the federal jurisdiction. While several Canadian provinces have similar pay equity legislation, only Ontario and Quebec have pay equity that is both pro-active and applicable to the private as well as the public sector (Wiener and Gunderson, 1990: 125; Quebec, 2000: 44). Enacted in 1987, Ontario's pay equity legislation requires employers to evaluate and compare jobs using criteria of skill, effort, responsibility and working conditions, and to pay people in female-dominated jobs the same as people in equivalent male-dominated jobs.

However, the mid-1990s brought a retreat from Canada's relatively vigorous policy response to systemic discrimination. The most blatant signal of this retrenchment was the acrimonious political campaign in Ontario 1995 resulting in the election of Mike Harris' Progressive Conservative government on a stridently neo-liberal platform. As he had promised, one of the Harris government's first acts was to pass legislation that repealed Ontario's Employment Equity Act, which had been in effect for only a few months (see the two chapters that follow for details). The Harris government then watered down the requirements of the Ontario Pay Equity Act (Pay Equity Commission, 1996) and significantly reduced the services and resources of the Ontario Human Rights Commission.

C. Agocs (ed.), Workplace Equality, 65–89.

The Liberal government in Ottawa, meanwhile, was also committed to stimulating the growth of the private sector while cutting government employment and services, with significant negative impacts on women's employment and incomes (Bashevkin, 1998: 220-226; Day and Brodsky, 1998). Moreover, a review of the federal Employment Equity Act (1986), resulting in a new Employment Equity Act in 1995, as well as in amendments to the Canadian Human Rights Act, proved to be a mixed blessing in that it strengthened some equity provisions while undermining or removing others. At the turn of a new century, as Canadian society and labour markets become increasingly diverse on the basis of race, ethnicity and gender, the political will necessary to prevent that diversity from becoming stratified into entrenched patterns of inequality has weakened. As a result the promising potential of Canada's earlier employment and pay equity initiatives has not been realized.

This chapter outlines Canadian experience with employment equity policy and its implementation, highlighting its fundamental purpose as a remedy for systemic discrimination in the workplace. Current federal employment equity legislation and policy are assessed with regard to their record and potential to provide an effective response to systemic discrimination. Available evidence regarding the results of employment equity as it has been implemented since 1987 is reviewed in an effort to identify both improvements in the status of the employment equity groups, and areas where results under the policy have been disappointing. The chapter concludes by proposing some explanations of the limited effectiveness of Canada's employment equity policy in addressing systemic discrimination, and posing some questions for the future.

CANADA'S EMPLOYMENT EQUITY POLICY FRAMEWORK

In Canadian society, research evidence, case law and advocacy have established that four populations have been persistently and significantly disadvantaged in employment. Indicators include disadvantage with respect to access to regular full time employment opportunities, fair compensation, an inclusive working environment, and representation at upper levels of management, among others (see Chapter 1). The groups recognized as disadvantaged in employment ("designated groups") are:

1) racial minorities, termed "visible minorities" in employment equity policy, predominantly composed of people who identify their ancestry as Black, Chinese or South Asian;[1]
2) aboriginal peoples, who include North American Indians or members of First Nations, Metis and Inuit;
3) persons with disabilities;[2] and
4) women, who of course may also be members of one or more of the other three populations.

Employment equity legislation requires employers to undertake pro-active measures to remove and counteract systemic discrimination affecting the designated groups within their workplace. Before there was employment equity legislation, both the Canadian Human Rights Act (1978) and the Charter of Rights and Freedoms of the Constitution of Canada (1982) permitted employers to implement voluntary affirmative action; however only a handful of firms did so (Agocs, 1986: 154-157). Furthermore, although the federal and some provincial human rights statutes allow human rights commissions to initiate complaints of systemic discrimination, this has rarely been done: the CNR case (1987) was a notable exception. Resources have generally not been allocated to this purpose and the Canadian Human Rights Commission (CHRC) has not used its statutory power to initiate systemic cases (Canadian Human Rights Act Review Panel, 2000: 16). As a result there have been few court or human rights tribunal decisions ordering employment equity programs as a remedy for systemic discrimination or for non-compliance with the Employment Equity Act.

Canada's first Employment Equity Act was passed in 1986 by the Progressive Conservative government of Brian Mulroney and took effect in 1987. The Act made employment equity programs mandatory for federally regulated employers of 100 employees or more, including federal crown corporations and private sector employers such as banks and firms in inter-provincial communication or transportation. About 595,000 employees, or 4.2 percent of the Canadian labour force, worked in 373 firms covered by the Act as of 1987 (Employment and Immigration Canada, 1988: 20); 333 firms and 586,588 employees, or about 3.8 percent of the labour force, were covered in 1999 (CHRC, Auditor General's report, 2000: Table 8). The 1987 Act's rationale and many of its fundamental concepts, including the name "employment equity" and the principle of creating a systematic policy response to the problem of systemic discrimination, were inspired by Justice Rosalie Abella's *Report of the Royal Commission on Equality of Employment Opportunity* (1984). (The Royal Commission was established by the preceding Liberal government of John Turner.) However, the 1986 Act failed to address significant recommendations of Abella's report, including an effective monitoring and enforcement capability, sanctions for failure to implement employment equity, coverage of the federal public service, and a supportive constellation of social programs such as publicly funded child care.[3] Furthermore, in response to "strong pressure from employers," the policy of the Canadian Human Rights Commission was to refrain from using its power under the Act to initiate complaints against employers whose results indicated a lack of action on the Act's requirements (Canadian Human Rights Advocate, 1988).

In 1986 the Government of Canada also initiated the Federal Contractors Program, which applies to employers that have 100 or more employees and who wish to sell goods or services to the federal government valued at $200,000 or more. Approximately 1,270 employers and a million employees (7 percent of Canada's workforce) were covered by the FCP in 1988 (Employment and Immigration Canada, 1989:2). As of 1998, 1,361 employers (of whom 769 were contractors) and 947,426 employees representing approximately 6.1 percent of the labour force were part of the Federal Contractors Program (personal communication, Federal Contractors Program).

In 1995, under the Liberal government of Jean Chretien, the Employment Equity Act (1986) was reviewed following a process of evaluation and public consultation, and a new Employment Equity Act (1995) was passed that took effect October 24, 1996. The most significant changes in the Act's requirements were the following:

1) Coverage of employers under the Act was expanded to include the federal public service, commissions and agencies (285,296 employees in 1999) (CHRC, Auditor General's Report, 2000: Table 8).
2) Beginning in 1997, employers covered by the Act are subject to compliance audits by the Canadian Human Rights Commission, and an Employment Equity Review Tribunal is empowered to enforce compliance using the existing tribunal structure under the Canadian Human Rights Act.
3) The Federal Contractors Program, previously under regulation, was brought under the Act.

4) Employers now are obliged to "consult" and "collaborate" with "employees' representatives", but these "are not forms of co-management" according to the Employment Equity Act, 1995 (Sec. 15).

Under the 1995 Act, as under the 1986 Act, employers are required to report annually to the Minister (Human Resources Development Canada [HRDC] after 1996) and their individual reports are supposed to be available to the public. Information from their reports is also summarized in a public annual report published by HRDC. Employers covered by the Federal Contractors Program are subject to compliance reviews by HRDC, but contractors are not required to submit their equity plans and reports to the Department and there is no public reporting on their results. Table 1 (page 69) summarizes the most significant provisions of the Employment Equity Act and the Federal Contractors Program as they are currently in force.

While the 1995 Act retained the framework of the 1986 Act, there were some changes in response to the research evaluation of the first five years' experience (ABT Associates, 1992). Critiques of the 1986 Act presented by organizations representing the designated groups, trade unions and others advocated a more vigorous legislative response to systemic discrimination (Johnson et al, 1991; Special Committee, 1992). Predictably, their views were countered by representatives of business and others who advocated limited employment equity legislation with few requirements, such as in the 1986 Act (e.g. deLaurentiis, 1991). While it contains more provisions for holding employers accountable than the 1986 Act, the 1995 revision of the Act also introduced weaknesses reflective of political compromises. These included a modification of the Canadian Human Rights Act such that a Tribunal may not order "positive policies and practices" or " goals and timetables" when an employer is found to have discriminated (Canadian Human Rights Act, as amended, 1995: Sec. 54.1). (This only reinforces Sec. 33 of the Employment Equity Act (1995) that forbids the Canadian Human Rights Commission or a Tribunal from imposing "a quota" on an employer, where "quota" is defined as "a requirement to hire or promote a fixed and arbitrary number of persons during a given period.") Had this section of the Canadian Human Rights Act been in place at the time of the landmark order of the Supreme Court of Canada in *Canadian National Rail v. Action Travail des Femmes* (1987), the order that CNR implement a hiring quota and positive policies and practices as a remedy for systemic discrimination could not have taken place. The 1995 Employment Equity Act also modified the Canadian Human Rights Act to disallow the use of data collected under the Employment Equity Act as the basis for a complaint, and the use of statistical evidence of under-representation as the sole basis for a complaint (Canadian Human Rights Act, as amended 1995: Sec. 40). The CHRC had used this data as a basis for negotiating voluntary agreements with employers to step up their equity activities (ABT, 1992:51).

Another change that resulted in the weakening of the employment equity policy framework was rooted in the principal priority of the Liberal government in the 1990s. Beginning in 1995 the Government reduced spending and stimulated the private sector by means of extensive cuts to the federal public service. The result was a downsizing of the government workforce in regular full time positions by 20 percent from 1994 through 1998 (Malizia and Booker, 1999: 2), as well as a downsizing of the private sector workforce covered by the Employment Equity Act. The resources allocated to the implementation and enforcement of the Act were also depleted at the same time that its requirements were somewhat strengthened.

Table 1. Employment Equity Act (EEA) and Federal Contractors Program (FCP) Primary Requirements (1995)

	EEA	FCP
Coverage:		
Firms in federal jurisdiction	X	
Federal crown corporations	X	
Federal Government	X	
Firms with 100+ employees bidding on federal contracts worth >$200,000		X
Commitment of senior management		X
Assignment of EE responsibility to senior personnel		X
Collection and tabulation of workforce data using voluntary self-identification	X	X
Comparison of designated group representation with relevant labour force availability data	X	X
Employment systems review to identify and remove discriminatory barriers	X	X
Establish numerical goals and timetables for hiring, training and promotion of designated groups	X	X
Establish a work plan for attaining goals	X	X
Inform employees about employment equity	X	X
Special measures and reasonable accommodation	X	X
Consultation and collaboration with employee representatives in preparation of EE plan	X	
Establish favourable climate for integration of designated group members		X
Monitor results and revise plan	X	X
Agreement to allow on-site review by HRDC		X
Compliance audit by CHRC	X	
Report annually to Minister using a set format	X	
Reports made public	X	

Sources: Human Resources Development Canada, "Federal Contractors Program – June 8, 2000 Statement of Requirements" June 8, 2000
Employment Equity Act, 1995

OVERVIEW OF RESULTS OF EMPLOYMENT EQUITY POLICY: AN EFFECTIVE RESPONSE TO SYSTEMIC DISCRIMINATION?

In Chapter 1, systemic discrimination was defined as "patterns of organizational behaviour that are part of the social and administrative structure, culture and decision-making processes of the workplace, and that create or perpetuate relative disadvantage for members of some groups and privilege for members of other groups." Systemic discrimination encompasses the complex and interrelated pattern of policies, institutionalized practices, norms and values that perpetuate exclusionary structures and relationships of power and opportunity within organizations and labour markets. At the level of the workplace, systemic discrimination may be embedded in decisions affecting access to employment, job assignment, terms and conditions of employment, training and development, compensation, promotion, performance appraisal, quality of work life, work-family relationships, and termination. Informal social relations, networks of communication, and the quality of workplace culture and climate may also perpetuate patterns of systemic discrimination.

This chapter is concerned with assessing the effectiveness of Canadian employment equity legislation, as it is currently designed and implemented, as a response to systemic employment discrimination affecting women, racial minorities, aboriginal peoples and persons with disabilities. Based upon the working definition of systemic discrimination proposed above, the following criteria for assessment are suggested:

1. *Numerical representation throughout the organization that approximates the labour market representation of the designated groups (i.e. their "availability");*

2. *Implementation of an employment equity plan.*
   The employer's plan includes measures to identify and remove discriminatory barriers in organizational decision making that limit the access, career development, full participation, and accommodation of the uniqueness of each of the four disadvantaged groups. Such a plan should also aim to create a workplace culture in which the four groups experience inclusion and belonging, supportive supervision, the possibility of full participation and freedom from harassment. The plan should contain goals for improved representation and career development of the designated groups and measures the employer will take to ensure attainment of these goals.

3. *Equality of results -- as measured by salary and representation in senior management for designated group members equivalent to that available to majority group members.*

The following paragraphs examine available information regarding results attained under employment equity policy so far with reference to each of the three criteria. Sources for this purpose include published research, reports on designated group representation in the federal public service from the Public Service Commission of Canada, compilations of employers' data summarized in annual reports published under the Employment Equity Act, and the annual report of the Canadian Human Rights Commission.

However, because of significant gaps in the information available, the review of results to date must be taken as suggestive. There is virtually no information available that relates to the creation of an inclusive workplace culture. Furthermore, since little information is publicly available concerning results achieved under the Federal Contractors Program, this overview focuses primarily on the policy provisions and the results attained under the Employment Equity Act (a research evaluation of the FCP, as required by the Act, is underway at this writing).

The data available in the annual reports published under the Employment Equity Act have notable deficiencies that impede efforts to assess progress. For example, the annual reports for 1998, 1999 and 2000 do not report data on hires, promotions and terminations separately for men and women who are members of visible minorities, persons with disabilities, or aboriginal persons, making it impossible to track results for women in these designated groups. This is a conceptual problem as well as an empirical limitation, since it tends to perpetuate the assumption that data on visible minorities, persons with disabilities, and aboriginal people are data about men, and that data on women are about white women. The result is that women who are aboriginal, or persons with disabilities, or members of racial minorities, are rendered invisible. Moreover, there is an implication of competition between "women" and the "other three" designated groups as to who wins and who loses under employment equity, making alliances in the struggle for change difficult to sustain (Bacchi, 1996: ch. 4).

Furthermore, disaggregated data for full time and part time employees are not published for 1997, 1998 and 1999, at a time when involuntary part time employment became an issue of growing concern for women. While 90 percent of positions in companies under the Act were full time in 1987, this proportion had decreased to 85 percent in 1998. Finally, available data are not as current as one would like. As of January 2001, the most recent annual report under the Employment Equity Act, published in 2000, covers 1998 data, which allows for only two years' experience under the 1995 Act.

In the paragraphs that follow, the available data -- with all their limitations -- form the basis of an effort to assess progress under employment equity in relation to the criteria identified above. For purposes of this analysis it is assumed that employers covered by employment equity legislation or regulation would be most likely to be leaders in employment equity implementation, given the strong evidence that very few employers undertake equity programs unless these are mandatory. For example, a recent study of 40 relatively large Calgary-based companies found that compliance with federal programs was the most common reason given for hiring a more diverse workforce; few companies gave attention to diversity for any other reason ("Calgary Firms", 1999; also Jain and Hackett, 1989). Research evidence reviewed in the discussion that follows notes that formalized and comprehensive equity programs are related to better results for designated groups. Since we are interested in what has been accomplished under employment equity, the lack of research systematically comparing covered employers with those that are not covered is not considered to be a pressing issue.

1) Numerical Representation of Designated Groups Reflective of their Availability in the Labour Market

As summarized in Table 1 (page 69), the Act and FCP both contain requirements related to numerical representation, which has traditionally served as the primary measure of the success of affirmative action or employment equity policy. Employers must conduct a workforce census based upon voluntary self-reports by employees as to their membership in the designated groups. Data on representation are reported by occupational and salary categories, and counts of designated group representation among employees hired, promoted and terminated are also required. Employers must identify areas of under-representation and set their own goals and timetables for improvement, and develop a plan specifying the measures they will take to address under-representation. The goals are to be set with reference to data, usually Census data provided to employers by Human Resources Development Canada, on the availability of designated group members with appropriate qualifications in labour markets relevant to their business.

Table 2 (page 73) presents data on changes in the representation of the designated groups in most sectors covered by the Employment Equity Act. The table includes data for 1987 because that was the first year for which data are available; 1996 was the last year the 1986 Act was in force, and 1999 is the most recent year for which data are available. The period from 1987 was covered by the 1986 Act, while the 1995 Act, with its enhanced enforcement provisions, was in force from 1997 forward.

Women's representation in the companies covered by the Employment Equity Act increased from 41 percent in 1987 to 45 percent in 1996 and remained constant in 1999 -- slightly below their labour force availability rate of 46.4 percent. In the banking sector women's representation was far above their representation in the Canadian workforce as early as 1987 and declined after that, reflecting the downsizing of clerical positions where women were concentrated. Women's representation among those hired increased somewhat from 1987 to 1999 but remained well below their availability. Their representation among those promoted exceeded their workforce rate and their rate of termination was less than their rate of representation in companies under the Act. However women's rate of promotion decreased and their termination rate increased from 1996 to 1999. Over two thirds of part time employees in companies covered by the Act were women.

In the federal public service, women's representation increased from 42 percent in 1987 to 51.5 percent by 1999. However, their representation remained low in some sectors and types of jobs including executive positions. A long-standing pattern of concentration of women of all designated groups in clerical/administrative support jobs continued; research by Pendakur at al (2000) found that over 58 percent of women in federal government employment were concentrated in the administrative support category. The downsizing of the federal public sector had an especially large impact on clerical occupations, and therefore on women, from 1991 through 1997 (Peters, 1999). Women made up 72.5 percent of all part time employment in the federal government workforce (Peters, 1999: 47), and continued to be hired into temporary positions much more frequently than men (CHRC, 2000a).

To summarize what the data show about the representation of women, there is improvement from the first year of employment equity (1987) to 1996, but no evidence of improvement under the 1995 Act. Indeed in 1999 women's representation among employees hired was less than their availability rate and their representation in the workforce under the Act remained constant. This is puzzling, since not only was the Act that took effect in 1996 somewhat stronger than the 1987 Act, but the overall rate of hiring and promotion increased noticeably in 1998 (HRDC, 1999:1).

The representation of visible minorities increased in the private sector under the Act from 5 percent in 1987 to 10.5 percent in 1999 -- slightly more than their availability rate of 10.3 percent. Their representation rates also vary considerably across sectors and occupations; visible minority women were concentrated in banking and among clerical and part time workers. The presence of visible minorities in senior management continues to be low. There was a notable increase from 1987 to 1999 in the representation of visible minorities among those promoted, but their share of hirings remained constant from 1996 to 1999.

The representation of visible minorities in the federal public service was only 5.9 percent in 1998-99 and their share of hiring was only 4.4 percent. The improvement from

Table 2. Representation of Employees Who Are Members of Designated Groups in Firms Covered by the Employment Equity Act, Canada, 1987, 1996 and 1999

Designated Group as Percent of:	Visible Minorities(2.4)			Persons with Disabilities(2,3,4)			Aboriginal People(2,4)			Women(total)(2)		
	1987	1996	1999	1987	1996	1999	1987	1996	1999	1987	1996	1999
Canadian Workforce(1)	6.3	10.3		5.4	6.5(3)		2.1	2.1		44.0	46.4	
Workforce Under the Act: Total	5.0	9.2	10.5	1.6	2.7	2.4	0.7	1.2	1.5	40.9	44.8	44.8
Banks	9.5	14.1	15.8	1.8	3.7	2.2	0.6	1.1	1.3	76.1	74.8	72.0
Communications	4.1	8.7	9.3	1.4	2.5	2.3	0.6	1.1	1.1	39.6	41.9	41.5
Transportation	2.6	4.8	7.1	1.4	1.6	2.5	0.7	1.2	1.8	16.9	21.8	25.2
Hires	5.3	10.6	10.6	0.7	1.1	0.9	0.6	1.7	1.5	37.4	39.4	39.9
Promotions	7.4	12.0	14.1	1.4	2.4	1.9	0.6	1.4	1.4	51.1	56.0	53.9
Terminations	3.3	8.4	9.9	1.2	2.6	2.0	0.6	1.6	1.6	36.4	39.0	40.9
Upper level/Senior Managers	2.1	3.0	3.1	1.6	2.5	1.8	0.2	0.3	0.5	4.7	14.9	17.3
Salary >$70,000	1.5	6.8	8.4	1.2	2.4	2.0	0.2	0.4	0.7	3.1	14.5	19.7
Salary <$30,000	7.0	13.4	13.9	1.7	2.9	2.2	0.8	1.7	2.1	56.0	65.6	63.0
Part-time Employees	6.4	10.0	11.2	1.2	2.4	1.7	0	1.5	1.6	74.6	70.0	68.0

Notes:
(1) Census of Canada, 1986, 1996
(2) Employment Equity Act, Annual Reports, 1988, 1989, 1997, 2000
(3) Health and Activity Limitation Survey, 1991
(4) includes women and men. 1987 data are for full-time employees: 1996 and 1999 data are for total employees, except salary data, which are for full-time employees only

4.1 percent in 1990-91 to 5.9 percent in 1999 was due in large part to the wave of retirements of white able-bodied males in the mid-nineties and a higher retention rate for visible minorities, not to an actual increase in their numbers (Booker et al, 2000: 2, 18). Improved self-identification data for 1997-1999 also contributed to the higher representation rate (Booker et al, 2000: 5). Visible minority men and women were both unevenly distributed among the occupational groups and departments of the public service in 1999. Thirty four percent of visible minority men (compared with 16 percent of non-minority men and 13 percent of visible minority women) were concentrated in scientific and professional jobs. Both visible minority women and non-minority women (43 and 44 percent respectively) were concentrated in the administrative support category (Booker et al, 2000: 8). There continued to be a very low representation of visible minorities in the executive (EX) group and in the key feeder groups leading to EX positions. Research by the Public Service Commission has shown that the problem of under-representation of visible minorities in the federal public service throughout the nineties is due in large part to a low rate of recruitment of this population (Booker et al, 2000:3). Barriers to recruitment include a lack of flexibility in the staffing process, lack of senior managers who are members of visible minorities, and the important role of informal social networks in the provision of career-related information and support (Samuels, 1996).

The representation of aboriginal people in the private sector covered by the Act was still only 1.5 percent in 1999 compared to an availability rate of 2.1 percent. Moreover, the hiring of aboriginal people remained far below their availability rate, and had declined or remained constant for five years in a row (CHRC, 2000a:19). Aboriginal people also suffered a disproportionately high share of terminations; in fact, their termination rate exceeded their hire rate in 1998 and 1999.

In the public service, aboriginal representation reached 2.9 percent in 1999; however there was a concentration of this group in the Department of Indian and Northern Affairs and a very low representation in most of the other departments (CHRC, 2000a:20).

Persons with disabilities comprised 2.4 percent of private sector employees in 1999, a decline from 2.7 in 1996. Their share of hiring also fell from 1996 to 1999, especially in banking, while their rate of termination continued to far exceed their hiring rate. They were significantly under-represented in all sectors even in comparison with an outdated 1991 availability rate of 6.5 percent. The representation of persons with disabilities would have decreased even more had it not been for improved self-identification results in 1998 (HRCD, 1999:31).

In the public sector, their representation stood at 4.6 percent in 1998 and hiring remained low. It is likely that the increased representation of people with disabilities from 1997 to 1998 was also due to improved self-identification (CHRCa, 2000:21).

To summarize, judging from evidence on numerical representation available to date, the 1996 Employment Equity Act has not delivered significant improvements over the 1986 Act. Representation rates remain far below even the underestimates of labour force availability that are normally used as a benchmark. Some improvements are evident for visible minorities and women, particularly white women, judging from the scant information available on gender differences. However the populations that are most disadvantaged -- people with disabilities and aboriginal people -- have benefited very little from employment equity to date.

2) Implementation of Employment Equity Plans

Both the Act and the FCP require the employer to conduct an "employment systems review." The ESR is a review of human resource management policies and practices, especially those that govern hiring, development and promotion, in order to identify and remove or replace those that create discriminatory barriers that are not necessary to the operation of the business. The 1995 Act also requires that unions be involved in employment equity implementation, and requires employers in non-unionized workplaces to consult with employee representatives, including those who are members of the designated groups. All of these requirements contribute to the foundation of an effective program to reduce systemic discrimination. A caveat is that seniority is deemed not to be an unacceptable barrier under the Employment Equity Act, even though there is research evidence that the probability of layoff is higher for designated group members (Singh and Reid, 1998).

In the context of its compliance audit process, the Canadian Human Rights Commission considers the employment systems review (ESR) to be a cornerstone of an employer's employment equity plan and program, since goal-setting and special measures to foster workplace equality follow from the diagnosis produced by the ESR. The Commission found in its first two years of experience under the 1995 Act that a majority of employers had failed to undertake employment systems reviews, and for this reason, compliance with the Act was at a low level (CHRC, 2000a).

Annual reports under the Employment Equity Act suggest that few employers have undertaken special measures sufficient to remove barriers and effectively address the under-representation of designated groups. Training of employees (particularly "diversity training") and changes in recruitment practices appear to be the most frequently adopted measures, although there is a lack of systematic public reporting of this information. Under the Vision Awards program employers are recognized for initiatives in employment equity. Banks, colleges and universities have been prominent among the winners, for such activities as flextime programs that benefit all employees, modifications to buildings to make them accessible, and partnerships with community organizations to assist aboriginal people, persons with disabilities and visible minority youth to enter employment. However Human Resources Development Canada has given merit awards for such activities as successfully conducting the required workforce census, posting job openings, training available to all employees, and distributing brochures (HRDC, 1999). Management accountability for equity results continues to be lacking even in the federal public service: ability to manage diversity is not on the list of required competencies for promotion to executive positions (Phillips, 2000).

Recent studies of the under-representation of visible minorities in the federal public service report that this group faces many barriers to their hiring and promotion. Barriers include a lack of recognition of educational credentials earned in other countries, a lack of inclusion in the culture and informal communication channels in the workplace, and a low level of effort to actively recruit minorities into executive positions (Samuels, 1996). The 1997 human rights tribunal case of *National Capital Alliance on Race Relations v. Health Canada* substantiated discriminatory barriers in formal decision-making processes and in the workplace culture faced by minorities with respect to career development and promotion. The Tribunal ordered Health Canada to implement an employment equity program including removal of barriers, training, and accelerated promotion and appointment rates for visible minorities.

There is evidence that when employers do implement formal employment equity plans there are positive outcomes for the designated groups. Leck and Saunders (1992) found that firms covered by the 1986 Act where there were formalized equity programs that included goals, timetables and plans, an employment equity administrator, and regular audits, and where these programs were comprehensive and supported by management, there was the most progress toward hiring a representative proportion of women into manual, supervisory, professional and management positions. In these firms the most representative hiring occurred for white non-disabled women, followed by women who were members of visible minorities, aboriginal women, and disabled women. In another analysis, Leck and Saunders (1996) found that the presence of formalized equity programs was related to increases in the representation of visible minorities in both management and non-management jobs, as well as to a decrease in occupational segregation in non-management jobs. However, Leck and Saunders (1992:209; 1996: 315) also found that a majority of organizations under the Act did not hire women or visible minorities in proportion to their availability in the labour market. Hence simply being covered by the Act, or even being in compliance with the Act's requirements, did not mean that a firm hires representatively. What makes a difference is employers' attempts to realize the purpose of the Act by means of formalized programs directed toward equity in the workplace, not minimal compliance with the legislation.

These findings are echoed in a study of 17 Ontario universities, 12 of them covered by the Federal Contractors Program. Stewart and Drakich (1995) found that the four FCP universities with the most vigorous employment equity programs also had the highest level of recruitment of women into entry level faculty positions. The universities showing the largest increases in the representation of women had implemented equity measures including affirmative searches and advertising, and peer monitoring of hiring processes at central and departmental levels. However, simply being a member of the FCP was not associated with institutional gains in the hiring of women (Stewart and Drakich, 1995: 444). Again, what counted was the implementation of actions designed to remove discriminatory barriers and get results, rather than mere participation in the FCP.

A survey of 99 FCP employers in Ontario soon after the FCP took effect found that only 13 percent had initiated equity programs prior to the FCP requirements; 17 percent had no plans to start such programs even though they were required to do so (Agocs, 1990). Only one company had set goals for the representation of women in management. However, those firms that had undertaken some of the activities required by the FCP were more likely to have women present in corporate decision making roles. There was a statistically significant relationship between corporate implementation of FCP requirements and a generally progressive approach to human resource management, including investing in management development, initiatives to create a woman-friendly workplace, and using performance-based criteria for staffing upper management positions. This suggests that equity measures are part of a generally progressive corporate human resources management strategy that benefits white able-bodied men as well as designated group members (e.g. see Leck, St Onge and LaLacette, 1995).

Available information about employers' implementation of employment equity requirements demonstrates the positive impact of employment equity policy when it is put into practice. Unfortunately the evidence suggests that few employers have taken serious and effective steps to ensure movement toward an equitable workforce. The requirements to implement employment equity are in place, and they have been shown to get results -- but all too often, they have not been put into practice.

3) Equality of Results

Effective employment equity programs should result in a lessening of the disadvantages faced by employees who are members of designated groups in terms of the distribution of power and rewards. For example, we might expect to see a closing of the gap in salary and in representation in senior management between designated groups and the white male able-bodied employees. Part-time employment generally offers little job security, few benefits and little career potential, and there is evidence that women are more likely than men to be in involuntary part time employment in Canada (Statistics Canada, 2000:104).

Table 2 (page 73) includes data on the representation of aboriginal people, visible minorities, persons with disabilities and women in upper level/senior management, at the upper and lower ends of the salary spectrum, and in part-time employment within firms covered by the Employment Equity Act in 1999, 1996 and 1987. Part time employees were predominantly women, as were employees who were paid less than $30,000 per year for full time work. Members of visible minorities were also represented in these categories at higher rates than their representation in the Canadian workforce, and at an increasing rate. Aboriginal people had a share of part time work and low salaries for full time work that exceeded their level of representation in the workforce under the Act.

At the other end of the spectrum, all designated groups were represented among senior managers, and in the highest salary group, at rates markedly below their representation in companies under the Act. Male employees who were not members of designated groups made up 80 percent of those earning $70,000 or more, and 37 percent of employees earning less than $30,000 (HRDC, 2000: Table 10).

Data on the salary gap between designated groups and all men who are employed full-time provide evidence of some progress, but also of persisting inequality in firms under the Employment Equity Act as of 1999. Women's salary was 77.6 percent of men's, up from 70.7 percent in 1987. Visible minority men received 92.4 percent of the salary of all men, men with disabilities received 94.8 percent, and aboriginal men received 86.8 percent. There was also a salary gap between all women and women who were members of the other designated groups, as follows: visible minority women, 96.4 percent, women with disabilities, 95.6 percent, and aboriginal women, 86.8 percent (HRDC, 2000).

Research by Pendakur et al (2000) on the federal public service from 1987 through 1998 found a pattern of concentration of the designated groups within the two lowest salary quartiles of each occupational category. The study also showed lower odds of promotion for all designated groups, compared with white males, in all job categories except the operational group.

Recent research by the Federal Public Service Commission has examined the representation and rates of appointment of designated groups in executive (EX) positions in the public service and in the ten key feeder groups from which people are promoted into EX positions. Table 3 shows the representation of the designated groups in the feeder positions, in EX positions, and in appointments to the feeder and EX groups. All the designated groups are represented in EX positions at rates well below their representation in the public service. There is evidence that women are being appointed to EX positions at a rate only slightly lower than their appointment to feeder positions. However for aboriginal peoples and visible minorities EX appointments are occurring at a much lower rate than appointments to feeder positions. Aboriginal persons in the feeder pool are concentrated in the Department of Indian and Northern Affairs, and their rate of appointment to EX positions actually declined from 1991-92 to 1998. Visible minorities demonstrate a particularly low representation in EX positions and appointments, and a decline from 5.3 percent of EX appointments in 1991-92 to 1.7 percent in 1998 (Nehme and Gorber, 1999: 12). The number of persons with disabilities in EX positions has been small throughout the study period, but was considerably greater in 1991 than it was in 1998. This is related to the dual impact of public service downsizing (Nehme and Gorber, 1999: 14-15) and failure to recruit new members of this group. In the future, the aging of the EX group will present opportunities for renewal and movement toward greater diversity through new appointments, provided that employment equity implementation is taken seriously.

Table 3. Designated Group Representation in EX positions and Top Ten Feeder Groups, Federal Public Service, 1998

	Representation in:			Appointments to:	
	Federal Public Service	EX Positions	Top 10 Feeder Groups	EX Positions	Feeder Groups
Percent:					
Women	48.1	24.3	31.2	40.6	44.0
Aboriginal people	2.4	1.7	2.9	1.1	3.0
Persons with Disabilities	3.7	2.5	3.2	2.8	2.9
Visible Minorities	5.1	2.6	3.7	1.7	3.8

Source: Malizia and Booker, 1999: 2, 11, 15

Research using wage levels as a dependent variable has made an important contribution to knowledge about the effects of employment equity. We would expect that reductions in the impact of systemic discrimination would result in a shrinking of the wage disadvantage suffered by women, visible minorities, aboriginal people and persons with disabilities. Indeed, an analysis of Labor Market Activity Survey data found that designated group members had a salary advantage of 7.2 percent in companies covered by the 1986 Act, compared with uncovered companies (Gunderson, Meug and Smith, 1996; Taggar, Jain and Gunderson, 1997: 331).

Using employer reports under the 1986 Act and telephone survey data, Leck, St.Onge and Lalancette (1995) compared relationships between average pay of the designated groups and employment equity activities reported by the firms to examine the effects of employment equity on the wage gap between 1989 and 1993. The analysis shows some reduction in the wage gap between white men and each of the designated groups in the lower and middle salary ranges, but an increase in the wage gap at higher salary levels. In firms that had the most formalized employment equity programs, the improvement in average pay of white, visible minority and disabled women as well as aboriginal men was greatest. Formalized equity programs were those characterized by goals, timetables, plans, audits and an employment equity administrator. Employment equity programs, then, were reducing the wage gap between white men and the four designated groups, with white women and minority men as the greatest beneficiaries.

Increases in the representation of the designated groups in senior management can be considered another indicator of progress toward employment equity. Senior managers are defined as "employees holding the most senior positions in large firms or corporations," and who are responsible for corporate policy, strategic planning and the direction and control of the organization's functions (HRDC, June 1999: 62).

Table 2 (page 73) summarizes data on firms covered by the Act. Census data for 1996 show that of senior managers in the Canadian workforce, 79.2 percent were men and 20.8 percent were women; as well, 2.6 percent were aboriginal and 7.3 percent were members of visible minorities (HRDC, Labour Branch, Dec. 1998). Available data on firms under the Act show that since the beginning of mandatory employment equity policy in Canada there has been very little improvement in the representation of aboriginal people in senior management. There was a small increase and then a decrease in the representation of persons with disabilities, mostly men. Visible minorities -- again mostly men -- gained one percent in representation in senior management, and are now present at far below their availability.

The representation of white women improved from 4.7 percent to 17.3 percent of senior managers, which was considerably below their representation in senior management in Canada. In their study of the wage gap, Leck, St. Onge and Lalancette (1995) found that although white women were increasing their representation in upper level management in firms under the Act, their earnings did not keep pace with those of men at that level. The wage gap between minority women and minority men also widened in the higher salary categories. The presence of a formalized employment equity program generally did not result in a narrowing of the wage gap at high salary levels.

In summary, under employment equity to date there is persisting evidence of a glass ceiling effect such that all the designated groups continue to face barriers to entry into senior management. Furthermore, women whose representation in management has improved generally do not receive salaries equal to those of men in these positions.

Results under the Employment Equity Act: Accomplishments and Shortcomings

The review of available information about results under the Employment Equity Act and the Federal Contractors Program shows that there has been some improvement in access to employment for women and racial minorities, but very little for persons with disabilities or aboriginal people. There are continuing concentrations of women in clerical and part time work, and of visible minorities in professional, scientific and technical occupations. There has been some improvement in the access of white able-bodied women to senior management, but their salaries do not match those of their male peers. There has been little progress in the representation of visible minorities in senior management, and none for aboriginal people and persons with disabilities. Rates of representation for all designated groups remain below even the outdated underestimates of their availability that are used as benchmarks.

However, research on the impacts of employment equity implementation shows that in workplaces that have formalized equity programs, women and visible minorities are more likely to be hired in proportions similar to their availability, to be present in management, and to benefit from a decrease in the wage gap. One significant concern is that persons with disabilities and aboriginal people have benefited only slightly. Another concern is that, generally speaking, the data suggest that few employers are implementing formalized, comprehensive and effective employment equity programs in the spirit of the legislation.

WHY THE LIMITED RESULTS?

In an attempt to account for the limited results attained under employment equity policy some critics point to limitations of the Act itself, citing what they consider to be flaws in its premises and strategy for addressing systemic discrimination. Others have argued that the strategy underlying employment equity policy is sound in theory, but specific provisions of the Act are weak, and resources for enforcement are inadequate, as a result of political compromises. As a result employers do not give priority to the implementation of employment equity and tend to do the minimum to comply with the Act's requirements. Both the specific weaknesses of the 1995 Act and its enforcement are limitations that might be explained by pointing to a lack of political commitment to employment equity in an era of neo-liberalism. In this context addressing systemic discrimination in the workplace is not a priority for either governments or employers.

Are There Weaknesses in the Logic and Strategy of Employment Equity?

Lum (1995) contends that the Act is ineffective as a policy instrument for dealing with systemic discrimination because of its inherent flaws, chief of which is its reliance on data collection as its central policy lever. In setting up the labour market of the recent past as the standard that firms are to match, the Act reinforces the very patterns of systemic discrimination that compliance with the Act is supposed to correct. As an example, a Public Service Commission forecasting model showed that "if goals are set at availability levels it would take many [federal] departments about 28 years before full representation of some designated groups is reached" (CHRC, 2000:6).

Lum (1995) also argues that the data-related requirements of the Act are undermined by the limitations of the availability data that employers rely upon to set numerical goals.

The quality of availability data was much improved with the 1996 Census of Canada, which included more valid indicators of aboriginal and visible minority status. However, resources were not allocated to a 1996 census on disability so availability data on disability dates back to 1991 (HRDC, 1999). The availability pool for people with disabilities is probably closer to 14.5 percent than to the 6.5 percent that is now used as a benchmark by employers and compliance agencies (Lum, 1995). Census data on the labour market representation of visible minorities is quickly outdated in light of immigration trends, and availability rates for visible minorities and aboriginal people vary widely among cities and provinces. For example, the 1996 census showed that nearly a third of Toronto's and Vancouver's populations were comprised of visible minorities (Statistics Canada, 1998). Generally, the size of the labour market of available members of the designated groups is understated, with the result that employment equity goals are set too low.

Lum also challenges weaknesses inherent in the self-identification process used to collect workforce data. For example, annual reports on results under the Act published by Human Resources Development Canada acknowledge that in some years, a large portion of the (small) increases in the representation of aboriginal people and visible minorities was attributable to increases in the rate of self-identification, not to employers' implementation of the Act's requirements. There have also been persistent problems in the definition and self-identification of persons with disabilities.

Others have criticized the Act for allowing employers to set their own goals, and for the opportunity they have to explain away a lack of results, for example by pointing to an unfavourable business climate. A major weakness is that the Act provides for sanctions only when employers fail to file their reports, not when employers show a lack of progress in implementing their own equity plans. However, the Canadian Human Rights Commission has the power to give an order that has legal force to an employer ("make a direction"), and to appoint a tribunal whose decisions are final, in cases of non-compliance with the Act -- as a last resort. Under the Federal Contractors Program, the sanction for non-compliance is that the employer loses the right to bid on future federal contracts.

These limitations suggest that the Act's requirements set the bar too low for employers and are too weak to result in acceptable progress toward the reduction of inequality in employment for the four designated groups. Yet even these requirements, inadequate as they may be, are not being fully and effectively implemented by many employers. There seems to be no practical alternative to requiring employers to set their own goals relative to the labour markets in which they hire. The appropriateness of those goals is assessed as part of the compliance audit. As to whether the Act's reliance on data on numerical representation is a weakness, it can be argued that there is no clear alternative if progress over time is to be assessed, and if it is recognized that there must be some generally accepted standard, at least as a lower limit, for setting goals. The problem is not the use of workforce and labour force data in principle, but the poor quality of currently available data. The 2001 census will provide more useful data for visible minorities provided that resources are allocated to its collection and publication. Better data for persons with disabilities should be available in 2003, following analysis of results of a special survey to be conducted in 2001 apart from the Census (HRDC, 2000). Furthermore, if there were the political will to make employment equity policy effective, weaknesses in specific provisions of the Act and its requirements could be corrected by amending the Act in conjunction with its pending legislative review.

An assessment of the underlying theory and strategy of employment equity must also question whether an assimilationist logic is built into the policy (e.g. Bacchi, 1996: 64), or whether it is, or can be, a strategy for transforming organizations to make them more equitable. In other words, is employment equity merely a program for fitting people who are "different" into a workplace designed for a traditional white able-bodied male workforce in ways that penalize "newcomers" and force them to conform to existing structures? Or does employment equity force dominant social groups in the workplace to change, to share power, to confront their biases, to subject existing structures to critical scrutiny, and to create new structures and policies that meet the needs of today's diverse workforce?

Results so far attained under employment equity policy indicate that change has been limited. However, the primary issue is not weaknesses in the premises and logic of employment equity policy, but a failure of employers to implement the policy as it is written. Until a high level of compliance with employment equity requirements is attained it would be inappropriate to attribute the disappointing results to the policy itself. Until employment equity policy is taken seriously as a priority of governments and employers its potential as a facilitator of organizational change remains unclear. One cannot fairly evaluate a policy that has not been put into practice.

Arrangements and Resources for Enforcement

Under the 1986 Employment Equity Act, when enforcement provisions were negligible, employers' implementation activity was weak. Three early studies undertaken soon after federal employment equity policy took effect in 1987 found that employers had made little progress toward implementation (Agocs, 1990; Drakich and Stewart, 1995: 444; Jain and Hackett, 1989). The 1992 research evaluations of results under the 1986 Act found that only about half the employers covered had set hiring goals and taken steps to remove systemic barriers. In contrast, the compliance review process for the FCP had significantly affected the level of employment equity activities among covered employers. Furthermore, the level of equity activity in FCP firms was higher than in firms covered by the Act (ABT, 1992: 54). Compliance reviews had a significant effect on inducing equity initiatives among contractors, who did little until they were identified for a compliance audit (ABT, n.d.: 37). This was true even though only two contractors were disbarred from the right to bid on contracts in 1988-89, and both were soon reinstated (ABT, n.d., 50).

The Canadian Human Rights Commission (CHRC) now has responsibility for the enforcement of the Employment Equity Act (1995). The CHRC is expected to use persuasion to get employers not in compliance to move toward compliance. A decision that the employer is in compliance with the Act's requirements means that the designated groups are equitably represented in the workplace, or that the Commission is satisfied that the employer's equity plan will result in "reasonable progress" toward that goal (CHRC, 2000a). The compliance audit process used by the CHRC involves a desk audit and a site visit for verification. If the employer is not in compliance the Commission prepares an interim report setting out the requirements to be completed within twelve months, and this undertaking is negotiated with the employer. Then the employer files a progress report and receives a follow-up audit. If the employer is still not in compliance the Commission issues a direction as to the work required and the time limit. After another follow-up audit, if the employer is still not in compliance the Commission may ask the Employment Equity Tribunal to issue an order that may be registered with a federal court. Audits take nine to eleven months each on average (CHRC, 2000a). In view of this lengthy process, with no sanctions for employers who delay, an employer may be able to avoid compliance with the Act for years.

The 1999 annual report of the CHRC notes that during the first two years of compliance audits under the 1995 Act, 111 initial audits were completed, and only four employers were found to be in compliance (CHRC, 2000a). Undertakings requiring follow-up audits were signed with 103 employers, and of these, eight more were found to be in compliance the following year. However two thirds of the follow-up audits found that employers were still not in compliance and most were granted extensions. Four employers, including one government department, had not accomplished enough to warrant an extension, so the Commission issued directions requiring these employers to act. It is too early to tell what the next steps will be in these cases. The CHRC may apply to the Tribunal for an order confirming the direction if an employer does not comply, but only as a last resort. As yet there have been no such cases.

A significant reason for employers' lack of action to implement employment equity may be the lack of meaningful sanctions for non-compliance. The Act specifically forbids the Commission to impose a quota on an employer or to order an employer to undertake actions that would cause undue hardship to the employer, or to hire or promote "unqualified persons", or to create new positions. A Tribunal can order an employer to cease discrimination and/or to comply with the Act's requirements, but is not permitted to order an employer to adopt a special program to achieve improved representation. The Act provides for a fine of $10,000 for a single violation or $50,000 for "repeated or continued violations" in the case of failure to file the required reports, or for false reporting. However there is no sanction for failure to improve the representation of the designated groups, provided that the required reports are submitted and that the employer can provide a plausible reason for slow or non-existent progress. For example, during its first two years of experience under the 1995 Act, the Commission found that many employers set goals that were lower than availability, and their representation levels did not improve relative to that benchmark (Canadian Human Rights Commission, 2000). As well, there are no sanctions for failing to remove job barriers identified in the employment systems review, or for hiring members of a designated group into a "job ghetto", or for paying them less than white male workers with equivalent qualifications are paid.

Employers are rarely in compliance on the first or even the second audit, leading to a cumulative workload that appears to quickly exceed the resources of the Commission ("more that 95 percent of employers require follow-up audits, most frequently because they are insufficiently aware of the requirements of the Employment Equity Act" [CHRC, 2000b:10]). The Commission's initial plan to audit every employer covered by the Act during the first five years has not been attainable. Moreover, there is obviously a need for more investment in the education of employers as to the Act's requirements and how to fulfill them – a function for which the Treasury Board Secretariat, the Public Service Commission and the Department of Human Resources Development Canada all share responsibility.

The enforcement of the Act is hampered by resource limitations, particularly for addressing systemic discrimination. The CHRC has budgeted for more cuts in spending from 1999 through 2002, at the same time that it faces a more complex and demanding mandate because of recent and anticipated changes in the statutory framework, and the fact that "an increasing number of issues it deals with reflect systemic practices rather than isolated incidents of discrimination" (CHRC, 2000b:4). However systemic cases apparently cannot be given priority since the CHRC has the statutory obligation to process every individual case that is filed under the Canadian Human Rights Act (approximately 1600 complaints files annually). This appears to be an impossible workload with current resources, resulting in an extensive backlog of cases whose resolution is a high priority. The complaint-related services of the Commission account for 53 percent of its resources for 2000-2001 (CHRC, 2000b: 9). The Commission's audit responsibilities under the Employment Equity Act, in contrast, receive only 12 percent of its budget for 2000-2001 (CHRC, 2000b: 10).

It is likely that a sector that knows it has a high probability of being audited will take measures to ensure that it will be in compliance. In part to address the problem of inadequate resources and maximize the impact of the audit program, the Commission plans to concentrate employment equity audits on larger employers, particularly federal government departments. The federal public service has also been in the spotlight following a Canadian Human Rights Tribunal finding that Health Canada practiced systemic discrimination against racial minority employees. The Tribunal ordered the department to implement a variety of equity measures (*National Capital Alliance on Race Relations and CHRC v. Health and Welfare Canada et al*, 1997). These events may partly explain the Public Service Commission's making employment equity one of its five priorities for the year 1999-2000, as well as its recent increases in equity-oriented research and outreach recruitment activities (PSC, 20000:7-9). The CHRC may have helped to initiate this attention to employment equity by commissioning a research study that documented barriers facing visible minorities in the public service (Samuels, 1996). In the mid-nineties, there appeared to be improvements in some companies under the Act, particularly the banks, as a result of the CHRC's program to negotiate agreements with employers to undertake more vigorous equity efforts rather than face legal action under the Commission's power to initiate systemic complaints.

The CHRC appears to be making effective and strategic use of the resources it has to pursue its mandate and get results. If the CHRC had the resources and the mandate to set standards, conduct studies, and actively enforce compliance with the Employment Equity Act, such that each employer covered had a high probability of facing an audit with consequences for non-compliance, results under the Act would no doubt improve significantly. Moreover, the Commission presently lacks the resources required to deliver the intensive educational and consulting services that employers appear to require: employers' lack of knowledge about employment equity and its requirements is a major barrier the Commission faces in getting compliance with the Act (Phillips, 2000).

Under the 1995 Employment Equity Act, compliance audits are more rigorous than they currently are for participants in the Federal Contractors Program (Rose, 1998). For employers covered by the FCP, failure to implement the requirements can result in loss of the opportunity to bid on future federal contracts. However this sanction has been rarely applied. Most Canadian universities are federal contractors: university equity officers and others who are most familiar with the employment equity compliance-related activities in universities are sometimes surprised when their organizations are found to be in compliance with the FCP requirements. Drakich and Stewart (1995:444) found that universities with representations of women on faculty that were below the provincial average had been found in compliance.

As in the case of the CHRC's enforcement of the Act, resources for enforcement of the Federal Contractors Program are also far too lean to meet the need. In 1999 only 6 full time positions were dedicated to HRDC's compliance review program, to track 860 contractor firms across the nation. More recently, most compliance-related activity was transferred from the Ottawa head office to 18 regional equity consultants, and staff at the Compliance Review Officer level in Ottawa were reduced from 6 to 3 (personal communication, Neil Gavigan, Director of Labour Standards and Workplace Equity, HRDC, July 25, 2000). Non-compliance cases are referred to the head office. The regional field staff are responsible for reviewing the compliance of FCP companies. In addition, regional HRDC staff provide availability data, consultation and information services to employers under both the FCP and the Act, as well as handling pay equity information and promotion. Given this workload it is understandable that current consultation and educational services to employers do not meet the need, judging from the CHRC's experience with compliance audits.

The employment equity policy framework, as it was established in the 1986 Act and carried forward into the 1995 Act, makes the assumption that public scrutiny as well as pressure brought about by advocates for the designated groups will be an important part of the implementation and enforcement functions. While the Employment Equity Act requires "consultation" with employees, it does not specify what form this should take. For example, equity committees are not required in the workplace, and employers are not required to consult with, and listen to, members of designated groups who, after all, are particularly knowledgeable about the existence of systemic barriers. The 1999 Annual Report under the Act notes that employers provided little information on their consultation efforts; indeed many said that no mechanisms existed, while others indicated that they had “informed” employees (p. 3). The Act's consultation requirement is not only vague, but it does not appear to be enforced with regard to either managements' or unions' role in employment equity (Gavigan, 2000).

This is a serious issue, since there is a large research literature demonstrating the efficacy of arrangements for the participation of stakeholders in the planning and implementation of organizational change, including equity-related change (Agocs, Burr and Somerset, 1992). Furthermore, there are working examples of success in the use of mandatory workplace committees to safeguard employees' rights and to monitor compliance, such as joint occupational health and safety committees. Organizations representing and assisting the designated groups have also played a central part in successful equity initiatives at the level of the workplace. For example, employers depend heavily on the assistance and educational work of organizations that assist people with disabilities in order to successfully recruit employees and arrange appropriate accommodation. The failure of employment equity so far to show results for persons with disabilities and aboriginal people suggests the need for much greater attention to policy development focussing on these groups. Consideration could be given to supplementing compliance-oriented efforts with support for the contribution that organizations serving the designated groups make to the successful implementation of employment equity initiatives, particularly for persons with disabilities and aboriginal people. Assistance could be provided by means of a federal program to support and encourage partnerships between organizations serving these designated groups and employers. Under the program, funding and expertise could be made available for initiating and maintaining successful joint equity initiatives between employers and designated group organizations.

Advocacy organizations at the community level have also played a leading role in employment equity policy development and in monitoring equity at the level of the workplace. The critical role of advocacy organizations in equity-related change by means of legal action is exemplified in the landmark Supreme Court of Canada case of *Action travail des femmes vs. CNR* (1987) as well as the tribunal case of *National Capital Alliance on Race Relations v. Health Canada* (1997). As in the domain of environmental damage and threat, the ability to bring class action suits would contribute to the enforcement framework for employment equity.

For vigorous public scrutiny and pressure on companies under the Act to occur, the data that firms are required to report must be easily available in a form that is usable by grass roots organizations. Furthermore, the media must be interested in reporting the employment equity results of companies under the Act so that the public is aware of progress and lack of progress. As mentioned previously, the annual report summarizing the data from companies has not consistently reported the same indicators from year to year. Furthermore, in recent reports statistics are highly aggregated so that, for example, users interested in the progress of women with disabilities, or in impacts on women of recent increases in part time employment, have no data to work with. Reports on individual companies are difficult to obtain. The publication of the annual reports is often virtually ignored by the media. In practice, then, there has been little evidence that on-going public scrutiny and advocacy using data reported by companies under the Act has brought significant pressure on companies to take employment equity seriously.

Throughout the 1990s, advocacy organizations have been faced with a multitude of issues of concern and diminished resources with which to address them; it was unrealistic to expect them to take the lead in the struggle for equity in employment. At the same time, in the political climate of the 1990s the media have perpetuated the damaging and ideological myths about employment equity that were part of right wing campaign rhetoric, particularly of the Harris Tories in Ontario and the Reform and Canadian

Alliance parties at the federal level. The misconceptions and distortions that shaped public opinion about employment equity as a result of this discourse need to be countered by a program to raise public awareness of the continued existence of systemic discrimination in employment, and of what is actually involved in employment equity policy and its implementation. Such a program to build understanding and support for employment equity and counter entrenched myths would require leadership and resources from governmental and corporate sources.

In summary, research on the relationship between employers' level of employment equity activity and results -- as indicated by level of designated group representation, presence in management and pay -- clearly shows that implementation of employment equity requirements makes a difference. This literature also demonstrates that employers' failure to implement employment equity requirements is linked to lack of results for the designated groups: just being covered by the Employment Equity Act or a contract compliance program is not enough to produce equity gains. Proactive education of employers and mechanisms to ensure participation of employees and their representatives, combined with vigorous enforcement -- including compliance audits and consequences for non-compliance -- are all critical to the effective implementation of policy. Decisions of courts and human rights tribunals have played and will continue to play a critical role in the development of more equitable workplace practices.

The legislative and policy framework for dealing with issues of occupational health and safety provides an example of elements contributing to effectiveness in producing change at the level of the workplace. Advocacy by unions and health advocates has framed the issues, educated the public, and put pressure on decision-makers. Court decisions resulting in consequences for employers put forward the reality of employer liabilities. Legislation with clear requirements and standards, including workplace committees in which employees and unions have a role in monitoring compliance, provides a framework for implementation. No doubt there have been gaps between the intentions of policymakers and implementation in the case of occupational health and safety, but many elements of an effective system appear to be in place.

Analysis of available information suggests that the theory of employment equity as a remedy for systemic discrimination provides a sound working basis for equality policy for Canadian society at the present time. Furthermore, in comparison with other countries, Canada's employment equity legislation is advanced, and broad in scope and coverage. However, there has been a gap between the promise of employment equity policy and the limited results achieved. Results under employment equity have been disappointing primarily because of lack of support for the implementation of employment equity by political leaders and employers. In effect, the implementation and enforcement of employment equity policy is being sabotaged by a lack of commitment and resources. Political compromises have weakened the compliance-related provisions of the Act, compounded by lack of resources for monitoring and enforcement. There is a need for sanctions when employers fail to make progress toward equity in the workplace, and for government and corporate leadership in informing the public about the realities, in contrast with the myths, of employment equity. The critical role that courts and human rights tribunals have played in clarifying employers' responsibilities and liabilities, as well as employees' rights, shows the need for continued development of the case law regarding systemic discrimination and its remedies.

The overview sketched here suggests that the promise of employment equity as a policy that can be effective in reducing the impacts of systemic discrimination in employment has not been realized to date. Its weaknesses need to be addressed, and new approaches need to be developed in parallel with changes in the nature of work, if employment equity is to realize its purpose. It will require political will to work toward a society in which systemic discrimination in employment is a part of the past rather than the future.

Carol Agocs is a Professor in the Department of Political Science, University of Western Ontario, London, Ontario, Canada.

NOTES

[1] In the Employment Equity Act (1995), "members of visible minorities" means "persons, other than Aboriginal peoples, who are non-Caucasian in race or non-white in colour". In the 1996 Census of Canada, 11.2 percent of the population responded that they were members of a visible minority specified in the regulations to the Act. Of the visible minority population, 27 percent indicated Chinese origin, 21 percent South Asian, and 18 percent Black (Statistics Canada, 1998). Thirty percent of those who identified themselves as visible minorities were born in Canada; the rest were immigrants.

[2]The term "persons with disabilities" is defined in the Act as "persons who have a long-term or recurring physical, mental, sensory, psychiatric or learning impairment and who (a) consider themselves to be disadvantaged in employment by reason of that impairment, or (b) believe that an employer or potential employer is likely to consider them to be disadvantaged in employment by reason of that impairment." The definition "includes persons whose functional limitations owing to their impairment have been accommodated in their current job or workplace" (Human Resources Development Canada, June 1999: 26, 28).

[3] Flora McDonald, Progressive Conservative Minister of Employment and Immigration who introduced the Employment Equity bill in Parliament, faced opposition in Cabinet and Caucus, "acrimonious debate" in Parliament, and the behind-the-scenes lobbying of business opponents who couldn't believe that "their government" would do this. The opposition parties (the Liberals and New Democrats) and advocates of employment equity applied vigorous public pressure in an attempt to strengthen the bill. The result was a compromise. In McDonald's view it was "better to achieve something concrete, limited as its scope may be, as long as it is fundamentally sound" (McDonald, 2000).

REFERENCES

Abella, Judge Rosalie Silberman. *Equality in Employment: A Royal Commission Report*. Ottawa: Supply and Services Canada, 1984.

ABT Research Associates, *Project Report: Evaluation of the Federal Contractors Program, n.d.*

ABT Research Associates. *Final Report: Evaluation of the Legislated Employment Equity Program*. Ottawa: Employment and Immigration Canada, Program Evaluation Branch, June 1992.

Agocs, Carol. "Affirmative Action, Canadian Style: A Reconnaissance." *Canadian Public Policy* 12.1 (1986): 148-162.

Agocs, Carol. "Employment Equity Activity Among Federal Contractors in Ontario." *Proceedings of the 26th AnnualConference of the Canadian Industrial Relations Association*, 1990, 517-529.

Auditor General of Canada. *Report on the Canadian Human Rights Commission, 1998*. Chapter 10. Ottawa, 1999.

Bacchi, Carol Lee. *The Politics of Affirmative Action*. London: Sage, 1996.

Bashevkin, Sylvia. *Women on the Defensive: Living Through Conservative Times*. Toronto: University of Toronto Press. 1998.

Booker, Douglas, Natalie Dole, Stan Lee, Kathy Malizia, Daniel O'Connor and Rhonda Nause. "Demographic Study of the Visible Minority Community in the Federal Public Service." Ottawa: Public Service Commission, Federal Task Force on Visible Minority Participation in the Public Service, February 2000.

"Calgary Firms Motivated by Compliance, not Bottom-line Benefit." *Workplace Diversity Update* (April 1999): 4.

Canada. Chapter 44, "An Act Respecting Employment Equity." assented to 15th December 1995.

Canada. House of Commons. "Minutes of Proceedings and Evidence of the Legislative Committee on Bill C-62, An Act Respecting Employment Equity, 1985.

Canada. House of Commons, Special Committee on the Review of the Employment Equity Act. A *Matter of Fairness.* May 1992.

Chicha, Marie-Therese. "Contract Compliance Programs in Quebec." paper presented to the Metropolis Conference, Vancouver, November 14, 2000.

Canadian Human Rights Act Review Panel. *Promoting Equality: A New Vision 2000.* Ottawa: Department of Justice. 2000.

Canadian Human Rights Advocate, 4.7 (August 1988).

Canadian Human Rights Commission (CHRC). *Annual Report, 1999.* Ottawa: CHRC, 2000 (a).

Canadian Human Rights Commission (CHRC). "2000-2001 Estimates, Part III - Report on Plans and Priorities." Ottawa: Treasury Board, 2000 (b).

Day, Shelagh and Gwen Brodsky. *Women and the Equality Deficit: The Impact of Restructuring Canada's Social Programs.* Ottawa: Status of Women Canada, March 1998.

deLaurentiis, Joanne. "Employment Equity: Eliminating Barriers." *Canadian Business Review* 18.2 (1991): 33ff.

Employment and Immigration Canada. *Employment Equity Act. Annual Report to Parliament 1988.* Ottawa: Minister of Supply and Services, 1988.

Employment and Immigration Canada. *Employment Equity Act. Annual Report 1989.* Ottawa, 1989.

Gagnon, Yves Chantal and Francine Letourneau. " L'efficacite des programmes d'acces a l'egalite pour les femmes." *Canadian Public Administration* 39.2 (1996): 136-156.

Gavigan, Neil. informal discussion on employment equity in Canada, Conference on Employment Equity Challenges and Opportunities. Regina, Saskatchewan, June 20, 2000.

Gunderson, Morley, R. A. Meng and D.A. Smith. "The Impact of Employment Equity Programs on Wages." unpublished paper, 1996.

Human Resources Development Canada [HRDC]. *Annual Report: Employment Equity Act, 1998.* Ottawa: Minister of Public Works and Government Services Canada, 1998.

Human Resources Development Canada [HRDC]. *1999 Employment Equity Act Annual Report.* Ottawa, 1999. At http://info.load-otea.hrdc-drhc.gc.ca/~weedis.

Human Resources Development Canada [HRDC]. 2000 *Employment Equity Act Annual Report.* Ottawa, 2000.

Human Resources Development Canada [HRDC]. "Federal Contractors Program -- Information for Suppliers and Organizations." 2000.

Human Resources Development Canada [HRDC]. "Key elements of the New Employment Equity Act and Regulations." n.d. (http://info.load-otea.hrdc-drhc.gc.ca/~weeweb/keyele.htm).

Human Resources Development Canada, Labour Standards and Employment Equity. *1996 Employment Equity Data Report (release no. 2).* June 1999.

Human Resources Development Canada. "Update on the Survey on Persons with Disabilities." Oct. 24, 2000.

Jain, Harish and Rick Hackett. "Measuring Effectiveness of Employment Equity Programs in Canada: Public Policy and a Survey." *Canadian Public Policy* 25.2 (1989): 180-204.

Jain, Harish, Simon Taggar and Morley Gunderson. "The Status of Employment Equity in Canada: An Assessment." paper presented to the 49th annual conference of the Industrial Relations Research Association, New Orleans, January 1997.

Johnson, Adrian, Carol McGregor, Roy Cunningham and Handel Mlilo. "Perspectives on Employment Equity." *Canadian Business Review* 18.2 (1991): 30 ff.

Leck, Joanne, Sylvie St. Onge and Isaelle Lalancette. "Wage Gap Changes Among Organizations Subject to the Employment Equity Act." *Canadian Public Policy* 21.4 (1995): 387-400.

Leck, Joanne and David Saunders. "Achieving Diversity in the Workplace: Canada's Employment Equity Act and Members of Visible Minorities." *International Journal of Public Administration* 19.3 (1996): 299-321.

Leck, Joanne and David Saunders. "Hiring Women: The Effects of Canada's Employment Equity Act." *Canadian Public Policy* 18.2 (1992): 203-220.

Lum, Janet M.. "The Federal Employment Equity Act; Goals vs. Implementation." *Canadian Public Administration* 38.1 (1995): 45-76.

Malizia, Kathy and Douglas Booker. "Demographic Profile of Key Executive Feeder Groups, 1991-1998." Ottawa: Public Service Commission of Canada, 1999.

McDonald, Flora. "Employment Equity -- Fifteen Years Later." keynote address, Conference on Employment Equity Challenges and Opportunities. Regina, Saskatchewan, June 20, 2000.

National Capital Alliance on Race Relations and Canadian Human Rights Commission v. Health and Welfare Canada, Public Service Commission and Treasury Board. Canadian Human Rights Tribunal Decision T.D. 3197/D.T.3/97, March 19, 1997.

Nehme, Micheline and Timna Gorber. "Demographic Study of the Executive Community, 1991-1998." Ottawa: Public Service Commission of Canada, Research Directorate, February 1999.

Ontario. Legislative Assembly. "An Act to Provide for Employment Equity for Aboriginal People, People with Disabilities, Members of Racial Minorities and Women." Royal Assent December 14, 1993.

Pay Equity Commission, Ontario. *Annual Report 1995-1996*. Toronto: Pay Equity Commission, 1996.

Pendakur, Ravi, Fernando Mata, Stan Lee and Natalie Dole. "Job Mobility and Promotion in the Federal Public Service." Ottawa: Strategic Research and Analysis, Canadian Heritage, and Research Directorate, Public Service Commission, Feb. 18, 2000.

Peters, Joseph. *An Era of Change: Government Employment Trends in the 1980s and 1990s*. Canadian Policy Research Network, June 1999.

Phillips, Rhys. "Canadian Human Rights Commission Employment Equity Compliance Audits. " presentation to the Metropolis Conference, Vancouver, November 2000.

Public Service Commission of Canada. "Estimates, Performance Report for the Period Ending March 31, 2000. " March 31, 2000.

Quebec Assemblee Nationale, premiere session, trente-sixieme legislature, projet de loi n. 143. "Loi sur l'acces a l'egalite en emploi dans des organismes publics et modifiant la Charte des droits et libertes de la personne. " Dec. 2000.

Quebec. *Report on Outcomes of the World Summit on Social Development: Social Development in Quebec, 1995-2000*, 2000.

Rose, Ghyslaine. "Update on the Federal Contractors Program." presentation to the Annual Conference of the Ontario Universities Employment and Educational Equity Network, Oct. 27, 1998.

Samuels, John. *Visible Minorities and the Public Service of Canada*. Ottawa: Canadian Human Rights Commission, 1996.

Singh, G. and Reid, F.. "Are Seniority-based Layoffs Discriminatory? The Adverse Impact of Layoffs on Designated Groups." *Relations Industrielles* 53.4 (1998): 730-749.

Statistics Canada. "1996 Census: Ethnic Origin, Visible Minorities." *The Daily* (Feb. 17, 1998) *(at* http://www.statcan.ca/Daily/English/980217/d980217.htm*)*

Statistics Canada. *Women in Canada 2000: A Gender-based Statistical Report*. Ottawa: Statistics Canada, 2000.

Stewart, Penni and Janice Drakich. "Factors Related to Organizational Change and Equity for Women Faculty in Ontario Universities." *Canadian Public Policy* 21.4 (1995): 429-448.

Taggar, Simon, Harish Jain, and Morley Gunderson. "The Status of Employment Equity in Canada; An Assessment." *Proceedings of the 49th Annual Meeting, Industrial Relations Research Association*. New Orleans, January 4-6, 1997.

Weiner, Nan. "Employment Equity and Pay Equity: Similarities, Differences and Integration." *Canadian Labour Law Journal* 2.1 (1993): 16-31.

Weiner, Nan and Morley Gunderson. *Pay Equity. Issues, Options and Experiences*. Toronto: Butterworths, 1990.

CHAPTER 5

ABIGAIL B. BAKAN AND AUDREY KOBAYASHI

EMPLOYMENT EQUITY LEGISLATION IN ONTARIO: A CASE STUDY IN THE POLITICS OF BACKLASH[1]

INTRODUCTION: THE EMPLOYMENT EQUITY PARADOX

Canada presents a paradoxical employment equity context. At the federal level, legislative commitment to the principles of employment equity, particularly regarding the public service, is one of the most extensive in the developed world (Agocs and Burr, 1996; Leck and Saunders, 1992a; 1992b; Jain, 1990; Jain, et al, 1990). At the provincial level, however, not only are employment equity policies and programs very poorly developed and unevenly applied, but there is extensive – and highly ideologically charged – debate over its existence. The Canadian context suggests very different standards and attitudes to employment equity in these different political jurisdictions.

At the centre of the paradox is the contrast between the normative institutional context regarding employment equity as a means to redress the effects of systemic discrimination, and a politically inspired action against the very concept. Federally, while the effects of implementation are not fully realised, the government has clearly indicated its ongoing support for the principles of employment equity. Improvement of employment equity policies was a significant item in the Liberal government platform, and therefore one for which the current government must have believed they had broad public support. The Ontario government under Premier Mike Harris, in contrast, has mounted explicit opposition to the recognition of systemic discrimination in employment. In its pre-election strategy, the Harris government presented employment equity policy as an unfair means of advancing the "special interests" of certain groups, based on the invalid claims of reversing unfair treatment where none actually exists.

Systemic discrimination has been recognised since the early 1960s in Canadian policy debates, and this recognition has fuelled the development of rights-based policy and legislation over the past four decades. The federal employment equity program stems from the 1983 Royal Commission on Equality in Employment and the subsequent report by Judge Rosalie Abella, *Equality in Employment* (1984), which explicitly endorsed the principles of employment equity, based on the recognition of women, Aboriginal peoples, persons in a visible minority, and persons with disabilities as the four "designated groups" considered to experience systemic discrimination rooted in oppressive practices. The federal government has continued to build upon those principles, with a major re-vamping of the program over the past four years. Most recently, the Treasury Board commissioned a Task Force on Visible Minorities in the Federal Public Service, with the mandate to develop an action plan to address the huge gap between availability and representation of

C. Agocs (ed.), Workplace Equality, 91–107.

members of visible minorities (Task Force on Visible Minorities, 2000). While it is too early to determine whether the action plan will have effective results, it is at the least an indication of some willingness at the federal level to go beyond policy towards implementation.

At the provincial level, there is a spectrum of divergent policies ranging from firm opposition to the principles and practices of employment equity, to binding legislative enforcement (Bakan and Kobayashi, 2000). No provincial legislature has mirrored the federal policy context precisely. Employment equity legislation, as distinct from general equity policy, has only been enacted in three provinces: Quebec has very recently passed legislation to cover the provincial public service; British Columbia's legislation governing public service employment has a clause requiring employment equity, but no separate legislation; and, Ontario has repealed what was once the most comprehensive legislation, covering both the public and private sectors.

The province of Ontario presents a curious combination of extremes regarding employment equity. This province has a unique and recent history not only of having had the most progressive employment equity legislation in any jurisdiction at any time, but also of the most profound backlash against employment equity that has ever occurred in Canada. Employment equity legislation was enacted under the New Democratic Party government led by Premier Bob Rae in 1993, only to be repealed in 1995 under the Ontario Progressive Conservative government led by Premier Mike Harris. The repeal of the law during the first year of the first Harris government was conducted in an atmosphere of ideological backlash that challenged not only the legitimacy of the legislation, but also the principles of employment equity policy in general.

The Ontario case moved from the legislative assembly to the courts with the presentation of a Constitutional challenge to the *Job Quotas Repeal Act (1995)*, the Harris government's legislation repealing the Employment Equity Act. The challenge was based on the terms of the Canadian Charter of Rights and Freedoms, part of the Canadian Constitution repatriated to Canada in 1982. The case was heard by the Ontario Court, General Division, in November of 1996. In July of 1997, the Court announced that the judge had dismissed the application, but the coalition immediately announced its intention to challenge the ruling before the Ontario Court of Appeal. In April of 1998, the case was heard; in December of the same year, the Ontario Court of Appeal, while acknowledging the existence of systemic discrimination in employment, dismissed the appeal on grounds that complaints could be lodged under the Human Rights Code. The Alliance responded by reiterating their insistence that complaints-driven legislation did not address systemic discrimination, and continued its legal challenge. The case was taken to the highest court in Canada, the federal Supreme Court, but in December of 1999, the Court declined to hear the appeal (Alliance for Employment Equity, Dec. 9, 1999).

Despite the defeat of the challenge, the claim that the repeal of the Ontario Act to Provide Employment Equity was unconstitutional, in violation of the *Canadian Charter of Rights and Freedoms*, poses important issues for equity advocates. It further highlights a point of contest between two normative conceptions of employment equity. For the advocates of the Charter Challenge, the employment equity legislation was seen as a means to provide relief from systemic discrimination, a form of discrimination that would otherwise not be met by human rights codes or other forms of legislation. Removing such protection amounted to creating, or contributing to, further discrimination. The legislation was a means to redress long-standing patterns of discrimination, in every aspect of employment, that result in barriers to full and equitable employment for qualified persons.

For the opponents, however, employment equity law was seen to be a concession that granted special privileges to undeserving employment applicants.

The Ontario Conservative government's ability to claim a legal victory in this case is also not to be ignored. The Harris government filed its objection to the leave to appeal before the Supreme Court on the grounds that the Alliance for Employment Equity was advocating "reverse discrimination" and "job quotas" (Government of Ontario, Feb. 5, 1999). These legal arguments followed on the same path established by the Ontario Progressive Conservative Party during the 1995 provincial election campaign, and later in passage of the repeal legislation. As Carol Agocs and Catherine Burr summarise:

> The Job Quotas Repeal Act (1995) was introduced in the aftermath of a political campaign in Ontario which relied heavily on the incitement of fears and anxieties during a time of high unemployment and extensive corporate downsizing and layoffs. The use of language such as "job quotas" and "reverse discrimination" in the campaign misrepresented the actual requirements of the Employment Equity Act (Agocs and Burr, 1996: 34).

The Ontario situation provides an example of the success of a backlash against employment equity, as a normative challenge to the notion of using the law as a means to redress systemic discrimination. The success of the backlash gives an implicit green light to oppressive practices – including racism, sexism, and discrimination based on ability – in the workplace in particular and more generally in society at large. The rapid transition from the implementation of employment equity legislation to its repeal in such a context of extreme backlash has profound implications for employment equity policy discussions taking place at every level of government, and in every province, across Canada. For example, the federal Opposition party, the Canadian Alliance, has proposed the repeal of the federal Employment Equity Act in Canada. Moreover, there are serious implications for members of the designated groups, within Ontario and in the country at large.

Drawing upon the Ontario example as a case study of the rise and fall of employment equity legislation, this chapter will consider the impact of this debate on the struggles to claim redress for systemic discrimination. It will be argued that backlash, though successful, has not occurred without challenge. Employment equity advocacy has not been quashed in the aftermath of the Ontario backlash. The relationship between the demise of the legislation, therefore, and the development of community responses, is not a simple or linear one. The perspectives and policies of the previous Ontario New Democratic Party Government, the Ontario Progressive Conservative Government, and community advocates for employment equity are intricately interconnected, and they are influenced by shifting political tides at least as strongly as they are by more deeply abiding social commitments to equity.

While we attempt to examine this issue with a wide purview, we do not claim to be neutral in the debate. As researchers, writers and activists, we are firm advocates for the successful implementation of employment equity policy, up to and including effective legislative measures at every level of government. That said, the presence or absence of employment equity legislation is only one of a number of factors that may play a role in achieving equitable workplace practices. We are concerned, therefore, to understand the entire context in which employment equity legislation and policies are enacted and implemented.

What follows is an analysis of the Ontario context from several perspectives. We maintain that the Ontario example is unique, and therefore notably important, in three distinct regards. First, when the employment equity legislation was in place, it marked the most extensive in any province to date, and was wider in its mandate than the federal legislation. Second, the extreme nature of the backlash against employment equity policy in Ontario is also unmatched in Canada. There are particular implications of this backlash for all designated groups, and for all those who experience any form of systemic discrimination in society (Bakan and Kobayashi, 2000). Third, Ontario also presents a uniquely organised, self-educated, and committed non-governmental community that has continued to advocate for employment equity principles and practices, albeit in very challenging and difficult circumstances. There are indications that the backlash, at least in some respects, is less successful than its supporters would like to claim. Each of these elements will be considered in the remaining sections of this discussion.

Methodologically, we do not present documented evidence of the workplace efficacy of employment equity policy. Available evidence suggests that employment equity legislation is difficult to measure in terms of its effectiveness in ensuring the elimination of barriers to equal access to jobs and promotions among the four designated groups – women, Aboriginal peoples, members of visible minorities and persons with disabilities. Moreover, interpretations vary regarding effective measurement (Bakan and Kobayashi, 2000: 15-18; Leck and Saunders, 1992b). Statistical measurement of workplace representation of members of designated groups has itself become a target of the backlash. One striking aspect of the Ontario repeal legislation was an explicit requirement to destroy workforce census data on the representation of the designated groups that employers had collected under the requirements of the employment equity act (Ontario Legislature, "An Act to Repeal Job Quotas," Dec. 1995). Data in the current Ontario context are therefore not available. We rely here on a multi-layered approach, combining policy analysis, a contextual emphasis on political culture, and a consideration of theoretical studies to date on the nature of backlash in general as a political and ideological phenomenon.

THE BACKLASH EFFECT

What then are the implications of the assault on employment equity legislation that has taken place in Ontario in recent years? What does it mean in normative terms for Canada's largest province to be the home of such an intensive and officially endorsed backlash?

The concept of "backlash" has become widespread in both popular discourse and social science literature during the past decade. The term is loosely applied to a wide range of conservative reactions to such things as affirmative action, immigration, environmentalism and taxation. It has become commonplace to use "backlash" to describe a putative right-wing response to "progressive" political trends. The most common metaphor associated with the backlash effect is that of the "trigger", activated by fear or by some other "irrational" emotional response, which sets off a reaction that is stronger than it would have been had the progressive event not taken place. For example, it is claimed that fear of success of the new regime in South Africa has triggered a backlash by the extreme right (Khumalo, 1992).

In the United States in particular, the spectre of backlash has become a major element in debates over "affirmative action", a term essentially equivalent to employment equity (Chavez, 1998; Lawrence and Matsuda, 1997). It is now commonly believed that a widespread reaction against affirmative action policies adopted during the post-civil rights era is responsible for the cutting back or cancelling of such programs in a number of states, most notably Texas and California. Susan Faludi's path breaking exposé (1991) documents a staggering series of challenges to advances of American feminism over the 1980s.

While the popular press adopts a largely uncritical assumption of the backlash effect, academic theorists advance a variety of explanations. John Ralston Saul, in *The Unconscious Civilisation* (1995), contends that corporatism, and the advancement of the individual at the expense of the public good, results in a series of backlashes. The threat of backlash is used, in his assessment, as a means of advancing particular interests. This position is supported by Hoey (1997), who suggests that in Australia the individual-society dichotomy is responsible for social tensions that result in backlash against Aboriginals, Asians and immigrants. Savran (1996) claims that backlash is strengthened by distortions of power and violence in such cultural representations as Rambo films, which encourage a sado-masochistic masculine identity. Such positions raise the question of whether moderation in attempts to promote equity claims will be effective in pre-empting backlash.

Alexander (1997) uses concepts of individualisation and reflexive modernity to explain backlash as a manifestation of social polarisation. He departs from the moderation model, however, by suggesting that backlash be used creatively to play a role in a radical synthesis, which he depicts as a Marxist vision of social development. Another radical interpretation suggests that backlash is a means of the powerful to retain power by opposing any move to improve the standing of the disenfranchised (Quadagno, 1996; Walker, 1996). A more complex analysis depicts backlash as a peculiarly post-modern intervention in a world in which superficially progressive policies such as colour blindness mask new forms of conservative reaction that interconnect increasing racial inequality with global economic and geopolitical trends.

There is a less developed literature on strategies to avoid backlash. Stilwell (1997) suggests a need for social balance among institutions, and for more spatial differentiation of the local, national and global effects of social and economic policy in order to offset the "backlash against the backlash." The risk is provoking arguments that are extreme, and then offsetting one extreme with an equally extreme counter-argument. Similar arguments by moderates suggest the need for progressive elements to adopt a pragmatic political strategy in order to avoid backlash (Annetts and Thompson, 1992; Cartwright, 1996).

Studies conducted primarily in the United States in the context of affirmative action, however, refute the claim that progressive policies produce a backlash effect. Belliveau (1996) finds that greater exposure in the work place to affirmative action policies actually leads to greater endorsement. Taylor (1995) studied white workers whose employers who did or did not use race-targeted policies, and found that there is no indication that the existence of affirmative action policies creates resentment on the part of white workers. Moreover, white workers in affirmative action settings are more likely to support interventionist policies.

Regarding the Canadian context particularly, the literature is rather sparse. Though opposition to advancement for women in particular has been well documented (see Burt, 1993; Bashevkin, 1993; 1998), there is to our knowledge no substantive analysis of the impact of the backlash effect on employment equity policy in Canada. Our research to date supports the position that the backlash effect is a social construction that is both deliberately used as a mechanism of reactionary politics, and complicitly accommodated by many others who otherwise favour the general aims of equity. And it would seem that, at least in the federal context, strengthening employment equity policies has not led to a perceptible increase in backlash. This is not, however, to suggest that it is a figment of someone's imagination. Backlash has very real and specific effects that need to be understood within specific – in this case regional and provincial – contexts. In other words, systemic discrimination presents itself differently in different contexts, a manifestation of geographically situated political cultures. Backlash therefore is variable in different contexts. It is an ideological and social construction that is remarkably flexible in its targets, but in all cases justifies the claim of a normative democratic equality that is challenged by the special interests of the oppressed. In general, backlash serves as an ideological justification for advancing or ignoring systemic discrimination.

Because backlash is an adaptable current, the context in which it arises is affected by local manifestations of political culture. To understand variations in political culture, we need to understand how those cultures engage issues surrounding systemic discrimination, toward which employment equity is one of a number of measures of redress. Recent geographical literature has shown that local manifestations of political culture also need to be connected to national and global processes that involve transnational culture and communication and the global re-location of capital and people. This point is especially important when considering the large metropolitan areas of, for example, Vancouver and Toronto, Canada's most cosmopolitan and most diverse cities, and in asking why the role of government is subjected to different sorts of discourse at the municipal, provincial and federal levels.

Our concept of political culture is distinct from that traditionally used in political science literature (Bell and Tepperman, 1979). By "political culture" we mean a recursive coalescence of political, social, historical, ideological and spatial processes that influence social relations and are therefore reflected in policy formation. These processes include political mobilisation, social movements, party politics and public discourse. We suggest that regional variations in political culture have been pivotal in shaping employment equity policy formulation at the provincial level in Canada.

We also suggest that different combinations of processes shape federal and provincial political cultures, including distinctive public discourses and regional attachments. For example, and rather curiously, the federal Employment Equity Act was enacted in Canada during the term of a Conservative government, and was subsequently revised and strengthened by a Liberal government. Both of these governing parties are on the moderate or far right of the Canadian political spectrum.[2]

The notion of systemic discrimination that informs employment equity policy is based on an understanding that processes inherent in the economic, social and political traditions of liberal democracies have tended selectively to discriminate against those who are members of a specific social group, resulting in systemic barriers to equal representation, distribution and workplace access. Abella describes "systemic discrimination" as a process that operates regardless of intent on the part of the perpetrator; indeed there may not even be a single perpetrator to identify. Instead, it

> suggests that the inexorable, cumulative effect on individuals or groups of behaviour that has an arbitrarily negative impact on them is more significant than whether the behaviour flows from insensitivity or intentional discrimination . . . Systemic discrimination requires systemic remedies. Rather than approaching discrimination from the perspective of the single perpetrator and the single victim, the systemic approach acknowledges that by and large the systems and practices we customarily and often unwittingly adopt may have an unjustifiably negative effect on certain groups in society (Abella, 1984: 9).

Yet not all policy packages designed and called upon for the purpose of redress of oppression are informed by this notion of discrimination. An individual rights-based model informs human rights codes at the provincial and federal levels, and certain interpretations of section 15 of the *Canadian Charter of Rights and Freedoms*. In these instances the underlying assumption is that all individuals are guaranteed substantive equality of access to rights as well as non-discriminatory practices. Where such equality is violated, complaints-driven mechanisms for redress are called upon. Such mechanisms presume individual victimisation and "point the finger" as it were at the alleged discriminatory body or person.

This notion of an individual rights-based condition of equality, as something that exists as an objective condition of democratic practices, tends to be hegemonic in modern western societies. In normative terms, the understanding is that those who suffer discrimination, even as part of a group, are individually aggrieved; having access to a complaints-based system of redress protects them. We suggest, however, that it is in precisely this judicial and ideological space that the backlash effect comes into play. Opponents of employment equity often attempt to take the high ground of "democracy" by reducing all forms of discrimination to a universal model of individual rights; systemic forms of discrimination are simply denied.

In other words, in the background of debates about systemic discrimination lie competing visions of social justice. What is discrimination, and what are the means to redress discrimination? What is just in a democratic society that strives towards equality? Iris Marion Young suggests examining *injustice* in terms of relations of domination and oppression, rather than the traditional notion of justice based on a distributive or allocative model (Young, 1990). Similarly, Kobayashi and Ray (2000) suggest the need to move from a rights-based model that specifies *de jure* possibilities, to a risk-based model that addresses actual conditions of lived oppression, addressing rights not as abstract objects but as what are necessary to live without oppression. Employment equity policy represents an example of the latter model. It is a proactive mechanism that redresses discrimination by challenging actual, historically constructed, systemic barriers identified as limitations on access to equality for oppressed groups.

Employment equity policy is thereby informed by a conception of systemic oppression that applies to a number of identified groups. How do various forms of oppression relate to one another from the point of view of explaining systemic discrimination? Over recent years, a series of studies inspired in particular by anti-racist scholarship have attempted to link women's oppression with other forms of oppression, particularly those based on race and class (Goetz, 1991; Mohanty, 1991; Williams, 1991; Yuval-Davis, 1997; Bhaba, 1996). Gender has become identified by a growing number of Canadian scholars as a factor influenced by, and influencing, the politics of citizenship and the relationship between local, regional and international issues, as well as questions of economic access, race, sexual orientation and nationalism (Chicha, 1999; Razack, 1998; Bakan and Stasiulis, 1997; Andrew and Rodgers, 1997; Agnew, 1996; Creese, 1996; Staehli and Clarke, 1995; Das Gupta, 1996; Jhappan, 1996; Cardinal, 1995; Monture-Angus, 1995; Bishop, 1994; Bristow et al, 1994; Giles and Arat-Koc, 1994; Daenzer, 1993; Banarji, 1993; Ng, 1993; Turpel, 1993). A common concern is to develop an approach to gender equality that does not exclusively emphasise gender in an artificial hierarchy of oppressions that risks blurring or denying other experiences of oppression.

It would be a mistake, however, to presume that all approaches that link multiple forms of oppression are the same. Government policy is designed to address the interests of the "public" as a whole, a generic whole that can be interpreted in various ways. Commonly, an inclusive approach implies that all citizens are equal, and therefore deserve universally equal treatment. Discrimination is seen as exceptional, a break in a norm that is essentially fair and egalitarian. Such a notion of a universal "public" erases the reality of systemic discrimination. By hiding racism, sexism and discrimination against persons with disabilities, such practices are implicitly legitimised and considered "normal". If discriminatory practices are not recognised to exist, they cannot, and should not, be challenged. The specific experiences of any one form of oppression or any specific combination of oppressions become blurred. Only in what are considered to be the most unusual cases, where the complainant can provide evidence of criminal activity resulting in bias, is discrimination accepted as a reality.

Within such a universalising discourse, difference may be recognised through so-called "diversity" policies, which accept social variation but do not recognise systemic discrimination. In such circumstances the result continues to be the erasure of systemic discrimination. Governmental policies or arguments that claim to achieve diversity ("equal treatment") without actively intervening to overcome systemic discrimination serve to fuel backlash by creating a comfortable environment in which the backlash effect can operate (Wilson, 1996). This is where an analysis of backlash specifically, and not only of oppression or discrimination, becomes critical to sustaining a progressive agenda.

The controversy over individual rights versus redress of systemic discrimination has been at the centre of debate over employment equity legislation in Ontario. The Ontario Charter challenge suggested the depth of the impasse in that province (Ferrel et al, 1998). The Alliance for Employment Equity brought together a broad group of stakeholders, including several organisations acting as interveners, to challenge the legality of the 1995 Ontario Conservative government's Act to Repeal Job Quotas and to Restore Merit-based Employment Practices in Ontario (Bill 8) on the ground that it violated the *Charter of Human Rights and Freedoms*. The interveners included the Women's Legal Education and Action Fund, the DisAbled Women's Network, the African Canadian Legal Clinic, the Toronto Chapter of the Congress of Black Women and the Ontario Federation of Labour. In challenging the constitutionality of the repeal of the Employment Equity Act, this coalition placed on the table the entire history of systemic discrimination in that province (Alliance for Employment Equity, 1998).

LEGISLATING EMPLOYMENT EQUITY: THE FEDERAL CONTEXT

The contrast between the heightened public debate regarding employment equity legislation in Ontario and the virtual silence regarding the federal level emphasises the Canadian paradox on this issue. Ontario employment equity advocates and practitioners are strikingly aware of this apparently contradictory situation. In this light, it is worth briefly summarising the federal legislative context before returning to the Ontario example.

The federal legislation is grounded in an established body of policy discussion, documentation, and legislative experience. From the outset, the mandate of the Royal Commission included the Crown corporations, but ultimately the investigation covered general employment practices in Canada with recognised focus on the federal government itself as an employer. More recently, in *Public Service 2000: A Report on Progress*, this established commitment to the principles of employment equity is identified and re-affirmed as part of the guidelines for future planning for the federal public service:

> Successive federal Governments have acknowledged since the early 1970s that the Public Service work force should be representative of the community it serves. In the 1970s and 1980s, the Public Service played a leadership role in recruiting, integrating and advancing designated groups . . . . In a continuous learning culture, members of designated groups should also have greater access to both formal and informal training and developmental opportunities to increase their chances of pursuing meaningful careers in the Public Service. Equitable representation is a goal that the Public Service continues to strive for; success will be within reach when managers look beyond numbers and focus on job and career opportunities for members of designated groups (Tellier, 1992: 59-60).

Since the mid-1980s, federal government employment equity initiatives have been developed to apply to three distinct jurisdictions, including the Federal public service, federally regulated employers, and federal contractors. The 1986 Employment Equity Act applied to some 350 federally regulated employers, including Crown corporations, with 100 employees or more. This Act, administered through Human Resources Development Canada (previously Employment and Immigration Canada), required employers to submit an annual report and an employment equity plan.

The Federal Contractors Program pertains to those employers, again with 100 or more employees, that bid for federal goods and services contracts of $200,000 or higher. Companies under this program are obliged: to undertake plans to remove discriminatory barriers; to increase the participation of members of the designated groups through hiring, training and promotion; to develop an employment equity plan; and to keep records of employment equity implementation. Human Resources Development Canada was mandated to undertake compliance reviews to ensure implementation.

The Federal Public Service was not officially covered under the 1986 Employment Equity Act; however, employment equity was implemented under the administration of the Treasury Board Secretariat. In 1986 the Federal Government adopted an employment equity program mandated by the *Financial Administration Act*, and specified in the *Public Service Employment Act*. According to the latter, departments and agencies were required to:

- Establish an environment that supports the principles of employment equity;
- Prepare and analyse statistical data on their work force to identify areas in which persons in the designated groups are under-represented;
- Analyse their employment systems to identify systemic barriers facing designated groups;
- Consult with employees and encourage persons belonging to the designated groups to participate in implementing employment equity initiatives;
- Develop three-year employment equity plans that include special measures to correct imbalances in the Public Service work force and contain quantitative and qualitative objectives, activities, schedules and monitoring mechanisms;
- Endeavour to meet numerical objectives for designated group representation and distribution, as they are defined by the Treasury Board target-setting strategy (Canada, Treasury Board Secretariat 1994:6).

The revised *Employment Equity Act* (1995) and the accompanying Employment Equity Regulations came into effect on October 24, 1996. Employers were required to comply with the requirements of the Act by October, 1997. Section 4 of the Act formally brings the Federal Public Service under its jurisdiction. Specifically, the Treasury Board and the Public Service Commission:

> each acting within the scope of its powers, duties and functions under the Financial Administration Act and the Public Service Employment Act, are responsible for carrying out the obligations of an employer under this Act...(Canada, Treasury Board. Secretariat 1994:4).

The new Act builds upon past experiences within the federal public sector to strengthen both the requirements and the procedures for achieving employment equity. One such requirement is for consultation between the employer and bargaining agents on issues concerning employment equity, through the National Joint Council on Employment Equity (NJC-EE.).

The employment equity responsibilities of the Federal Public Service, including its departments and agencies, remain essentially the same under the new Employment Equity Act as under the former Financial Administration Act. Compliance monitoring, however, is now assigned to the Canadian Human Rights Commission. In February 1997, a Memorandum of Understanding between the Secretary of the Treasury Board and the Chief Commissioner of the Canadian Human Rights Commission was signed, with the objective of increasing co-operation between the two agencies in implementation of the 1995 Employment Equity Act. The Commission has been given the power to conduct audits of departments and agencies in order to ensure that they are in compliance with the Act.

The recent changes in the federal context, including the 1995 replacement of the previous 1986 *Employment Equity Act*, therefore indicate, at least formally, a renewed and increased emphasis on the central principles of employment equity as a workplace model for the public sector, and for any corporation that relies on significant public sector funding.

These requirements bring the federal public sector as a whole under extensive, rigorous, and long-term employment equity practices. At the same time, the emphasis on the public sector is not presented as exceptional, but rather as exemplary of fair employment practices in Canada. As Weiler summarises:

> The public sector has typically been a leader in introducing workplace equity whether by incorporating principles of a meritocracy or by voluntarily implementing pay or employment equity. While equity-seeking groups tend to find progress in the public sector slow, it is generally recognised the public sector leads the private sector. (This in itself creates higher expectations for public sector organisations) (Weiler, 1986:63).

(UN-LEGISLATION): THE ONTARIO ACT

The Ontario government's *Act to Provide Employment Equity for Aboriginal People, People with Disabilities, Members of Racial Minorities and Women* passed third reading in the Ontario legislature in December of 1993, and was proclaimed into law in 1994. By December of 1995, the Act had been repealed. Meanwhile, a provincial election had taken place and Premier Mike Harris and the Ontario Progressive Conservatives had replaced the New Democratic government led by Premier Bob Rae. The Tories challenged a wide array of political positions held by the NDP in what was titled the "Common Sense Revolution." Employment equity policy was part of the platform under attack.

The brief period that Ontarians lived under provincial employment equity legislation was one in which election campaigning had increased the intensity of ideological positioning. Public debate produced hostile ideological challenges to the principles of employment equity in particular, and the politics of judicial redress for systemic oppression in general. The backlash was in full sway, and Ontario's Act to Provide Employment Equity was considered by many to be an open target.

We do not intend to present an in-depth comparative analysis of the similarities and differences between the federal and provincial employment equity policy contexts. The point to emphasise here is simply that there has been a clear divergence in the pattern, both at the legislative and ideological levels, regarding the public policy direction of employment equity. In 1995, while the Ontario Act underwent intense and severe ideological challenge for going too far in "forcing" employers to follow the principles of employment equity, the Federal Employment Equity Act, without public protest and almost without even public notice, was extended and strengthened.

Another notable distinction is the mandate of the Ontario Act, which applied to the provincial government and all its agencies, public sector employers of ten or more employees (including municipalities, school boards, universities, hospitals and all other health care facilities), as well as private sector employers with more than 50 employees. The size of the workplace, measured by the number of employees, rather than status as a public or private employer, was made the criterion for inclusion. This was a new application of the principles of employment equity in the Canadian context. Ontario was thus distinguished from, for example, British Columbia, the only province currently with employment equity legislation in place, affecting only the public service sector. While the federal law is extensive in its mandate regarding the public sector (that is, the federal public service and federally regulated employers such as those in the financial, transportation and communications industries) and private sector government contractors, in the Ontario case the legislation included many employment sites that would have evaded the mandate of the federal legislation.

From the perspective of many employment equity advocates, the legislation implemented in Ontario was slow to develop and far more limited in scope than hoped for. From the perspective of private sector defenders of the free market, however, the Ontario law was a sweeping imposition. The law compelled employers to operate in a fair, accountable manner, actively challenging historic practices of systemic discrimination. As the extent of the backlash was later to indicate, this requirement violated the normative primacy of private entrepreneurial authority. Two different concepts of justice, fairness and equality came into open conflict. According to the corporate opponents of employment equity legislation in Ontario, "business benefits" rather than "a legal or moral standpoint based on fairness" needed to be restored as the "driving force" in human resource allocation (Alliance of Manufacturers and Exporters Canada and Min. of Cit., 1997:3,10).

A brief outline of the mechanisms of the *Act to Provide Employment Equity for Aboriginal People, People with Disabilities, Members of Racial Minorities and Women* is in order. The Ontario employment equity law was designed to be pro-active. Despite claims to the contrary by its opponents, however, it fell short of requiring specific representational targets, or quotas, for each of the designated groups. Instead, employers were required to develop an "employment equity plan in accordance with the regulations." Such a plan was to indicate steps towards the elimination of systemic barriers to equity in the workplace. Moreover, positive measures had to be delineated, and measures supportive of members of each of the four designated groups had to be outlined. Such measures had to be indicated for every stage of workplace hiring and retention, from recruitment of applicants for new positions through to promotion. Workplace surveys assessing the levels of representation of each of the designated groups, and specific timetables with goals set by the employer were required in the employment equity plans.

Some flexibility was incorporated into the legislation. For example, more than one employment equity plan per workplace could be developed. Recognising variations within workplaces and industries, allowance was made for differential targets and timetables. There were, however, consequences for non-compliance. The Employment Equity Tribunal, a body separate from the Employment Equity Commission, was created to address monitoring and enforcement. This body was given a permanent mandate under the Ontario Act. While the Tribunal's existence was short-lived, it had legislative teeth. According to the *Act to Provide for Employment Equity*,

> The Tribunal will act as mediator and adjudicator. It will review and enforce orders of the Commission. It will adjudicate disputes about joint responsibility and respond to complaints

> that an employer has not lived up to its obligations under the employment equity plan. If an employer fails to comply with an order of the Tribunal, it may be prosecuted in the courts and face a fine of up to $50,000 (Ont. Min. of Cit, 1993: n.p.).

The Ontario legislation was clearly aimed at employers, public or private, with a view to ensuring that the vast majority of workers in Ontario were subject to the principles of employment equity. The Ontario NDP government, with a clear majority and elected with considerable public support, made its intention to implement employment equity legislation clear in the first Speech from the Throne in November 1990 (Ont. Min. of Cit., 1993; Bakan and Kobayashi, 2000). By March of 1991, an Ontario Employment Equity Commissioner, Juanita Westmoreland-Traoré, was appointed. Bill 79, the first formal draft of the law, was introduced for First Reading on June 25, 1992. Public consultations were held through all phases of the legislative process.

The new legislation was widely recognised to rationalise many laws extant in Ontario that already included employment equity provisions, some of which, including policy for Ontario public service employees, had been operative for many years prior to the NDP's election. Bill 79 was therefore building not only on perceived public support, but also on existing policy. The legislation could be justified in part as a streamlining and centralising effort on the part of the new government. This process of rationalisation, however, was also used to advantage by the advocates of backlash. When Bill 8, *An Act to Repeal Job Quotas and to Restore Merit-based Employment Practices in Ontario,* was introduced and passed in the Legislature within the three-month period between October and December of 1995, none of the previous employment equity provisions were preserved. Instead, employment equity policy in Ontario was virtually eliminated with a single piece of sweeping legislation.

THE BACKLASH IN ONTARIO

Another unique, and tragic, aspect of the Ontario experience is the level of formal success of an ideological and legislative backlash, expressed through the Ontario Provincial Progressive Conservative Party under the leadership of Mike Harris. This government is currently into its second mandate. The period surrounding the 1995 provincial election, and the subsequent Tory government's first term in office, saw the most serious blows struck against employment equity (Henry and Tater, 2000).

The title of the bill, officially referred to in short form as the Job Quotas Repeal Act, reveals much about the ideological context in which it was introduced. Though the *Act to Provide for Employment Equity* did not require job quotas, the Tory government, as in its pre-election platform, has repeatedly and insistently maintained that it did. In an argument characteristic of the backlash in Canada and internationally, the claim was made that those who had suffered from demonstrated systemic discrimination in employment and in society as a whole were only trying to gain unfair advantage. The government's *Job Quotas Repeal Act* was put forward to correct this imputed imbalance, to replace a system based on privileging "special interest groups" with one based on "merit". Bill 8 did not merely see through the repeal of the previous employment equity law. The *Police Services Act* and the *Education Act* were also amended to ensure removal of all employment equity measures.

Further, the *Repeal Act* required all information gathered in connection with the previous law to be destroyed (Ontario Govt., *An Act to Repeal Job Quotas:* 1,5). The subsequent destruction of demographic data on representation of members of the designated groups in hiring, retention and promotion, had the additional impact of rendering implementation of voluntary programs very difficult, and of making it impossible to get any clear picture of what impact the legislation has had on the employment of members of the designated groups.

The repeal of the employment equity legislation took place in the context of a generalised, and very rapid, series of government sponsored attacks on equity seeking groups in Ontario. Having promised to return to the principle of "merit" in the election campaign, government funding cuts coincided with ideological attacks. Significantly, the elements of the employment equity law that were specifically designed to address systemic discrimination faced by women, people with disabilities, members of racial minorities and Aboriginal peoples were now rendered null and void. Any public, official recognition of sexism, discrimination based on ability, or racism was now virtually eliminated. For example, the Anti-racism Secretariat was eliminated, and severe funding cuts slashed the budgets of the Ontario Women's Directorate, the Office of the Ontario Human Rights Commission, and the Office of the Pay Equity Commission.

In the face of this massive assault, it is a tribute to the advocates of employment equity policies in Ontario that the debate continued, in the public and in the courts through the Charter Challenge mentioned above. Employment equity advocates in Ontario have not emerged from the period of backlash silenced. On the contrary, because the backlash effect is actually about a competition of visions of democratic practices and social justice, the battle lines have been drawn on two sides: despite the backlash against employment equity, the voice of advocacy remains in the province. There remains an organised community in the province, highly educated in the political issues associated with employment equity. This community continues to advocate for the implementation of employment equity at every level of government policy and legislation. To this end, the awareness of the Canadian paradox, the apparent contradiction between the directions of federal and provincial employment equity policies, is not insignificant.

CONCLUSION: LINGERING EFFECTS OF BACKLASH IN ONTARIO

The argument developed here maintains that the rise and fall of employment equity legislation in Ontario is not only a story of legislative debate. The history of the development of employment equity policy is a living one that has a lingering effect despite the weight of the backlash, and acts as a major channel for public discourse and the negotiation of social norms. While the elimination of the legislation upon the election of the Harris Progressive Conservative government in 1995 was rapid and dramatic, the same cannot be said of the process that led to its original establishment by the previous NDP government.

After the Ontario Employment Equity Commissioner was appointed in November 1991, numerous public fora on employment equity were held in cities across the province, including three rounds of public hearings and extensive consultations,. Over 400 written briefs were received by the Office of the Employment Equity Commissioner prior to first reading of Bill 79; after the bill was tabled, a further 100 presentations were heard and an additional 184 written briefs were submitted (Ont. Min. of Cit., 1993). Even before the legislation had been developed, the Ontario Human Rights Commission estimates that fourteen government offices were already responsible for administering some form of employment equity policy (Frazee, 1992).

The policy vacuum that has been left in the aftermath of the repeal is therefore profound. The Ontario government has developed an alternative "Equal Opportunity" policy that stresses "diversity" as a benefit to business productivity. This policy, however, is explicitly *not* about the redress of systemic discrimination. In a guidebook to the policy titled *Business Results Through Diversity*, notably published jointly by the Alliance of Manufacturers and Exporters Canada and the government of Ontario, equal opportunity is explained as "a new model – not employment equity or affirmative action" (Alliance of Manufacturers and Exporters and Min. of Cit., 1997: 11). The policy guidelines continue to distinguish this merit-based program that applies to all employees on a voluntary basis from a quota system that offers "special privileges" with "bureaucratic requirements" as a human resource program (Alliance of Manufacturers and Exporters and Min. of Cit., 1997: 11).

If the backlash has been institutionalised at the government level, issues of discrimination continue to affect racial minorities, Aboriginal peoples, people with disabilities and women on a daily basis in the workplace environment and beyond. The struggle against such discrimination continues. A wide array of community based organisations and, significantly, important sections of the Ontario labour movement have become highly sensitised to issues of systemic discrimination and the need for pro-active workplace processes to ensure redress. Years after the repeal of the employment equity law, Ontario displays a concentration of self-educated, highly trained employment equity experts, who in turn represent or are part of wider pro-employment equity communities. This is not to presume that the backlash has no support within the Ontario population; indeed, this goes without saying. But it is the continued support for employment equity principles that commonly goes unnoticed. The debate regarding the development and implementation of employment equity continues (Infantry, 1999; Henry and Tator, 2000). Ontario is then not only unique in its manifestation of the backlash, but also in its level of polarisation around this issue.

If the Ontario example is unique, this does not mean that it is exceptional. Every provincial context has characteristics specific to its political culture, but the impact of the rise and fall of provincial employment equity legislation also sets an example for other provinces. At the same time, the spectrum of policy debate is not static. The terrain of debate regarding employment equity policy in other provinces in the rest of Canada is changing and unstable. As British Columbia enters an election period, for example, a backlash against employment equity could emerge. Certainly in that province there is already evidence of backlash targeting the rights of Aboriginal peoples, immigrants and visible minorities. Ontario's experience may prove to be an unfortunate bellwether of what lies in the future for British Columbia; but there is nothing inevitable or pre-determined in this. If the Ontario experience offers a lesson to those who oppose employment equity, it is also rife with lessons for those of us who continue to insist on the rights of equity-seeking groups. The expression of an outspoken constituency of employment equity advocates, as exists in Ontario, could hinder the success or slow the momentum of a potential backlash in British Columbia or other provinces.

Moreover, these provincial contexts do not exist in a vacuum. The Canadian paradox continues. The formal endorsement of employment equity legislation at the federal level runs counter to the type of backlash that has found expression in Ontario. In the November, 2000 federal election in Canada, the main challenger to the incumbent Liberal Party was the Canadian Alliance Party led by Stockwell Day. Day is a former minister in the Conservative government of the province of Alberta, with an established record of anti-equity positions. The Alliance, as it is commonly called, now the Official Opposition, is opposed to the extant federal employment equity legislation on the same ideological grounds put forward by the Ontario Progressive Conservative government. In fact, the

Alliance, previously the Reform Party, challenged the 1995 federal Employment Equity Act in Parliament by drawing explicit references to the Ontario experience.

As long as there is systemic discrimination, the struggle to challenge racism and sexism and bigotry in all its forms will not stop. Even when there are setbacks, however, our research indicates that there is no room in the Canadian political and social spectrum for opponents of employment equity to claim unqualified success.

Abigail B. Bakan is Professor of Political Studies and Women's Studies at Queen's University, where she has been teaching as a Queen's National Scholar since 1985.
Audrey Kobayashi is Professor of Geography and Women's Studies at Queen's University.

NOTES

[1] Research for this study is supported by the Social Sciences and Humanities Research Council of Canada. This chapter is written jointly and equally by the authors, whose names appear in alphabetical order.

[2] Certainly the Liberal federal government's recent pay equity dispute with the Public Service Alliance of Canada should give us pause to question the level of commitment to the principles of equity in general. On July 29, 1998, the Canadian Human Rights Tribunal issued a decision in support of PSAC's pay equity claim, a decision that if implemented would grant equal pay for work of equal value to 200,000 current and former Federal government employees. Between 1991 and 1997, there were 262 days of hearings before the Canadian Human Rights Tribunal regarding this issue. On August 27, 1998 Federal Justice Minister Anne McLellan and Treasury Board President Marcel Massé announced that the government intended to appeal the decision of the Canadian Human Rights Tribunal. The Supreme Court of Canada ruled in favour of the PSAC in October 1999, and a settlement was agreed upon between the federal government and the Public Service Alliance of Canada, where the demands of the union were substantially met and retroactive pay identified as the "largest pay equity settlement in the world" was awarded to the women workers (PSAC, 1999).

REFERENCES

Abella, Rosalie Silberman. *Equality in Employment: A Royal Commission Report.* Ottawa: Minister of Supply and Services, 1984.

Agocs, Carol and Catherine Burr. "Employment Equity, Affirmative Action and Managing Diversity: Assessing the Differences." *International Journal of Manpower*, 17.4/5 (1996).

Agnew, Vijay. *Resisting Discrimination: Women from Asia, Africa and the Caribbean and the Women's Movement in Canada.* Toronto: University of Toronto Press, 1996.

Alexander, Don. "The Backlash Caused by the Past." *Social Alternatives* 16. 4 (1997): 30-31.

Alliance for Employment Equity. News Release. "Charter Challenge Update - 9 December, 1998. Appeal Court's Decision Released 8 December: Court Dismisses Appeal on Government's Repeal of Employment Equity Act (April, 1998)". (December 9, 1998).

Alliance for Employment Equity. News Release. "Supreme Court of Canada Denies Leave to Appeal Charter Challenge." (December 9, 1999). <http://www.web.net/~allforee/chalenge.htm>

Alliance of Manufacturers and Exporters Canada and the Ministry of Citizenship, Culture and Recreation. *Business Results Through Diversity: A Guidebook.* Queen's Printer for Ontario, 1997.

Andrew, Caroline and Sandra Rodgers. *Women and the Canadian State/ Les femmes et l'état canadien.* Montreal and Kingston: McGill-Queen's University Press, 1997.

Annetts, Jason and Bill Thompson. "Dangerous Activism?" in Ken Plummer, ed. *Modern Homosexualities: Fragments of Lesbian and Gay Experience.* London: Routledge, 1992: 227-236.

Infantry, Ashante. "You don't have to be black to suffer prejudice. You just have to sound black." *Toronto Star*, July 7, 1999. <http://www.geocities.com/CapitolHill/2381/tobeblack.html>

Bakan, Abigail B. and Audrey Kobayashi. *Employment Equity Policy in Canada: An Interprovincial Comparison*. Ottawa: Status of Women Canada, 2000.

Bakan, Abigail B. and Daiva Stasiulis, eds. *Not One of the Family: Foreign Domestic Workers in Canada*. Toronto: University of Toronto Press, 1997.

Banarji, Himani, ed. *Returning the Gaze: Essays on Racism, Feminism and Politics* . Toronto: Sister Vision Press, 1993.

Bashevkin, Sylvia. *Toeing the Lines: Women and Party Politics in English Canada*. Toronto: University of Toronto Press, 2nd. ed. , 1993.

Bashevkin, Sylvia. *Women on the Defensive: Living Through Conservative Times*. Chicago: University of Chicago Press, 1998.

Bell, David and L. Tepperman, *The Roots of Disunity: A Look at Canadian Political Culture*. Toronto: McClelland and Stewart, 1979.

Belliveau, Maura A. "The Paradoxical Influence of Policy Exposure on Affirmative Action Attitudes." *Journal of Social Issues* 52.4 (1996): 99-104.

Bhabha, Jacquelin. "Embodied Rights: Gender Persecution, State Sovereignty, and Refugees", *Public Culture* 9 (1996) : 3-32.

Bishop, Anne. *Becoming an Ally: Breaking the Cycle of Oppression*. Halifax: Fernwood Publishing, 1994.

Bristow, Peggy, et al. *"We're Rooted Here and They Can't Pull Us Up": Essays in African Canadian Women's History* Toronto: University of Toronto Press, 1994.

Burt, Sandra. "The Changing Patterns of Public Policy" in *Changing Patterns: Women in Canada*, Sandra Burt, et al eds. Toronto, McClelland and Stewart, 1993: 212-241

Canada, Treasury Board Secretariat. *Annual Report*. 1994.

Cardinal, Linda. "Making a Difference: The Theory and Practice of Francophone Women's Groups, 1969-82" in Joy Parr ed. *A Diversity of Women* Toronto: University of Toronto Press, 1995.

Cartwright, D. "The Experience of French Language Rights in Ontario 1968-1993: The Uses of Territoriality in a Policy of Gradualism." *The Canadian Geographer* 40.3 (1996): 238-257.

Chavez, Lydia. *The Color Blind: California's Battle to End Affirmative Action*. California. University of California Press, 1998.

Chicha, Marie-Therese."The Impact of Labour Market Transformations on the Effectiveness of Laws Promoting Workplace Gender Equality." in *Women and Work*. Richard P. Chaykowski and Lisa M. Powell eds. Kingston: McGill-Queen's University Press, 1999: 283-304.

Creese, Gillian and Laurie Peterson. "Making the News: Racializing Chinese Canadians." *Studies in Political Economy*. 51 (Fall 1996): 117-145.

Daenzer, Patricia. *Regulating Class Privilege: Immigrant Servants in Canada, 1940s-1990s* Toronto: Canadian Scholars Press, 1993.

Das Gupta, Tania. *Racism and Paid Work* Toronto: Garamond Press, 1996.

Faludi, Susan. *Backlash: The Undeclared War Against American Women*. New York: Crown Publishers, 1991.

Ferrel, Marilyn et al and Attorney General of Ontario. Respondent on Appeal. Court of Appeal for Ontario. Factum of the Intervenor Ontario Federation of Labour. Court File No. C27917. December 7, 1998

Frazee, Catherine, Chief Commissioner. Submission of the Ontario Human Rights Commission to the Office of the Employment Equity Commissioner in Response to "Working Towards Equality: the Discussion Paper on Employment Equity Legislation." February 13, 1992.

Giles, Winona and Sedef Arat-Koc, eds. *Maid in the Market: Women's Paid Domestic Labour* Halifax: Fernwood Publishing, 1994.

Goetz, Anne Marie. "Feminism and the Claim to Know: Contradictions in Feminist Approaches to Women in Development" in Rebecca Grant and Kathleen Newland eds., *Gender and International Relations* Bloomington: Indiana University Press., 1991.

Hansard, English (Recorded debates in the House of Parliament, Canada), Government Orders, 15415 <http://www.parl.gc.ca/english/hansard/previous/240_95-10-16/240GO2E.html> October 16, 1995.

Hoey, Les. "Is Backlash Only a Modern Social and Political Phenomenon?" *Social Alternatives* 16. 4 (1997) : 23-25.

Henry, Frances and C. Tator, *Racist Discourse in Canada's English Print Media*. Canadian Race Relations Foundation, Toronto, 2000.

Jain, Harish. "Affirmative Action/Employment Equity Programs in Canada: Issues and Policies", *Labour Law Journal*, 41 (1990): 487-92

Jain, Harish , et al, eds. *Equality for All: National Conference on Racial Equality in the Workplace: Retrospect and Prospect*. Hamilton: MacMaster University, 1990.

Jhappan, Radha. "Post-Modern Race and Gender Essentialism or a Post-Mortem of Scholarship". *Studies in Political Economy*. 51 (Fall 1996): 15-63.

Khumalo, Fred. "White Backlash: The Fear that Mandela and de Klerk will Eventually Reach Some Accommodation has Prompted a Massive Backlash by Extreme White Wing." *New African.* (April 1992): 12-13.

Kobayashi, Audrey and Brian . "Civil Risk and Landscapes of Marginality in Canada: A Pluralist Approach to Social Justice." *The Canadian Geographer* (forthcoming).

Lawrence, Charles R. and Mari J. Matsuda. *We Won't Go Back: Making the Case for Affirmative Action.* Houghton Mifflin, 1997.

Leck, Joanne D. and David M. Saunders. "Hiring Women: the Effects of Canada's Employment Equity Act". *Canadian Public Policy*, 18, 2 (1992a): 203-20.

Leck, Joanne C. and David M. Saunders. "Canada's Employment Equity Act: Effects and Employee Selection", *Population Research and Policy Review*, 11, 1 (1992b): 21-49.

Mohanty, Chandra Talpade. *Third World Women and the Politics of Feminism.* Bloomington: Indiana University Press, 1991.

Monture-Angus, Patricia. *Thunder in My Soul: A Mohawk Woman Speaks.* Halifax: Fernwood Publishing, 1995.

Ng, Roxana. "Sexism, Racism, Canadian Nationalism," in Himani Banarji ed. *Returning the Gaze: Essays on Racism, Feminism and Politics.* Toronto: Sister Vision Press, 1993: 223-241.

Ontario Government. News Release. "Government to Oppose Job Quotas Coalition." (February 5, 1999) <http://www.web.net/~allforee/govt90205.htm>

Ontario Government of. An Act to Provide for Employment Equity for Aboriginal People, People with Disabilities, Members of Racial Minorities and Women. *Statutes of Ontario*, Chapter 35: 611-640. December, 1993

Ontario, Government of. "An Act to Repeal Job Quotas and to Restore Merit-based Employment Practices in Ontario". *Statutes of Ontario,* Chapter 4:1499-1503. December, 1995.

Ontario Ministry of Citizenship. "The Employment Equity Consultation Process: A Backgrounder". (December, 1993).

Ontario Ministry of Citizenship. *A Guide to Bill 79: The Employment Equity Act.* (December 4, 1993).

Public Service Alliance of Canada (PSAC). "National Women's Conference Celebrates Pay Equity Victory." 1999. <http://www.psac.com/COMM/UPDATE/Vol11-21/11-21-e.htm#5>

Quadagno, Jill. "Race and American Social Policy." *National Forum.* 76.3 (1996): 35-38.

Raulston Saul, John. *The Unconscious Civilization.* Concord, Ontario: Anasi, 1995.

Razack, Sherene. *Looking White People in the Eye: Gender, Race and Culture in Courtrooms and Classrooms* Toronto: University of Toronto Press, 1998.

Savran, David. "The Sadomasochist in the Closet: White Masculinity and the Culture of Victimization." *Differences* 8. 2 (1996): 126-152.

Staehli, Lynn A. and Susan E. Clarke. "Gender Place and Citizenship" in *Gender in Urban Research.* Thousand Oaks, California: Sage Publications (1995): 3-23.

Stilwell, Frank "Reform, Backlash and Social Balance." *Social Alternatives* 16.4 (1997): 18-22.

Task Force on Visible Minorities in the Federal Public Service. *Report.* Ottawa: Minister of Supply and Services, forthcoming.

Taylor, Marylee C. "White Backlash to Workplace Affirmative Action: Peril or Myth?" *Social Forces* 73.4 (1995): 1385-1414.

Tellier, Paul M. *Public Service 2000: A Report on Progress.* Ottawa: Minister of Supply and Services Canada: 1992.

Tepper, Elliot L. *Changing Canada: The Institutional Response to Polyethnicity. The Review of Demography and Its Implications for Economic and Social Policy.* Ottawa: Carleton University, 1988.

Turpel, Mary Ellen "Patriarchy and Paternalism: the Legacy of the Canadian State for First Nations Women," *Canadian Journal of Women and the Law*, 6 (1993).

Walker, Richard. "California's Collision of Race and Class." *Representations* 55 (1996): 163-183.

Weiler, Joseph M. "The Role of Law in Labour Relations," in Ivan Bernier and Andrée Lajoie, eds., *Labour Law in Canada* . Toronto: University of Toronto Press, Royal Commission on the Economic Union and Development Prospects for Canada, and Supply and Services Canada: 1986.

Williams, Patricia J. *The Alchemy of Race and Rights* Cambridge, Mass.: Harvard University Press, 1991.

Wilson, Trevor. *Diversity at Work: The Business Case for Equity.* Etobicoke: John Wiley and Sons, 1996.

Young, Iris Marion. *Justice and the Politics of Difference* Princeton, New Jersey: Princeton University Press, 1990.

Yuval-Davis, Nira. "Women, Citizenship and Difference." *Feminist Review.* 57 (Autumn 1997): 4-27.

CHAPTER 6

CHILE EBOE-OSUJI AND ELIZABETH MCISAAC

REPEAL OF THE ONTARIO EMPLOYMENT EQUITY LAWS: DENIAL OF EQUAL PROTECTION OF THE LAW

INTRODUCTION

The spring and summer of 1995 were election time in Ontario. The incumbent government was of the New Democratic Party (NDP), under the leadership of Premier Bob Rae. One of the most memorable achievements of the Rae Government was the enactment of the Ontario *Employment Equity Act*, 1993, which was informed by the same principles as found in affirmative action programs in the United States and Australia.

The Progressive Conservative Party (the Tories) led by Mike Harris were contenders for the governance of Ontario. The Tories began their 1995 election campaign with a document entitled the *Common Sense Revolution*, which was drawn up in 1994 as their manifesto for the purposes of the 1995 elections. It was a dry document full of charts and statistics stating how the Tories would cut social programs and improve life in the province. The *Common Sense Revolution* was devoid of any reference, directly or indirectly, to the Ontario *Employment Equity Act*.

In the middle of the campaign, however, the Tories made an effort to inject new life into their campaign. They did not have to look farther than what their fellow conservatives in the United States had done successfully. The Republican Party led by Newt Gingrich had swept into Congress by, among other things, mounting a spirited and effective attack against affirmative action programs. They had attacked affirmative action as imposing quotas, subverting merit and generally causing reverse discrimination against white able-bodied males.

The success of the 'Gingrich Revolution' in this regard gave the Ontario Tories just the idea they needed to boost their campaign. So on 5 May 1995, in a news release entitled "Mike Harris and Equal Opportunity," the Tories formally launched their attack against the Ontario *Employment Equity Act*, 1993. The document opens with the statement that "Hiring by quota is just as wrong as any other form of discrimination and will end with a Harris government's *Equal Opportunity* program ..."[1] They went on to promise that, if elected, they would "replace reverse discrimination and quotas in the NDP's Bill 79 with the merit principle in hiring and promotion."

From that point on, the Tories' pre- and post-election speeches dwelt upon the simple repeated affirmation, without any elaboration, that the *Employment Equity Act* imposed quotas, undermined merit and caused reverse discrimination against white able-bodied males. In so doing, the Tories showed little care for the accuracy and effect of their statements. Mike Harris, the Tory leader, was caught on tape saying, "There is *nothing* in that piece of legislation. It is *all* quota-based" [emphasis added].[2] The Act in fact

C. Agocs (ed.), Workplace Equality, 109–137.

contained fifty-five sections and no mention of quotas. A Tory Cabinet document claimed that "the N-D-P legislation said employers couldn't hire based on merit. They were forced to hire based on quotas."[3] As will be shown later in this chapter, this assertion had no basis in fact.

Just as the Tories exercised little restraint in the rhetoric they used against the Act, they also expressed innuendoes against those for whom the Act was designed to afford protection. Some of these utterances appeared geared to prey on the fears and prejudices of sections of the population. For example, they portrayed the Act as involving "special favours and special privileges from the Bob Rae government" to "special interest groups."[4] In one instance, as he criticised the Act for causing reverse discrimination against white able-bodied males, Premier Harris was reported in the press to have declared that "people's lives are at stake here" (Wallace, 1995). And speaking of the Act and other programs like it, one Tory politician lashed out against "special interest groups who hijacked *our* province" [emphasis added].[5] A reporter noted that "the [job quota] label stuck, making it the issue that best defines the politics and philosophy of the Progressive Conservative reign" (Toughill, 1995). As another reporter put it:

> Wherever he went, Mr Harris denounced unfair discriminatory job quotas. In the end, the myths surrounding job quotas may have proved to be the most persuasive issue of the campaign. Typical was Don Thrasher, campaign manager for the Conservatives in the Southwestern Ontario riding of Middlesex.
>
> As he explained to a visiting reporter last Sunday, 'A lot of people are saying why don't we just hire the best person for the job' instead of worrying about hiring equally qualified members of minorities, as the law specified.
>
> Mr. Thrasher then cited various newspaper job advertisements that said that 'White Males Need Not Apply.' Under questioning, he conceded he had never seen such an ad, nor had he met anyone who had actually claimed to have seen one. But people are talking about it and they believe it, he said (Grey, 1995:A10).

In the end, the Tories effectively rode to electoral victory the myths against the *Employment Equity Act*. And upon assuming office, they promptly repealed the Act.

Upon the repeal, Marylin Ferrel, an Ontario woman with cerebral palsy, led a group of Ontario residents in litigation seeking judicial declaration that the repeal was unconstitutional. The first author of this chapter represented her as her lead counsel. What follows is a discussion of the Ontario Employment Equity Act itself and the grounds on which, it is argued, its repeal violated the Canadian Charter of Rights and Freedoms. Although the views expressed in the following pages are based on thorough and exacting legal research, the reader is warned that the arguments made herein are presented from the point of view of persuading the reader that the repeal of the 1993 Act was unconstitutional.

BILL 8 -- AN UNCONSTITUTIONAL ENACTMENT

Bill 8 is Ontario legislation by which the *Employment Equity Act* was repealed. It was passed on 14 December 1995, and received Royal Assent, becoming law, the very next day. The full title of the Act is "An Act to repeal job quotas and to restore merit-based employment practices in Ontario." Because of the stereotypes involved in the titles of this Act it will henceforth be referred to only as 'Bill 8'[6]. By this law, the following pieces of legislation were repealed:

1. the Ontario *Employment Equity Act*, 1993;

2. sections of the Ontario *Education Act* which required school boards to implement employment equity in the education system;
3. sections of the *Ontario Human Rights Code* which harmonised that Code with the Ontario *Employment Equity Act*; and
4. sections of the Ontario *Police Services Act* that required police services to implement employment equity for their employees.

Although Bill 8 repealed other pieces of legislation as well, the discussion of the unconstitutionality of Bill 8 in this paper will be restricted to the context of the *Employment Equity Act*, as this is the Act that best defines the essence and the socio-political context of Bill 8.

THE ONTARIO EMPLOYMENT EQUITY ACT, 1993

The Ontario *Employment Equity Act*, 1993, was informed by overwhelming evidence that people with disabilities, women, Aboriginal people, and racial minorities face the unending scourge of discrimination in the workplace.[7] Some of the impacts of this discrimination include the following:

- higher rates of unemployment or higher representation in part time employment (when full time work is desired) or both;
- lower pay for equal qualifications and for work in the same occupational classifications;
- under-representation in management relative to similarly qualified white able-bodied men;
- near absence from senior decision-making positions in private and public sector organisations;
- concentration in a narrower range of occupations;
- under-representation in the kinds of jobs and functions that lead to advancement in managerial careers;
- subjected to harassment in the workplace because of gender, race, disability or a combination of these characteristics; and
- experience more discrimination than other people in finding employment, in retaining employment and in being promoted on the job.

For racial minority groups, these and other kinds of employment discrimination persist in the face of studies which show that they are as qualified as—and sometimes even more qualified than—the average white able-bodied male (see Smith, 1996; Kelly 1995; Human Resources Development Canada, 1995).

Many of these disadvantages result both from systemic discrimination or adverse impact discrimination, and from a deliberate will to discriminate. As Judge Abella expressed in her Royal Commission Report (1984:2):

> Discrimination in this context means practices or attitudes that have, whether by design or impact, the effect of limiting an individual's or group's right to the opportunities generally available because of attributed rather than actual characteristics. ...
> It is not a question of whether this discrimination is motivated by an intentional desire to obstruct someone's potential, or whether it is the accidental by-product of innocently motivated practices or systems. If the barrier is affecting certain groups in a disproportionately

negative way, it is a signal that the practices that lead to this adverse impact may be discriminatory.

With the recognition that systemic discrimination or adverse impact discrimination has often meant that Aboriginal people, persons with disabilities, members of racial minorities and women (hereinafter referred to as the "designated groups") are frequently overlooked or denied opportunities in the workplace, without regard to their merit, the previous Legislature of Ontario under the Rae Government enacted the Ontario *Employment Equity Act* in 1993. The aim was to cure and prevent these conditions of disadvantage which members of the designated groups experience in employment. As a means to this objective, the 1993 Act required employers to undertake effective and practical measures carefully designed to eliminate discrimination from workplaces across Ontario.

Obligations Under the Ontario Employment Equity Act

The Ontario *Employment Equity Act*, 1993 is not a one-dimensional statute, singularly pre-occupied with boosting the workforce numbers of designated group members. Apart from the requirement to set equitable numerical goals, the Act required other measures aimed at rooting out the causes of discrimination or inequality in the workplace. To better understand the various measures required as employers' obligations, and to see them in their proper perspectives, it is suggested that the Act be seen as containing at least *two tiers* of measures. The *first tier* of measures involves an identification of what has to be done at the first level. The *second tier* involves measures that are required in order to implement each of the *first tier* measures.

First Tier Measures

In brief, the requirements of the Ontario *Employment Equity Act*, 1993 include the following measures at the first level (see the "General Regulations", Employment Equity Act, 1993):

i) provision of information to all employees about the objectives, values, and process of employment equity [employee education];
ii) a survey of the workforce based on voluntary self-reporting by employees of their membership in the designated groups, with the view to determining the extent to which members of the designated groups are employed in the employer's workforce [workforce survey];
iii) a review of formal and informal policies and practices used to make decisions about all aspects of human resource management, in order to identify any policy or practice that may constitute discrimination [review of employment policies];
iv) preparation of an Employment Equity Plan, including equitable goals and timetables, for removing discriminatory barriers where they are found, and to implement measures to address disadvantages [Employment Equity Plan]; and,
v) monitoring and assessing progress in light of experience, with revision of the equity plan every three years in order to make it as effective as possible [monitoring].

Second Tier Measures: The Employment Equity Plan

The Act and its *General Regulations* prescribed details of the second tier of measures to be undertaken in order to implement each of the first tier of measures identified above. The Employment Equity Plan, as a first tier measure, has attracted the most attention of all the first tier measures, specifically because of its requirement of numerical goals as a component of its second tier of measures. Yet equitable numerical goals and timetables are only one of at least six other second tier measures involved in the Employment Equity Plan. As s 12 of the Act shows, the second tier of measures involved in the Employment Equity Plan are as follows (see the *Employment Equity Act*, 1993, and Westmoreland-Traoré, 1992:52-55):

(a) elimination of discriminatory barriers identified as a result of a review of employment policies [barrier elimination measures];
(b) implementation of positive measures with respect to the recruitment, hiring, retention, treatment and promotion of members of the designated groups. Such measures include job vacancy advertising in community media of designated groups, non-traditional outreach programs targeting educational institutions, etc [positive measures];
(c) implementation of supportive measures with respect to the recruitment, hiring, retention, treatment and promotion of members of the designated groups. These are intended to include policies aimed at balancing family and work responsibilities, anti-discrimination and anti-harassment policies including training and education, mentoring, etc [supportive measures];
(d) implementation of measures to accommodate members of designated groups in the workforce. These are intended to include provision of appropriate assistive devices and access to updated and appropriate technology and software required to perform the job, flexible hours and modified job duties, accessibility of buildings and all facilities and areas in the work environment, dress codes which accommodate women and cultural minorities, etc [accommodation measures];
(e) specific goals and timetables for the measures referred to above in clauses (a) to (d);
(f) specific goals and timetables with respect to the equitable composition of the employer's workforce, and
(g) such other matters as may be prescribed by the regulations.

Given then that the requirement to set equitable numerical goals to increase the composition of members of the designated groups is only one of at least six other measures required as a second tier of measures, it is hardly justified that Premier Harris or any other critic of the Act should assert that "there is nothing in that Act. It is all quota-based."

THE CONSTITUTIONAL VIOLATION

This chapter argues that as an instrument for the repeal of the 1993 Act, Bill 8 is a violation of s 15 of the *Canadian Charter of Rights and Freedoms*; that is to say, it is a law inconsistent with the Canadian Constitution. Section 15 of the *Charter* makes the following provisions:

> 15 (1). Every individual is equal before and under the law and has the right to the equal protection and equal benefit of the law without discrimination and, in particular, without

> discrimination based on race, national or ethnic origin, colour, religion, sex, age or mental or physical disability.
>
> 15 (2). Subsection (1) does not preclude any law, program or activity that has as its object the amelioration of conditions of disadvantaged individuals or groups including those that are disadvantaged because of race, national or ethnic origin, colour, religion, sex, age or mental or physical disability.

Bill 8 violates s 15 of the *Charter* because it removed a piece of legislation which attempted to give "equal protection of the law" to people with disabilities, women, Aboriginal people, and members of racial minority groups. There are three theories to the violation in question:

1) violation of s 15 by removing a protective shield,
2) violation of s 15 by encouraging backlash, and
3) violation by breach of an original duty.

FIRST THEORY OF VIOLATION: REMOVING A PROTECTIVE SHIELD

Given the overwhelming evidence of employment discrimination against members of the designated groups, the previous legislature under the Rae Government felt a need to put in place a protective shield around the designated groups, against these forces of discrimination. This special protection entirely accords with the idea of 'substantive equality' as recognised by the Supreme Court of Canada in *Andrews* v *Law Society of British Columbia*. This special protection would, among other things, enable these vulnerable groups to reach a 'critical mass' in the workforce.[8] This critical mass, then, would make the designated groups less susceptible to discrimination.

In removing this shield of protection, Bill 8 effectively left members of the designated groups exposed—or re-exposed—to the forces of discrimination, when they could have been enjoying equal protection or equal benefit of the law. This idea of violation of the right to equal protection and equal benefit of the law has been recognised by the Courts on previous occasions. For instance, *Blainey* v *Ontario Hockey Association* recognises the principle that a statutory provision will be found in breach of the right to equal protection and equal benefit of the law, where a citizen would have enjoyed that right but for the impugned provision.[9] In that case, a young girl challenged a provision of the *Ontario Human Rights Code* that had exempted single-gender athletic clubs from the Code's prohibitions of discrimination on grounds of sex. This provision prevented the girl from participating in the Ontario Minor Hockey League that was an all-male league. The Court of Appeal for Ontario agreed with the girl that the impugned provision of the Code violated the girl's right to equal protection and equal benefit of the law, as guaranteed by s 15 of the *Charter*. And in *Re Manitoba Council of Health Care Unions & ors* v *Bethesda Hospital & ors* it was held that a statutory provision will be seen as discriminatory if it legislatively sanctions continued discrimination against people traditionally discriminated against.[10] This is a chief flaw of Bill 8. The *Employment Equity Act* was designed to compel employers to, among other things, review their employment systems in order to identify practices, procedures and attitudes which have continued to cause adverse impact or systemic discrimination against members of designated groups. No other piece of legislation was that far-reaching. In repealing the Act and effectively allowing a continuation of those practices, procedures and attitudes which have continued to cause adverse impact or systemic discrimination against members of designated groups, Bill 8 permitted the types of discrimination at issue.

Finally, in *R* v *Edwards Books & Art Ltd*, Dickson CJC, gave the following caution:

> In interpreting and applying the *Charter* I believe that the Courts must be cautious to ensure that the it does not simply become an instrument of better situated individuals to roll back legislation which has as its object the improvement of the condition of less advantaged persons.[11]

The repeal of the 1993 Act is both directly and indirectly ensnared by this caution. First, the Tories claimed that one of the reasons that they repealed the Act was because it was discriminatory against white able-bodied males; this clearly an assertion that the Act violated the right of white able-bodied males as contained in s 15(1) of the *Charter*. This approach is flawed not only because it is ensnared by Dickson CJC's caution as appears above, but also because it ignores the provisions of s 15(2) of the *Charter* which provides that no law or program is discriminatory if it was designed to ameliorate the conditions of those who have traditionally been disadvantaged in society. Furthermore, Dickson CJC's caution is as applicable to the exercise of legislative power found elsewhere in the Canadian Constitution as it is to the purported exercise of the *Charter*-guaranteed rights and freedoms of those "better situated individuals." In other words, if better situated ordinary individuals are cautioned against employing the *Charter* to roll back legislation ameliorative of conditions of the disadvantaged, then better situated individuals should also be cautioned against attempts to achieve the same objective by the simple device of electing their political agents who then repeal ameliorative legislation, alluding to their constitutional or political power to legislate such a repeal.

SECOND THEORY OF VIOLATION: ENCOURAGING BACKLASH

A simple repeal of the Ontario *Employment Equity Act*, 1993 was enough to make Bill 8 vulnerable to attack as a piece of unconstitutional legislation. The Tories did not, however, simply repeal the Act. There is evidence that the manner in which Bill 8 was brought about resulted in backlash against the members of the designated groups, thus putting them in a position worse than they experienced before the passage of the Employment Equity Act.[12] The occurred by means of a campaign of calumny - much publicised in the media[13]- against the Ontario *Employment Equity Act* and against those to whom the Act afforded equal protection of the law. This was achieved by the simple process of the Tories repeatedly alleging that the Ontario *Employment Equity Act* required "quotas," "provided against merit" and legislated "reverse discrimination," for the benefit of "special interest groups" who had "hijacked the province," and to the detriment of white able-bodied males whose "lives were at stake." Even as they won the 1995 election, the Tories could not resist branding their campaign rhetoric into the title of Bill 8, as is apparent from the short and long titles of Bill 8.

What's in a Name? Perpetuation of Stereotypes by Unreasonable Characterisation

The Harris government made a conscious decision to give Bill 8 a title that entrenched the negative Tory campaign rhetoric against employment equity. Its short title is the *Job Quotas Repeal Act*. Its long title is "An Act to repeal job quotas and to restore merit-based employment practices in Ontario." There are two points of note here. First, these titles clearly do not address either the title or the content of the *Employment Equity Act*, 1993. In the realms of legislative drafting the characterisation of Bill 8 is quite unusual. One would expect its proper title to be the "Employment Equity Repeal Act," the "Employment Equity Laws Repeal Act," the "Employment Equity Act and Relevant Provisions Repeal Act", or some other such title. It was neither necessary nor relevant to entitle Bill 8 as either the *Job Quotas Repeal Act* or *An Act to repeal job quotas and to restore merit-based employment practices in Ontario.* Such titles quite properly expose Bill 8 to charges of stereotyping. Secondly, there is evidence that the characterisation of Bill 8 was entirely deliberate, as shown in two pieces of evidence. The first is found in a Ministry of Education memorandum of 13 September 1995, a briefing memorandum to the Minister of Education from the Assistant Deputy Minister in charge of Policy Priorities and Curriculum Development. In this memorandum, the following pieces of vital information appear:

- The original short title to Bill 8 appears as the '*Employment Equity Repeal Act;*' 'The purpose of the briefing is to seek [the Minister's] approval of the Compendium to the *Employment Equity Repeal Act* to be included in a submission from MCCR [Ministry of Citizenship, Culture and Recreation] to the Leg/Regs Committee for discussion on September 21, 1995. This material must be submitted by MCCR to Leg/Regs Committee by noon on Thursday, September 14.' [Emphasis added]
- The attached Compendium is entitled 'Compendium to the *Employment Equity Repeal Act, 1995.*' [Emphasis added]
- An attached explanatory note is entitled '*Employment Equity Repeal Act, 1995.*' [Emphasis added]
- The attached draft bill bears the following long title: '*An Act to repeal the Employment Equity Act, 1993 and to make related amendments to the Education Act, the Human Rights Code and the Police Services Act.*' [Emphasis added]
- 'The intention is to introduce this bill as one of the first pieces of legislation when the House begins sitting.'
- 'Included in the package is the timing of the repeal bill developed by MCCR.'

The second piece of evidence of the deliberate characterisation of Bill 8 in a manner reflective of the stereotypes of lack of merit for members of the designated groups is found in a government document entitled "Confidential Briefing Note - Cabinet Meeting - October 4, 1995." In this document the following pieces of information appear (emphasis added):

Item:

Report from Cabinet Committee on Legislation and Regulations pertaining to the *Employment Equity Repeal Bill* - Section 1(5).

Recommendation:

That Cabinet approve Section 1(5) of the *Employment Equity Repeal Bill* as follows:

Every person in possession of information collected from employees exclusively for the purpose of complying with Part III of the *Employment Equity, 1993* shall destroy the information as soon as reasonably possible after this Act comes into force.

Background:

- On September 6, 1995, Cabinet approved the policy directions for a *bill to repeal employment equity.*
- *The draft legislation was reviewed by the Cabinet Committee on Legislation and Regulations on September 21, 1995.* The Committee decided to refer Section 1(5) pertaining to the treatment of information collected from employees under Part III of the *Employment Equity Act,* back to Cabinet for discussion.
- At the Cabinet meeting of September 27, the draft legislation was approved except for 1(5). ...

It is clear then that the original title for Bill 8 was proposed as '*Employment Equity Repeal Act*, 1995', for short, with the long title of "An Act to repeal the Employment Equity Act, 1993 and to make related amendments to the Education Act, the Human Rights Code and the Police Services Act." These titles remained the case even on 4 October 1995. Somehow, somewhere, the titles changed to the *Job Quotas Repeal Act*, 1995, and "An Act to repeal job quotas and to restore merit-based employment practices in Ontario," which will forever appear in the statute books of Ontario. The stereotyping implication of this unnecessary manner of characterising a piece of legislation is clear.

The anti-stereotyping dicta of the justices of the Supreme Court of Canada in *Andrews*, *Turpin* and *Egan* are sufficient to support a claim that the Harris government violated the s 15 rights of members of the designated groups. They did this not just by their election campaign rhetoric of 1995, but also by reflecting such stereotypes in the long and short titles of Bill 8.

A Clear Intention to Discourage Voluntary Employment Equity

The Harris government did not limit their efforts to attacks against the 1993 Act that they criticised as legislation of job quotas. The government also displayed a clear intention to discourage employers from voluntarily embarking upon employment equity initiatives in general, even though such employers may have been doing employment equity long before the 1993 Act required them to do so. This intention appears, first, from the requirement in Bill 8 that employers destroy data collected for the purposes of compliance with s 10 of the Ontario *Employment Equity Act*, 1993. These data include workforce survey data required by the Act. The immediate purpose of the data collection exercise was to enable employers to ascertain the extent of general under-representation of members of the designated groups in their workforce, as well as the extent of particular under-representation at the various occupational levels in the workforce. The ultimate aim of the data collection process was to enable employers to implement employment equity plans that were required by the 1993 Act. There is no doubt that following the repeal of the Act, these data would have been useful to those employers who might otherwise not have got around to collecting the data, but who may be predisposed to implementing voluntary employment equity plans. The Harris government was quite mindful of this, as shown in a background information brief on the "Federal Contractors Program for Employment Equity" (attached to the Confidential Briefing Note re the Cabinet Meeting of 4 October 1995):

> [Apart from a given list of Ontario companies who are shown as having contracts with the federal government, under the Federal Contractors Program for Employment Equity] '*[o]ther Ontario employers may wish to voluntarily continue their employment equity programs*, even though they are not federal contractors. We do not know how many in this category have already collected workforce data, but we do know that *approximately 5500 private and broader sector companies are required to submit employment equity plans by March1, 1996 so it is reasonable to assume that some of them have collected data and are continuing their programs*. [Emphasis added.]

Secondly, and related to the requirement to destroy data, there is further evidence of the Harris government's intention to discourage employers from voluntarily embarking upon or continuing with employment equity initiatives, quite apart from the requirements of the 1993 Act. The Government's 'Top Ten List of Questions for Job Quotas Repeal' (Ministry of Citizenship, Culture and Recreation) states, in Question 9 and the answers to it:

> Q: Some employers had equity programs before the act was brought down. With the repeal, are you telling them this was the wrong thing to do? Are they going to have to get rid of them? What if they keep their programs?
> A: We believe that quotas are wrong. Businesses don't want quotas and employees want hiring decisions to be based on merit. Any action by employers to support the merit principle has the full support of this government.
> Q: Supplementary: So you're telling employers to scrap their Employment Equity Plans?
> A: And support Equal Opportunity instead. *Yes, you've got it!*

The information cited in the two government documents cited above leads to the conclusion that the government not only intended to abolish the 1993 Act, because they perceived it as *legislation* of quotas; rather the government's primary motive was to eradicate the *practice* of *employment equity* in Ontario.

Debunking the Myths and Misconceptions

As will be seen presently, the Tory criticisms of the 1993 Act were based on myths not borne out by the true wording, principles and intention of the Act.

i) The Employment Equity Act, 1993 Does Not Impose Quotas

The Ontario *Employment Equity Act*, 1993, did not require quotas. A quota may be defined as a peremptory numerical factor, which must be 'set aside',[14] regardless of considerations of merit or substance. This point has been made very clearly by M. David Lepofsky of the Ontario Ministry of the Attorney General, who wrote that 'Quotas' are numerical, fixed, and inflexible as to time and are externally imposed (1993:4).[15] 'Quotas' are not imposed, nor even mentioned, in the 1993 Act. Instead, the Act required employers to establish 'goals' for the achievement of measures identified in their employment equity plans. This is quite consistent with the recommendations of the Abella Report (1984) and the Westmoreland-Traoré Report (1992). The key elements of goals are as follows:

- goals are qualitative as well as quantitative: employers are required to set goals for removal of discriminatory barriers, as well as for hiring;
- goals are set by employers themselves, not imposed by any external authority;
- goals are flexible and responsive to the employer's circumstances;
- numerical goals are established by employers only in relation to job openings, which means hiring or promotion opportunities—not creation of new positions unrelated to the employers demands;
- the achievement of these equitable 'goals and timetables' is informed by the supply of qualified designated group members;
- goals are not absolute, but employers are required to make all reasonable efforts to achieve their self-created goals.[16]

Critics of employment equity programs concede that the only offensive aspects of the programs are the aspects that require goals. They accept as proper the other aspects of equity programs. As Finkle and Strom wrote:

> Most affirmative action programs have several elements such as: compelling employers and schools to refrain from using discriminatory criteria based on sex or race; providing remedial programs; and creating a more congenial and supportive environment through the use of flex-time and day-care. *These aspects of affirmative action are unimpeachable.* [Emphasis added.] (1990:82)

Most of the measures identified above as obligations under the 1993 Act are entirely consistent with aspects of the programs which Finkle and Strom have declared 'unimpeachable'. It is the use of goals that has been the focus of controversy. In this connection, critics have refused or failed to make any distinction between 'quotas' and 'goals' (Finkle and Strom, 1990:82).

Yet there is a need to distinguish 'equitable goals' from 'quotas'. This distinction begins with dictionary definitions. In the *Concise Oxford English Dictionary*, 'quota' is mainly defined as "1. the share that an individual person or company *is bound* to contribute to or entitled to receive from a total; 2. a quantity of goods etc. which under official controls *must* be manufactured, exported, imported, etc. [Emphasis added.] Two things must be noted here, contrary to popular misconceptions. First, neither the 1993 Act nor its regulations determined the actual goals and imposed them on employers. Rather the employers were required to determine these goals themselves, using reasonable yardsticks—such as data from Statistics Canada -- indicating the numbers of qualified members of the designated groups in the particular employer's localities, industries, companies and occupational levels. In setting their goals, employers were expected to take into account their own particular circumstances. Second, the Act placed no absolute responsibility on employers to meet any such goal. All that the Act required is that "every employer shall make all *reasonable efforts* to implement each of the employer's Employment Equity Plans and to achieve goals set out in each plan in accordance with the timetables set out in the plan" (S 14) [emphasis added].

One reason that critics of employment equity equate goals with quotas is because the 1993 Act and its regulations contain a penalty for non-compliance. This, critics say, is unacceptable because it entails government regulation, which means governmental interference with the free will of employers. Having noted, however, that the Act only required employers to make reasonable efforts to achieve their goals, a legislative stimulus in setting such goals ought not to be seen as unacceptable. The reason for this should begin with an appreciation of the meaning of 'goals'. According to the *Concise Oxford English Dictionary*, 'goal' is defined chiefly as "the object of a person's ambition or effort; a destination; an aim." Given this definition, it hardly seems improper for the government to require employers to set these aims or 'objects of ambition'. Nor should it be improper for the government to establish guidelines for the parameters of these goals. It must particularly be noted that employers had generally failed to set these goals voluntarily throughout the years before the enactment of the Act. Another reason for legislative incentive to set goals is to provide uniformity of rules applying to all the employers who are regulated by the Act.

Although the 1993 Act was not intended to result in fixed hiring goals externally imposed on employers who comply with their ordinary obligations under the Act, such hiring goals have indeed been recognised at the Supreme Court of Canada as valuable in certain circumstances. The *locus classicus* in this regard is *Action travail des femmes* v *CNR.*[17] In that case, the Supreme Court of Canada unanimously gave the following dicta which underscore both the necessity and effectiveness of peremptory employment equity programs (*Action travail des femmes* v CNR (1987, 40 DLR (4th) 193 (SCC) pp 210-216):

- To combat systemic discrimination, it is *essential* to create a climate in which both negative practices and negative attitudes can be challenged and discouraged...

- When confronted with ... a case of 'systemic discrimination', it may be that [imposing on CNR a hiring goal of 25% until the goal of 13% female involvement in the non-traditional work-force had been achieved] is the only means by which the purpose of the *Canadian Human Rights Act* can be met...
- In any program of employment equity, there simply cannot be a radical dissociation of 'remedy' and 'prevention'. Indeed there is no prevention without some form of remedy...
- [A peremptory] employment equity program ... is designed to break a continuing cycle of systemic discrimination. The goal is not to compensate past victims or even to provide new opportunities for specific individuals who have been unfairly refused jobs or promotion in the past, although some such individuals may be beneficiaries of an employment equity scheme. Rather, an employment equity program is an attempt to ensure that applicants and workers from the affected group will not face the same insidious barriers that blocked their forebears....
- An employment equity program thus is designed to work in three ways. Firstly, by countering the cumulative effects of systemic discrimination, such a program renders future discrimination pointless. To the extent that some intentional discrimination may be present, for example, in the case of a foreman who controls hiring and who simply does not want women in the unit, a *mandatory* employment equity scheme places women in the unit despite the discriminatory intent of the foreman. His battle is lost... Secondly, by placing members of that group that had previously been excluded into the heart of the work place and by allowing them to prove ability on the job, the employment equity scheme addresses the attitudinal problem of stereotyping. ... Thirdly, an employment equity program helps to create what has been termed a 'critical mass' of the previously excluded group in the work place. This 'critical mass' has important effects. The presence of a significant number of individuals from the targeted group eliminates the problems of 'tokenism'. ... The 'critical mass' also effectively remedies systemic inequities in the process of hiring ... . In other words, once a 'critical mass' of the previously excluded group has been created in the work force, there is a significant chance for the continuing self-correction of the system....
- For the employment equity program [involved in this case] to be effective in creating the 'critical mass' and in destroying stereotypes, the goals had to be expressed in terms of actual employment. [Emphasis added.]

As we have seen, the Supreme Court of Canada held in *Action travail des femmes* v *CNR* that "faced with systemic discrimination," it may be that imposing a fixed goal of a certain percentage is the only way to achieve the objectives set out in the statute at issue in that case. A similar reason may justify such an approach to dealing with a recalcitrant employer who refuses to undertake the ordinary measures prescribed in the 1993 Act. However, this approach could be expressly forbidden in the Act, even as a measure of dealing with recalcitrant employers, by means of amending the Act. The federal government adopted this approach in its own employment equity statute as amended in 1995.[18] Rather than total repeal, the Tories could very well have followed the lead of the federal government in similarly amending the 1993 Act, if perceived quotas were the real concern.

ii) The Employment Equity Act, 1993 is Consistent with Merit

Employment equity is based on the premise that there are qualified people with talent, skills and knowledge among all groups regardless of disability status, gender, race or ethnicity. It does not accept the assumption that hiring and promoting more women, persons with disabilities, racial minorities and persons of Aboriginal ancestry will result in the lowering of standards of performance. On the contrary, employment equity is intended to open up the employment process to fair competition by fairly allowing opportunities to groups that have been traditionally excluded in the past because of discrimination.[19]

Employment equity does not undermine the merit principle; it establishes merit based hiring where it does not exist. For example, research by Billingley and Muszynski found:

> *Without exception*, organisations that have engaged in racial minority recruitment efforts have *been deluged* with qualified applicants. One respondent whose organisation has recently completed such a program reported:

> We have *extremely well-qualified* Non-White applicants to fill any vacancies [in the organisation] for the next two years;
> Another remarked:
> This business about racial minorities not being qualified is a lot of crap. *We got so many people with the right expertise, and education* replying to our ads for minorities in professional positions [to serve our minority clients] that *we had a hard time choosing.*
> [Underlined emphasis in original., other emphasis added.] (1985:33-34)

Furthermore, studies from Statistics Canada have shown that visible minorities tend to be more educated than the average population, and yet more likely to be unemployed or under-employed (Kelly, 1985: 8). From a recent American study on faculty posts for new PhD holders, the following report appears, in spite of years of affirmative action in America (Smith, 1996:B3-B4):

- Minority PhDs, even those who were found to be 'among the most elite of the new scholars, almost all of them receiving both undergraduate and graduate degrees from the country's most selective universities,' continued to suffer from discrimination.
- More than half these people do not get hired. So they are often driven to pursuing *post-doctoral* studies—even three and four times over—and, yet many continue to face unemployment at the end of it all.
- This trend has several negative effects: it delays the development of serious careers[;] it ratchets up what new faculty members require of their institutions in order to continue their research[;] and it makes it difficult for PhDs who cannot afford to take post-doctoral positions to find jobs. This can hurt all new faculty members, but it has a particularly *severe* impact on the hiring of minority-group [candidates.]'
- 75% of white male PhDs in the study continued to find 'faculty positions with which they were quite satisfied.'
- A number of these white males in these faculty positions commented on the resistance, they saw, to diversify the faculty. As one of them said: 'There is a lot of talk about diversifying, but when push comes to shove, there is still a lot of hiring of white males.'

Above all, there is credible evidence that employment equity produces positive results for employers and the economy in general.[20] In a 1991 study by a team of staff reporters of *Business Week*, the American business magazine found that as a result of the American version of employment equity, "Individual businesses and the economy have profited, not lost" (Gleckman et al., 1991: 62).

iii) Reflection of "Representation" in the Community - A Question of Construction

A recurring criticism of the 1993 Act is the perception that it required an employer to reflect the percentages of members of the designated groups in the employer's community. This, it is feared, would lead to the absurdity of employing and promoting people who do not merit their employment and promotions. This criticism derives its base from the second principle in the Act as set out in s 2:

> Every employer's workforce, in all occupational categories and at all levels of employment, shall reflect the representation of Aboriginal people, people with disabilities, members of racial minorities and women in the community.

Bringing the applicable principles of statutory interpretation to bear, this provision ought not to be feared as a requirement to employ unqualified people. Without delving too much into the principles of statutory interpretation, it will suffice that both the 'golden rule' of statutory construction and resort to preambles should effectively assuage this fear. First, the value of the 'golden rule' is best said in the words of Parke:

> It is a very useful rule, in the construction of a statute, to adhere to the ordinary meaning of the words used, and to the grammatical construction, unless that is at variance with the intention of the legislature, to be collected for the statute itself, or leads to any manifest absurdity or repugnance, in which case the language may be varied or modified, so as to avoid such inconvenience, but no further [*Becke* v *Smith* (1836) 2 M & W 191, at p 195. See also *R* v *Tonbridge Overseers* (1884) 13 QBD 339 at p 342, per Brett LJ.].

The 'golden rule' of statutory interpretation is the fountain of such other rules of statutory interpretation as the rule of avoidance of unreasonable results. In the words of Danckwerts, "An intention to produce an unreasonable result is not to be imputed to a statute if there is some other construction available." [*Artemiou* v *Procpiou* (1966) 1 QB 878 at p 888].

Clearly then the 'golden rule' affords the means of avoiding such interpretations of the 1993 Act as would lead to the 'absurdity', 'inconvenience' or 'unreasonable result' of requiring, say, a hospital to employ a blind man with no medical training to perform eye surgery on someone else.

Coupled with the 'golden rule', the preamble to the Act provides an employer with another construction that saves the employer from employing unqualified people. As Lord Normand wrote in *Attorney-General* v *HRH Prince Ernest Augustus of Hanover* about the preamble of a statute:

> When there is a preamble it is generally in its recitals that the mischief to be remedied and the scope of the Act are described. It is therefore clearly permissible to have recourse to it as an aid to construing the enacting provisions [*Attorney-General* v *HRH Prince Ernest Augustus of Hanover* (1957) AC 436 [HL] at p 467].

But more important, section 8 of the *Interpretation Act* of Ontario provides as follows:

> The preamble of an Act shall be deemed a part thereof and is intended to assist in explaining the purport and object of the Act.

Turning then to the role of the preamble of the 1993 Act, the word "representation" in the Second Principle of the Act must derive its proper meaning from the mischief which the Act set out to remedy, as well as the object of the Act. This mischief and object are clearly set out in the preamble to the Act. After describing the general nature of the discrimination and employment inequity faced by members of the designated groups, the Act makes the following declaration in the second paragraph of the preamble:

> ... *People of merit* are too often overlooked or denied opportunities because of this discrimination. The people of Ontario recognise that when *objective standards* govern employment opportunities, Ontario will have a workforce that is truly *representative* of its society [Emphasis added].

This is a clear indication that, first, the Legislature never intended by the Act to force unqualified members of the community onto any employer. Secondly, when the Second Principle of the Act declares that every employer's workforce shall "reflect the representation" of members of the designated groups in the community, the preamble indicates that the Legislature had in mind reflection of the 'representation' of people who are 'people of merit'. This is the proper route to the aspiration of the *Employment Equity Act* of Ontario; that is, to have a 'workforce that is truly *representative* of its society.'

iv) The Employment Equity Act, 1993 is not "Reverse Discrimination"

The fourth Tory myth was the allegation that the Act engendered reverse discrimination against white able-bodied males. Again this is unfounded in terms of the intention of the Act and the proven consequences of similar programs in other jurisdictions. Employment equity is designed to remove *existing* barriers based on considerations unrelated to performance (Lepofsky, 1993:9-11). It is not designed to *erect* barriers to any group. In terms of consequences of similar programs elsewhere, studies have shown that white able-bodied males are not truly disadvantaged.[21] Employment equity seeks to create a workplace in which employment decisions are made openly and on the basis of objective, fair and relevant criteria.

As we have seen, these four false myths and the manner in which they were publicised by the Tories, in their efforts to repeal the Act, without any effort to show the arguments and evidence against those myths, resulted in backlash against members of the designated groups.[22] The resultant backlash constitutes a violation of s 15.

THIRD THEORY OF VIOLATION: BREACH OF AN ORIGINAL DUTY

Under this theory of violation, a number of questions arise. Did the repeal amount to a reviewable action or is it a mere omission? If it was a mere omission, does the *Charter* apply? And is there an original duty on the state to eliminate systemic discrimination?

It is tempting to view the repeal of the Ontario *Employment Equity Act*, 1993, as a mere omission. It is further tempting to argue that as a mere omission, the *Charter* does not apply. But that view is mistaken. To repeal a piece of legislation is not a mere omission. It takes a series of positive legislative actions to enact a statute that repeals another. These positive legislative actions include cabinet decisions, cabinet approvals, introduction into the legislature, first reading, committee procedures at various stages, second reading, third reading, passage, and royal assent. This series of positive legislative actions is identical to the steps involved in enacting a constitutive statute. Therefore it cannot be argued that repealing a statute is a mere omission. Notwithstanding these features that repeal and enactment have in common, the Tories also actively campaigned against the 1993 Act.

Even if repeal were to be seen as mere omission, it does not follow that the *Charter* will not apply to a legislative omission of repeal. Quite apart from any judicial precedent directly bearing on this point in the context of the *Charter*, it is well established that the corpus of Anglo-Canadian law, including tort law,[23] criminal law and the *Charter*[24] recognises that a wrong may be done by omission, as by commission.

With particular reference to discrimination, Canadian Courts have held on various occasions that an omission to include vulnerable and discrete groups under the equal protection, or allow them the equal benefit, of laws amounted to violation of their rights as guaranteed by s 15 of the *Charter*. For instance, in *Brooks* v *Canada Safeway Ltd*, Safeway's group insurance plan disentitled pregnant women from receiving accident or sickness benefits under the plan for seventeen weeks. Among Safeway's arguments was that the plan was not discriminatory; rather it was merely under-inclusive of the potential risks it could conceivably insure. In rejecting this argument, Dickson CJC, wrote for the Court:

> In Canada, as I have said, discrimination does not depend on a finding of invidious intent. A further consideration militating against the application of the concept of underinclusiveness in this context stems, in my view, from the *effects* of so-called 'underinclusion'. *Underinclusion may be simply a backhanded way of permitting discrimination* (*Brooks* v *Canada Safeway Ltd* (1989), 59 DLR (4th) 321 (SCC) at pp 336-337.) [Emphases added].

Other cases in which under-inclusiveness was held to violate s 15 include *Schacter* v *Canada* (failure to include adoptive parents as parents who may receive parental benefits under the *Unemployment Insurance Act*);[25] *Haig and Birch* v *Canada* (failure to include sexual preference as grounds for valid complaint of discrimination under the *Canadian Human Rights Act*);[26] and *Re Blainey and Ontario Hockey Association* (exclusion of membership or participation in athletic activities as grounds for complaint of gender discrimination under the Ontario *Human Rights Code, 1981*).[27]

More recently, it has been held that legislatures may not escape scrutiny under the *Charter* merely by choosing the avenue of permissive rather than the prescriptive legislation. In *Vriend* v *Alberta, supra,* Hunt JA held:

> It is clear that governments cannot avoid the impact of the *Charter* through using one legislative technique rather than another. In my opinion, nor should they necessarily be able to avoid the *Charter* in all cases by refusing to act or by choosing to ignore legitimate problems that are presented to them. (*Vriend* v *Alberta* [1996] AJ No 182; Appeal No 9403-0380-AC (Alta CA) dated 23 February 1996 (unrptd) para 140 *per* Hunt JA [dissenting]).

Justice Hunt's dictum was also informed *inter alia* by the following dictum of Wilson JSC in *Lavigne* v *Ontario Public Service Employees Union, supra*:

> [I]t must be recognised that if this court were to hold without qualification that the *Charter* does not apply to permissive legislation, the door would surely be open to widespread abuse at the hands of the government. This court has already acknowledged that technical avoidance of the application of the *Charter* is to be avoided. ... By analogy, it is easy to envision that government may avoid its duty to respect the guarantees embodied in the *Charter* through the vehicle of permissive legislation. This, of course, is a result which this court should seek to avoid. What qualifications therefore need to be added to the general principle that permissive statutory provisions standing alone are insufficient to call the *Charter* into play? As a general observation, I would think that in each case all the circumstances would have to be carefully examined to determine whether government had significantly encouraged or supported the act which is called into question. Depending upon the context, the enactment of the permissive provision may indeed support a finding of governmental approval or encouragement of a particular activity sufficient to invoke the protective guarantees of the *Charter* (*Lavigne* v *Ontario Public Service Employees Union* (1991), 81 DLR (4th) 545 (SCC) at pp 570-571).

Even in America, there is a line of authorities recognising that the state is liable for breach of citizens' rights by their fellow citizens, where such breaches followed either the state's failure to protect vulnerable citizens or the state's withdrawal of protection from such citizens. For instance, in *Lynch* v *United States*, the police were felt to be guilty of culpable official inaction and thus responsible for a beating administered to a prisoner by a mob while the police looked on passively.[28] In *NAACP* v *Alabama, ex rel Patterson*, the state was said to be responsible for private injuries likely to be triggered when it withdraws protection for anonymity;[29] and in *Feiner* v *New York*, the US Supreme Court held that the state abridges speech if it fails to give a speaker reasonable police protection from a hostile audience.[30] In *United States* v *Hall*, it was held that a mere 'omission to protect' may amount to 'denying ... equal protection.'[31]

The Supreme Court of Canada has held on several occasions that in determining whether any given law has violated the *Charter* in general, and the right to equality in particular, the Court must assess the impact of the law upon the complainant, in addition to the content and purpose of the law. As Dickson CJC ruled in *R* v *Big M Drug Mart Ltd*:

> In my view, both purpose and effect are relevant in determining constitutionality; *either* an unconstitutional purpose *or an unconstitutional effect* can invalidate legislation. All legislation is animated by an object the Legislature intends to achieve. This object is realised through the impact produced by the operation and application of the legislation. Purpose and effect respectively, in the sense of the legislation's object and its ultimate impact, are clearly linked, if not indivisible. Intended and actual effects have often been looked to for guidance in assessing the legislation's object and thus, its validity.[32] (*R* v *Big M Drug Mart Ltd* (1985), 18 DLR (4th) 321, at p 350) [Emphasis added.].

Thus, the *Charter* does apply where an avoidable omission is seen to result in discriminatory effect.

The Principle of Duty

The repeal of the Act calls into question the reneging of a state obligation. There is a duty upon the government to pass legislation aimed at preventing or eliminating the causes of discrimination. There are numerous legal principles that will anchor this doctrine of a duty.

No useful discussion of this subject can reasonably be explored without recalling the following dictum of Wilson JSC in *McKinney* v *University of Guelph*:

> It has been argued by the respondents as well as by some of the interveners that this limit upon the reach of the Code does not offend the Charter because the province was under no obligation to provide any protection against discrimination in the first place. They say that absent such an obligation there is no room for constitutional scrutiny of the state's failure to go far enough in legislating human rights protection. It is not self-evident to me that government could not be found to be in breach of the Charter for failing to act. Whether the Constitution is implicated when the state fails to do something is a question which has plagued the American courts for many years. Indeed, Laurence Tribe has commented that it is precisely when the state has not acted that the court is called upon to make the most difficult determinations regarding the scope of the Constitution: see *Constitutional Choices* (Cambridge 1985) at pp. 246 et seq. Since this is not an instance where the province has completely failed to act, we are happily relieved from deciding such a difficult question on these appeals, and I refrain from doing so. I do, however, consider it axiomatic that once government decides to provide protection it must do so in a non-discriminatory manner. It seems clear to me that in this instance the province has failed to provide even-handed protection. The contention that the Charter has no application in this circumstance must therefore be emphatically rejected: see *Re Blainey and Ontario Hockey Association* (1986), 54 O.R. (2d) 513 (C.A.). (*McKinney* v *University of Guelph* (1990) 76 DLR (4th) 545 at pp 624*g*—625*b*).

It is instructive that this question of duty is one that has vexed American Courts since the Fourteenth Amendment to their Constitution in June 1866, and vexes them still. If the American Courts have still not put this issue to rest, and if such eminent American jurists as Professor Laurence Tribe are still suggesting the existence of such a duty, it surely must seem quite presumptuous of Canadian judges to be seen to have already dismissed—in a few short *obiter dicta*, in a few years of their experience with the *Charter*—the idea of the existence of such a duty.

On proper consideration of all the theories of law available, it would seem that there is indeed a duty upon the government to make all its best and reasonable efforts, in good faith, with the view to eliminating the causes of discrimination.

The Meaning of Right

An appreciation of the principle of duty herein contemplated must include consideration of the characterisation of the jural notions entrenched in the *Canadian Charter of Rights and Freedoms*. The first thing to consider in this regard is the essence of the title, Charter of Rights *and* Freedoms. There is no reason to suppose that that the drafters of the *Charter* would give the document a tautological title. It must be presumed instead that the drafters of the *Charter* recognised that the notion of 'right' has a meaning essentially different from that of 'freedom'.

The term 'right' refers to an interest recognised and protected by the law, respect for which is a *duty*, and disregard of which is a wrong. Every *right* has a correlative *duty* which will facilitate that right. The duty to facilitate a right is upon the person against whom a right is claimed (Paton, 1972; Harding, 1989). 'Freedom' means the ability to act without hindrance or restraint. 'Freedom' lacks the same jural correlative of *duty* which 'right' enjoys (Paton, 1972:291). When interpreting sections of the *Charter*, the Court must bear these distinctions in mind in order to remain systematically sensitive to the context and purpose of the particular language of any provision of the *Charter* (see Paton, 1972:291). The constitutional prohibition against discrimination and the provision for equal protection and equal benefit of the law are in the nature of a 'right.' As a 'right' then, there is a correlative duty on someone else to ensure that the beneficiaries of the right do in fact enjoy that right. S 15(1) of the Canadian *Charter* has been declared by the Court of Appeal for Ontario -- and noted with approval at the Supreme Court of Canada -- as "a compendious expression of a *positive right* to equality in both the *substance* and the administration of the law. It is an all-encompassing right *governing all legislative action*"[33] [emphasis added]. As a 'compendious expression of a positive right,' s 15 of the Canadian *Charter*, it must be noted, contains no word of limitation, excluding a duty (upon the state) as the jural correlative of the positive right to equal protection of the law.

Although this may not have been so clearly articulated by Canadian Courts, especially in the context of s 15, there have been other contexts of *Charter* application where the Courts have implicitly recognised the existence of a correlative duty on the state to facilitate or actualise *rights* guaranteed by the *Charter*. For instance, s 10(b) guarantees to the citizen, first, the *right* to retain and instruct counsel, and, secondly, the *right* to be informed of the right to retain and instruct counsel. Section 10(b) does *not* speak literally in terms of any 'duty' on the state to inform the citizen of the right to retain and instruct counsel. However, consider first that the existence of a right imports the existence of a correlative duty on somebody else to facilitate that right; and, second, that the state is the entity in the closest jural position to facilitate a citizen's right to be informed of the right to retain and instruct counsel. The Supreme Court of Canada in *R* v *Brydges* and *R* v *Bartles* exposed the duty on the state to facilitate that right. In this connection, the Court has held that the right in question also extends to the right to be informed of the existence of legal aid and duty counsel where they are available.[34]

In recognising that there is a correlative of duty to the 'rights' guaranteed in s 15, the Court would have been interpreting s 15 in a manner which involves more than simply adding judicial gloss as if it were dealing with the equivalent of ordinary legislation. Proper interpretation of s 15 requires more. It 'will establish what the legislature can or *must* do under the Constitution thereby constraining its powers'[emphasis added] (*Miron* v *Trudel* (1995), 124 DLR (4th) 693 (SCC) at pp 701*e*—*g* and 718*f*).

Where There is a Right There is a Remedy

Apart from the jurisprudential postulation of duty as a correlative of right, the common law has traditionally recognised that wherever there is a right, there will be a remedy. This is traditionally expressed in the phrase *ubi jus ibi remedium,* wherein remedy is the means by which the violation of a right is prevented, redressed, or compensated. Thus, as s 15 of the *Charter* has guaranteed the right to equality and freedom from discrimination, the state must do its best to remedy the lot of people who have traditionally been discriminated against. The Supreme Court of Canada recognised, in *Action travail des femmes* v *CNR*, that in any program of employment equity there cannot be a radical dissociation of 'remedy' and 'prevention'. Indeed there is no prevention without some form of remedy (*Action travail des femmes* v *CNR* (1987), 40 DLR (4th) 193 (SCC) at 212.).

A principle which is related to the *ubi jus* principle is encapsulated in the phrase *ubi aliquid conceditur, concenditur et id sine quo res ipsa esse non potest* [where anything is granted, that is also granted without which the thing itself is not able to exist]. Thus, where s 15 of the *Charter* has guaranteed a right to equality and freedom from discrimination for people traditionally discriminated against, there is also a duty on the state to actualise such a right for its intended beneficiaries. Considering then that it is only the government that can give citizens equal protection and equal benefit of the law, the duty to afford that right will clearly lie with the government.

Furthermore, the right to equal protection and equal benefit of the law is a right 'guaranteed.' S 1 of the *Charter* reads; "The *Canadian Charter of Rights and Freedoms* guarantees the rights and freedoms set out in it subject only to such reasonable limits prescribed by law as can be demonstrably justified in a free and democratic society." The verb 'guarantee' imports an undertaking "with respect to (a contract, the performance of a legal act, etc.) that it shall be duly carried out; ... *hence* to assure the existence or persistence of ...'. 'To engage to do something; to warrant or ensure that something will happen or has happened" (The Concise Oxford English Dictionary).

Duty Imposed by International Law

Under various international treaties it is recognised that "[a]ll persons are equal before the law and are entitled, without discrimination, to the equal protection of the law. In this respect, the law shall prohibit any discrimination *and guarantee* to all persons equal and *effective protection* against discrimination on any ground such as race, colour, sex,... national origin, ... or other status" [emphasis added].[35] Canada and Ontario are bound by international law to take necessary steps, in accordance with Canadian constitutional processes, to adopt such legislative or other measures as may be necessary to give effect to the rights recognised in international law.[36]

Apart from the province of Ontario under the Rae Government, other jurisdictions and governments in the common law world have legislated employment equity in their respective jurisdictions. In Canada, the federal Government passed employment equity legislation in 1986. In 1995, the Canada *Employment Equity Act* was amended to make it stronger. In the U.S., the federal government has peremptory employment equity programs. In 1995 a Presidential Review Commission recommended continued implementation of such programs.[37] In Australia, the federal government commenced legislated employment equity in 1986 with the passage of the *Affirmative Action (Equal Employment Opportunity for Women) Act*, 1986. A year later, they passed a more comprehensive statute called the *Equal Employment Opportunity (Commonwealth Authorities) Act*, 1987. This latter statute was more comprehensive in the sense that, quite like the Ontario *Employment Equity Act*, it extended the protection of employment equity legislation to other 'designated groups.'[38]

The community of nations in general, and the respective federal governments of Canada, Australia and the United States in particular, see a need to employ the force of legislation in order to advance the principles of employment equity for those members of society who have traditionally suffered the scourge of employment discrimination.

Duty Arising from Power

In law, a duty may arise simply from the enjoyment of power. It is part of the law in Canada as well as other Commonwealth countries that power may be coupled with a duty to exercise that power, if proper regard is had to the nature of the thing empowered to be done, the object for which the power is conferred, the conditions under which the power is to be exercised, or the circumstances of the person(s) intended to be benefited by the exercise of power. Some of the considerations that have been held as coupling a power with a duty are as follows:

- that the beneficiaries of the exercise of power would have been exposed to prejudice and hazard; or
- that the thing to be done is for the public benefit or in advancement of public justice.

This is a principle well recognised in common law.[39] In Ontario, the power to provide equal protection of the law lies with the Legislative Assembly. The duty to use this power for the benefit of those who have not been enjoying equal protection of the law must necessarily lie with the Ontario Legislative Assembly.

A Duty Arising from the Rule of Law

According to the preamble to the *Canadian Charter of Rights and Freedoms*, Canadian society is founded upon principles that recognise the rule of law. When s 15 of the *Charter* speaks of equal *protection* of the law, it contemplates equal protection according to the rule of law. The rule of law emanates, in turn, from the idea of the social contract. By this contract, individuals yield to the state the right to take the law into their own hands.[40] Thus, the state enjoys the power to govern the individuals, as well as the moral and legal duty to make laws in order to protect the individuals who have yielded to the state the right to protect themselves as they see fit.[41]

In connection with this theory of violation arising from a duty, there is a need to address a line of dictum that appears to be gaining currency among some Canadian judges. In *Thibaudeau* v *Canada*, L'Heureux-Dubé JSC stated, "[Section] 15 of the Charter does not impose upon governments the obligation to take positive actions to remedy the symptoms of systemic inequality" (1995, 2 SCR 627 at 655).

This has led some to assert that 'the Supreme Court of Canada' has determined that s 15 of the *Charter* imposes no duty on the state to take action in an effort to eliminate systemic discrimination[42]. This view of the law arises out of an improper analysis of s 15 of the *Charter* and of Madam Justice L'Heureux-Dubé's dictum in *Thibaudeau* v *Canada*. First, the dictum was given in the context of a hypothetical scenario she posed in her dissenting judgement. Second, the question of whether s 15 raises a duty does not appear to have been canvassed by the parties in that case. In this regard, therefore, her remark must be seen as *obiter*, and not the judgement of the Court. As has been said by the House of Lords, "[I]t is not everything that falls from a noble and learned Lord in advising the House [of Lords] which is to be considered as the opinion of the House."[43] There is a stronger reason for this stricture to apply to *obiter dicta* of the justices of the Supreme Court of Canada made in the course of their dissenting judgements. And, to the extent that there is as yet no case in the Supreme Court in which the parties have canvassed the question of whether s 15 raises a duty in the state to eliminate the causes, or indeed symptoms, of discrimination, any dictum from that Court on that point must also be seen as *obiter*. This is in accord with a recent pronouncement of L'Heureux-Dubé JSC herself in *R* v *O'Connor* (1995, 103 CCC (3d) 1 at p 49) where she said that certain of her colleagues' pronouncements on matters not canvassed before the Court were *obiter*.[44]

Quite apart from the value in *stare decisis* of L'Heureux-Dubé's *obiter* in *Thibaudeau* v *Canada*, it is also imperative to note that analysis of her language should not lead to the observation that there is no duty on the state to eliminate systemic discrimination. What she did say is that there is no duty to eliminate the "symptoms of systemic inequality." This could not easily be seen as saying that there is no duty on the state to eliminate the *causes* of systemic inequality, nor indeed of discrimination itself.

EQUALITY, DEMOCRACY AND THE POLITICS OF SELF-INTEREST

The repeal of the *Employment Equity Act* of Ontario and the constitutional challenge of that repeal raise a very important question. The Act was repealed by an elected government that was voted into power by a majority of the electorate in part because they had promised to repeal the Act once in office. These questions then arise: On what authority must the Courts reverse the will of the electorate? Is this lawsuit not contrary to the principles of democracy?

The answer is no. It is perfectly in accordance with the constitutional cohabitation of the rule of law and democracy that certain actions of the majority be challenged by politically weak and vulnerable minorities in order to restrain democracy from breeding oppression or despotism for the politically weak and vulnerable.

Democracy

The end of democracy is to give political power to the majority in a civilised, non-violent and acceptable way. Modern society, however, is forever wary of two chief evils associated with political power: the usurpation of political power and the abuse of it. To a large extent, the democratic process solves the former problem, but not the latter, particularly when the majority and the minority are wedged against each other in politics of self-interest.

As a means to the acquisition of power, the democratic process provides inadequate checks on the abuses in the exercise of that power. This is especially the case when the victims of such abuses are politically weak and vulnerable minorities. Hence there is a need to restrain the excesses of democracy that tend to be oppressive to weak and vulnerable minorities.

Therein lies the role of the Rule of Law. It keeps democracy within proper bounds. The contemporary notion of the rule of law emphasises the importance of the principles that the exercise of the discretionary power of rule-making and adjudication should be controlled by impartial tribunals. These are to operate in the light of stated general principles designed to ensure that the power should be exercised fairly and within the limits prescribed by law (*Fontana Dictionary of Modern Thought,* 1988: 466).

Understandably, the principles of the rule of law emphasise the need to maintain the notion of equality through legislation and adjudication. As Rousseau wrote, "It is precisely because the force of circumstances tends continually to destroy equality that the force of legislation should always tend to its maintenance" (Rousseau, quoted with approval in Abella, 1984:193).

The rule of law operates best in a society where there is separation of powers between the different branches of government; and where there are checks and balances between those branches of government, in order to guarantee individual rights and freedom.[45] Hence the role of the Courts becomes all the more significant, in that they uphold the most fundamental law of the land.

Thus, in a battle over equality between members of the majority and members of the minority, and where there is a challenge to the will of the majority to roll back legislative schemes that were designed to prevent discrimination and the causes of inequality, things cannot be left on the altar of electoral power. As Henderson CJ of the US District Court of the Northern District of California wrote recently in his order temporarily restraining the operation of California's anti-affirmative action Proposition 209 (a case very similar to the Employment Equity case in Ontario):

> In a case of this nature, the issue is not whether [the] Court should reject or respect the 'will of the people.' Rather, the issue is whether the challenged enactment complies with the laws of our Constitution and Bill of Rights [*Coalition for Economic Equity, et al* v *Pete Wilson, et al*, unrptd No C 96 4024 TEH, per Henderson CJ, TRO delivered on 27 November 1996].

Similar sentiments have been expressed in the past by justices of the Canadian Supreme Court and of the Supreme Court of the United States. In the Canadian case of *Collins* v *R*, for instance, Lamer JSC, endorsed the idea that the Courts have a duty, under the *Canadian Charter of Rights and Freedoms*, to protect the politically weak and vulnerable minorities from "the shifting winds of public passion."[46]

In *R* v *Edwards Books & Art Ltd*, Dickson CJC cautioned that in interpreting and applying the *Charter*, the Courts must ensure that the *Charter* does not simply become an instrument of better situated individuals to roll back legislation which has as its object the improvement of the condition of less advantaged persons.[47] This caution is as applicable to the exercise of legislative power found elsewhere in the Canadian Constitution as it is to the purported exercise of the *Charter*-guaranteed rights and freedoms of those 'better situated individuals'. It must be seen as unacceptable for the better situated individuals to do through the backdoor what they are forbidden to do through the front door. In other words, it must not be acceptable that better situated individuals may negate legislation ameliorative of conditions of the disadvantaged by simply electing political surrogates who then use their legislative powers to roll back legislation that ameliorates the conditions of the disadvantaged, because this legislation was seen by the better-situated persons as resulting in reverse discrimination against them. It has been held by the Supreme Court of the United States that "one aspect of the judiciary's role under the Equal Protection Clause is to protect 'discrete and insular minorities' from majoritarian prejudice or indifference."[48]

All these strictures are in harmony with the Constitution of Canada which, apart from being the supreme law of the land (together with its guarantee of the right to equality without discrimination), also declares that Canada is a nation founded on principles that recognise the Rule of Law (see the preamble to the *Canadian Charter of Rights and Freedoms*). Thus, the Canadian Courts have begun in recent times to recognise fully their role with respect to checks and balances.

The Canadian Compromise

In the Canadian constitutional arena, however, the idea of checks and balances is limited. There are instances where, although rights and freedoms may be infringed, the Courts are constitutionally barred from adjudicating, as well as instances when they ought to defer to the elected officials. This is seen in s 33 of the *Charter* as well as in s 1. This is a

Canadian compromise devised, perhaps, to soothe Canadian legislatures when the *Charter* was introduced in 1982 to curtail their sovereignty.[49]

Under s 33 of the *Charter*, the legislatures have a power to 'inoculate' their statutes against constitutional challenge in Courts, even if such statutes violate certain rights guaranteed under the *Charter*—including the right to equality. A legislature can do this by the simple process of expressly declaring in the statute that the statute must operate notwithstanding the provisions of s 2 nor of ss 7 to 15 of the *Charter*. This manner of 'inoculation' effectively immunises the statute in question from challenge on grounds of violation of the rights guaranteed in s 2 and ss 7 to 15 of the *Charter*.

Apart from the legislative preserve of s 33, the Courts will also refrain from interfering with a statute or other government action, where such statute or action is seen to violate *Charter* rights or freedoms, but the violation is a legal prescription that is reasonably justified in a free and democratic society. To achieve judicial deference to Bill 8 under s 1, however, there are certain considerations that must be brought to bear on the adjudication. First, there are certain yardsticks by which the Courts have traditionally measured violation of rights as justifiable or not under s 1. In order that the limitation of any guaranteed right or freedom may be held as reasonably and demonstrably justified, the state must prove the following:

a) There was a legitimate social objective to the measure that violated a right or freedom.
b) That the legitimate social objective in question is of sufficient importance to warrant over-riding a right or freedom guaranteed by the constitution. The standard must be high in order to ensure that objectives that are trivial or discordant with the principles integral to a free and democratic society do not gain s 1 protection.
c) That the means chosen to achieve the objective are proportional to the objective sought in the sense that;
   i) the measures adopted must have been carefully designed to achieve the objective in question; they must not have been arbitrary, unfair or based on irrational considerations; they must be rationally connected to the objective;
   ii) even if rationally connected to the objective as in (b)(i) above, the means should impair the right or freedom in question in as little a manner as possible; and
   iii) there must be a proportionality between the *effects* (of the measures which are responsible for limiting the right or freedom guaranteed by the *Charter*) and the objective that has been identified as of pressing and substantial: in other words, there must be a proportionality between the discriminatory effects of the impugned legislation and the salutary effects of the distinction.
   iv) (*R* v *Oakes* (1986), 24 CCC (3d) 321 (SCC) at pp 348—349; *Dagenais* v *CBC* (1994), 120 DLR (4th) 12 (SCC) at pp 45*a*—46*f*.).

The Tory government should find it difficult to validate Bill 8 under either s 33 or s 1 of the *Charter*. In the first instance, Bill 8 does not contain a 'notwithstanding clause' for purposes of s 33. With respect to s.1, there is no rationale for the total repeal of the *Employment Equity Act*. The government said that they had to repeal the Act because they said that it contained quotas, legislated against merit and entrenched reverse discrimination. Section 1 would require the government to prove that amendment would have been insufficient to solve these problems, if indeed the Act had been as flawed as the government made it out to be. As has been noted above even critics of employment equity programs concede that the only problematic aspects of the programs are their requirements of goals (see for example Finkle and Strom, 1990). They accept as proper the other aspects of the programs.

Second, where politically weak and vulnerable minorities mount a challenge to a statute or other governmental measure which accords with the will of the majority, an analysis of such a measure under s 1 must be done in such a manner as to give as much importance to the phrase 'free society' as to the phrase '... democratic society', because the limitation of s 1 relates to the values of 'a free *and* democratic society.' In other words, s 1 analysis cannot be done solely from the perspective of the majority (who want to enjoy unlimited all the advantages of the democratic process), at the expense of politically weak and vulnerable minorities (who are entitled to enjoy a full measure of freedom in the society in which they live). In these circumstances, therefore, s 1 calls for a delicate task of balancing these competing values. The need for this balancing, it must be noted, has not escaped the Supreme Court of Canada. As Dickson CJC wrote in *R* v *Oakes*:

> It is important to observe at the outset that s. 1 has two functions: first, it constitutionally guarantees the rights and freedoms set out in the provisions which follow; and, second, it states explicitly the exclusive justificatory criteria (outside of s 33 of the *Constitution Act*, 1982) against which limitations on those rights and freedoms must be measured. Accordingly, any s 1 inquiry must be premised on an understanding that the impugned limit violates constitutional rights and freedoms -- rights and freedoms which are part of the supreme law of Canada. As stated in *Singh et al* v *Minister of Employment and Immigration*, *supra*, at p 218: '... it is important to remember that the courts are conducting this inquiry in light of a commitment to uphold the rights and freedoms set out in the other sections of the Charter.'
>
> A second contextual element of interpretation of s 1 is provided by the words 'free and democratic society'. Inclusion of these words as the final standard of justification for limits on rights and freedoms refers the Court to the very purpose for which the Charter was originally entrenched in the Constitution: Canadian society is to be free and democratic. The Court must be guided by the values and principles essential to a free and democratic society which I believe embody, to name but a few, respect for the inherent dignity of the human person, commitment to social justice and equality, accommodation of a wide variety of beliefs, respect for cultural and group identity, and faith in social and political institutions which enhance the participation of individuals and groups in society. The underlying values and principles of a free and democratic society are the genesis of the rights and freedoms guaranteed by the Charter and the ultimate standard against which a limit on a right or freedom must be shown, despite its effect, to be reasonable and demonstrably justified (R v *Oakes*, (1986), pp. 345-346).

It is quite clear that the *Employment Equity* Act was motivated by the following values, among others: respect for the inherent dignity of the human person; commitment to social justice and equality; accommodation of a wide variety of beliefs; and respect for cultural and group identity. Given that the chief objectives of the Act were, among other things: a) to give members of the designated groups faith in the social and political institutions of Ontario, and b) to enhance their participation as individuals and groups in the Ontario society, the onus should be on the government to convince the Court that the repeal of the Act, in the circumstances of Bill 8, are entirely in accord with the foregoing values identified by Dickson CJC in *R* v *Oakes*. This would indeed be very difficult for the government to establish.

CONCLUSION

From the point of view of equity and good conscience, a state of darkness shrouds employment practices in Ontario. This much was essentially conceded by the Harris Government when, in the context of the *Ferrel* case, they acknowledged that '[d]iscrimination is a significant problem in both Canada and the United States.'[50] As this has been the state of affairs for many years, there is little doubt that the modern Ontario society has grown accustomed to this environment of social darkness, an environment that is prone to unjust relations and practices rooted in discrimination. This environment, it must be stressed, can never be excused by the simple argument that the environment is dark; all are handicapped by it; so there is not much that can be done at the moment to improve the circumstances of those who are disadvantaged by it. Nor may it be soundly argued that change must be left to the slow process of nature—from darkness to dawn and light—by which one hopes for a better view. These arguments fail for a number of reasons including the following. First, the darkness here is self-induced and wilful blindness is no excuse. Furthermore, even a natural state of darkness may not excuse a defendant from the consequences of a wrongful act where the defendant could easily have afforded herself or himself the light (s)he needed to operate safely.

The Ontario Legislature in 1993 passed the Ontario *Employment Equity Act*. The Act was designed as a beacon of light which would enable Ontario employers to see more clearly the quality of merit in women, aboriginal people, people with disabilities and members of racial minority groups, who have for generations endured "chronic adverse treatment" (Lepofsky, 1993:15) As such, the Act constitutes a classic instance of equal protection or benefit of the law for those in need. This is the essence of s 15 of the *Canadian Charter of Rights and Freedoms.*

In view of a tradition of employment inequity, the success of an employment equity initiative depends on proper education (Lepofsky, 1993:15). No one is in a better position to carry out this function of education than the government and those who aspire to govern. Government acts become vulnerable to constitutional scrutiny where the government embarks upon the task of educating people with a view to undermining an initiative informed by a motive to give people their full measure of a constitutional right. This is particularly so where this mis-education is motivated by a desire to mobilise popular sentiment against the constitutionally-informed initiative, in order to enable an easy abolition of that initiative. This was the fate of the employment equity laws of Ontario.[51] The focus of any constitutional scrutiny in the circumstances will not only be on the actual repeal of employment equity legislation, but the manner and form must be equally questioned.

Chile Eboe-Osuji LLB, LLM has been called to the bars of Ontario, British Columbia and Nigeria, and was lead counsel in Ferrel et al v Attorney General of Ontario. He has been serving as prosecution counsel at the United Nations International Criminal Tribunal for Rwanda since 1997. *Mr Eboe-Osuji would like to thank Mark Hart Esq, his co-counsel in Ferrel. He also wishes to thank the many scholars and lawyers who expressed very useful thoughts on some of the arguments which form aspects of this paper. They include but are not limited to Professor Peter Hogg, QC, Professor Bruce Ryder, Professor Juanita Westmoreland-Traore, Ms Judith Keene, Dr Mary-Ellen Symonds, and Ms Nisha Naidoo.*

Elizabeth McIsaac MA has taught courses on Employment Equity and Human Rights at the community college level in Ontario. She is currently involved in community advocacy initiatives around issues related to access and equity for foreign-trained professionals in Ontario.

NOTES

[1] Progressive Conservative Party, 'Mike Harris and Equal Opportunity' News Release [Toronto, 5 May 1995]. The *Employment Equity Act* of Ontario is colloquially known as Bill 79.

[2] CBC-TV, short documentary on Marylin Ferrel, evening news 25 November 1996.

[3] Ministry of Citizenship, Culture and Recreation, 'Top Ten List of Questions for Job Quotas Repeal'. Answer to Question 2.

[4] See for example Premier Harris's statements in Assembly on 4 December 1995: Ontario Legislative Assembly, *Hansard* (Toronto, 4 December 1995) p 1181.

[5] Ontario Legislative Assembly, *Hansard* (Toronto, 4 October 1995) p 113.

[6] Strictly speaking, however, in Canada a 'bill' is only a draft of a proposed piece of legislation, which upon receiving Royal Assent, becomes an 'Act' of the legislature.

[7] See The Ontario *Employment Equity Act*, Preamble (1993); see generally Westmoreland-Traoré (1992); Lewis (1992); Abella (1984); Ontario Employment Equity Commission (1991); Canadian Human Rights Commission (1996); Steele (1995); Statistics Canada/Kelly (1995); Human Resources Canada (1995); Social Planning Council of Metropolitan Toronto/Henry and Ginzberg (1985); and, Social Planning Council of Metropolitan Toronto/Billingsley and Muszynski (1985)

[8] See *Action travailes des femmes* v *CNR* (1987), 40 DLR (4th) 193 (SCC), at pp 214-216.

[9] See *Blainey* v *Ontario Hockey Association* (1986), 54 OR (2d) 513 (Ont C A) at p 526*c*; leave to appeal denied (1986), 58 OR (2d) 274 (SCC).

[10] *Re Manitoba Council of Health Care Unions & ors* v *Bethesda Hospital & ors* (1992), 88 DLR (4th) 60 at p 67*h* [Man QB].

[11] *R* v *Edwards Books & Art Ltd* (1986), 35 DLR (4th) 1 at 49. See also *McKinney* v *University of Guelph* (1990) 76 DLR (4th) 545 at p 616*a-b*.

[12] see Affidavit of Michael Smith, paras 11 to 18—tab M of the Application Record (vol..2) , and Affidavit of Rafia Haniff, paras 13 and 15—tab K of the Application Record (vol.1).

[13] see affidavit of Michael Smith, paras 11 to 18—tab M of the Application Record (vol.2). In this connection, the Court of Appeal for Ontario has taken judicial notice of the 'influence of negative stereotyping on all of the citizens of Ontario' especially given the fact that the media helps create out of our society a 'global village': *R* v *Wilson* (1996), 29 OR (3d) 97 at 102*a* (Ont CA, *per* McMurtry CJO).

[14] A better understanding of the elements of a quota system will be apparent upon an examination of the American cases of *Richmond* v *J A Croson Co* 488 US 469 (1989) [USSC] and *Regents of the University of California* v *Bakke*, 438 US 265 (1978) [USSC]. It is clear from these cases that quota involves setting aside for a group a definite percentage of a total figure. See also *Fullilove* v *Klutznick*, 448 US 448 (1980) (US SC) at pp 475-478; *Richmond* v *J A Croson*, 488 US 469 (1989) (US SC); and *Regents of the University of California* v *Bakke*, 438 US 265 (1978) at pp 320 and 412—421.

[15] See also City of Toronto: *City of Toronto Equal Opportunity 1982-83 Review* (Toronto, 6 December 1984) 'goals and timetables' and 'quotas' as defined in paras 4 and 6, at p 5, and 'Myth 1' at p 2; and s 33 generally, and especially s 33(1)(e) and s 33(2), of the *Canadian Employment Equity Act*, 1995.

[16] S 12(1)(f) of the *Employment Equity Act*, 1993; ss 18 and 19 of *O Reg 390/94*; Lepofsky (1993:4); Westmoreland-Traoré (1992:51-52, 193 -194, 214 and 255); s 33 generally of the *Canadian Employment Equity Act*, 1995.

[17] *Action travail des femmes* v *CNR* (1987), 40 DLR (4th) 193 (SCC).

[18] See s 33 of the Canada *Employment Equity Act*, as amended in December 1995.

[19] Para 2 of the Preamble—and First Principle at s 2—of the *Employment Equity Act*, 1993; Lepofsky (1993:6-9); Abella, 'Employment Equity—Implications for Industrial Relations' [Kingston, 1987] see pp 2 to 3.

[20] See House of Commons Canada, *Employment Equity: a Commitment to Merit*, p 5; also see generally Conference Board of Canada/Taylor, *Dimensions of Diversity in Canadian Business* [Ottawa, 1995]; Ondrack and Fletcher, 'The Impact of a Voluntary Program of Employment and Pay Equity on Job Satisfaction and Commitment Among Female and Male Employees' (Toronto, 1987), p 11; The White House, *Affirmative Action Review*: Report to President Clinton (Washington, 1995) especially at p 87.

[21] House of Commons Canada, *Employment Equity: a Commitment to Merit*, p 7; see also 'Study Finds Little Evidence of Reverse Discrimination] *Washington Post* [31 March 1995]; see generally The White House,

Affirmative Action Review: Report to President Clinton [Washington, 1995] p 37; Gray, 'Harris's pledges attracted Middle Ontario' *Globe and Mail* [9 June 1995].

[22] Affidavit of Michael Smith, paras 11 to 18—tab M of the Application Record (vol.2) , and Affidavit of Rafia Haniff, paras 13 and 15—tab K of the Application Record (vol 1).

[23] *Donoghue* v *Stevenson* [1932] AC 562 at p 580; and Flemings, *The Law of Torts* (8th edn, 1992) pp 146-149.

[24] See *eg* s 11(g) of the *Canadian Charter of Rights and Freedoms*; see also David Selbourne, *The Principle of Duty* (London, 1994), paras 237 and 243.

[25] *Schacter* v *Canada* (1990), 66 DLR (4th) 635 (Fed Ct of App) at pp 640*g*—646*h*.

[26] *Haig and Birch* v *Canada* (1992), 9 OR (3d) 495 (Ont CA) esp at p 506*a*—*b*.

[27] *Blainey* v *Ontario Hockey Association* (1986), 54 OR (2d) 513 (Ont C A); leave to appeal denied (1986), 58 OR (2d) 274 (SCC).

[28] *Lynch* v *United States*, 189 F 2d 476 (5th Cir), at 479-480, *cert denied* 342 US 831 (1951).

[29] *NAACP v Alabama, ex rel Patterson*, 357 US 449 at pp 462-463 (1958).

[30] *Feiner* v *New York*, 340 US 315 at pp 325-327 (1951).

[31] *United States* v *Hall*, 26 Fed Cas 79 at 81(CCSD Ala 1871) (No 15,282).

[32] See also *Andrews* v *Law Society of British Columbia* (1989), 56 DLR (4th) 1 (SCC) at 18*c*; *Miron* v *Trudel* (1995), 124 DLR (4th) 693 (SCC) at pp 702*e*, 742*d & h* and 745*e*; *Egan* v *Canada* (1995), 124 DLR (4th) 609 (SCC) at pp 621*c*—*f*, 623*g*, 631*h*—632*b*, 635*a*—*c* and 646*g*.

[33] *Blainey* v *Ontario Hockey Association* (1986), 54 OR (2d) 513 (Ont C A) at p 524*e*; leave to appeal denied (1986), 58 OR (2d) 274 (SCC); see also *Andrews* v *Law Society of British Columbia* (1989), 56 DLR (4th) 385 (SCC) at 15*f*—*g*.

[34] *R* v *Brydges* (1990), 53 CCC (3d) 330 (SCC) at p 347 (*per* Lamer JSC as he then was); *R* v *Bartle* (1994), 92 CCC (3d) 289 at pp 301—302 (SCC).

[35] Article 26 of the *International Covenant on Civil and Political Rights*. See also articles 2, 5, 7 of the *International Convention on the Elimination of All Forms of Racial Discrimination*; and articles II and III of the *International Convention on the Elimination of All Forms of Discrimination against Women*.

[36] Article 2(2) of the *International Covenant on Civil and Political Rights*; articles 2, 5, 7 of the *International Convention on the Elimination of All Forms of Racial Discrimination*; Articles II and III of the *International Convention on the Elimination of All Forms of Discrimination against Women*. See also Cohen and Bayefsky, 'The *Canadian Charter of Rights and Freedoms* and Public International Law'(1983) 61 *Can Bar Rev* 265.

[37] The White House, *Affirmative Action Review*: Report to President Clinton [Washington, 1995].

[38] See ss 6 and 7 of *Equal Employment Opportunity (Commonwealth Authorities) Act*, 1987, whose long title is 'An Act to *require* certain Commonwealth authorities to promote equal opportunity in employment for *women and persons in designated groups* and for related purposes.' [Emphasis added.] According to the *Public Service Act*, 1922, Section 7(1) designated group members include: a)members of the Aboriginal race of Australia or persons who are descendants of indigenous inhabitants of the Torres Strait Islands; b)persons who have migrated to Australia and whose first language is a language other than English, and the children of such persons; c) persons who are physically or mentally disabled; and d) any other class of persons declared by the regulations to be a designated group for the purposes of this definition …

[39] See *Julius* v *Oxford (Bishop)* (1880) 5 App Cas 214 (HL) at pp 222—225 and 229—230; *Padfield* v *Minister of Agriculture* [1968] AC 997 (HL) at pp 1032—1033; *Bradley* v *Commonwealth* (1973) 128 CLR (HC Aust); *R* v *Wilkinton (Churchwardens)* (1729), 94 ER 155; *R* v *St Luke's Vestry, Chelsea* (1862) 1 B & S 903.

[40] Sir Ivor Jennings, *The Law and the Constitution*, (5th edition) pp 42-45. See also Rousseau, *The Social Contract or the Principles of Political Right* [Translated and Introduced by Christopher Betts] (Oxford, 1994) pp 45-61; Hobbes, *Leviathan*, [Introduced by Kenneth Minogue] (London, 1987 reprint) pp 63-66.

[41] Selbourne, *The Principle of Duty*, (London, 1994), paras 4, 20, 235, 237, 243 and 247

[42] See paragraph 75 of the Factum of the Attorney General of Ontario in *Ferrel & ors* v *Attorney General of Ontario*, Ontario Court (General Division) File No RE/6078/95. See also the endorsement of the interlocutory motion Judge in *Ferrel* v *Attorney-General of Ontario* dated 28-29 December 1995 [Ontario Court (General Division) File No RE/6078/95]; and *Masse* v *Ontario (Minister of Community and Social Services)* [1996] OJ No 363 at pp 66—67, Court File No 590/95, dated 8 February 1996.

[43] *Mersey Docks Trustee* v *Gibbs* [1866] LR 1 HL 93 at 127.

44 L'Heureux-Dubé JSC observed at paragraph 98 of her judgment:

> As a preliminary matter, it should be noted that the issue before us relates to the production of private records held by third parties. We are not concerned here with the extent of the Crown's obligation to disclose private records in its possession, or with the question whether privacy and equality interests may militate against such disclosure by the Crown. Although my colleagues Lamer CJ and Sopinka SCJ deal with these questions at great length in their reasons, I prefer not to pronounce on these issues as they do not arise in this appeal and were not argued before us. Any comment on these questions would be strictly obiter. On another occasions, the Supreme Court of Canada has refused to follow earlier pronouncements of the Court on an issue because such pronouncements were made in 'casual and indirect manner.'

See *Rothman* v *R* [1981] 1 SCR 640 at p 674), or because the pronouncements were made '[i]n the absence of a more definitive statement or a more extensive analysis of the issue …' (see *DeSousa* v *R* [1992] 2 SCR 944 at p 960). In other words, the earlier pronouncements were statements in the nature of mere *obiter dicta* (see Ehrcke, 'Stare Decisis' [1995] 53 *The Advocate* 847 at pp 854-855.)

45 "Montesquieu, Charles Louis de Secondat, Baron de la Brede et de," *Microsoft® Encarta® 96 Encyclopedia.* © 1993-1995

46 *Coalition for Economic Equity, et al* v *Pete Wilson, et al,* [unrptd No C 96 4024 TEH, per Henderson CJ, TRO delivered on 27 November 1996].

47 *R* v *Edwards Books & Art Ltd, supra,* p 49. See also *McKinney* v *University of Guelph*, *supra,* p 616*a—b*.

48 See *Richmond* v *J A Croson Co* 488 US 469 (1989) [USSC] at p 495. See also *United States* v *Carolene Products Co* 304 US 144 (1938) [USSC] at p 153 n 4.

49 For details of this discussion see Hogg, *Constitutional Law of Canada* 3rd edition [Toronto, Carswell, 1992] chapter 12.

50 Ondrack, paragraph 5 of Affidavit, Respondent's Application Record, vol 1, in *Ferrel & ors* v *A-G* [Ontario Court (General Division) File No RE/6078/95]. Ondrack was the Government's expert witness. Following his theme, counsel for the Attorney-General submitted in their factum that 'discrimination in society, be it in employment or other fields is a significant problem …'. [See paragraph 7(iii) of Statement of Fact and Law of the Respondent, The Attorney-General of Ontario in *Ferrel & ors* v *A-G* [Ontario Court (General Division) File No RE/6078/95].

51 *Ferrel et al v Attorney General of Ontario*, the case inspired by some of the thinking in this chapter was not auspicious in the Canadian Courts. Justice Dilks of the Superior Court of Ontario dismissed the constitutional challenge to the repeal of the Employment Equity Act: the Ontario Court of Appeal upheld his decision; and the Supreme Court of Canada denied leave to appeal the case to that court. Further details on the history of this case may be found at www.web.ca/~allforec. For all intents and purposes that is the end of the road for the case in Canada. There remains, however, one last forum for the applicants to make this case. That forum is the United Nations Human Rights Committee, any decision which it may render, contradicting the decision of the Canadian courts will not have the effect of reversing the decision of the Canadian Courts on the case. However, any such decision will be binding on Canada and Ontario at the international level, and failure to comply with it will be seen as a violation of international law.

REFERENCES

Abella, Rosalie. 1987. *Employment Equity: Implications for Industrial Relations*. Kingston: Industrial Relations Centre, Queen's University.

Abella, Rosalie. 1984. *Report of the Commission on Equality in Employment.* Ottawa: Supply and Services Canada.

Billingsley, Brenda, and Leon Muszynski. 1985. *No Discrimination Here?* Toronto: Social Planning Council of Metropolitan Toronto.

Bullock, Allan, and Oliver Stallybrass, eds. 1988. *Fontana Dictionary of Modern Thought*, 2nd Edition. London: Fontana Press.

Canadian Human Rights Commission. 1996. *Annual Report 1995*. Ottawa: The Commission.

Cohen, Maxwell and Anne F. Bayefsky. 1983. "The Canadian Charter of Rights and Freedoms and Public International Law." *Canadian Bar Review*, 61, March, 265 - 338.

Finkle, Peter, and Torsten Strom. 1990. "Affirmative Action, Natural Law and Justice." *Windsor Yearbook of Access to Justice*, Vol. 10, 79-101.

Gleckman, Howard, Tim Smart, Paula Dwyer, Troy Segal, and Joseph Weber. "Race in the Workplace: Is Affirmative Action Working?" *Business Week*, 8 July, 1991, 50-63.

Gray, John. "Voters give a firm no to more of the same." *The Globe and Mail*, 9 June, 1995, A1 and A10.

Harding, A.J. 1989. *Public Duties and Public Law*. Oxford: Clarendon Press.

Henry, Frances, and Effie Ginzberg. 1985. *Who Gets the Work? A Test of Racial Discrimination in Employment*. Toronto: Social Planning Council of Metropolitan Toronto.

Hogg, Peter. 1992. *Constitutional Law of Canada*. 3rd Edition. Toronto: Carswell.

House of Commons. Canada. Parliament. Standing Committee on Human Rights and the Status of Disabled Persons. 1995. *Employment Equity: A Commitment to Merit. A Report of the Standing Committee on Human Rights and the Status of Disabled Persons*. Ottawa: Canada Communication Group.

Human Resources Development Canada. *Towards Equity*. Ottawa-Hull, 1995.

Kelly, Karen. 1995. "Visible Minorities: a Diverse Group." *Canadian Social Trends*. Ottawa: Statistics Canada, Summer. http://www.statcan.ca/english/ads/11-008-XPE/vismin.html

Lepofsky, M. David. 1993. "Understanding the Concept of Employment Equity - Myths and Misconceptions." *Canadian Labour Law Journal*, Summer, 1-15.

Lewis, Stephen. 1992. *Report on Race Relations in Ontario*. Toronto: Government of Ontario.

Ontario. *Employment Equity Act*. S.O. 1993, c.35.

Ontario Employment Equity Commission. "A Look at the 1991 Employment Equity Populations of Toronto CMA (and other major Ontario cities)".

Ontario. Office of the Employment Equity Commissioner. 1992, *Opening Doors: A Report of the Employment Equity Consultations*. Toronto: Ministry of Citizenship.

Paton, George W., and David P. Derham. 1972. *A Textbook of Jurisprudence*. 4th Edition. Oxford: Clarendon Press.

Smith, Daryl G. "Faculty Diversity When Jobs Are Scarce: Debunking the Myths." *The Chronicle of Higher Education*, September 6, 1996, B3.

Steele, Scott. 1995. "Women at Work: Room to Improve: A New Study Shows the Continuing Gender Gap." *Macleans*. August 21, Vol. 108, No. 34, 28-29.

Toughill, Kelly. "Quashing of 'Quota Law' a Defining Moment: Job equity bites the dust as Tories deliver on promise that won the hearts of voters." *The Toronto Star*, December 16, 1995, E1 and E4.

Stephanopoulos, George, and Christopher Edley, Jr. 1995. *Affirmative Action Review: Report to the President*. Washington, D.C.: White House.

Wallace, James. "White Males Face 1st Layoffs: NDP equity hirings protected." The *Toronto Sun*, March, 17, 1995, p. 4.

CHAPTER 7

HARISH C. JAIN AND C.S. VENKATA RATNAM

GENDER EQUALITY IN INDIA

INTRODUCTION

India has, since ancient times, held its women in high esteem. Hindus, who constitute the majority community, typically pray to the goddess Saraswati for knowledge and learning, goddess Lakshmi for wealth and goddess Durga for the strength to fight evil forces. Indian women have excelled in various walks of life, including as saints (Meera Bai) and warriors (Rani Jhansi and Rani Rudrama Devi). Swami Vivekananda, one of the greatest exponents of Hindu culture, exhorted that a civilisation is known by the manner in which it treats its women.

India is a dominantly patriarchal society. Still, some states like Kerala in southern India and several states in northern India, which are advanced states in the country in terms of UNDP's Human Development, are matriarchal societies.

Mythologically, women enjoyed a special status in India. Constitutionally there is no discrimination against women. Yet, demographic, social and economic indicators point out that women continue to be disadvantaged in terms of their access to education and employment. Attitudes about gender roles, social belief systems, customs and physical infrastructure have perpetuated the relative backwardness and vulnerability of women in society.

This paper presents a study of gender equality in India with particular reference to the application of the concept of equal remuneration in India. As for equal remuneration, Indian legislation falls short of the concept of equal pay for work of equal value. Enforcement of the equal remuneration legislation is studied with reference to case law before the labour adjudication machinery and higher judiciary. The limitations in and the barriers to the application of the concept of equal remuneration and the measures taken by the government to strengthen its enforcement are briefly reviewed.

The data provided in this section provide the basic framework for gaining an insight into and analysing gender-related issues in India. An alarming feature of India's demographics is the steady decline in the sex ratio (females per 1000 males) from 972 in 1901 to 927 in 1991. Even though both male and female infant mortality rates (IMR) have been going down over the years (from 98 to 73 for females and 96 to 70 for males between 1985 and 1997), the IMR for females have consistently been higher than the corresponding male rates. This suggests differential access to the care of male and female infants. Also, it is widely known that female infanticide continues in some states in India due to traditional preferences for a male child. Furthermore, as Swapna Mukhopadhyay (IAMR, 2000:260-261) observes, "The higher rates of female mortality for the 15-29 population age groups

C. Agocs (ed.), Workplace Equality, 139–164.

can be explained by persistently high rates of pregnancy-related mortality, most of which is preventable."

As seen from Table 1 (page 159) at the end of the chapter, the incidence of illiteracy is higher among women than men, both in rural and urban areas. Table 2 (page 160) shows that the incidence of illiteracy is higher among the workforce than in the population, both for men and women. Table 3 (page 161) shows women's employment in the organised and unorganised sectors. The Employment Market Information (EMI) Programme of the Directorate General of employment and Training (GET), Ministry of Labour, Government of India, defines the organised sector as comprising all establishments in the public sector and those establishments in the private sector which employ 10 or more persons on any day of the reference period (usually three months). All other economic activities, by implication, could be considered unorganised. In common parlance, unorganised sector activities comprise those that are not:
(a) organised systematically; (b) made formal through mandatory registration or licence; (c) covered by legislation to protect minimum labour standards in employment; and (d) unionised. As per the 1991 Census, women account for 28.58 percent of the workforce; 4.21 percent of women workers are employed in the organised sector as against 10.23 percent of male workers. Women's participation rate is less because those who are not in paid jobs (such as household work) are not considered to be working! As a British economist observed, "If you employ a woman for domestic work, the GDP goes up, if you marry her, the GDP goes down." Tables 4 and 5 (page 161) show data on labour force participation rates by level of education and women employed in the organised sector by major industry groups. Labour force participation is low among those who drop out after secondary school and before graduation. It is relatively higher among the less educated and among graduates. Overall, women's access to education and employment (as indicated by labour market participation rates) continues to be low. (The data shown in the tables are based on the 1991 census. The 2001 census commences in February and its preliminary results will be released in August-September 2001.)

Table 6 (page 162) shows information on industries that employ more females than males. Most of the industries where females outnumber males are in relatively low-paying sectors/occupations with very limited opportunities for career advancement. Swapna Mukhopadhyay (IAMR, 2000:559-561) observes that "Despite putting in long hours of labour as revealed by time-use studies, large chunks of work performed by women are not adequately captured by official data-gathering systems, leading to very low recorded work participation by women." Banning women from working on night shifts and in underground mines has further reduced the scope of employment for women. Trade unions are generally opposed to lifting the ban on working of women on night shifts even though there is a great potential for employment in information technology-related areas involving tele-work in call centres, medical transcription, etc., where round-the-clock work is the norm.

The data are revealing in that the representation of women in formal/organised sector occupations is abysmally low. Women are predominantly engaged in informal/unorganised sector activities where wages and working conditions are inferior, largely unsecured and mostly devoid of social security benefits. Women outnumber men in the primary (agriculture) sector, both in relative and absolute terms.

Three-fourths of the migrant women have migrated on account of marriage, which often means giving up either studies or employment if they had been pursuing either or both. Less than 3 percent of females migrate for reasons of education or employment, while the corresponding percentage for males is nearly 32 percent (Table 7, page 162).

Until recently, women were denied property and successor rights and, except in urban areas, they were housebound. While in traditional Muslim families women cover themselves fully and do not let themselves be seen by "others", in some orthodox Hindu families there was a time when it was said, with some exaggeration though, that the grandmother did not look at the face of her husband till the first child was born. All this conveys how subservient women were to male domination in the past; that they took a long time even to make eye contact with their husbands. One other unique feature was that, in the past, women themselves perpetuated female subjugation and mothers-in-law often discriminated viciously against their daughters-in-law. Also, one often hears of mothers in poor families discriminating in favour of sons in terms of allocating family resources for education, food, etc. A widower could remarry, but a widow had to, until recently, sacrifice her life by placing herself on the pyre of her deceased husband or lead a life of rigor and sacrifice, shave her head, wear white clothes, eat tasteless food and deny herself all pleasures and comforts of life. Sex-based discrimination is rampant, though women and, to a considerable extent children too, constitute the majority of breadwinners in rural areas and predominantly among the poorer strata of society. But, over the years, such barbaric customs and practices have been changing, due to the pioneering efforts of social reformers and progressive legislation.

Education and urbanisation are slowly changing the scenario. The percentage of females joining the workforce increased from 14 percent in 1971 to nearly 23 percent in 1991. Their representation in decision-making roles continues to be low, as indicated (Table 8, page 163) in an empirical study of media organisations (Patel, 1994).

Traditional sexual division of labour is pervasive. Some employers have got over the "males for sales" syndrome (which means that only males should be recruited for sales positions in the corporate sector even though in rural India it is mainly the women who undertake the sale of agricultural and fishery products). They now allow not only young females but also married women to pursue a career. However, women continue to face a number of hurdles. Symbolically, women are now employed "everywhere" except in men's rooms. In the past, their own ambitions were through the success of their husbands or even children (Jain, 1992). But now they wish to experience such success themselves. Jain (1992) asserts that the middle class in India wants more out of life: "an extra holiday, a flat, a Maruti car, and Nike shoes for their children. So young women are being coaxed into the workforce by their parents or husbands. Jain found that nearly 20 percent of the Sunday matrimonial advertisements are for working wives".

ROLES OF SOCIAL PARTNERS

Government

The Indian Constitution seeks to establish an enlightened and egalitarian society. It gives women adult franchise and property rights, equal access to education, and equal right to run for public office. The Constitution of India upholds the principle of equality. It also makes affirmative action through quotas/reservations and other positive measures like preferential access to education and employment constitutional. Table 9 (page 164) shows how the Indian Constitution, legislative framework and administrative framework seek to enforce international labour standards concerning gender equality.

Way back in 1971, the Government of India constituted the Committee on the Status of Women in India. The Committee observed that despite constitutional guarantees and legislative protections, social and economic inequities faced by women in demographic ratios, access to education and work and wages were growing and disturbing. It also noted that special clauses for women workers in India were aimed at (a) regulation of employment in dangerous occupations and operations, (b) prohibition of night work, (c) maternity protection, and (d) special welfare provisions and amenities for workers with family responsibilities. The decline in the proportion of women in organised work and the increased presence of women in unorganised work where wages and working conditions are inferior have been major causes for concern.

Until the 1970s, the government's approach to women was one of munificence. Since the 1970s there has been a shift in approach from "welfare to development". The Sixth Plan (1975-80) focused a chapter on women, recognising their potential as agents of development. Subsequently, central government and several state governments set up separate departments at the state level and statutory committees at the district level for women and child development.

In 1987, the report of the government-appointed National Commission on Self-Employed Women and Women in the Informal Sector highlighted problems of working women. The National Commission on Rural Labour appointed in 1992 echoed the observations of the earlier-mentioned two commissions and stated that, "Labour in the context of women has to be construed in a more comprehensive sense to include: (a) help in family economic activity relating to agriculture, dairy, poultry and cottage industries, (b) raising and rearing a family, and (c) a variety of consumption-related activities required for the home, including fetching water, fuelwood and fodder and all kinds of domestic chores" (Government of India, 1992). In 1992, the government established the National Commission on Women as an apex statutory body to review the constitutional and legal safeguards for women, recommend remedial legislative measures, facilitate redress of grievances and advise government on all policy matters affecting women.

Emulating the Soviet model, India has, under the leadership of its first Prime Minister, Jawaharal Nehru, pursued the path of economic planning with socialist objectives. This has continued till the country's economy opened up in 1991. The successive five-year plans have focused on protection and welfare of women. However, the activities under the UN Decade for Women in the 1970s, the World Conference on Women in Beijing, the Social Summit in Copenhagen in 1995, and the subsequent efforts of the UN system, including the ILO, have both influenced and been influenced by Indian contributions. The result has been conceptual advancement in planning women's development mainly in three ways (Mazumdar, 1998): (1) establishing cells within various sectoral development/planning agencies at different levels; (2) earmarking a share of various sectoral allocations for investment in women; and (3) promoting rural employment and development through women's own collective organisations, at the grassroots.

The economic reforms of the 1990s are widely perceived to have had some negative effects on women's employment, while the significant growth prospects of new economy industries — information, communication and entertainment — have meant more opportunities and greater possibilities for women.

The 73rd and the 74th Constitutional amendments in 1992 granting 33 percent of the seats in local self-government institutions at the village level – panchayati raj – and the enhanced empowerment of these local bodies have also opened up new possibilities for women's political empowerment and emancipation (Kapur, 1999). Today, in 2001, one of three members and one out of three chairpersons in the panchayat raj institutions and municipal corporations throughout the country is a woman. Parliament is seized with the issue of reserving 33 percent of the positions for legislators at the state (legislative assemblies) and central (members of Parliament) levels for women. The two dominant political parties – the Bharatiya Janata Party (heading the ruling coalition) and the Congress (the main opposition party) - are unanimous on this issue. Still, it is delayed because of questions raised by some other parties on sub-reservations based on caste. Some state governments announced reservations for women in education and public employment. As in many other fields, here too implementation lags behind the intent.

Employers

Major national and regional organisations of employers and chambers of commerce have women's wings. For instance, the Federation of the Indian Chambers of Commerce and Industry (FICCI) has the FICCI Ladies Organisation (FLO), the Associated Chambers of Commerce and Industry (ASSOCHAM) has the Forum for Women in Business and the Indian Merchants' Chamber has the Ladies Wing. In the public sector, women employees have established a forum called Women in Public Sector (WIPS) for regular interaction and exchange of experiences. Its activities include development of a database, setting up of an information network, providing training and development opportunities, and support services including counselling, entrepreneurial training, etc. Today, women in the public sector are occupying senior positions in non-conventional functions like marketing, industrial relations and vigilance, etc. With the support of the Standing Conference of Public Enterprises (SCOPE) and the Department for International Development (DFID) of the UK, springboard activity (training programs to help women help themselves to move up the corporate hierarchy) was established to provide training and career counselling for women employees to go up in the hierarchy and break the glass ceiling.

Organised industry and the services sector, particularly the public sector and multinationals, usually discriminate on the basis of gender. Hence, very few women are able to reach beyond the middle levels. Women still find it difficult to get a foothold in some areas like mechanical and civil engineering. In the unorganised sector, women's work remains low paid or even unpaid and unaccounted for with the result that women usually remain invisible bread-earners for the family.

The problem is largely social rather than legal. Also, in many cases, the environment is still hostile to women and the civic infrastructure too weak and inadequate. As a Member of Parliament commented recently, there is a need for adequate provision of separate toilet facilities for women members.

A report on women managers based on 400 respondents (men and women) from 100 Indian corporations carried out by the Association of Management Development Schools in South Asia (as quoted in *Savvy*, July 2000) states that only 3.6 percent of the male executives surveyed believe that it is harder for women to climb the corporate ladder, as against 22 percent of women executives. The study also finds that the following factors contribute to women's success: consistently exceeding expectations (77 percent) and seeking out of difficult assignments to prove oneself (50 percent). Women executives believe that the factors that hold women back from top management include male stereotyping and preconceptions about women (52 percent); exclusion from informal networks of communication (49 percent); and lack of significant general management/line experience (47 percent).

"A change of heart is imminent", according to management consultant Sushil Chandra (quoted by Bhargava and Herr, 1996:157), "as employers' own daughters go out to work and as younger men grow up watching their own strong, articulate working mothers. Till then, women want only considerations, not concessions; alternative night shifts instead of three in a row, a notice before travel, and so on."

Bhargava and Herr (1996) identify the following best practices in their survey on corporate approaches to managing gender bias:

- Rid the mostly-male top management of its inherent prejudices against women.
- Accept the fact of maternity and help women employees through it.
- Eradicate male intimidation by establishing redressal forums.
- Offer both women and male managers flexible working hours and work-from-home options.
- Regard women managers as an investment that will be repaid only in the long term.

The following are some examples of corporate initiatives for promoting equal opportunity and for achieving work-life balance.

A Hotel Chain: Company C has several five-star hotels in various locations across India. It is one of the few in the services sector that positively discriminates in favour of women in terms of recruitment for several positions. Its advertisements seeking applications for various jobs invariably mention the following:

- We take special care of our women employees.
- We provide creche, nursery and other day-care facilities to the children of our employees.
- We allow periodic breaks during a working day to let mothers take care of their infants.
- We have separate rest rooms for women.
- We provide escort facilities to women who come to or leave office after dusk and before dawn.

USV Ltd: Until recently, pharmaceutical companies, like most other large companies, never recruited women for sales jobs. The only exception is vendors of fish and vegetables, and door-to-door salespersons of consumer's goods like detergents and cosmetics. In recent years, several pharmaceutical companies have started opening up sales representative positions to women as well.

One such company, USV Ltd., advertised for female medical communicator positions exclusively for housewives with a B.Sc. in biological sciences and in the age group 30-40 years. An except from the advertisement is:

> Once upon a time you passed your B.Sc. with biology or chemistry. You thought of a career in marketing or the medical field. Suddenly, something went nice, you got married, you liked him, he liked you, then there was an addition in your family, you were occupied, you grew in responsibility… 10 years flew like a dream, you are now 35 maybe 40. Today you think you have missed something you always wanted to do. We at USV Ltd. think we can help you to use your talents and the sense of responsibility at the same time you earn handsomely. The job: Four hours a day at your convenience and moreover, there is no boss, no train travelling, no late-mark. It means there is no office. On top of it you earn Rs 3,500 (*The Hindu*, 1996).

State Electricity Board: This is a state government undertaking engaged in the production and transmission of electricity. Recruitment in this company is based on marks in the qualifying examination, seniority in the employment exchange register and position on the caste roster (nearly two-thirds of the positions are filled through caste-based reservations in this state). There is no written test. The interview is a mere formality to verify the certificates. The medical test also is usually just a formality. Over the last few years several women were recruited. When some of these women were posted to rural areas as junior engineers, the unmarried and single among them found it extremely difficult to find accommodation. Also, these women engineers found that it was difficult and dangerous to venture out at night without a proper male escort to attend to emergency duties like transformer breakdowns.

Industrial Credit and Investment Corporation of India (ICICI): ICICI is a Rs 65,390 (Rs 47 = 1 US$) crore (one crore is equal to 10 million) company and is one of the leading financial institutions in India. It is also one of the very few companies in India that treats men and women as equals. Many of its key operations are now (in the year 2001) being handled by women achievers who are driving the future of the organisation (*Business India*, December 11-24, 2000). Besides Lalitha Gupte, deputy managing director, four of the eight general managers are women with brilliant academic credentials. Some of them hold independent charge as chief executive officers of key strategic business units such as ICICI Capital Services and ICICI Web Trade.

Media Organisations

An empirical study (Patel, 1994) on employment patterns in media organisations -- Doordarshan (government-run Television Corporation) and All India Radio -- reveals that despite some increase in recent years, the employment of women at all levels has been abysmally low. Doordarshan, a relatively newer broadcasting organisation, appears to have a slightly better representation of women than All India Radio (AIR). Nevertheless, in both organisations women lag behind men in terms of employment.

The gender composition of the workforce in these organisations is pyramidal. With the exception of a handful of women in senior positions, women continue to be denied an effective role. Most women employees are concentrated in "feminine" occupations and in the lower levels of the organisational hierarchy. For instance, the representation of women in jobs directly related to program production is far from satisfactory in both Doordarshan and AIR. The absence of women in key positions dealing with decision-making in program production (Table 8, page 163) implies that women have limited power in changing gender bias in media content.

To ensure improvement in women's employment in the public broadcasting system, the study makes the following recommendations:

- Create a database on women's employment in state-owned media organisations in order to monitor the gender composition of the media workforce and influence recruitment policies and practice.
- In-house training and retraining of women media professionals is also essential to enable women to achieve competence in the fields that they have been denied entry into.
- Gender-sensitive training is crucial for all media professionals in male-dominated media organisations.
- Systematic research is required on women's participation in media organisations in order to influence employment policies and change the organisational work culture and practices.

Civil Service

For the first time in history, in December 2000, a woman was appointed as the Foreign Secretary of India. Also, for the first time in history a woman became the Chairperson of the Central Board of Direct Taxes in late 1990s.

Management Schools

In the 1960s, when a leading management school in India wanted to consider a woman as its founding director, a premier management school in the US, which was the collaborating institution of the former, did not support the idea. Even in the 1970s, management programs in India had barely a few candidates. In contrast, since the late 1990s nearly 40 percent of the students in management schools are women. There is a view that while men can be fair and firm, women, besides being fair and firm can also be compassionate. Though family responsibilities hold them back, women are generally no less committed than men.

Parvez Agarwal, managing director of DBS Corporate Services Private Limited, reportedly observed thus:

> When I first got married into a conservative Agarwal family they didn't like the fact that I was a working daughter-in-law. But over the years, I became a role model for the younger girls of the family. They too have broken through stereotypes and are in fairly powerful positions today. In large cities women have already overcome the gender divide. A lady boss is no longer a novelty (*Savvy*, July 2000).

Family-friendly Policies

At ICICI, meetings may be rescheduled if an executive – man or woman – has to attend to family issues like parent-teacher meetings in his or her children's school. Those who work on weekends can bring their children to the kiddies club so that children can have fun while their parents work.

At NIIT, an IT training and software company, a special allowance is paid to employees if their dependent parents or in-laws stay with them. In doing this, the company is not just being altruistic. A young, dual career workforce with family responsibilities need not worry about routine childcare and other issues connected with family responsibilities if there are some elders to take charge at home. The allowance not only serves as a motivation to take care of the aged and promote family values, but also considerably eases the tensions associated with family responsibilities and lets employees concentrate better on their job.

Most women are both family and career oriented and therefore familial issues like childcare and flexible work schedules should be seen not just as women's issues, but also business issues. Some organisations like NIIT, for instance, offer half-day jobs and special allowances for new parents to take a three-wheeler auto-rickshaw (instead of a bus) to go home to check on the baby during the lunch hour. A few Indian companies have started giving paternity leave voluntarily, in addition to the statutory maternity leave.

Sexual Harassment

In a landmark judgement in 1997 in the case of Visakha vs. Others, the Supreme Court made up for the lack of guidelines for action against sexual harassment. Since then, this judge-made law has resulted in the formulation of guidelines in government and other organisations. The Industrial Standing Orders (Regulation of Employment Conditions) Act, 1948, was amended to include sexual harassment in the definition scope of "misconduct". Committees were set up in several hundred organisations with a senior woman executive as chairperson and with representatives from women's organisations/non-governmental organisations as members. The provision for outsiders in monitoring committees was aimed at giving voice to people who otherwise might be intimidated into silence. However, not many cases have been reported since then. This does not mean that the problem does not exist. According to a survey of 150 organisations carried out by Sakshi, an NGO, 80 percent denied having had to deal with any such problem, even though 70 percent of the 2,500 respondents from these 150 organisations categorically stated that they had faced such a situation – either a hostile environment or a quid pro quo offer, covert or otherwise - at least once.

A number of non-governmental and international organisations have started conducting a series of programs on gender sensitivity, dealing with sexual harassment, etc.

Trade Unions

In India, women who work to earn have triple responsibilities. Besides work at the office and in the house, they have to take care of the spouse, the children and in some cases, even the in-laws. Alongside this, to take up the responsibility of mobilising members or leading trade unions is certainly tough. Women's participation in trade unions is low and their presence in leadership positions is even less. This is so even in unions where women outnumber men, such as nursing and teaching. In a study of over 200 collective agreements signed by about 1000 union leaders it was found that less than 10 were women (Venkata Ratnam, 2001).

Trade unions have also not taken much initiative to find out why women (and even youth) join or do not join unions. The collective bargaining agenda does not adequately reflect the concerns of women and workers with family responsibilities. It is only in recent years that unions have started demanding paternity leave. Banking is the only industry where there was an agreement in 1987 to the effect that pregnant women may refuse to work before computer terminals.

Of late, however, trade unions have established women's wings and started mobilising women into trade union activity. One of the national centres has recently announced that if their affiliates send nominations for representation at various levels in the union hierarchy without a woman member in the panel, they will not consider the entire panel suggested by them.

What is even more disconcerting is the rather lackadaisical attitude of even non-governmental organisations and women's fora that have been vested with the right to pursue cases of continued discrimination in pay and remuneration and in fighting sexual harassment. In the recent debates on lifting the ban on night work for women, many trade unions and several women's organisations have preferred the status quo ante.

Mention should; however, be made of some women's organisations which function both as trade unions and as non-governmental organisations (Venkata Ratnam and Sinha, 2001). They include Self Employed Women's Association (SEWA) based in Ahmedabad, which has received world-wide recognition for its initiatives in mobilising women in many unorganised occupations and Women Workers Forum operating in four southern states in the country. In the wake of the recent earthquake in Gujarat, the state government has asked SEWA to co-ordinate all the relief work organised by the non-governmental organisations. It is a measure of the standing and reputation of the organisation built by Ela Bhat. SEWA itself was started in 1970s as part of Textile Labour Association (the latter founded by Mahatma Gandhi) but had to branch out of it and become independent as the environment within TLA was not conducive enough to cater effectively to the needs of women workers in the unorganised sector.

Pay Equity

ILO Convention No.100 on Equal Remuneration deals with sex discrimination only. India ratified the convention in 1958 and enacted the Equal Remuneration Act (ERA) in 1976, which was celebrated as the International Women's Year. The Indian legislation is based on the concept of same or similar work, not work of equal value. It excludes professional workers, places the burden of proof on the employee, and allows differences on the basis of skills and qualifications, but not job content. Thus the Indian legislation takes a very restricted view of the subject, unlike the concept of equal pay for work of equal value which aims at comparison across jobs based on four factors: skill, effort, responsibility and working conditions.

Though the enforcement is weak, a positive feature of the Indian legislation concerns the constitution of advisory committees and empowerment of selected women's organisations/non-governmental organisations to file complaints on behalf of the affected parties even though they themselves are not party to discrimination.

Studies on the enforcement of the legislation in the centre and select states indicate that the frequency of inspections under the ERA is rather low compared to that under other legislation on pay matters (for instance, see: Thorat, 1994; Pandey, 1989), but higher than under the Maternity Benefits Act. Most significantly the number of prosecutions disposed of have been very few, and convictions none, during the period 1987-96. The complaints against employers concern mainly the use of different designations for males and females with a view to consider the latter's jobs as less skilled or unskilled and keeping most jobs held by women under a piece-rate system.

Apart from inspection, the Labour Department also attempts to mediate or adjudicate disputes under the ERA. One major case decided by the Labour Department under the Delhi Administration related to pay discrimination in the Super Bazaar. In this case packers and packing cleaners were doing similar work, but paid differential wages and the Super Bazaar was discriminating against women employees by designating them as packing cleaners. There was evidence to suggest that males who were doing the cleaning work were designated as packers. The Labour Court upheld the claim of the petitioner for an amount of Rs.5210-40 for the period of 1984 to March 31, 1987.

Another case concerned the appointment of the Ms. Artika Goel as Project Officer in the Adult Education Branch of the Education Department under the Delhi Administration. Here also the petitioner was not paid wages at rates equal to those of workers of the opposite sex for the same work or work of similar nature. Ms. Goel was paid Rs.1,500 whereas the men were being paid Rs.2,000 to Rs.2,900 during October 1990 to October 1993. Ms. Goel demanded that Rs.66,176 should be paid to her as the value of relief. The case was filed on December 21, 1993. The employer, however, contended that there had been no discrimination and she was paid what was promised to her at the time of appointment.

There are many instances where women appointed ten years ago have not been regularised to date while male workers appointed in the same year were not only regularised but also promoted. For instance, Ms. Jamila was appointed as a peon in the Horticultural Department of the Delhi Government Authority (DDA) in May, 1984. Till May 1994 she had not been regularised and was being paid minimum wages, while two male peons who were appointed on the same date were regularised in June 1986. According to the Act, no employer shall discriminate against women in any conditions of service subsequent to recruitment such as promotions, training and transfer. The petitions submitted to the Labour Department state that while male casual workers were regularised within a span of two years, female workers continued to work as casual labourers. Ms. Jamila submitted in her petition that two coolies were appointed in 1988 and promoted to peons in 1989. They were regularised in 1991 while she was still waiting for her regularisation. The Delhi Administration might contend that there were thousands of male causal workers also waiting to be regularised and that there was no discrimination against females, but this cannot explain Ms. Jamila's case. She has an appointment letter saying that she will be confirmed within six months of appointment and even during her probation period her salary will be equal to that of regular workers. Her case is yet to be settled (*The Pioneer*, June 24, 1994).

Court Cases

There have been several judgements on the Equal Remuneration Act, 1976 (see Appendix 1, pages 154 -158). The first and the major judgement of the Supreme Court in this regard in the year 1987 concerned the case of Makinnon Mackenzie vs. Audrey D'Costa. Ms. D'Costa, who was working as a "Confidential Lady Stenographer," sued her company on the grounds that she was paid less than her male counterparts. She won the case in the Bombay High Court. The judgement also laid down guidelines to decide whether a particular job is the same or similar in nature as another job:

> In deciding whether the work is the same or broadly similar, the authority should take a broad view; next, in ascertaining whether any differences are of practical importance, the authority should take an equally broad approach for the very concept of similar work implies differences in details, but these should not defeat a claim for equality on trivial grounds. It should look at the duties actually performed, not those theoretically possible. In making comparison the authority should look at the duties generally performed by men and women. Where, however, both men and women work at inconvenient times, there is no requirement that all those who work at inconvenient times (e.g., at night), shall be paid the same basic rate as all those who work normal day shifts. Thus a woman who is working day shifts cannot claim equality with a man or higher basic rate for working nights if in fact there are women working nights on that rate too, and the applicant herself would be entitled to that rate if she changes shifts. We do not suggest that there can be no discrimination at all between men and women in the matter of remuneration. There are some kinds of work which women may not be able to undertake. Men do work like loading, unloading, carrying and lifting heavier things, which women cannot do. In such cases there cannot be any discrimination on the ground of sex: discrimination arises only where men and women doing the same or similar kind of work are paid differently. Wherever sex discrimination is alleged there should be a proper job evaluation before any further enquiry is made. If the two jobs in an establishment are accorded an equal value by the application of those criteria that are themselves non-discriminatory (i.e., those criteria look directly to the nature and extent of the demand made by the job), as distinct from criteria which set out different values for men and women employed on these jobs and are paid differently: then sex discrimination clearly arises.

The Supreme Court, in the case of Randhir Singh V/s Union of India (1982), held that

> Article 39(d) of the Constitution (of India) proclaims equal pay for 'equal work for both men and women'. It means equal pay for equal work for everyone and as between the sexes. Directive Principles, as had been pointed out in some of the Judgements of the Supreme Court, have to be read into the fundamental rights as a matter of interpretation. Article 14 of the Constitution enjoins the state not to deny any person equality before the law or the equal protection of the laws and Article 16 declares that there shall be equality of opportunity for all citizens in matters relating to employment or appointment to any office under the State...".

Unlike in several industrialised countries, courts in India have held that the doctrine of "equal pay for equal work" applies only where employees are equal in every respect, in educational qualifications, duties, functions and measure of responsibilities, and yet they are denied equality in pay. But if the classification for prescribing different scales of pay is founded on a reasonable nexus the doctrine will not apply (Markandeya vs. and others V/s State of Andhra Pradesh and others 1989-I-LLNP.815). Two years earlier, the Bombay

High Court had held the principle of equal pay for equal work is deducible from the equality provision contained in Articles 14 and 16 of the Constitution of India. Employees discharging the same work in different departments are entitled to equal pay scales (Pachghare K U vs. Viswesvaryya Regional College of Engineering, Nagpur and another, 1987-I-LLN-p.678).

The Supreme Court of India also held that similarity in the nature of work alone would not justify equal pay for equal work if there is a qualitative difference in performance of the work. Management can classify the posts and fix different scales of pay, as it is for the management to evaluate the work of the employees and not for the courts (Umesh Chandra Gupta and others vs. Oil and Natural Gas Commission and other. 1989-I-LLN-p.74).

The following trends militate against the effective enforcement of ERA:

1) Problems in the definition of pay; whether and how to take into account employee benefits, pensions, etc.
2) Gender neutral job evaluation not being common in most enterprises.
3) Even where job evaluation exists, occupational segregation and other biases in job evaluation (for example, giving more weight to physical than mental stress) lead to discrimination.
4) Emphasis on multi-skills and compensation for additional skills.
5) Tendency to link payment to qualifications.
6) Introduction of two-tier wage systems through collective bargaining.
7) Shift away from full-time to part-time and short-term contracts, with greater feminisation in the latter type of contracts that makes comparisons between male and female earnings even more difficult.
8) Shift away from collective bargaining to individual contracts of employment.

TOWARDS GENDER EQUALITY

We conclude this essay with the assertion that there is a need for initiatives at the company level based on the belief that equality at work between men and women means:

- not letting discrimination be an obstacle to getting the best candidates for the jobs at hand;
- enhanced competitiveness through developing more productive human resource policies;
- more flexibility for both the enterprise and its workers, especially now that new technology has removed many of the constraints placed on mothers who wish to participate in the labour market;
- proactively addressing possible gender-related barriers that exist at all levels on account of work design, institutional policies, traditional approaches or even mere lack of awareness;
- equality of opportunity in providing challenging assignments and vertical mobility based on candidates' merit and choice rather than on managers' preconceived notions arising from a gender-typed division of labour.

Companies' commitment to equality of men and women

Companies should prohibit discrimination on grounds including gender, race, ethnic origin, religion, political belief, age, region, caste, language, etc. They must seek to develop innovative and creative ways to remove barriers faced by women in selection, recruitment, placement, training, retraining and promotion and shall undertake positive measures and set up specific goals and timetables to prevent discrimination of any kind that is not based on job requirements, qualifications, merit and performance. They should also prevent any direct or indirect discrimination on the basis of marital status or family responsibilities. Doing so benefits them in the following ways:

- widest possible pool of talent will be available from which to select;
- greater transparency in selection through a pre-determined and fair means will establish management credibility and provide employees goodwill;
- benefits to the business from diversity of approach, background and priorities;
- fair and merit-based selection without discrimination based on gender will improve training and retraining and promotion processes;
- establish a good image.

Comply with legal framework

Companies should fully comply with their constitutional and legal obligations in respect of non-discrimination, equality of opportunity in employment and occupation, training/retraining and career prospects, pay equity, facilities during pregnancy and maternity, and prevention of sexual harassment.

They should consciously review and monitor the relations between women and men so as to put them on an equal footing and leave no chance for prejudice, discrimination or harassment, either covertly or overtly. The company will expect its employees to understand, value, respect and abide by its policy of equality between men and women in every sense, both in letter and in spirit. The company also expects its employees to be responsible and accountable for such behaviour as would promote and contribute to the furtherance of the company's policy of ensuring equality. Employees whose behaviour is wanting in this regard and those who indulge in discrimination and in disregard of a company's policy guidelines will be liable for disciplinary action.

Positive human resource practices

To bridge the existing gaps, if any, in terms of gender parity at any and every level, other things being equal, companies should give preference to women. They will need to develop gender-neutral job descriptions and candidate specifications. They should also identify and provide for adequate arrangements to increase access of women employees to further education, training and retraining to enhance their prospects for equal opportunity for promotion in their careers.

Companies need to develop dual career plans for working couples in accordance with the established principles and practices of reasonable accommodation, balancing the needs of the organisation and individuals, particularly in matters of placement, promotion and transfers. They should not discriminate between men and women in the matter of pay and fringe benefits. They should endeavour to take care of the special needs of workers with family responsibilities and develop a co-operative and flexible approach to facilitate a woman's to return to work, without any disadvantage, within a designated period following the birth of her child and, where possible, provide other options for part-time or home work and career breaks.

Companies also should establish a committee and complaint processing mechanism as per the guidelines of the Supreme Court in Visakha vs. others case in 1997, mentioned above. The company should amend its standing orders to make sexual harassment a serious form of misconduct liable for disciplinary action. They should take measures in this regard to safeguard the rights of privacy and provide for impartial investigation and private counselling.

Best practices

Companies should believe not only in compliance, but be committed to exceeding the minimum requirements under relevant constitutional and legal obligations of employers. They should develop an effective system of two-way communication for a regular flow of information. They should constantly look for creative and innovative ways of addressing and removing barriers to gender equality, monitor inter-firm practices on gender equality and consciously endeavour to improve upon the best practices in the industry.

Dr. Harish Jain is Professor at McMaster University, Hamilton, Canada and Dr. C..S. Venkata Ratnam is Professor at the International Management Institute, New Delhi, India.
The authors acknowledge the assistance received from Dr. (Ms) V. Chandra, Assistant Professor, International Management Institute and Mr. D.K. Panigrahi, Research Associate, International Management Institute.

REFERENCES

Bhargava, S. and Herr, H.. "How to Manage Gender Bias." *Business Today* 7.21 (January 1996): 154-7.

Eyraud e. al. "Equal Pay Protection in Industrialised Market Economies: In Search of Greater Effectiveness." Geneva : ILO, 1993.

IAMR. "Manpower Statistics, 2000." New Delhi: Institute for Applied Manpower Research, 2000.

ILO. "Equal Remuneration: General Survey by the Committee of Experts on the Application of Conventions and Recommendations." Report presented at the 72nd Session of the International Labour Conference, Geneva : ILO, 1986.

ILO. "Report of the Committee of Experts." Geneva: ILO, 1994:.306-7.

India (Government). "Annual Report on the Working of Equal Remuneration Act 1976 for the Year Ending 1992." New Delhi: Office of the Chief Labour Commissioner (C), Ministry of Labour, Government of India, 1974, Mimeo.

India (Government). "Towards Equality: Report of the Committee on the Status of Women India, 1974-75." New Delhi., 1975.

India (Government). "Shramshakti: Report of the National Commission on Self-Employed Women and Women in the Informal Sector." New Delhi, 1988.

India (Government). "Report of the National Commission on Rural Labour." New Delhi, 1992.

India (Government). "Standard Note on Women Labour". New Delhi : Women's Cell, Ministry of Labour, Government of India 1995, Mimeo.

India (Government). "Ministry of Labour – Annual Report, 1999-2000." New Delhi, 2000.

Jain, M. "The Changing Woman." *India Today* (15 July 1992): 52-61.

Kapur, A. *Women Workers' Rights in India: Issues and Strategies: A Reference Guide*, New Delhi: Training and Information Dissemination on Women Workers' Rights – India Project, International Labour Organization, 1999.

Mazumdar, V. "Women from Equality to Empowerment." In H. Karlekar. *Independent India, The First Fifty Years.* New Delhi: Oxford University Press, 1998.

Mukhopadhyay, S. "Locating Women Within Informal Sector Hierarchies." *The Indian Journal of Labour Economics* 40..3 (1997):.383-492.

Pandey, P N. "Implementation of Equal Remuneration Act, 1976 in the State of Uttar Pradesh." Lucknow: Giri Institute of Development Studies, 1989, Mimeo.

Patel, I. *Gender Differences in Employment Patterns of Doordarshan and All India Radio*, Media Advocacy Group and Friedrich Ebert Shiftung, New Delhi, 1994.

Thorat, M. "Labour Administration Enforcement and Gender." in C. Joseph and K. V. E. Prasad (eds.). *Women, Work and Equality*, Noida, National Labour Institute, 1994.

Venkata Ratnam, C. S. "Collective Bargaining – A Response to Liberalization." New Delhi: International Management, 2001.

APPENDIX 1

Analysis of Selected Court Judgements

NATURE OF DISPUTE	INDUSTRY	OCCUPATION	TYPE OF LEGAL INSTITUTION & DATE OF DECISION	DECISION: PRINCIPLE OF PAY EQUITY
Confidential Lady Stenographer paid less than male Stenographers, though nature of work is same	Private Enterprise	White collar	Supreme Court of India. 1987. Makinnon MacKenize V/s Audrey D'Costa	Upheld
Daily wage earners discharging same duties as other Class-IV employees	Government	Blue collar	Rajasthan High Court. 1991. Gulati and others V/s Sate of Rajasthan	Upheld
Qualifications, duties and functional responsibilities similar, though holding charge as Development Officers in different industries of the same employer	Government Leather and Gur Development	White collar	Punjab and Haryana High Court, 1991. J L Jaggi V/s State of Haryana	Upheld
Comparison between State Government and University employees in the same state	Teaching	(White collar) – Craft Instructors	High Court of Bihar. 1991. S Kumar V/s Chancellor, University of Bihar	Upheld
Social service society government staff who are claiming employees parity with government staff	Federal Government Department	White collar Social Service workers	Supreme Court of India. January 1, 1991. Grih Kalyan Kendra Workers' Union V/s Union of India and Others	Not upheld
The Issue of Job Classification in post restructuring of the department which gave higher functional grade to some officers	Federal Government Department	White collar, Account and Audit staff	Supreme Court of India. February 4, 1992. Union of India and Others V/s The Secretary, Madras Council Audit and Accounts Association	Not upheld

NATURE OF DISPUTE	INDUSTRY	OCCUPATION	TYPE OF LEGAL INSTITUTION & DATE OF DECISION	DECISION: PRINCIPLE OF PAY EQUITY
Higher pay for teachers of engineering subjects than those teaching other subjects – whether rational nexus exists or value judgment is irrational	Teaching	(White collar) Professional	Kerala High Court	Not upheld
Junior employee getting higher pays than the senior employee. Junior had higher qualifications ; recruited from a different source ; paid higher pay on recruitment and this pay was protected even after the merger of two department	Andhra Pradesh Electricity Board	White collar (lower division) clerk	Andhra Pradesh High Court. September 13/1993 R B Subrahmanya M and others V/s AP State Electricity Board	Not upheld
Employee question-ing job classification. Employer arguing that duties and classification for two job categories are different	State Electricity Board	Blue collar skilled	High Court of Himachal Pradesh. January 15/1993. Punjab State Electricity Board V/s Darshan Singh Rana and Others	Not upheld
Parity principle applies where the cadre is common and jobs within the cadre across departments are interchangeable and where no differences in qualifications exists	Municipal Corporation	Blue collar technical staff / machine operators	Supreme Court of India. March 17/1993. Narendra Kumar and another V/s Dharain Dutt and another	Upheld for certain categories but not for others
Agrogamies claming 'priority in scale' firemen in West Bengal. Supreme Court ruled that merely because of academic and physical requirements of both are similar – but their duties and functions are not same. Hence, denied higher pay scale of agragamies is unwarranted	State of West Bengal 'Civil Emergency Force'	'Agragamies' same as Firemen	Supreme Court of India, February 3/93	Upheld – Set aside Calcutta High Court and the Division Bench decisions

NATURE OF DISPUTE	INDUSTRY	OCCUPATION	TYPE OF LEGAL INSTITUTION & DATE OF DECISION	DECISION: PRINCIPLE OF PAY EQUITY
College Librarian pay compared with Librarian working at District Library. Also claimed that jobs interchangeable, to equal pay	Odd Institution (Library)	Professor While collar Librarian	High Court of Gujarat, 3/93. State of Gujarat and another V/s N B Patel	Upheld
ER Act, 1976 Sec 2(4). Same work or work of similar nature	Government	Several (36) Writ petitions	High Court of Rajasthan. September 6/93. A K Garg V/s State of Rajasthan	Not upheld Appeal dismissed
Casual / daily rated workmen doing same work as regular workmen and for equal number of hours claim equal pay	Muncipal Corporation	(Blue collar) workmen	High Court of Delhi. November 26/93. Muncipal Corporation of Delhi V/s Ganesh Razak and another	Upheld
Pay parity between statutory and non-statutory canteen employees	Calcutta Port	Blue color canteen staff	Supreme Court of India. April 27/93. Board of Trustees for Port of Calcutta V/s A K Mondal and others	Decision withheld
School mother appointed on temporary basis receiving fixed pay only and not given salary and allowances payable to school mothers appointed on regular basis	State Government Education School	School mother	High Court, Gauhati, Assam (Agarthala Bench in Tripura State). September 30/93	Upheld. Court also directed the State Government not only to pay regular salary but also to terminate the petitioner's services. The services have to be regularized by employer as and when vacancies occur
Though work is same, the Third Pay (Government) Commission of Federal Government fixed two different grades based qualifications	Government Pharmaceutical	White collar skilled Pharmacists	Supreme Court of India. February 8/94. Shyam Babu Verma V/s Union of India	Not upheld
Helper officiating as tractor-cum-driller claiming equal pay	Agriculture Irrigation Department	Blue collar manual tractor-cum-trailer driller	High Court of Calcutta. February 14/94. Gopal C Ghosh V/s State of West Bengal and others	Not upheld

NATURE OF DISPUTE	INDUSTRY	OCCUPATION	TYPE OF LEGAL INSTITUTION & DATE OF DECISION	DECISION: PRINCIPLE OF PAY EQUITY
Volunteer police constable doing the same job as a regular police constable claiming equal pay	State Police Force	Blue collar volunteer Police Constable	Supreme Court of India. March 16/94 State of West Bengal V/s Hari Narayan Bhowal and others	Not upheld
Labour enforcement officer prosecuted the bank because a branch office did not maintain register in relation to workers employed by it as required by Section 8 of Equal Remuneration Act	Bank	Not applicable	High Court, Kerala. February 24/97. Lord Krishna Bank Lgd. V/s Labour Enforcement Officer	Not upheld. It is enough if the head office of the Bank is maintaining the register.
Women claimed equal remuneration with their respective male counterparts	Pharmaceutical	Junior executive in accounts department	High Court, Bombay. January 220/97. Irene Fernandes V/sNeo Pharma Pvt. Ltd.	Decision withheld and case remanded to Assistant Labour Commissioner with the directive that applicants show evidence that the skill, effort and responsibility required to carry out the work done by them are the same as required to be carried out by a member of the opposite sex.
Casual workers working for more than 240 hours in a calendar year seeking parity in pay with regular employees engaged by the employer for work of similar skill and responsibility	Public sector enterprise	Casual workers	High Court, Andhra Pradesh. November 28/95	Upheld as a right flowing from the principle of equal protection of law and equality before law as in Article 14 of Indian Constitution
Despatchers claiming pay scale of Junior Clerk as they were doing the work of Junior Clerk	Ahmedabad Municipal Corporation	Office staff	High Court of Gujarat July 16/98. Ahmedabad Municipal Corporation V/s Ahmedabad Municipal Nokar Mandal & others	Not upheld. Posts are different. For getting post of Junior Clerk, candidate has to go through process of selection. Despatchers failed in the process. Hence they are not entitled to get pay scale of Junior Clerk

NATURE OF DISPUTE	INDUSTRY	OCCUPATION	TYPE OF LEGAL INSTITUTION & DATE OF DECISION	DECISION: PRINCIPLE OF PAY EQUITY
Doctors appointed on contract basis as Junior Medical Officers in various government hospitals and dispensaries claiming same pay as is payable to regular Junior Medical Officers	Hospitals and dispensaries run by Government of National Capital Territory of Delhi	Doctors appointed on contract	High Court of Delhi, Sept 11/98. Govt. of National Territory of Delhi & others V/s DR. V.S. Chauhan	Upheld. The employees should not be made to suffer for taking up employment on contract basis for short term on account of force of circumstances.
Person appointed as Biochemist made to work as lecturer, including setting and evaluating examinations	Visvesvaraya Regional college of Engineering, Nagpur	Biochemist functioning as lecturer	High Court, Bombay, December 2/98. Sakhaullah V/s Visvesvaraya Engineering College, Nagpur	Upheld for the period he actually worked as lecturer. Also awarded periodic increments and consequent retirement benefits.
District and Sessions Judges in Union Territory of Goa drawing same pay as that of their counterparts in Union Territory in Delhi in 1982. In that year pay of the latter was increased. The former claimed parity in pay	Judicial officers in the State of Goa	District and Sessions Judges	Supreme Court of India April 23/99. Alvare Noronha Ferriera & another V/s Union of India & others	Upheld for a limited period when the employer was common.
Laboratory assistants working in schools claiming parity of scales of pay with primary teachers	Government schools	Laboratory assistants	High Court, Delhi. May 14/99	Not upheld. Qualifications, duties and responsibility of both posts different
Sales girl appointed on contact basis on consolidated pay seeking parity in pay with other workers	Government handicrafts corporation	sales staff	High Court, Delhi. August 11/99. Priti Chopra V/s Managing Director, M.P. HastshilpVikas	Not upheld. Petitioner not taken as regular employee. Procedure for appointment on regular basis not followed. No particulars given in writ petition about duties performed by her and duties performed by regular employees. Not possible to arrive at any definite conclusion.

Table 1. Percentage of Male and Female Population by Educational Level, 1991

Educational Level	Rural			Urban			Total		
	Female	Male	Person	Female	Male	Person	Female	Male	Person
Illiterate	75.15	52.93	63.69	46.15	31.24	38.28	67.83	47.25	57.15
Literate without educational level	8.25	12.81	10.60	10.99	11.74	11.38	8.94	12.53	10.80
Primary	8.64	14.14	11.48	14.36	15.04	14.72	10.08	14.38	12.32
Middle	4.89	10.17	7.61	11.46	14.08	12.84	6.55	11.19	8.95
Secondary/Higher Secondary	2.61	8.04	5.41	11.99	18.40	15.38	4.98	10.75	7.97
Non-Technical diploma or Certificate not equal to degree	0.04	0.09	0.07	0.13	0.13	0.13	0.06	0.10	0.08
Technical diploma or Certificate not equal to degree	0.06	0.22	0.14	0.25	0.89	0.59	0.11	0.40	0.26
Graduate and above	0.36	1.60	1.00	4.67	8.48	6.68	1.45	3.40	2.46
Total (Million)	100.00	100.00	100.00	100.00	100.00	100.00	100.00	100.00	100.00
	301.53	321.27	622.80	101.83	113.94	215.77	403.36	435.21	838.57

Excludes Jammu and Kashmir

- Includes figures for educational levels not classifiable.

Source: Registrar General of India, 1991 Census.

Table 2. Percentage of Male and Female Main Workers by Educational Level

Educational Level	Rural			Urban			Total		
	Female	Male	Percent	Female	Male	Percent	Female	Male	Percent
Illiterate	82.33	50.07	58.20	46.96	22.84	25.98	77.78	43.27	51.02
Literate without educational level	4.70	9.49	8.28	5.34	6.43	6.29	4.78	8.72	7.84
Primary	6.93	15.90	13.64	9.49	15.53	14.74	7.26	15.81	13.89
Middle	3.30	11.89	9.72	6.69	16.29	15.04	3.73	12.99	10.91
Matriculate/ Secondary	1.52	7.62	6.08	9.06	17.31	16.24	2.49	10.04	8.34
Higher Sec./Inter./Pre University	0.40	2.44	1.93	4.19	6.68	6.36	0.89	3.50	2.91
Non-technical diploma or certificate not equal	0.10	0.13	0.12	0.76	0.18	0.25	0.18	0.14	0.15
Technical diploma or Certificate not equal to degree	0.18	0.28	0.26	1.62	1.33	1.37	0.37	0.54	0.51
Graduate and above	0.54	2.18	1.77	15.89	13.41	13.73	2.52	4.99	4.43
	100.00	100.00	100.00	100.00	100.00	100.00	100.00	100.00	100.00
Total (Million)	56.00	166.29	222.29	8.27	55.37	63.64	64.27	221.66	285.93

Excludes Jammu and Kashmir.
Main workers are those who work for 183 days or more in a year.
Source : Registrar General of India, 1991 Census.

Table 3: Employment in the Organised and Unorganised Sectors, 1991

	Organised	Unorganised	Total (in lakhs+)
Male	229.53 (10.23)	2014.11 (89.77)	2243.64 (71.42)
Female	37.81 (4.21)	859.86 (95.79)	897.67 (28.58)
Total	267.34 (8.51)	2873.87 (91.49)	3141.31 (100.00)

+ Lakh = 1/10th of a million

Table 4. Labour Force Participation Rates by Rates of Educated Persons (Percentage)

	Educational Level	Male		Female	
		Rural	Urban	Rural	Urban
1983	Below Matric	88.5	84.2	38.2	18.9
	Matric	74.3	71.7	23.8	13.8
	Graduate	88.3	87.4	37.6	35.3
1987-88	Below Matric	88.9	83.5	53.5	23.8
	Matric	74.2	70.7	26.3	16.2
	Graduate	90.1	86.4	39.9	37.7

Source CMIE, 1996

Table 5. Women's Employment in the Organised Sector by Major Industry, 1995

Major Industry	Total in '000s	Women in '000s	Percentage of total employment in the industry
Agriculture	1433.2	490.3	34.2
Mining	1118.7	80.6	7.2
Manufacturing	6262.2	731.5	11.3
Electricity, Gas, Water	975.8	36.8	3.7
Construction	1217	64.8	5.3
Trade, Hotels	470.5	39.3	8.3
Transport, Storage & Comm.	3164.1	160	5
Financing, Insurance	1576	204.5	12.9
Community Social & Personal	11107.4	2420.1	21.7
Services	27524.7	4227.9	15.36

Source: Quarterly Employment Review Jan-March 1995 Director General of Employment and Training (DGE&T), Ministry of Labour (Ministry of Labour), New Delhi.

Table 6. Industries Which Employ More Females than Males, 1991

	Description	NIC Group	Number of workers: Female	Male	Percent Female
1.	Processing , canning and preserving of fish, crustacean and similar foods	203	14,215	13,938	51
2.	Processing of edible nuts	215	61,761	31,092	67
3.	Manufacture of bidi	226	1,454,224	648,316	69
4.	Cotton spinning other than in mills (charkha)	231	150,159	109,718	58
5.	Preparatory operations (including carding and combing) on coir fibres	252	17,975	9,471	65
6.	Spinning, weaving and finishing of coir textiles	255	53,936	30,974	64
7.	Manufacturing of matches	307	91,638	40,816	69
8.	Welfare services rendered by organisations operating on a no profit basis for the promotion of welfare of the community such as relief societies, creches, homes for the aged and physically handicapped, etc.	941	170,177	99,921	63
9.	Domestic services	960	562,396	410,527	58

Source: Registrar General of India, 1991 Census

Table 7. Percentage Distribution of Migrants by Reasons

Reasons	1981		1991	
	Female	Male	Female	Male
Employment	1.9	31.8	1.8	27.0
Education	1.0	5.1	0.8	4.8
Family Moved	14.3	30.3	11.0	26.6
Marriage	73.4	3.3	76.1	4.0
Others*	9.4	29.5	10.3	37.6
Total	100.00	100.00	100.00	100.00
Total (Million)	145.2	62.5	167.8	64.3

*includes business, natural calamities like drought, floods, etc.
Source: Registrar General of India.

Table 8. Women's Representation in Decision-Making Roles in Media Organisations

	Doordarshan		AIR		Others		All		
	Female	Male	Female	Male	Female	Male	Female	Male	Total
Senior staff									
Director-General		1		1			1	1	
Deputy Director		1						1	
Senior posts[a]					2	8			10
Managerial staff									
First level	4	13	15	173	3	12	22	198	220
Second level	6	40	21	386	2	34	29	460	489
Third level	28	112	25	424	5	49	58	585	643
Total	38	165	61	983	10	95	109	1,243	1,352
Advisory committees	(18.7)	(81.3)	(5.8)	(94.2)	(9.5)	(90.5)	(8.1)	(91.9)	(100)
Board of management					3	36	3	36	39
Board of governors					4	77	4	77	81
Total					7 (6.4)	102	7 (6.4)	102 (93.6)	109 (100)

Notes:
[a] As positions among senior staff vary in other media organisations, the total number of senior staff is presented
Figures in parentheses are percentages of the total number in a specific organization(s)

Both Doordarshan (Television corporation) and All India Radio (AIR) are owned and managed by Government.

Source: Patel (1994)

Table 9. International Labour Standards and Indian Legal Framework

International Labour Standard	Indian Constitution/laws
Discrimination (Employment and Occupation) Convention (No. 111), 1958	Constitution of India, 1950 stresses the principle of equality and makes gender-based discrimination unconstitutional. Guidelines laid down by the Supreme Court in the case of Visakha vs. State of Rajasthan, 1997.
Human Resource Development Convention (No. 142), 1975	Some state governments provide for 30 percent reservation for women in educational institutions.
Employment Promotion and Protection(Unemployment Convention (No. 168), 1988	Affirmative action for recruitment, training and promotion of women. Several government departments and public sector organisations now prepare and monitor gender ratios in these matters. Factories Act, 1948 and Mines Act, 1952 provide that women may not be engaged in night work in factories and mines. There are also legislative provisions prescribing maximum weight loads assignable to woman and young workers. Childcare facilities: creche if more than 30 women workers are employed in the workplace under the Factories Act. Creche facility if more than 50 workers are working under the Plantation Labour Act, 1951 and Building and other Construction Workers (Regulation of Employment and Conditions of Service) Act, 1996.
Employment Policy Recommendation (No. 169), 1084	Higher income tax rebate/exemption level for women employees.
Equal Remuneration Convention (No. 100), 1951	Equal Remuneration Act, 1976.
Maternity Protection Convention (Revised (No. 103), 1952	Maternity Benefits Act, 1961 providing 12 weeks' paid leave. Two nursing breaks till the child is 15 months old. A worker on maternity leave cannot be dismissed from service during her absence.
Workers' with Family Responsibilities Convention (No. 156), 1981	Dual career planning and common postings/transfers in government. Paternity leave in government and in some companies through collective agreement or otherwise. Some companies provide for career breaks, part-time/home work and flexible hours for workers' with family responsibilities.

CHAPTER 8

FOLKE J. GLASTRA, PETRA E. SCHEDLER AND ERIK KATS[1]

BETWEEN PUBLIC CONTROVERSY AND MARKET INITIATIVE: THE POLITICS OF EMPLOYMENT EQUITY AND DIVERSITY IN THE NETHERLANDS

INTRODUCTION

Inequality seems endemic to the working of the labour market. After all, the process of selection and allocation of individuals in workplaces implies the unequal distribution of career possibilities and, consequently, of life chances (Van Hoof, 1990), whether one likes it or not. However, when certain categories within the labour force appear to be systematically excluded or disadvantaged, a broad, if differentially motivated, consensus among politicians, employers and pressure groups may arise that seeks to remedy their situation. Various policies are used to improve the position of such ethnic minority groups in the labour market. Among such policies, equity legislation is by far the most controversial (Braham et al., 1993). Usually this kind of legislation introduces measures that oblige organisations to produce data on the representation of certain designated groups in their workforce and make the data available for inspection to some external institution, and it applies negative sanctions to documented failures to achieve results or demonstrate good faith effort.

Opposition to equity legislation may stem from employers who resist interference in their recruitment and selection practices, from traditionally more privileged groups in the labour market who feel threatened by what they see as reverse discrimination (Blakemore and Drake, 1996: 207), and from those who favour a much more restricted welfare state. It may also come from nationalists who fear the disuniting of the nation state and argue that equity legislation has de facto resulted in the perpetuation of the minority status (Schlesinger Jr., 1992), and from a varied collection of social groups who reject preferential treatment in the labour process for meritocratic reasons (D'Souza, 1995: 314 ff.). Equity legislation is not without controversy among ethnic minorities either. Here, perceptions of the arbitrary, homogenising and stigmatising character of the registration procedures in use clash with the upsurge of individualism and achievement orientation in late modern societies (Beck, 1992). Although some might find bureaucratically entrenched minority preferences an indispensable support, those who have made it may not want to be covered by measures that lump them together in collectivities that they did not define or choose on their own terms (Hollinger, 1995). Others, however, evaluate equity legislation in light of social justice. They oppose such legislation for the reason that it is still much too weak and ineffective (Veraart, 1992; 1994). They point at the fact that it is the rhetoric of equity policies that evokes false images of effective preferential treatment and produces resentment, while in actual practice nothing much is being accomplished. Often criticism is directed against so-called equal opportunities policies which focus on like treatment and procedural justice for each individual, instead of stimulating a redistribution of collective outcomes in favour of designated groups

C. Agocs (ed.), Workplace Equality, 165 –179

(Blakemore and Drake, 1996: 11).

The forces supporting equity legislation for the labour market in the Netherlands as much as elsewhere seem to be confronted by a formidable and many-headed opposition. A reconstruction of the historical development of equity policies in the Netherlands may clarify the nature of resistance against this controversial approach. In this article, we will analyze the developments and discussions which led to the adoption of the employment equity laws in the Netherlands, and the accompanying political turmoil.

We start with a short note on the demographic composition of the Netherlands and the terminology we use.

ETHNIC MINORITIES IN THE NETHERLANDS

Since the sixteenth century, many immigrants from different countries have come to the Netherlands, where they looked for work and struggled to overcome the existing barriers in a country that was reputed to be relatively tolerant. Famous early examples are the Flemish from Belgium, the Huguenots from France and Jewish people from Portugal and Middle and Eastern Europe, who made important contributions to the development of the Dutch economy (Lucassen and Penninx, 1985). According to population statistics, 16 million people are currently living in the Netherlands, of whom some 9 percent are officially labelled ethnic minorities in view of their immigrant backgrounds in combination with their marginal position in Dutch society. The largest categories among them, counting first and second generations, are the Surinamese (1.9 percent in 1999) and Antilleans/Arubans (0.6 percent) from the former Dutch colonies who immigrated in large numbers from 1980 onward, Turks (1.9 percent) and Moroccans (1.6 percent) who were recruited in Netherlands as "guestworkers" in the 1960s in order to fill in labour shortages, and asylum seekers (39,000 requests in 1999 and an expected 45,000 in 2000) and refugees (an estimated 0.8 percent in 1998) . The minority status was conferred on all of these groups around 1980, when at last the Dutch government acknowledged that these groups would stay in the Netherlands permanently, and that it was high time to do something about their marginal situation. We will use the terms "ethnic minorities" and "immigrants" interchangeably for these groups. We will refer to the (mostly) white Dutch population as the "indigenous" population.

THE DUTCH MINORITIES POLICY CONTEXT

The minorities policy of the Dutch government developed from the end of the 1970s onward, when large numbers of immigrants from the former colony of Surinam entered the country, and it was, hesitatingly, acknowledged that the Turkish and Moroccan guestworkers, who were recruited in the 1960s, would not return to their home countries. The policy was initially aimed at three goals: the individual and collective emancipation of ethnic minority groups, equal treatment and equality in legal rights, and proportional social and economic participation in Dutch institutions. The general drift of the policy was the integration of ethnic minorities while retaining the cultural identities of their countries of descent. This policy, which has distinctly multiculturalist overtones (cf. Vermeulen, 1997; Kymlicka, 1995), has become the object of controversy since the end of the 1980s (cf. Penninx and Vermeulen, 1994). By that time, unemployment among ethnic minorities had increased alarmingly and kept growing, even when more jobs were available with the economic recovery in the second half of the 1980s. Ultra right-wing parties appeared on the political stage, and asylum seekers (who, unlike refugees, have a transitory and uncertain status in the Netherlands) and illegal aliens became issues of public debate. The general feeling among influential politicians, policy-makers and minorities specialists was that the minorities policy followed hitherto had been a failure.

Against this background, the Scientific Council for Government Policy (SCGP), an independent advisory body to the Dutch government, published a report in 1989 that was very critical of the multicultural minorities policy of the government and what it had brought during the 1980s. It argued that the government had been far too lenient towards ethnic minorities, had treated them as "categories of care" (WRR, 1989: 9) and that sustaining cultural identities of ethnic groups should no longer be acknowledged as a legitimate matter of government concern. Labour market and educational policies were identified as the preferred means for achieving the integration of ethnic minorities (WRR, 1989). Many of the measures that the Council proposed were premised on a deficit analysis (see Glastra, Schedler and Kats, chapter 9 in this book) and aimed at adapting ethnic minorities to the Dutch society and especially to the labour market. A proposal concerning employment equity legislation constituted the main exception to this rule.

THE CANADIAN EXAMPLE

In 1987, the Social Economic Council (SEC) called on the government and the business community to make a voluntary effort in order to improve the employment participation of ethnic minority groups. The SEC is the most important advisory body of the Dutch government in the field of socio-economic problems with regard to economic growth, labour participation and income distribution. The SEC is formed by representatives of the organisations of employers and the labour unions, and by independent members appointed by the Crown. Unanimous advice coming from the SEC gives a government a clear indication of support or resistance among employers and labour unions with regard to a policy measure. In this case the advice urged government and Parliament not to resort to equity legislation and allow time for local corporate initiatives and regular evaluation of outcomes and experiences.

However, two years later the SCGP concluded that the situation of ethnic minorities in the labour market had only worsened. In its 1989 report (WRR, 1989: 36) the SCGP concluded that in order to enhance the accessibility of work organisations for ethnic minorities, it does not make sense to impose quotas on employers. It states that experience in the case of the disabled has shown that the recruitment of certain categories of personnel is not readily enforceable. It argues however that this does not diminish the public responsibility of the government. The Canadian Employment Equity Act is embraced as an "original approach of the problem" in which "public and private responsibilities are interconnected in a complementary way". The Council summarises the core elements of the Canadian act as a "*non-sanctioned* obligation of the employer" to bring about employment equity and to produce an annual employment equity plan with goals and timetables, and a "sanctioned obligation of a yearly report" on the representation of designated groups in the workforce of employers.

In a revealing motivation for its preference, the Council writes: "The (...) attractive aspect of this type of legislation is that, with the use of very light interventions, it stimulates employers to acknowledge and account for their co-responsibility for the proportional employment of women and other minority groups. The single obligation to publicly account for their actions means that employers also have to motivate in public, why they have given less or more salience to their responsibility towards the underrepresented groups in their human resources policy. Thus indirect social pressure takes the place of direct government coercion." (WRR, 1989: 36). The Council argued that legislation along the lines of the Canadian example would offer the government a way out of "the dilemma between compulsion and voluntariness" (WRR, 1989: 137) and enhance the co-responsibility between the private and the public sectors.

TOWARDS EMPLOYMENT EQUITY DUTCH STYLE

However, the coalition government of Christian Democrats and Social Democrats was not in favour of legislative intervention. Because the Parliament threatened to take legislative steps on its own initiative along the lines suggested by the SCGP, employers and unions, united in the Labour Foundation (LF), voluntarily signed an agreement in 1990 (STAR, 1990). The LF is a private national platform of three central organisations of employers and three central labour unions in the Netherlands, usually referred to as the social partners. They discuss themes with regard to labour problems and labour relations, and they advise employers and labour unions. They also advise the government on such matters and have tri-partite consultations twice a year that result in authoritative agreements on wages. It is one of the strongholds of the Dutch poldermodel (Schedler, Glastra and Kats, 2001). The stated goal of the LF agreement was the realisation of "a proportional labour position for the ethnic minority population compared to the indigenous population" (STAR, 1990: 8), through the allocation of 60,000 jobs for ethnic minorities in a period of five years. It was meant for Moluccans, Surinamese, Antilleans, Arubans, Turks, Moroccans, Tunisians, refugees, Gypsies, Italians and Spanish living in the Netherlands. Note that immigrants from Italy and Spain are not regarded as ethnic minorities in the Netherlands since the 1980s. The agreement states that ethnic minorities constitute "a social category that is not (originally) born in the Netherlands and whose members are, according to objective measures and in the majority of the cases, in a situation of socio-economic deprivation" (STAR, 1990: 8). By means of this agreement, the danger of legislation seemed to be averted (Veraart, 1992: 11). The government promised the Parliament that it would reconsider its position with regard to legislation if the LF agreement did not succeed in bringing about the desired results (Pattipawae, 1992: 7).

As a result of interim evaluations of the LF agreement, it became apparent that the agreed number of jobs for ethnic minorities would not be reached in time. When the rate of unemployment among ethnic minority groups remained four times as high as that of the non-minority population, members of Parliament argued in favour of legislation. Representatives of the left-wing parties, together with the liberal and the liberal-conservative party in Parliament, jointly presented a private member's bill concerning employment equity. Although ethnic interest organisations and even an advisory body of the government had urged that employment equity measures be accompanied by a policy of contract compliance (Van der Burght and Pattipawae, 1989: 44; TWCM, 1994: 33), there was not enough support to secure passage of such extended legislation in Parliament. Furthermore, the government had declined this possibility already in 1991, arguing that it would jeopardise the voluntary LF agreement for which it had pressed for so long (Brassé, 1997: 14).

FEATURES OF THE DUTCH EQUITY ACT OF 1994

In June 1994, the Law on the Stimulation of Proportional Labour Participation of Ethnic Minorities (henceforth referred to here as the Equity Act) became effective for a period of five years. It obliged employers with more than 35 employees in the private and the public sector to aim at a more proportional representation of ethnic minorities both in numbers and in distribution over different function levels, relative to the situation in the regional labour market. Ethnic minorities are defined in the Act as "those coming from abroad who have taken up their residence in the Netherlands, and their children". This would, for instance, include Americans and Japanese. However, the Act is expressly directed at ethnic groups that have a disadvantaged position in the labour market. If an employee or one of his or her parents was born in Aruba, the Dutch Antilles, Ethiopia, Iran, Iraq, Morocco, Turkey, Somalia, Surinam, Vietnam or the former Yugoslavia, he or she belonged to the designated groups under the Act. In contrast to Canadian practice, the Act does not pertain to the position of women or people with disabilities in employment, and it is, in that sense, less general in scope.

Employers are to register the ethnic identities of their personnel. This means setting up a separate personnel administration system which documents the personnel number of the employee, the country in which he or she was born, the country where each of his or her parents was born, membership of one of the designated groups, function level and full-time or part-time employment. It is not relevant for the registration of ethnic identities what the nationality of the employee is, or whether he or she self-identifies as an indigenous Dutch citizen. The employer draws the conclusion about the employee's designated status purely from factual data on the birthplace of the employee and that of his or her parents. Employees are legally obliged to provide such data to their employers. However, if they lodge an objection against registration in writing, the employer may not integrate their data into the administrative system. This strange twist in the legislation is the result of political compromise concerning the right of privacy (Kuijer and Stulemeijer, 1995: 34). The rejection of self-identification as a method for determining ethnic identity follows from an earlier government standpoint on the registration of minority data. The government stated in 1992 that it would not allow adding self-identification data to person registrations for the sake of positive action, since it would conflict with the need for the protection of privacy. It would also increase the risk of stigmatisation of the persons involved and the subjective nature of self-identification would only stress difference (Handboek, 1994 nr. 16: 11).

On the basis of the registration ethnic representation statistics have to be publicly reported on an annual basis to the Chambers of Commerce, where they may be checked and publicly exposed by ethnic interest groups and other interested parties. Employers must also write annual action plans on employment equity, in co-operation with the employees' councils. The latter are involved in the process in order to broaden social support in the work force. These plans must evaluate the representation of designated groups in the workforce, describe relevant HR-policies and define possible barriers for ethnic employees, provide a specification of target figures for the coming year, and state concrete measures to improve the situation. The action plans have to be filed with the state funded employment agencies, and these plans are not to be disclosed to the public. The idea is that these agencies can direct their mediation activities according to these plans. In practice, it turns out that they hardly make use of this possibility (Handboek, 1996 nr. 12: 9; Berkhout et al., 1996: iv).

Employers who consciously manipulate the data in the year report, who fail to publish the year report or to *file a copy* of their annual action plan with the employment agency of their region are liable to punishment under criminal law. It must be noted, however, that the failure to *produce* an action plan is *not* sanctioned. When the Equity Act came into effect, statements by the Minister of Social Affairs and Employment led business experts to infer that controlling compliance would not be a high priority with the police or the judiciary (Kuijer and Stulemeijer, 1995: 58). Employers who do not comply with the obligations of the act can also be sued by stakeholders such as minority organisations and labour unions under civil law. In reaction, employers have pointed at the risk of "people's tribunals" (Kuijer and Stulemeijer, 1995: 62).

THE RECEPTION OF THE EQUITY ACT

The Equity Act cannot be said to rest on a broad basis in Dutch society. In public debate, the organisations of employers criticised the Equity Act from the start, as they have always rejected the very idea of equity legislation. They remained in favour of the voluntary and market-driven road towards integration of ethnic minorities, paved with lower minimum wages, investments in the competitive capacity of the economy that would ensure job growth, and directing education at improving qualifications of minorities. The employers and their organisations characterised the Equity Act as yet another bureaucratic monstrosity that would cost too much and would not have the intended effect (Veraart, 1994; Handboek, 1996, nr. 7: 4). They pointed out that the Canadian Equity Act was only relevant for "a couple of hundreds of enterprises" as against "many tens of thousands" in the Netherlands, and they added that, again in contrast to the Dutch case, the "influx of foreigners in Canada is fiercely regulated (...) and restricted." (De Volkskrant, 27 October 1993).

However, if the organisations of employers had been the only ones criticising and opposing the Equity Act, they might not have been very successful (Veraart, 1992: 11). Although the Dutch federation of labour unions had pleaded for the introduction of affirmative action in the past, support for such legislation appears to be primarily located in the executives of the labour unions. Union activists and employees' councils in corporations, which consist almost totally of indigenous employees (SZW, 2000), have generally been unsympathetic to the idea. In the period preceding the passage of the Equity Act, the labour unions were conspicuously silent, while the employers' organisations actively and at great length lobbied against legal action. It seems fair to conclude that the LF, in which the silence of the unions was matched by the outspoken resistance of the employers on an organisational level, has played an important role in delaying the introduction of the Equity Act (Veraart, 1992: 8).

Organised interest groups of ethnic minorities constituted another political force in the controversy. However, they were never very sympathetic towards legal interventions such as the Equity Act (Veraart, 1994: 10). They felt that such a law required too little of employers, and they claimed that only quota measures would be effective. Their starting point was that Dutch employers, given their freedom of choice in an ample labour market and their conservative hiring politics, cannot be trusted to act on their own initiative. Other critics pointed out that employers should not merely be judged according to the quantitative standards of ethnic representation, but more specifically by their efforts to implement their action plans (cf. Schildmeijer, 1995: 188). Contrary to what the Equity Act prescribes, critics argued that the reports about these implementation efforts ought to be disclosed and publicly discussed. Those who felt that the Equity Act was not strong enough warned that the influence and, in the end, the results of the Act had been made too dependent on the pressure of societal organisations and groups. Although they did not want to underestimate the influence of, for instance, ethnic interest organisations beforehand, they stated that the responsibility for ensuring the implementation of the law should, first of all, be made the concern of government and political parties (Veraart, 1994: 11; Van Vught, 1995: 49).

The issue of identification and registration turned out to be the major concern of advocates and opponents of the Equity Act alike. The chairman of one of the most influential organisations of employers made use of existing feelings in Dutch society by stating that everyone with some historical consciousness pertaining to World War II had to oppose any form of ethnic registration (Veraart, 1994: 9). Some ethnic interest groups argued that stigmatisation could very well be an unintended consequence of ethnic registration. Furthermore, many members of ethnic minority groups claimed to be well-integrated into the Dutch society, and did not wish their identities to be registered in a period in which a more forceful approach to the so-called minorities problem and the sharpening of regulations and procedures applying to asylum seekers were officially endorsed. The advocates of the Equity Act argued, however, that the debate on ethnic registration was misguided in emphasising means and neglecting ends, i.e. the goal of enhancing the labour participation of ethnic minorities. According to them, the disproportionately high rate of unemployment among ethnic minorities would have far more stigmatising effects than the act of registration as such.

The criticism and the resistance did not die down after the Equity Act came into force. Especially the organisations of employers kept on protesting, and they publicly contested the practicability of the law. They continued to stress that a joint responsibility involving employers, labour unions, organised ethnic interest groups and the government, as already realised in the 1990 LF agreement, was to be preferred above what they habitually called a "centrally imposed registration law" which laid all the responsibility on employers (STAR, 1994). In Parliament, the Christian Democrats and the smaller right wing parties argued that a law that was the object of so much controversy had better be repealed. A new coalition government of social democrats, liberal conservatives and liberals took over the defence of the law without hesitation from August 1994 onward. The Minister of Social Affairs and Employment argued that it would take some time before the Equity Act would become established practice, and the Minister of the Home Office stated that he was not impressed by the criticism of the employers and threatened them with quota measures (NRC Handelsblad, 11 May, 1995).

EVALUATING THE IMPLEMENTATION OF THE EQUITY ACT

In the spring of 1995, the first dim predictions that the Equity Act would not work reached the media, and in the fall of that year they were confirmed. Only about 10 percent of the employers fulfilled their reporting obligation under the law. With some satisfaction, employers in trade and industry concluded that most of the ministries could also be reproached for negligence in this respect. Nevertheless, the employers feared the possibility of more severe legislation. In the autumn of 1995, they proposed a continuation of the LF agreement. The allocation of 12,000 jobs for ethnic minorities in 1996 should help to finally reach the number of 60,000 jobs that the original agreement was aiming at (STAR, 1996a).

At the end of 1996, the first two years of the Equity Act were evaluated. Research (Berkhout et al., 1996: 95) showed that 57 percent of the employers had complied with the required registration of ethnic employees, 26 percent had filed their annual report at the Chambers of Commerce, while only 12 percent had produced action plans. None of the employers who were not in compliance with the legislation was sued by the state or the stakeholders. Neither minorities' organisations nor state-funded employment agencies developed any monitoring activity with regard to representation statistics or action plans, for fear of jeopardising their relationships with employers. The researchers involved in evaluating the Equity Act explained the continued resistance by referring to the dominant opinion among employers that the weak position of ethnic minorities on the labour market is a supply-side rather than a demand-side problem. Employers argued that they were not prejudiced against employing ethnic minorities at all, but that they were unable to find workers among them who were qualified for the Dutch service and information economy. The researchers also pointed out that, in comparison to the Canadian example, a clear enforcement policy was lacking (Berkhout et al., 1996). The researchers determined that a minority of 11 percent of the employers who complied with one of the obligations of the Equity Act had made some amendments in their HRM policies, most notably in recruitment and selection practices. They also stated that it was too early to answer the question whether the Act had in fact enhanced the employment of designated groups (Berkhout et al., 1996: 95).

Against the background of these results, the Equity Act was discussed in the LF, and as a consequence, the government promised adjustments according to the wishes of employers and labour unions. At the same time, the social partners admitted that the LF agreement, and its continuation, had failed to improve the employment participation of ethnic minorities. They pointed to the lack of influence of the agreement on the most crucial policy level, i.e. the micro level, as one of the main explanations (STAR, 1996b: 7). The Labour Foundation proposed a far more decentralised approach to minority unemployment, in which collective bargaining agreements and intercultural management play pivotal roles, while quantitative goals on a macro level were de-emphasised (STAR, 1996b: 19). In a joint letter to the individual employers, the LF and the government characterised the existing Equity Act as a law that in its implementation primarily remained an administrative affair anyhow, and stimulated action insufficiently.

A REVISED EQUITY ACT

The new law, which was passed in Parliament 27 November 1997 and became effective in January 1998 for a period of four years, was to ease the administrative burden on the employers and was meant to support the 1996 Labour Foundation agreement mentioned above. Instead of two separate reports, only one annual report is required containing both ethnic representation data and action plans to improve employment equity. The employees' council is allowed to attach its judgement about the annual report as an integral part of it. The basis of the report continues to be the registration of the personnel in a separate administration system. However, the employer is now given a choice between two registration procedures: whether or not employees belong to the designated groups must be determined either according to the objective procedure outlined in the old Equity Act, or following a procedure of so-called restricted self-identification. This latter procedure states that if the country of birth of one or both of the parents differs from that of the employee and at least one of the stated countries belongs to the group of designated countries, the employee may choose whether he or she wants to belong to the designated groups under the law, or not. The employer may choose one registration procedure only and is obliged to apply it to all his or her employees. The new rules concerning registration methods are included in the Act in order to meet complaints of employees who feel that they are unjustly categorised as belonging or not belonging to the designated groups. Note, however, that it is the employer who must decide if employees are allowed a chance of self-identification. Note also that the variation in registration procedures will make comparisons between different annual reports less valid.

The annual report is no longer filed at the Chambers of Commerce but at the regional employment agencies. The intention is that consultants of these agencies who specialise in work mediation for ethnic minorities can use these data for the structuring of their work. The public's access to these data is restricted. The Labour Inspectorate monitors compliance with the law. It is part of the Ministry of Social Affairs and Employment and it controls whether employers and employees comply with laws and regulations with regard to labour. Legal enforcement no longer resides under criminal law, but will be dealt with under civil law, which would conform better to the character of a law that is directed to consciousness raising (Staatscourant, 1997).

Organisations of employers and employees are to encourage their members to improve the labour participation of ethnic minorities. Collective bargaining and hitherto largely inactive employees' councils (Berkhout et al., 1996; Beckhoven and Mevissen, 1996) are to play important roles in a more decentralised approach. The letter from the Minister of Social Affairs and Employment, informing the Parliament about the intended changes to the Equity Act, is co-signed by the most influential organisations of employers and labour unions. After the failure of the LF agreement, broader social support for an admittedly compromised Equity Act developed at last and cautiously, at the national level. The new law is called Wet Stimulering Arbeidsdeelname Minderheden (the Stimulation of Employment Participation of Minorities Act). The Dutch word SAMEN (Together) is used as the - all too symbolic - shorthand term (henceforth we will refer to this law as the revised Equity Act). The Act considers as designated groups persons who are born in Turkey, Morocco, Surinam, the Dutch Antilles, Aruba, Moluccans, the former Yugoslavia or in other countries of South and Central America, Africa, or Asia, with the exception of those born in Japan or the former Netherlands East Indies, and their children. As an answer to requests by the employers, who wanted their employees from other third world countries to count as belonging to designated groups too, the number of groups had already been greatly extended through a ministerial enactment under the original Equity Act.

The revised Equity Act contains less obligations, and is meant to complement the voluntary involvement of employers in encouraging the employment of ethnic minority groups. The voluntary approach already favoured by the SEC in 1987 and in 1992 has prevailed over mandatory interventions. The old Equity Act was never really and effectively implemented as intended. In a striking exemplification of the theory of the self-fulfilling prophecy, the employers made the law the dead letter that they said it would be. They forced those who aimed at restoring the primacy of political decision making in an area of evident stagnation back into the traditional structures of the Dutch corporative economy, where employers and labour unions negotiate agreements with as little government involvement as possible. The 1994 Equity Act was not given much time to prove itself in practice. On the other hand, it has not been repealed altogether, but it was amended in the process of broadening its social support beyond the boundaries of an always shaky Parliamentary coalition. For it is clear that, with the reduction of the obligations and the administrative burden, the removal of sanctions, and, last but not least, the introduction of a more pronounced co-responsibility of the labour unions through the employees' councils, employers' organisations have no reason to continue their lobby against equity legislation and have in fact changed their policy.

That is not to say that the implementation of the revised Equity Act has become much easier. An evaluation of two years of experience with the new act (Zandvliet, 2000) shows that employers still predominantly perceive it as an administrative burden. Of 21,000 employers under the Act, three quarters run a registration system, and 49 percent filed their annual report in 1999, of whom three quarters have specified target figures and equity measures. The majority of the measures proposed in the reports pertain to recruitment and preferential treatment; a minority is directed at career mobility and the prevention of discharge from the workforce. Effects of the Act in terms of changes in HRM policies, in recruitment practices, and in consciousness of the problematic situation of ethnic minorities are not impressive and differences between enterprises who do and who do not comply with the Act are small. The proportion of ethnic minorities in the workforce of complying organisations has increased by 30 percent against 23 percent with non-complying organisations. This lightly positive effect of the act is statistically not significant. Research evidence again points out that stakeholders hardly play any role in furthering equity with the use of the possibilities that the law gives them. Only in two thirds of the filed reports have employees' councils attached their judgements and these were almost never critical of the employer's perspective. Neither minority organisations nor labour unions took legal action against non-complying employers. They are looking for chances of dialogue rather than playing the watchdog. The overall picture is that compliance has improved somewhat since the revision of the Act, but significant effects for corporate policies and for ethnic minority employment remain to be demonstrated (Zandvliet, 2000).

In a letter to the Parliament of 28 June 2000 the Minister of Social Affairs and Employment introduces a series of discussions and agreements with the top management of large factories on the issue of ethnic minority employment as a reaction to the evaluation research report. He points at the recent agreement concerning 20,000 jobs for ethnic minorities in the sector of small and middle-sized business. He also states that governmental institutions will be forced to take their exemplary roles much more seriously. It has turned out, for example, that only 55 percent of the municipalities have filed their annual report as against 49 percent of the private enterprises in 1998 (SZW, 2000: 43). The minister has come to an agreement with the social partners that states that the LF will address individual employers in an information campaign that stresses compliance with the revised Equity Act, which, as he writes in his letter, will be prolonged for two more years until the end of 2003. The general background of these ministerial moves is that although the unemployment of ethnic minorities has decreased from 26 percent in 1994 to 14 percent in 1999, this figure stays roughly between 4 and 5 times larger than the unemployment percentage of the indigenous labour population (SZW, 2000: 19 ff.). As a consequence, the notion of many employers (Zandvliet, 2000) that shortages on the labour market and opportunities on the consumer markets have a bigger impact on employment equity than equity legislation is clearly mistaken. Whether this implies that equity acts can do a better job remains to be seen.

PUBLIC CONTROVERSIES AND CORPORATE AMENDMENTS?

In the short history of initiatives, plans and policies to enhance employment equity for ethnic minorities in the Netherlands the central struggle has been over the question of which parties should be involved and what their roles and responsibilities should be. The private member's bill of 1994 broke through the routine handling of socio-economic affairs in the well-established tripartite consultation network of government, central organizations of employers and labour unions, when this network failed to make visible progress with regard to equity. The Equity Act pointed to the employers as the social actors *par excellence* who should make an effort to employ more ethnic minorities. The employers have defended themselves and pleaded for a return to joint responsibility by pointing at the 1990 LF agreement with the labour unions and its follow up, to enhance equity in business. Their argument was that things should be left to the social partners with as little government involvement as possible: to the private sector where a combination of market forces, social responsibility and voluntary initiative would bring far better results than a peremptory and unwieldy Act could. The ensuing discussions had a distinct Dutch flavour. In the United States and in Ontario, debates about quotas and reverse discrimination figured as the central and often effective arguments against equity legislation and policies (Glastra et al., 1998). In the Netherlands, a country where the massive abduction of the painstakingly registered Jewish population during World War II is an open nerve in the nation's historical consciousness, the registration issue proved to be much more explosive in public debate. The central employers' organisations referred to the history of registration regularly in order to find room for a non-bureaucratic, decentralised and market-driven approach to employment equity. The changing demographic composition of labour and consumer markets, and the globalisation of economic activities, would ensure an extra push towards this voluntary engagement (Schedler et al., 2000). Following this perspective, one could come to the conclusion that, whereas equity is steadily growing in the industrial field as a result of purely pragmatic motives, the fate of equity legislation is especially vulnerable in the political arena where constituencies have to be won over by ideological arguments.

However, the image of silent, private progress and public controversies with regard to equity policies must be qualified. First, in the Netherlands, where equity policies lack the historical momentum that can be found in America and, to a lesser degree, in Canada, employers rather than politicians led the way in the resistance against the 1994 Equity Act and contributed to a public controversy. Second, equity policies have far less resonance in smaller scale firms (Handboek, 1996 nr. 13: 4 ff.), which in a period of downsizing and subcontracting, employ an ever growing part of the labour force. Such firms often lack the human resources capacities to answer legal requirements (Mevissen, 1991). There is little evidence of progress in this sector. Third, although an empirical overview is still lacking, available research (Zandvliet, 2000) suggests that, on the whole, public sector employers are not doing worse than private sector employers, even if large corporations among the latter have made the most progress. Fourth, even when the original Equity Act was revised according to the wishes of the central organisations of employers in the LF, they did not succeed in influencing individual employers to comply with the Act, or to implement their own LF minorities policies in significant ways (STAR, 1998). Fifth, the notion that the opportunity of public scrutiny and public accountability in the 1994 Equity Act would forestall a control role for the government vis à vis the employers, as the SCGP considered when it recommended the Canadian example, turned out to be a total failure. Both labour unions and ethnic minority organisations preferred harmonious relations with employers to creating a public controversy. Finally, the resistance of the employers has resulted in a restoration of the tripartite consultation model at the national level, where the LF policies and the revised Equity Act are officially understood to supplement each other, where the sharp edges of the initial act have been carefully removed, and where the implementation of the Act is to some extent improved. The struggle over the equity legislation in the Netherlands has focussed most of the public attention on the question of social support for the implementation of both equity acts and has, ironically, put questions of their effectiveness in a secondary position. We have argued above that those effects, which were only measured after five years of equity legislation, are quite small and statistically insignificant. However, also the new LF policy with regard to ethnic minority employment has remained an instrument at the national level with very little impact on the HRM practices of individual employers (STAR, 1998).

It seems that the three parties – the government, the employers' organisations and the labour unions -- that work together so smoothly at the national level, are faced with the increasing problem of reaching and convincing their constituencies. Union members in the employees' councils have not done much to foster the implementation of the Equity Act, individual employers did not know of the equity policies of their central organisations, and citizens of all creeds protested against the registration of their ethnic identity. Therefore, in the face of the continued marginal position of ethnic minorities in the labour market, equity legislation and employment policies of the social partners are not enough as long as these are arrangements at the national level. The active involvement of individual employers, labour union members, and ethnic minority groups seems to be a conditio sine qua non. And this is where managing diversity comes into play.

EQUITY AND DIVERSITY: AWKWARD ATTRACTIONS

The practice of managing diversity, which is quickly turning into big business in the USA, Canada and the Netherlands, is suggested as a natural complement, or even as the solution to the underemployment of ethnic minorities, that affirmative action or employment equity could not bring (Kandola et al., 1995). Managing diversity is concerned with establishing a corporate environment in which increasing and multifarious differences among employees can be accommodated in an inclusive organisation, and be made productive for employers and rewarding for the individuals concerned (cf. Thomas Jr., 1990). Diversity management is the business of consultants and industrial trainers who direct their activities at managerial attitudes and skills, and at interpersonal relations in firms. It promises productivity, social justice and employee development.

Whatever one may think of these promises (cf. Glastra, 1996; 1999; Prasad et al., 1997), managing diversity has several strong points working for it, too. They are, among others, that it has access to many firms and can penetrate into local corporate situations where inequality is reproduced and responsibility is located. Moreover, diversity management is better adapted to dominant management cultures of individual competitiveness and achievement, and indeed to the more generalised upsurge of individualism in late modern societies, than equal opportunities policies are (Blakemore and Drake, 1996: 205). Diversity management goes beyond the bureaucracy of the numbers game that some equity measures require of employers, and in terms of sanctions it replaces sticks by carrots. By focusing on individual differences of any kind rather than singling out designated groups, it is inclusive instead of potentially divisive, even though it is in danger of underestimating determinants of conflicts on a collective level. And as a bonus, it appears to be the market solution to a seemingly incurable public embarrassment, i.e. the continued failure of official integration and equity policies with regard to ethnic minorities from 1983 onward and the gradual emergence of an ethnic underclass in the Netherlands.

However, in the Netherlands, managing diversity is hardly part of regular HRM practices in corporations. It is rather a set of additional services, mostly in the areas of training and consulting. Its predominant form is that of a commodity to be bought and sold on the market and therefore its blessings will never be enjoyed across the board. Those supplying diversity management services remain dependent on and limited to the needs and requirements of corporations and institutions with large purchasing power. If the issues of numerical representation and access to employment and promotion are not addressed, there will be little diversity in the organisation to manage. The results of the endeavours of diversity consultants tend to be very localised and hard to measure, or to compare across organisations. If, and to what extent they have contributed to labour participation and career mobility of ethnic minorities will remain an open question. Moreover, without adequate documentation of the relevant differences constituting the diversity in the workforces that consultants work with, it will be hard to monitor how inclusive, productive or rewarding their interventions are.

Nevertheless, the conclusion that managing diversity cannot be effective without equity legislation, and that both strategies simply complement or include each other, overlooks some thorny questions. First, in comparison with equity policies, managing diversity highlights cultural differences instead of inequality. In that context, it has a tendency to value all differences, such as age, religion, education, professional background, as well as gender, race or ethnicity, as equally important. This proliferation and dilution of differences may be helpful in the construction of a flexible and resourceful workforce, but it obscures and negates systematic and enduring differences in opportunities between specific categories of employees (cf. Nkomo and Cox, 1996). Second, the great stress on cultural differences in managing diversity may inadvertently jeopardise the social basis for equity policies among minority groups, through the fuelling of identity politics, the drawing and defence of ever sharper group boundaries, and a focus on claims for cultural recognition rather than equal treatment in socio-economic and professional career terms (cf. Hollinger, 1995). Third, bureaucratic classifications of minority groups in the context of institutionalised equity policies tend to evoke collective cultural identifications among involved groups which run counter to the more individualised notions of identity that managing diversity is fostering (Kymlicka, 1995: 16 ff.).

Although there are no easy solutions for the frictions and problems mentioned above, it is clear that equity policies and managing diversity do not completely exclude each other. In some publications, managing diversity is presented as an encompassing strategy. However, in practice, it is primarily concerned with changing the mindsets and behaviours of individual managers and employees through education, training and advice (cf. Thomas Jr., 1991: 38). In that sense, it may be said to be dealing with issues of organisational culture. It does not generally deal with the numbers, the proportional representation of designated groups throughout the work force. Therefore, equity legislation cannot be dispensed with. Agocs and Burr (1996: 36) state, in addition, that managing diversity does not generally seek to ensure behavioural change by altering organisational processes or structures. It is not about power differentials, inequalities and privileges. However, these phenomena of employment systems are not adequately dealt with by existing equity legislation and policies either. A further development of managing diversity to address this sensitive area seems to be indicated, if it is to fulfil its promises with regard to the inclusiveness of organisations.

Employment equity and managing diversity intervene on different levels in labour relations and interethnic relations. In the Netherlands, managing diversity can fulfil a useful function in supplementing equity legislation and national equity policies of the social partners at more local levels and with a specific eye for organisational structures and cultures. If it wants to play its role in a fruitful way it should have a keen awareness of the risks mentioned above (see also our chapter "Multiculturalism with a Price Tag" elsewhere in this book) and of the socio-political context in which it operates.

Folke J. Glastra is an Associate Professor at the Centre for Learning and Communication in Organisations, Faculty of Social and Behavioural Sciences, Leiden University, Leiden, The Netherlands. Petra E. Schedler is an Associate Professor at the Centre for Learning and Communication in Organisations at Leiden University. Erik Kats is an Associate Professor at the Centre for Learning and Communication in Organisations at Leiden University.

NOTES

[1] The authors are indebted to the Canadian ministry of foreign affairs and to NUFFIC for research grants that supported the present paper.

REFERENCES

Agocs, C. and C. Burr. "Employment Equity, Affirmative Action and Managing Diversity: Assessing the Differences." *International Journal of Manpower*. 14.4/5, (1996): 30-45.

Beck, U. *Risk Society; Towards a New Modernity.* London, Thousand Oaks, New Delhi: Sage, 1992.

Beckhoven, A.P.M. and J.W.M. Mevissen. *Aan de grenzen van het haalbare; Achtergronden van de invloed van ondernemingsraden op de maatschappelijke betrokkenheid van ondernemingen.* 's-Gravenhage: SZW.

Berkhout, A., et al.. *Bereik en effecten WBEAA.* 's-Gravenhage: SZW, 1996.

Blakemore, K. and R. Drake. *Understanding Equal Opportunity Policies.* London: Prentice Hall, 1996.

Braham, P., A. Rattansi, and R. Skellington. (Eds.). *Racism and Antiracism. Inequalities, Opportunities and Policies.* London: Sage, 1993.

Brassé, P. Arbeidsmarktbeleid etnische minderheden. In *Handboek Minderheden.* 3/1050. Houten, Zaventem: Bohn Stafleu Van Loghum, 1997, 1-34.

Broeckaert, B. Positieve actie-plannen voor migranten: een goed idee? *Tijdschrift voor sociologie.* 13.2, (1992).

Burght, F. van der and N. Pattipawae. *Positieve actie bedingen. Contract compliance in Nederland.* Utrecht: LBR, 1989.

Cox, T. jr. *Cultural Diversity in Organizations. Theory, Research and Practice.* San Francisco: Berrett-Koehler, 1994.

Glastra, F. Intercultureel management en de calculatie van het verschil. *Opleiding en ontwikkeling.* 9.6, (1996): 13-20.

Glastra, F.J., Schedler, P.E. & Kats, E.. "Employment Equity Policies in Canada and the Netherlands. Enhancing Minority Employment Between Public Controversy and Market Initiative." *Policy & Politics.* 26. 2, (1998): 143-156.

Glastra, F.J. (red.). *Organisaties en diversiteit. Naar een contextuele benadering van intercultureel management.* Utecht: Lemma, 1999.

D'Souza, D. *The End of Racism. Principles for a Multiracial Society.* New York: The Free Press, 1995.

Handboek Minderheden. Registratie. nr. 16. Houten/Zaventem: Bohn Stafleu Van Loghum, 1994.

Handboek Minderheden; Snelle berichtgeving. nr. 7. Houten/Zaventem: Bohn Stafleu Van Loghum, 1996.

Handboek Minderheden; Snelle berichtgeving. nr. 12. Houten/Zaventem: Bohn Stafleu Van Loghum, 1996.

Handboek Minderheden; Snelle berichtgeving. nr. 13. Houten/Zaventem: Bohn Stafleu Van Loghum, 1996.

Hollinger, D. *Postethnic America. Beyond Multiculturalism.* New York: Basic Books, 1995.

Hoof, J.J. van. *De arbeidsmarkt als arena. Arbeidsmarktproblemen in sociologisch perspectief.* Amsterdam: SUA, 1990.

Kandola, R., J. Fullerton, and Y. Ahmed. "Managing Diversity: Succeeding Where Equal Opportunities has Failed." *Equal opportunities review.* nr. 59 (jan/feb 1995).

Kuijer, A., and M.N. Stulemeijer. *Evenredige arbeidsdeelname van allochtonen.* Alphen aan den Rijn/Zaventem: Samson Bedrijfsinformatie, 1995.

Kymlicka, W. *Multicultural Citizenship. A Liberal Theory of Minority Rights.* New York: Oxford University Press, 1995.

Lucassen, J. & Penninx, R. *Nieuwkomers. Immigranten en hun nakomelingen 1550-1985.* Amsterdam: Meulenhof, 1985.

Mevissen, J.W.M. *De vraag naar arbeid en het moeilijk plaatsbare aanbod; Een eerste verkenning van*

mogelijkheden voor een meer vraaggericht arbeidsmarktbeleid. Amsterdam: Regioplan, 1991.
Nkomo, S.M. and T. Cox. Diverse Identities in Organizations. In Clegg, S.R. et al. (eds.). *Handbook of Organization Studies.* London/Thousand Oaks/ New Delhi: Sage, 1996, 338-356.
Pattipawae, N. Wetsvoorstel bevordering arbeidskansen allochtonen. *LBR Bulletin.* nr.3, (1992).
Penninx, R. and H. Vermeulen. Pluriformiteit en gelijk(waardig)heid; empirische en theoretische overwegingen over het opnameproces van immigranten en minderheden in de samenleving. *Migrantenstudies.* 10.4 (1994): 198-212.
Prasad, P. et al. (eds.). *Managing the Organizational Melting Pot. Dilemmas of Workplace* Diversity. Thousand Oaks, London, New Delhi: Sage, 1997.
Schedler, P.E., F.J. Glastra and E. Kats. Ervaringen en ontwikkelingen in Canada. Lerende organisaties en de interculturalisering van het arbeidsproces. *Sociale interventie*, 9.1 (2000): 42-52.
Schedler, P.E., F.J. Glastra and E. Kats. "Policymaking as a Communicative Enterprise. On the Boundaries of the 'Polder model' in the Late Modern Society." *Policy & Politics.* (2001, in press).
Schildmeijer, R.J. Toepassing van de Wet Bevordering Evenredige Arbeidsdeelname Allochtonen. In G.W.M. van Vugt (Red.). *Werken in multiculturele organisaties.* Houten, Diegem: Bohn Stafleu Van Loghum, 1995.
Schlesinger Jr., A.M. *The Disuniting of America: Reflections on a Multicultural Society.* New York: W.W. Norton & Company, 1992.
Staatscourant. 27 May, nr. 97, (1997): 1.
STAR (Stichting van de Arbeid). *Méér werk voor minderheden.* Publ. nr. 6/90. Den Haag: STAR, 1990.
STAR (Stichting van de Arbeid). *Derde interimevaluatie van het Stichtingsakkoord `Meer werk voor minderheden'.* Publ.nr. 5/94. Den Haag: STAR, 1994.
STAR (Stichting van de Arbeid). *Vierde interimevaluatie van het Stichtingsakkoord `Meer werk voor minderheden'.* Publ.nr. 1/96. Den Haag: STAR, 1996a.
STAR (Stichting van de Arbeid). *Met minderheden meer mogelijkheden. Vervolgnota over het minderhedenbeleid na ommekomst van het Stichtingsakkoord `Meer werk voor minderheden'.* Publ.nr. 8/96. Den Haag: STAR, 1996b.
STAR (Stichting van de Arbeid). *Interimevaluatie van het 2e Stichtingsakkoord `Met minderheden meer mogelijkheden'.* Publ.nr. 6/98. Den Haag: STAR, 1998.
SZW (Ministerie van Sociale Zaken en Werkgelegenheid). *Arbeidsmarktbeleid voor etnische minderheden. Plan van aanpak 2000-2003.* Den Haag: Ministerie van Sociale Zaken en Werkgelegenheid, 2000.
Thomas Jr, R.R. "From Affirmative Action to Affirming Diversity." *Harvard Business Review.* 90.2, (1990): 107-117
Thomas Jr., R.R. *Beyond Race and Gender.* New York: Amacom, 1991.
TWCM (Tijdelijke Wetenschappelijke Commissie voor het Minderhedenbeleid). *Etnische minderheden en de toegang tot de arbeidsmarkt.* 's Gravenhage: SDU-DOP, 1994.
Veraart, J. Banen voor allochtonen 2. *LBR Bulletin.* nr.6, (1992).
Veraart, J. Een wet met scherpe tanden. *LBR Bulletin.* nr.2, (1994).
Vermeulen, H. (ed.). *Immigrantenbeleid voor de multiculturele samenleving? Integratie-, taal- en religiebeleid voor immigranten in vijf West-Europese landen.* Amsterdam: IMES, 1997.
Vugt, G.W.M. van De multiculturele samenleving, overheidsbeleid en werkgelegenheid. In G.W.M. van Vugt (ed.). *Werken in multiculturele organisaties. Theorie en praktijk van intercultureel management.* Houten, Diegem: Bohn Stafleu Van Loghum, 1995.
WRR (Wetenschappelijke Raad voor het Regeringsbeleid). *Allochtonenbeleid.* 's Gravenhage: SDU, 1989.
Zandvliet, C.Th., et al. *Evaluatie wet SAMEN : eindrapport.* 's-Gravenhage : Elsevier bedrijfsinformatie, 2000.

CHAPTER 9

FOLKE GLASTRA, PETRA E. SCHEDLER AND ERIK KATS

MULTICULTURALISM WITH A PRICE TAG: ON THE THEORY AND PRACTICE OF INTERCULTURAL MANAGEMENT IN THE NETHERLANDS[1]

INTRODUCTION

In the United States and Canada, diversity has become a marketable commodity. As a concept, diversity is increasingly used to refer to the variety of individuals and groups with whom work places in these countries are confronted both in their labour and their consumer markets. Diversity should penetrate companies and institutions to their very cores, according to its advocates. Generally, differences in skin colour, ethnicity, gender, sexual orientation, religion, physical ability and age are at stake. Such characteristics are used by people in late modernity to define and demarcate their own and others' position and identity (Cox, 1993). Diversity, in the somewhat breathless consultancy jargon, is a challenge that can bring competitive advantage to business. More often than not, this claim is followed immediately, and somewhat ominously, by the statement that this promise will only come true if diversity is managed well (Cox and Finley, 1995). And this is where managing diversity, or, as it is usually called in the Netherlands, intercultural management comes into play. This practice of organisational consultants, instructors, trainers and human resources personnel has become big business in North America and is quickly gaining ground in the Netherlands too. Intercultural management, the Dutch term that we will use henceforth, is, above all, aimed at helping managers and employees of work places to deal with cultural differences. It should, thereby, also bring about inclusive organisations, work communities in which nobody is privileged or disadvantaged on account of irrelevant characteristics such as skin colour or ethnicity, and where people can develop their talents and contribute to the realisation of corporate goals (Thomas Jr., 1991).

The Dutch debate on and practice of intercultural management is primarily concerned with ethnic groups, and much less with gender, sexual orientation or disabilities (Van Kooten et al., 1994; Van Vugt, 1995). Dutch population statistics today reveal that almost 9 percent of the total population are identified as ethnic minorities. Among these, the Surinamese, the Turks, the Moroccans and the Antilleans/Arubans are the largest ethnic minority groups, while asylum seekers and refugees constitute a large and increasing category as well (for more specific information, see our chapter on employment equity in the Netherlands in this book). More than anything else, intercultural management constitutes a new practice in the field of social integration, which in circles of policy makers has come to mean the regular employment of ethnic minorities (cf. WRR, 1989). This practice is emerging in a period in which it has become clear that the Netherlands have de facto become an immigration country,[2] and that existing integration policies are ineffective and only lead to controversy. Intercultural management attracts both organisational

C. Agocs (ed.), Workplace Equality, 181–199.

consultants who are always looking for new markets, and activists and agents from the sector of minorities institutions, who have felt the wind of government budget cuts and privatisation and found their own way towards the market for diversity management services.

Intercultural management in the Netherlands may be directed at the entry, the acceptance in everyday work life, the mobility and the outflow of members of ethnic minority groups in work organisations. In that context, it addresses both the Dutch population and the immigrants among the employees. Intercultural management practice is characterised by decentralised initiatives and projects, which are guided by a supply and demand market and in which various partners, among them intercultural management agencies, co-operate with their customers. So far, intercultural management has not yet gained a structural position within institutions and companies, even though special posts for officers for designated groups have been created in some work organisations. In general, the gurus and practitioners of intercultural management define their pursuit in terms of a double challenge: (1) enhancing *social justice* by stimulating the acknowledgement and valuing of cultural differences, and by a more equal distribution of chances of fulfilling employment, and (2) increasing flexibility, creativity and, in the end, *productivity and profitability*, through the cultural diversification of work places.

In this article we will refer to the Surinamese, the Turks, the Moroccans and the Antilleans/Arubans, asylum seekers and refugees living in the Netherlands as ethnic minorities and we will speak of the mostly white Dutch population as the indigenous population.

PROMISES OF A ROSE GARDEN

The reader of the literature on intercultural management and the brochures of the agencies involved will find a host of promises that refer to these twin goals. Thus a business firm will be able to realise *competitive advantage* by broadening recruitment channels, enhancing the attractiveness of the organisation as an employer, deploying as yet unknown capacities and talents, diversifying products and marketing strategies; all of this will help to prepare the organisation for a global marketplace. At the same time, intercultural management is said to contribute to a *humane and decent organisation* since prejudice is counteracted, barriers are broken down and a social climate is developed in which there is equal representation and acceptance of ethnic minorities. *Personal growth* is claimed to be another product of intercultural management. It is triggered and stimulated by knowledge of one's own and other cultures, the development of one's cultural identity, and by the increased necessity of flexibility and improvisation in the face of cultural differences. And, as a consequence, the goal of *organisational development* is brought within view. Intercultural management claims to help employers to use their human resources more effectively. By evaluating and mobilising existing organisational routines and corporate cultures, it urges them to specify the common ground of the organisation (cf. Handy, 1994: 120), and it strengthens the *necessity of training and education* among the indigenous labour force as well. In a remarkably exuberant variant of what the Dutch labour sociologist Van Hoof (1991) has called "convergence thinking", intercultural management seems to work in many ways at once.

Of course, exaggerated promises raise questions (cf. Prasad and Mills, 1997; Shadid, 1998). Is personal growth a real possibility for flex-workers who face a glass ceiling and are insecure about their jobs (Kee, 1997)? And isn't exclusivity rather than inclusivity the word that best fits the current trend of lean production and downsizing? Can every firm and each function endure the loss of the taken for granted, routine order, which the introduction of cultural diversity may bring with it (cf. Verkuyten, 1997: 80)? And, lastly, if there is so much competitive advantage to be gained by recruiting and retaining ethnic minorities, why then hasn't that been done from the start?

WHY INTERCULTURAL MANAGEMENT IS NECESSARY

Notwithstanding the above questions, intercultural management must be taken seriously. It is expected that ethnic minorities will make up 14 percent of the population of the Netherlands by 2015 (SCP, 1999), and in the metropolitan area in the western parts of the country this percentage will rise to 45 percent even sooner. However, the situation of ethnic minorities is not to be envied. From 1985 onward, unemployment among ethnic groups has been three to four times higher than among the indigenous labour population, even if some groups are doing better than others. This situation continues even in the current period of economic boom and job creation in the Netherlands. In addition, the educational performance of ethnic minority youngsters has certainly improved over the last years, but, unfortunately for them, so has that of their majority contemporaries (Veenman, 1994). Industries such as metals, shipbuilding and textiles, on which immigrants traditionally depended for their employment, are disappearing very fast in the Netherlands. In their place a knowledge and information economy is growing, where ever higher qualifications are required and the better educated displace the lesser educated (Van Hoof, 1993). Finally, recruiting and retaining ethnic minority employees is still seen as a risk for business, even when employers are faced with a tight labour market. As a consequence of these developments, the risk of a society divided along ethnic lines is increasing (SCP, 1999).

The Dutch government has tried to avert this threat by means of a policy with regard to immigration, education, labour market and integration, which confronts ethnic minority immigrants and asylum seekers with restrictive and mandatory measures, and by introducing redistribution measures such as the Dutch employment equity acts (cf. Glastra, Schedler and Kats, chapter 8). On a national level, employers and labour unions have also made some important efforts. Thus, in 1990 they made an agreement to create 60,000 jobs for ethnic minorities, and to make this an important issue for collective bargaining. Many of these measures have not contributed to a more equal distribution of employment over population categories, not in the least because they polarised relations between the government and employers. The government has eased obligations for employers in the recent revision of the Employment Equity Act, and after the failure of the 60,000 jobs plan, the employers together with the labour unions have decided to revert to a decentralised approach of which intercultural management is one of the cornerstones (cf. Glastra et al., 1998). Intercultural management must be taken seriously, because dealing with the existing problems on a national scale and under the central supervision of government and/or national employers organisations and labour unions has not brought significant improvements, and has proved very controversial indeed. In the Netherlands, intercultural management has found its way into many prominent corporations, and it is presented and embraced by the government, employers and unions as the soft way out of the present stalemate in the debate about structural unemployment among ethnic minorities.

CHANCES FOR DIVERSITY

If intercultural management is assigned such a central position by the most important players in the field (i.e. government and social partners), and given the fact that the problems for which it should provide a solution have proved resistant to the endeavours of many parties involved, it should have convincing credentials. It should be said, though, that research concerning the conditions influencing the chances of success or failure for intercultural management projects and endeavours is scarce in the Netherlands. Although much is still unclear, there is evidence supporting the observation that projects cannot accomplish much without the co-operation and involvement of top management (Van Twuyver, 1995: 163). Furthermore, research in health care institutions demonstrates that projects initiated by institutions themselves, and propelled by a clearly perceived corporate interest, such as solving job vacancy problems or opening up new markets, are more successful in attracting and retaining ethnic minority employees than projects that are initiated by external actors, such as national or local governments, for reasons of full employment or equity (Topaz, 1996; Schedler et al., 1999). More specifically, companies and institutions may voluntarily initiate intercultural management programs to address job vacancy problems, a decreasing demand for their services or products, or the diversification of needs and expectations of clients, customers and employees. For public institutions, however, the goals of full employment or equity may have a bigger salience, most certainly where they have led to legislation, as in the case of the Dutch Equity Act (SZW, 2000). It is also a well-established fact that much of what is gained in terms of equity and diversity in corporations is easily lost in times of recession and downsizing (Van Twuyver, 1995: 154; Sloane and Jain, 1983). This is predominantly explained by the working of the seniority rule prescribing that the last employee entering the organisation should be the first to leave it when it comes to personnel reduction, and by the fact that setbacks are mostly absorbed in the flexible buffer of organisations in which, comparatively, many workers from ethnic minority groups are employed.

Furthermore, small firms, the economic driving force in the Netherlands, do not constitute a fertile ground for the incorporation of ethnic workers (Berkhout et al., 1996). Small firms are inclined to attach great weight to harmonious relations among the employees and with management. As a consequence, filling vacancies is primarily achieved through informal recruitment by the current employees.[3] Since small firms do not usually have a human resources department, they generally lack a human resource policy and they are not in a position to benefit from subsidies concerning the hiring of designated groups.[4] Much depends here on the attitude of the boss. Educational and training activities are known to have low priority in the budgets of middle and small-scale businesses (cf. Van Hoof, 1993; Handy, 1994: 116).

Of course, there needs to be a sufficient supply of qualified and motivated labour in regional labour markets, including workers who perceive regular or partly subsidised work as an opportunity and a sensible life fulfilment. In circles where long term unemployment is a widespread phenomenon, this may not be the case, as Dutch poverty research has shown (Engbersen et al., 1993). Next to this problem of labour supply, there is a growing lack of readily accessible jobs. Statistics with regard to the development of the labour market (CPB, 1995) demonstrate that the transition from an industrial to an information and knowledge economy has created many jobs for women, who seem to benefit more than ethnic minority workers from the increasing demand for flexible and part-time contractual employees. And, finally, a certain acceptance with regard to such values as equal opportunities, equal treatment and mutual respect of people from the top to the bottom of organisations is a condition sine qua non. Approachability is influenced by the dominant political and ideological climate in a nation state (Verkuyten, 1997: 155 ff.)

There is a significant lack of clarity about other conditions for the adoption of equity- and diversity-related initiatives by employers. Does the nature of the production process or the character of the commodities or services produced constitute an important incentive for realising diversity in work organisations? Is there evidence for the claim that Tayloristic organisations are detrimental, whereas flat or adhocratic organisations are friendly to diversity (cf. Golembiewski, 1995)? Do the interethnic bridges that intercultural management aims to build stand a better chance in the core of tenured employees and high potentials in businesses than in the periphery, where the employees involved quickly fall back on familiar group relations against a background of job insecurity? Is the introduction of diversity more difficult in traditionally male-dominated organisations such as the police (cf. Ott, 1985; Elias, 1997: 23)? Or is this not an iron-clad rule, as the case of the American army seems to demonstrate (cf. Patterson, 1997; Shipler, 1997)? Do the relatively vague functional requirements in the sphere of personality and social skills, which become ever more important in a knowledge and service economy, function as an ethnocentric sieve, or will they be defined in specific ethno-cultural ways that will enhance the opportunities of ethnic minorities? And, lastly, does the current trend towards making business units responsible for results constitute an advantage for immigrant workers, because only their performance will count in the end? Or will business units build existing barriers even higher because the managers of such units are less prepared to take what they see as risks (cf. Golembiewski, 1995: 152)? There are many questions to which answers are lacking.

THEORETICAL PERSPECTIVES ON INTERCULTURAL MANAGEMENT

In the body of thought with regard to intercultural management in the Netherlands, differing approaches may be discerned which are not mutually consistent. Three main approaches are: (1) a differentiation approach, which stresses cultural differences; (2) a discrimination approach focusing on neglect, on the unequal treatment, the deprivation and exclusion of minorities from opportunities; and (3) a deficiency approach which makes deficits in qualifications the central issue (cf. Glastra, 1996; 1999).

Figure 1: Theoretical approaches to intercultural management

Approaches	**Versions**	**Central issues**
Differentiation	- Culturalisation - Individualisation	- Collective cultural differences - Individual cultural differences
Discrimination	- Prejudice - Systemic	- Attitudes and neglect - Social structure and neglect
Deficiency		- Deficits in qualifications

The *differentiation approach*, which is dominant in the Netherlands, can be subdivided into a culturalising and an individualising version. In the case of *culturalisation*, learning about collective cultural differences is most important (cf. Trompenaars, 1993; Pinto, 1994). Human thinking and action is primarily explained and understood in terms of their original ethnic or national culture. In this context, the influential Dutch investigator Hofstede (1980; 1995) even speaks of mental programming; people are defined by their cultural heritage. From this perspective, the intermingling of cultures within territories or organisations leads to misunderstandings and frictions. Therefore, it is imperative that members of the indigenous population, but also immigrants, learn about each other's cultures and develop intercultural communication skills. However, one should avoid a situation where learning about cultural differences turns into the institutionalisation of stereotypes, and the notion of cultural difference is made into a self-fulfilling prophecy (Human, 1996; Weiner, 1997). Culturalisation may in that case end in an intensification of the well-known situation in which people like each other across racial or ethnic borders as individuals, but vilify each other as collectivities (cf. Verkuyten, 1997; Shipler, 1997: 7). Culturalisation represents people one-sidedly as cultural heirs who belong to a certain collective culture in an unequivocal way. However, people are always producers of culture at the same time. Moreover, culturalisation fails to appreciate cultural ambiguity and the well-known phenomenon of changing identities and bi-culturality, for instance in alternations between leisure and work (cf. Koot, 1994; Shipler, 1997: 18).

Individualisation, the version of differentiation that was introduced in the Netherlands under the name of managing diversity and predominant in the conceptualisation of Roosevelt Thomas Jr., stresses the importance of learning about individual cultural differences and identifications. According to Thomas Jr. (1991), managers in particular should develop a mindset, which enhances the emergence of inclusive organisations. In such organisations, values and structures are induced that accord with the configuration of cultural identities, needs and competencies of the employees. Modern, individualistic employees no longer want to exchange their unique cultural identities at the firm entrance for the straitjacket of a corporate identity in the colours of the majority. It is not so much cultural knowledge that is needed here, but a management that facilitates and empowers. The risk involved in this version of differentiation is that late modern tendencies of tribalisation (cf. Bauman, 1995) and ethnification, which feed precisely on conflicts about the distribution of scarce goods such as waged labour (cf. Bader, 1995), are neglected. Furthermore, the flexibility of organisational structures and cultures and the flexing powers of managers are seriously overestimated.

In general, we may conclude that both versions of differentiation are inclined to define culture from the perspective of a form of capital that is, literally, incorporated in individuals or groups (cf. Bourdieu, 1992). We call this an atomistic conception of culture. In the differentiation approach this incorporated capital is lifted out of its social context, which includes other sorts of capital, which people have at their disposal, and various fields in which differing forms of capital may be more or less valuable, so that its importance and significance is easily overstated. And finally, the differentiation approach neglects the active involvement of companies and enterprises themselves in the day to day cultural development of their employees, which is underpinned by normative images of the model worker, and by organisational reward systems.

The *discrimination approach* concentrates on prejudice and ethnic exclusion in enterprises. As a solution, it offers racism awareness courses for individuals (Oomkes, 1993: 337). Sometimes such training is supported by a policy that provides for sanctions, as well as an information campaign, and by more general strategies directed at the institutional sources of inequality in organisational structures. The *prejudice version* involves the struggle against a mental enemy, which manifests itself in both individuals and in group processes. Confrontation with often repressed racist feelings and unconscious discriminatory behaviour are central issues. Notions of tolerance for the other and the principle of equality are used in order to argue the right of equal treatment. The central issues here are the attitudes and behaviour of the indigenous population, which result in forms of direct discrimination. The *systemic version* emphasises the historical, institutional and systematic aspects of the social structure, which maintain unequal social relations between ethnic groups in enterprises. Vested interests, power differences and routines that have not been critically examined result in ethnic disadvantage and exclusion (Van Dijk, 1993; Van Beek, 1993; Schuyt, 1995: 85). Here, the production of disadvantage is fused with organisational structures to a degree that intercultural management is only of use as part of a significant democratisation of work relations. The discrimination approach is the most controversial strategy in the Netherlands. As one intercultural practitioner said: "There have been many consultants who, like ourselves, have adopted consciousness-raising about existing racism as the point of departure for their training programmes. Most of them have been unsuccessful because it is so difficult. You have to make participants aware of racist aspects of their own behaviour. This evokes an enormous resistance" (Bouman and Hogema, 1995: 54).

The *deficiency approach* focuses on the perceived general lack of qualifications and the inability of ethnic minorities to adjust to organisational cultures in Dutch enterprises. The dominant structure of job requirements and organisational traditions are taken as given factors. Ethnic minority employees should be helped specifically to overcome deficiencies in their command of the Dutch language, in job search and interview skills, and in acquiring work experience in Dutch work places. Education, training and guidance are regarded as compensatory measures. It is argued that intensive forms of individual guidance must be used to facilitate the entry of immigrants into the labour market (Van den Berg et al., 1997). In this approach, participation in work is viewed as a question of opportunities. Access to, promotion within, and exit from firms are dependent on the relative assets of the person involved in terms of qualifications and work experience. This meritocratic reasoning suggests that an individual possessing the required talents, or investing in them, will progress far in a system, which knows no fundamental barriers. In this human capital theory of productivity (cf. Dagevos, 1997) the responsibility, and consequentially often the blame, for a lack of progress is located within the group or individual involved.

INTERCULTURAL MANAGEMENT PRACTICES

The literature on intercultural management in the Netherlands still consists to a large extent of general discussions, handbooks and case descriptions. Research with regard to the practice of intercultural management is slowly beginning (cf. De Vries, 1993; Nijhof and Abma, 1994; Boessenkool, 1994; Pettigrew and De Vries, 1994: Derveld. 1995; Van Twuyver, 1995; Glastra, 1996; Glastra et al., 1996; Meerman and Van der Vlist, 1996; Abell et al., 1997; Van Twuyver et al., 1997; Glastra, 1998; Meerman, 1999; Bovenkerk et al.,

1999; Glastra, et al., 1999; Van Putten, et al. 2000). This body of work enables us to indicate crucial defining characteristics.

In the practice of intercultural management, elements of the approaches mentioned above are often mixed and fused, but the main emphasis is on cultural differences. This specific definition of problems with regard to the multicultural nature of work organisations has become institutionalised in intercultural management as the business run by mostly private agencies in the field of intercultural training and consultancy. This specific institutionalisation of intercultural management reinforces the idea that it makes sense to deal with problems concerning the relations between majorities and ethnic minorities in isolation from the multifariousness of social bonds and relations in work places. Its additional service nature also limits the opportunities for intercultural management to develop into an integral corporate practice, and advances the idea that intercultural management should be no more than a quick fix to be bought on the market whenever and as long as extraordinary circumstances prevail. Diversity management should secure or restore business as usual, and is in that sense essentially defensive. The emphasis on cultural differences veils its potentiality to develop into an integral and innovative corporate practice.

Within this context, it is well-nigh impossible for intercultural management agencies to confront a firm or a department with discriminatory tendencies in its policies or in the interactions between colleagues. Open and direct discrimination is usually condemned, but is seldom perceived to happen in the everyday work situations of the mostly indigenous employees involved. Discrimination is thought to be elsewhere (Meerman, 1999). At the other end of the spectrum, suspicion of preferential treatment of minorities, for instance based on the texts of employment advertisements, stirs up bad feelings too. Combining the insensitivity to discrimination against ethnic minorities in the workplace, and sensitivity about their preferential treatment, restricts the operational area of intercultural management severely. Hence they concentrate on mutual acceptance, enhancing corporate communication, learning to deal with cultural differences, and making up for deficiencies in the qualifications or the smooth adaptation to new work environments of ethnic minority employees.

In the market for intercultural management, many agencies recruit and select ethnic job-seekers for the labour market, prepare these candidates for integration in work places through skill training, and teach linguistic skills and provide guidance during on-the-job professional schooling. Some agencies have started to provide career counselling (cf. Besamusca-Janssen, 1997). In addition, agencies are sometimes commissioned to assist in the development of a diversified human resources policy. Moreover, training is provided from management to shop floor, in cultural awareness, intercultural management and communication. Contributions are made to the development of methods and instruments (for instance in health care) that enhance professional activity in a multicultural environment, and sometimes conflict resolution services are provided. The main targets of the practice of intercultural management are problems of recruitment and selection and the quality of interethnic relations in everyday work situations. Vertical or horizontal mobility are rarely issues that are tackled as yet by intercultural management, urgent as they are.

There are but few companies and institutions that make serious efforts to become culturally diversified organisations, or try to adapt the structuring and definition of their tasks and their corporate strategy to the new realities (cf. Van Twuyver et al., 1997). More specifically, larger enterprises, organisations in the service and consumer goods sectors, media-sensitive institutions and corporations, and organisations such as the police and the prison system that have to compete at the lower end of a tight labour market, are beginning to define workforce diversity as a strategic target (cf. Bovenkerk et al., 1999; Glastra et al., 1999; Glastra, 1998). In general, the public and non-profit sectors are more active as buyers on the market for intercultural management than the private sector (Abell et al., 1997: 38).

Training and to a lesser extent organisational consultancy are the favourite methods in use. Eliminating deficits in qualifications among ethnic employees is often left to the educational sector, although it must be said that intercultural management agencies increasingly adopt a complementary and co-ordinating role, certainly where schooling in the context of access to jobs is concerned. Frequently, there is not much time or room allocated to thorough observation and analysis of the situation in a work place preceding the intervention. An extended interview with the customer must usually suffice in order to fill in cash-and-carry-training-modules with some couleur locale. Most corporations want quick solutions and have more than one reason to keep the agencies' room for in-depth analysis as limited as possible. Most agencies and consultants in the field of intercultural management bend to the discipline of the market. As a consequence of restrictions in analysis and time budgets, intercultural management projects are generally not capable of penetrating profoundly or broadly into organisations, nor are they, as a rule, allowed to organise follow up activities (cf. Abell et al., 1997). There is a preference for top-down interventions and an emphasis on employee attitudes, cognitions and behaviour. The specific content and the intensity of the intervention are geared to the positions that different groups occupy inside the organisation. The top is usually too busy for more than hearing the business case for diversity (cf. o.c.: 37). In practice, it turns out to be very difficult to reach the strategically positioned stratum of the middle managers in order to train them in managing a diverse workforce. In their output-driven business units, they are notoriously short of time. They have set priorities in terms of their targets and are only concerned with such professional and organisational requirements as will be helpful to realise those targets (cf. Meerman, 1999). The shop floor will receive a course in Dutch as a Second Language and be engaged in cultural or racism awareness or intercultural communication training. Usually this takes place during work hours and often participation is voluntary. In the Netherlands, the emphasis is on intercultural interaction attitudes and skills, and on the significance of cultural differences for personal performance and everyday interactions on the job (cf. Abell et al., 1997: 25). Organisational structures, work routines and corporate strategy are too often ignored and, hence, intercultural training shows a lack of embeddedness in the broader policies of companies and enterprises.

The above sketch does not imply that the development of intercultural management practices in the Netherlands is problematic across the board, and less still, that only the conceptions, methods and goals of the agencies involved are to be blamed for shortcomings. Often intercultural management practitioners cannot control or even influence working conditions in the labour market, and in companies and institutions they are confronted with worn routines, outright resistance, and the hard consequences of business calculations. All this is not to say that there are no long-term projects, which succeed in enhancing ethnic minorities' access to workplaces, and make the employees involved sensitive to the necessity of diversity and the adaptation of their tasks and services (cf. Topaz, 1996).

Despite the diversity of origins and backgrounds of the agencies operating in the field of intercultural management, distinctive traits, and what Bourdieu (1992) has called a doxa, are developing: a set of presuppositions about the nature of central problems and preferred solutions, which are no longer debated. In the construction of the field of intercultural management, professionalisation has begun to develop. Evidence of this includes specialised higher educational courses, the recent establishment of chairs in intercultural management (cf. Burggraaf, 1998) and intercultural communication, national and international exchanges and seminars (as in the national and international branches of the Society for Intercultural Education, Training, and Research), the mapping and monitoring of agencies and projects, support and network development (by the state-financed Institute for Multicultural Development, FORUM), and pleas for benchmarking and quality control. The emerging doxa shared by those working in the field of intercultural management consists of two assumptions: (1) incorporation into the regular labour system is the royal road to the integration of ethnic minorities in the eyes of the government, and (2) productivity and flexibility are number one priorities for employers. Diversity and, more rarely, inclusiveness, are catchwords bridging these exigencies of a humane society and a profitable market for most players. To make the necessity of integration a virtue of productivity a thorough understanding and management of individual and/or collective cultural differences is needed. In addition obstacles to an unprejudiced use and development of talents and competencies must be tackled. In this way, core premises of the former multiculturalist policy, carefully mothballed by the national government, return in privatised form, custom made for the market and the corporation (cf. Glastra, 1998).

Intercultural management practices must operate in a field with a history in which strategies to change interethnic relations have tended to end in disappointment and controversy time and again. Therefore, quick results cannot be expected. The routines reproducing ethnic inequalities are too deeply engrained for that. Cultural diversity is not just a coming together of various cultural and ethnic backgrounds and bonds that can be forged into a productivity factor by means of smart and culturally sensitive management. There can be a considerable amount of friction and conflict among those different social bonds within the department, the organisation, the ethnic peer group, and the nation state. Diversity is embedded in multipolar relations of power exerting their influence within and outside of organisations. Such relations impregnate the practices and the body of thought of intercultural management itself. This is, first of all, evident in the different approaches we sketched in the foregoing discussion, which are obviously based on different and even contradictory political analyses. But more important, the multipolarity of power relations manifests itself in a number of fundamental dilemmas for practitioners of intercultural management, whether they are aware of it or not. For example, must intercultural management induce people to find, (re)fabricate and mutually respect their ethno-cultural roots, or rather, are simultaneous tendencies of individualisation and the formation of plural and hybrid identities to be encouraged (Hollinger, 1995; Nederveen Pieterse, 1995; Bauman, 1998)? Are corporations indeed the social arrangements for a powerful realisation of the ideal of an inclusive and diversified society, or do those corporations, as a consequence of the very parameters underlying their operations, in fact continuously undermine the stability of the membership of society (cf. Handy, 1994)? Must intercultural management confess to cultural relativism or will Western values be assumed to be beyond debate (Koch and Scheffer, 1996)? Can the goals of equal treatment irrespective of ethnic or other backgrounds on the one hand, and unlike treatment on the basis of the acknowledgement of differences, be reconciled in the practice of intercultural management (Taylor, 1995)?

Even a short enumeration of such dilemmas makes it crystal clear that intercultural management is not a *deus ex machina.* In its present state intercultural management is too much bound and restricted both by its dependent position in the field that it seeks to change and its theoretical and methodical orientations. Our assertion would be that the arduous task of promoting and enhancing diversity and equity in the workplace would be more effectively undertaken if the intellectual scope and the repertory of methods of intercultural management were broadened and its political and social relations strengthened. In the context of this chapter we can only briefly stipulate what we have in mind.

TOWARDS A BROADER THEORETICAL PERSPECTIVE

If intercultural management is to make a contribution towards diversity and equity in the workplace, it is in need of a broader intellectual scope that enables practitioners and students of intercultural management to put the significance of deficits, prejudice and cultural differences in a broader perspective. In figure 2 we specify key elements of such a perspective.

First, in our opinion, a contextual approach to intercultural management is necessary (cf. Glastra, 1996; 1999). The contextuality referred to here primarily pertains to the political, social and economic contexts in which both corporations and practices of intercultural management operate. We dealt with them briefly in the foregoing discussion under the heading of chances for diversity. Reflecting on the significance of this multifarious environment is helpful in keeping projects on a fruitful course. Elsewhere (see Schedler and Glastra, 1998; Schedler et al., 1998; Glastra, 1999), we have detailed an analytical framework that is to be put to such uses drawing on the field theory of Pierre Bourdieu (1992).

Figure 2: Broadening the intellectual scope

. towards a contextual approach to intercultural management
. from organisations towards an analysis of political and economic contexts
. from group characteristics towards organisational features
. from cultural determination towards power dynamics
. not just cultural difference or discrimination as explanatory frameworks
. tracing situational logic by varying analytical perspectives

Second, interethnic relations should also be analysed in light of the dynamics of specific organisations. In cases of conflict or problems where majority and minority workers are involved, one should not in advance look for explanations in terms of prejudice or cultural difference, even though such variables will often play a role in the current circumstances. Immigrants and indigenous people are not brought together in firms as autonomous citizens. They have to co-operate and compete on the basis of the structure, the rules, the ends and the means, which have made the organisation what it is. And organisational features may vary widely, and empirically speaking, so do the circumstances under which migrants and indigenous inhabitants of the Netherlands meet each other in work situations (cf. Bader, 1995). The team of street sweepers that is composed of people recruited through a workfare scheme within the municipality of the Hague is not the same kind of group as the expert meeting of minority's specialists at the Ministry of the Interior. Aspects such as the duration and stability of the labour contracts, the hierarchical order in the work organisation, the educational levels involved and the nature of the work leave their mark on the evolving interactions. We argue that organisational features should be taken much more seriously. When frictions or conflicts arise, one should, first of all, look for a situational logic. More often than not, various problems, interests, perspectives and articulations of different social groups, institutional units or individuals are at stake at the same time. Ordinary explanations concerning labour circumstances, control over the arrangement of work processes and the quality of management should not be overlooked, as was found in an analysis of a conflict at the Amsterdam Municipal Transport Company (Glastra et al., 1996). In such cases, a training course with regard to cultural differences will not suffice, or can even be wide of the mark, because it doesn't address underlying structural and organisational dimensions of inequality.

The analytical perspective on problems of diversity and equity in organisations should be varied frequently. Intercultural management should not merely be informed by theories about ethnic attitudes, identity formation, cultural differences and intercultural communication, but also by insights concerning the labour market, organisational cultures and structures, leadership and management, and learning in organisations (cf. Glastra, 1999). In this way, various aspects of problematic or successful co-operation can be brought to the surface, while avoiding the pitfall of concentrating on attitude change and improving everyday interactions without ensuring that the intended results will be sustained by structural arrangements in the organisation (cf. Cohen, 1992). An organisation constitutes a dynamic practice of living and working together, kept intact by its own social and cultural order for as long as it is capable of realising the strategic goals defining its raison d'être. It is of the utmost importance to engage in the analysis of the relationships of power and interest, and the ways in which employees relate to the cultural and social order of the organisation, and reproduce or transform that order. Thus, it is possible to locate mechanisms of change and sources of conservatism.

Our argument may look like an *oratio pro domo*, a plea to turn finances for training and education into research grants, but it is not. Analysis and intervention should go together and structure each other in this endeavour (cf. Kats, 1996). And this brings us to the question of methods.

BROADENING THE REPERTORY OF METHODS

It could be the conclusion of an organisational analysis that the conditions for the fruitful introduction of some form of intercultural management are absent. Intercultural management would then be a waste of money, as is the case in strongly task-oriented organisations, which consider all risky learning processes of a longer timeframe to be dead weight. However, such conclusions are rarely drawn. Intercultural management agencies will usually provide training of short duration. Working with standard modules, which permit a limited measure of local colouring, facilitates the transaction and the implementation for both providers and customers, but also enhances superficiality. A modish appearance of custom-made solutions is created, which brings the relief of the limited intervention where a more holistic approach of general organisational characteristics is needed. The practice of learning about cultural differences and moral attitudes in isolation should be left behind, even though that will be difficult under the current market conditions. In fact, one can speak of a twofold danger inherent in much intercultural training. The central themes of intercultural management are extracted from the discourse of the work place, but by their transposition into the training form, also from everyday practice and the relationships that hold there. For the employees involved it becomes doubly difficult to translate and practice what is learned, model knowledge in model circumstances, in their own work situation (cf. Kessels, 1996).

Figure 3: Broadening the repertory of methods

. from training towards integrated forms of working and learning
. from interaction and personality towards structural embedding
. from short interventions towards long-term development projects
. acknowledging and reflecting on the political nature of interventions

Intercultural management in the Netherlands has so far, unjustly, ignored the tendency towards on-the-job-training (Van Onna, 1992) and the creation of so-called powerful learning environments (cf. Lodewijks, 1993) in the current debate about organisational learning and industrial training. Developments with regard to the ever more popular Dutch-on-the-shop-floor language programs constitute an important exception. Such programs have advantages over intercultural communication training and certified language courses in that they can be kept much closer to everyday working practices and to the skin of a living community of employees. Witte (1995) and Verhallen (1995), among others, have stressed the importance of directly linking second language acquisition to everyday work situations, which makes illustrative learning possible. As a consequence, they specify criteria for the description of tasks, the arrangement of the workplace and communication patterns in enterprises and companies. Work environments which are deprived of language as a consequence of segregation, routine labour or paternalism, will very soon induce the loss of what has been learned in terms of language command. Intercultural management should pay more attention to forms of learning - by the traditional workforce and ethnic minorities - which are integrated in the organisation in which working together and living together are two sides of the same coin and are closely associated with acquiring professional competencies. Elements of this type of learning were found by Glastra, Meerman and De Vries (1999) in their research with regard to diversity in penal institutions in the Netherlands. Here, weekly work consultations among members of diversified teams in some prisons were informally used to develop and share intercultural knowledge and competencies. These forms of spontaneous diversification of professional knowledge, competencies and attitudes on the shop floor were not acknowledged or sustained by management. Such local strategies may be the starting points of a more broadly based diversity policy.

In addition mentoring, a practice in which newcomers to an organisation or a department are assigned a mentor, is important. A mentor familiarises the employee involved with organisational rules and routines, and gives advice with regard to the social relationships and the work that is to be done (cf. Ragins, 1995; Lazeron, 1994). Of course, mentoring is not without dangers. It can contribute to the stigmatisation of newcomers, it can lead to jealousy and backlash, and it can also be a powerful instrument for the conservation of the traditional organisational culture (cf. Garvey, 1994). Nevertheless, a mentor relationship may eventually result in forms of mutual counselling and coaching between more or less equal professionals. Since informal social networks are of increasing importance for both getting jobs done and realising horizontal or vertical mobility in organisations, these should be paid much more attention than is currently the case in Dutch intercultural management practices and literature (Stephenson and Lewin, 1996; Elias, 1997). The acquisition of social capital can be advanced by mentor systems and by social networks. The latter have been formalised in American corporations such as IBM and Xerox in diversity councils and diversity networks. In the Netherlands, ethnic minorities' councils operate predominantly as pressure groups, and informal support groups aim at developing survival strategies for members of ethnic minority groups in work places.

Moving still further in the direction of changes in organisational structure is the introduction of employment systems reviews, which aim at identifying and removing organisational barriers against access, mobility and development of minority workers, and developing procedures for complaint and appeal. It is also possible to incorporate the minimum conditions and qualifications necessary for access or promotion to management and leadership positions in a multicultural organisation in task and function descriptions and, more generally, in everyday control and reward routines. This happens, for instance, in the Canadian Bank of Montreal, where bank branches are structured according to the concept of community banking. This means that the employees of a branch are a more or less precise reflection of the ethnic composition of the population of the neighbourhood where it is located (Schedler, et al. 2000). Thus the standard practice of leaving decisions about the selection of personnel to the personal views and preferences of local managers is left behind, for they have to take the neighbourhood composition into account.

And, finally, the notion that with intercultural management a better world and increased productivity are introduced at the same time should be called into question. In workplaces, many power relations are simultaneously in effect. A change agent, who succeeds in curbing a shop floor culture of practical jokes and machismo, and in instilling some respect and tolerance, will usually be quite content with such results. However, this may not be the only effect of the intervention. It may well have eroded the system of boundary markers that enabled workers on the shop floor to keep the office and the control of the manager at bay, and to realise a certain measure of self regulation of the work process (cf. Van den Broek, 1998). Intercultural management will never merely be the push in the right direction that it pretends to be. It is always concerned with thoroughly political interventions, and it had better be aware of the fact. This brings us to the social and political context of intercultural management.

STRENGTHENING POLITICAL AND SOCIAL RELATIONS

One could say that the practice of intercultural management has adopted core elements of the former minorities policy of the Dutch government, such as proportional participation, equal treatment, but most of all, integration while retaining the cultural heritage. These elements were exchanged in the first half of the 1990s for a social obligations conception of citizenship, especially where newcomers are concerned (cf. Engbersen, 1994; De Beus, 1996). Multiculturalism was privatised and introduced on the market, adorned with a price tag. As the commercial guardian of this cultural baggage, intercultural management should avoid concentrating on and realizing the priorities of businesses and institutions, which constitute its clientele. Insofar as it contributes to productivity, diversity is indeed a business issue. However, work organisations do not have a natural or inherent stake in a more just distribution of labour. This is aptly illustrated by the plea of the organisation of employers in small and medium-sized businesses in the Netherlands to compensate for the current under-supply of workers in the labour market by lengthening the working week and recruiting in neighbouring EC countries. According to the organisation, the existing so-called silent reserve of unemployed workers does not fit the employers' demand (NRC Handelsblad, 3 March 1998).

The practice of intercultural management cannot hope to accomplish much in the way of an equal distribution of opportunities in the labour market or the creation of inclusive organisations, if it cannot be based on adequate policies in the fields of education, labour market and the struggle against discrimination. Otherwise it will run the risk of become the playball of stronger market forces. Intercultural management will turn into a luxury commodity available in return for the spending power of public relations sensitive firms and institutions. Diversity then becomes window dressing for persistent job ghettos at the bottom end of the labour market. The supporters and suppliers of intercultural management cannot keep on reacting against the centre of power, and more specifically against governmental employment equity policies and legislation, even if such resistance apparently makes some sense in the light of the opposition from the employers. In our view, the strength of intercultural management should be to provide an integrative structure for the policy domains mentioned before and a network in which employers, publicly financed job agencies, the educational sector, authorities and organisations of ethnic minorities can be linked. In the Netherlands, most intercultural management projects are carried out in relative isolation, even though there are some encompassing and government financed projects which are firmly linked up with the main players in the field (cf. Topaz, 1996). The project of intercultural management is also threatened by a reverse risk, that of politisation, as the controversial introduction and inadequate implementation of the Dutch employment equity act has amply demonstrated (cf. Glastra, Schedler and Kats, chapter 8 of this book).

For the practice of intercultural management this means that it should leave the relative safety of its niche market for training and consultancy if it wants to take its own goals seriously. In that case, balancing on a tight rope becomes a necessity. The occasional fall must be taken as the opportunity to learn that the Dutch practice of intercultural management has avoided so far.

Folke J. Glastra is an Associate Professor at the Centre for Learning and Communication in Organisations at the Faculty of Social and Behavioural Sciences, Leiden University, The Netherlands. Petra E. Schedler is an Associate Professor at the Centre for Learning and Communication in Organisations at Leiden University, The Netherlands. Erik Kats is an Associate Professor at the Centre for Learning and Communication in Organisations at Leiden University, The Netherlands

NOTES

[1] Parts of this chapter were previously published in F. J. Glastra, M. Meerman, P. E. Schedler and S. de Vries, "Broadening the Scope of Diversity Management: Strategic Implications in the Case of the Netherlands," *Relations Industrielles/ Industrial Relations*, 55(4), 2000, 698-724.

[2] It is only recently that the Dutch minister of metropolitan areas and integration policies has stated that it would be better if the Netherlands were to acknowledge that it is an immigration country.

[3] However where small businesses are operated by ethnic minorities, such word-of-mouth recruitment creates employment niches for members of their community.

[4] The Dutch Equity Act pertains to firms and institutions that employ 35 employees and more. Subsidies for the training of ethnic minority job candidates flow from public funds. The government has set targets for the publicly financed labour mediation institutions and pays extra for the mediation, training and job experience of ethnic minorities. Firms who take on unemployed ethnic minorities may profit from wage subsidies and tax deductions.

REFERENCES

Abell, P., A.E. Havelaar, and M.M. Dankoor. *The Documentation and Evaluation of Anti-discrimination Training Activities in the Netherlands*. International Migration papers. Geneva: ILO, 1997.

Agocs, C., C. Burr, and F. Somerset. *Employment Equity*. Scarborough, Ontario: Prentice-Hall Canada, 1992.

Bader, V.M. Rassismus, Etnizität, Bürgerschaft. *Soziologische und Philosophische Überlegungen*. Münster: Westfälisches Dampfboot, 1995.

Bauman, Z. *Life in Fragments. Essays in Postmodern Morality*. Oxford and Cambridge: Blackwell, 1995.

Beek, K. van (1993). *To be Hired or not to be Hired, the Employer Decides. Relative Chances of Unemployed Job-seekers on the Dutch Labour Market*. Amsterdam: s.n.

Berg, H. van der, Denolf, L. & Veer, K. van der (1997). *Het kleine verschil. Slaag- en faalfactoren bij traject-bemiddeling van allochtonen*. Amsterdam: Jan Mets.

Berkhout, A., et al. *Bereik en effecten WBEAA*. 's-Gravenhage: SZW, 1996.

Besamusca-Janssen, M."Doorstroom en loopbaan-ontwikkeling." In Besamusca-Janssen, M. et al.. *Intercultureel management in de zorgsector*. Hilversum: Teleac/NOT, 1997, 99-110.

Beus, J. de. "Patriëring van oude en nieuwe Nederlanders." In Koch, K. and P. Scheffer (eds.). *Het nut van Nederland. Opstellen over soevereiniteit en identiteit*. Amsterdam: Bert Bakker, 1996, 161-186.

Boessenkool, J. "Think global - Act local: fictie of werkelijkheid?" *Mens & Onderneming*, 48.2, (1994): 161-174.

Bouman, H. and I. Hogema. "De markt van multiculturele misverstanden." *Intermediair*. 31.15 (1995): 53-55.

Bourdieu, P. *Opstellen over smaak, habitus en het veldbegrip*. Amsterdam: Van Gennep, 1992.

Bovenkerk, F., M. van San, & S. de Vries. *Policing a multicultural society*. Apeldoorn: LSOP, 1999.

Broek, L. van den. "Intimidatie op de werkvloer." In Haffmans, M. and B. Sijsjes (eds.). *Verborgen drempels*. Utrecht: Forum, 1998.

Burggraaf, W. *Intercultureel management; Over culturen en de multiculturele organisatie*. Breukelen: Nijenrode University Press, 1998.

Cohen, Ph. "'It's Racism What Dunnit'. Hidden Narratives in Theories of Racism." In Donald, J. and A. Rattansi (eds.). *'Race', Culture and Difference*. London: Sage/The Open University, 1992, 62-103.

Cox, T. H. Jr. *Cultural Diversity in Organisations*. San Francisco: Berrett-Koehler, 1993.

Cox, T.H. Jr. and J.A. Finley. 'An Analysis of Work Specialization and Organisation Level as Dimensions of Workforce Diversity." In Chemers, M.M., S. Oskamp, and M.A. Constanzo (eds.). *Diversity in Organisations. New Perspectives for a Changing Workplace*. Thousand Oaks, London, New Delhi: Sage, 1995, 62-88.

CPB (Centraal Planbureau). *Macro Economische Verkenningen 1996*. Den Haag: SDU, 1995.

Dagevos, J. "Economen over de positie van werkende allochtonen." *Migrantenstudies*. 13.4, (1997): 209-223.

Derveld, F.E.R. *Intercultureel management in perspectief*. Groningen: SIV, 1995.

Dijk, T.A. van. *Elite Discourse and Racism*. Newbury Park/London/ New Delhi: Sage, 1993.

Elias, M. (1997). *Onder dienders*. Amsterdam: Balans.

Engbersen, G., C.J.M. Schuyt, J. Timmer, and F. van Waarden. *Cultures of Unemployment*. New York: Westview Press, 1993.

Engbersen, G. "Zin en onzin van de culturele factor; sociale en institutionele voorwaarden voor inburgering." In Zwan, A. v.d. and H.B. Entzinger. *Beleidsopvolging minderhedendebat. Advies in opdracht van de Minister van Binnenlandse Zaken.* 's Gravenhage, 1994.

Garvey, B. "Mentoring: ervaringen in een groot bedrijf." In Kessels, J.W.M. and Smit, C.A. (eds.) *Opleiders in organisaties.* Capita Selecta. Afl. 19, Deventer: Kluwer Bedrijfswetenschappen, 1994, 93-105.

Glastra, F.J. "Intercultureel management en de calculatie van verschil." *Opleiding & Ontwikkeling,* 9.6, (1996): 13-20.

Glastra, F.J., M. Dewkalie, and M. Soons. "Pluriform personeelsbeleid en arbeidsconflicten in het openbaar vervoer." *Opleiding & Ontwikkeling,* 9.6, (1996): 27-32.

Glastra, F.J., P.E. Schedler, and E. Kats. "Employment Equity Policies in Canada and the Netherlands. Enhancing Minority Employment Between Public Controversy and Market Initiative." *Policy & Politics.* 26.2, (1998): 143-156.

Glastra, F.J. "Multiculturalisme met een prijskaartje. Over gedachtengoed en praktijk van intercultureel management in Nederland." In Gent, B. van and Zee, H. van der (eds.). *Competentie en arbeidsmarkt.* Den Haag: Delwel, 1998.

Glastra, F.J. (ed.). *Organisaties en diversiteit. Naar een contextuele benadering van intercultureel management.* Utecht: Lemma, 1999.

Glastra, F.J., M. Meerman, & S. de Vries. "Allochtonen en detentie." Den Haag: Ministerie van Justitie/WODC, 1999.

Golembiewski, R.T. *Managing Diversity in Organisations.* Tuscaloosa, Alabama: The University of Alabama Press, 1995.

Handy, C. *The Age of Paradox.* Boston, Massachusetts: Harvard Business School Press, 1994.

Hofstede, G. *Culture's Consequences. International Differences in Work-related Values.* Beverly Hills, London: Sage, 1980.

Hofstede, G. *Allemaal andersdenkenden. Omgaan met cultuurverschillen.* Amsterdam: Contact, 1995.

Hollinger, D. *Postethnic America: Beyond Multiculturalism.* New York: BasicBooks, 1995.

Hoof, J.J. van. "Balanceren tussen prestaties en tegenprestaties. Een bijdrage aan de discussie over de veranderende rol van het personeelsbeleid." *Tijdschrift voor Arbeidsvraagstukken,* 7.3, (1991): 56-63.

Hoof, J.J. van. "Arbeidsmarkt en arbeidsmarktbeleid in de jaren negentig." In Asch, A.W. van and Boonstra, J.J. (eds.). *Personeelsvoorziening in een turbulente arbeidsmarkt. Inspelen op personeelsbehoeften en veranderende beroepskwalifikaties.* Utrecht: Lemma, 1993.

Human, L. "Managing Workforce Diversity: A Critique and Example from South Africa." *International Journal of Manpower.* 17.4/5, (1996): 46-64.

Kats, E. *Metaforen en methodologieën. Ontwikkelingen in praktijkgericht onderzoek.* Groningen: Wolters-Noordhoff, 1996.

Kee, P. "De verklaring van de relatief hoge werkloosheid onder migranten in Nederland." *Migrantenstudies.* 13.2, (1997): 198-208.

Kessels, J.W.M. "Het corporate curriculum. Oratie." Rijks Universiteit Leiden: Leiden, 1996.

Koch, K. and P. Scheffer (eds.). *Het nut van Nederland. Opstellen over soevereiniteit en identiteit.* Amsterdam: Bert Bakker, 1996.

Koot, W. "Ambiguïteit en wisselende identiteiten." *Mens & Onderneming,* 48.2, (1994): 113-127.

Lammers, C.J. *Organisaties vergelijkenderwijs.* Utrecht: Spectrum (vierde druk), 1989.

Lazeron, A.H. (ed.). "Mentoring en coaching." In Kessels, J.W.M. and C.A. Smit (eds.) *Opleiders in organisaties.* Capita Selecta. Afl. 19, Deventer: Kluwer Bedrijfswetenschappen, 1994.

Lodewijks, J.G.L.C. *De kick van het kunnen; Over arrangement en engagement bij het leren.* Nijmegen: Oratie K.U.N., 1993.

Meerman, M. and R. van der Vlist. "The Integration of Ethnic Minorities in Organisations: First Steps." *Concepts and Transformation.* 1.2/3, (1996): 175-191.

Meerman, M. Gebroken wit. *Over acceptatie van allochtonen in de arbeidsorganisatie.* Leiden: Universiteit Leiden, 1999.

Nederveen Pieterse, J. "Globalization as Hybridization." In Featherstone, M., Lasch, S. and Robertson, R. (eds.). *Global Modernities.* Thousand Oaks, London, New Delhi: Sage, 1995, 43-68.

Nijhof, W.J. and H.J. Abma. "Diversity in Nederlandse bedrijven." *Opleiding & Ontwikkeling,* 7.6, (1994): 17-22.

Onna, B. van." Informal Learning on the Job." In Tuijnman, A.C. and Kamp, M. van der (eds.). *Learning Across the Lifespan. Theories, Research, Policies*. Oxford: Pergamon Press, 1992, 125-136.

Oomkes, F.R. "Interculturele training." *Opleiding & ontwikkeling*, 6.5, (1993).: 13-17.

Oomkes, F.R. "Training als beroep; Sociale en interculturele vaardigheid. Deel 3. Oefeningen in interculturele vaardigheid." Boom: Amsterdam, 1994.

Ott, M. *Assepoesters en kroonprinsen. Een onderzoek naar de minderheidspositie van agentes en verpleegkundigen*. Amsterdam: Sua, 1985.

Patterson, O. *The Ordeal of Integration. Progress and Resentment in America's 'Racial' Crisis*. Washington: Civitas/Counterpoint, 1997.

Pettigrew, T.F. and S. de. Vries. "A Comparative Perspective on Affirmative Action: Positieve Aktie in the Netherlands." *Basic and Applied Social Psychology*, 15.1&2, (1994): 179-199.

Pinto, D. *Interculturele communicatie*. Houten/Zaventem: Bohn Stafleu Van Loghum, 1994.

Prasad, P. and A.J. Mills. "From Showcase to Shadow." In Prasad, P. et al. (eds.). *Managing the Organisational Melting Pot. Dilemmas of Workplace Diversity*. Thousand Oaks, London, New Delhi: Sage, 1997, 3-27.

Putten, L. van, F.J. Glastra, and P.E. Schedler. Ondersteunen op afstand.Een evaluatie van het Infopunt Kleurrijk Korps en een verkenning van mogelijkheden om diversiteitsbeleid bij de politie te ondersteunen. Den Haag: Ministerie van Binnenlandse Zaken en Koninkrijksrelaties, 2000.

Ragins, B.R. "Diversity, Power, and Mentorship in Organisations. A Cultural, Structural and Behavioral Perspective." In Chemers, M.M., S. Oskamp, and M.A. Constanzo (eds.). *Diversity in Organisations. New Perspectives for a Changing Workplace*. Thousand Oaks, London, New Delhi: Sage, 1995, 91-132.

Schedler, P.E. and F.J. Glastra (eds.). *Voorlichting in veldtheoretisch perspectief*. Utrecht: Lemma, 1998.

Schedler, P.E., F.J. Glastra, and E. Kats. "Public Information and Field Theory." *Political Communication*. 15.4, (1998): 445-461.

Schedler, P.E., Suasso, I. & Van der Venne, C. "Instromen in de thuiszorg. Een evaluatie van een project voor allochtonen." *Opleiding en ontwikkeling*, 12. 12, (1999): 27-30.

Schedler, P.E., F.J. Glastra and E. Kats. "Ervaringen en ontwikkelingen in Canada. Lerende organisaties en de interculturalisering van het arbeidsproces." *Sociale interventie*, 9.1 (2000): 42-52.

SCP (Sociaal en Cultureel Planbureau). Rapportage minderheden 1999. Den Haag: VUGA, 1999.

Schuyt, C.J.M. *Tegendraadse werkingen. Sociologische opstellen over de onvoorziene gevolgen van verzorging en verzekering*. Amsterdam: Amsterdam University Press, 1995.

Shadid, W.A. *Grondslagen van interculturele communicatie. Studieveld en werkterrein*. Houten/Diegem: Bohn Stafleu Van Loghum, 1998.

Shipler, D.K. *A Country of Strangers. Blacks and Whites in America*. New York : Alfred A. Knopf, 1997.

Sloane, P.J. and H.C. Jain. "Use of Equal Opportunities Legislation and Earning Differentials: A Comparative Study." *Industrial Relations Journal*, 21, (1990): 221-229.

Stephenson, K. and D. Lewin. "Managing Workforce Diversity: Macro and Micro Level HR Implications of Network Analysis." *International Journal of Manpower*. 17.4/5, (1996): 168-196.

SZW (Ministerie van Sociale Zaken en Werkgelegenheid). Arbeidsmarktbeleid voor etnische minderheden. Plan van aanpak 2000-2003. Den Haag: Ministerie van Sociale Zaken en Werkgelegenheid, 2000.

Taylor, Ch. De politiek van erkenning. In Gutman, A. (ed.). *Multiculturalisme; De politiek van erkenning nader onderzocht*. Amsterdam Meppel: Boom, 1995, 43-95.

Tennekes, J. *Organisatiecultuur. Een antropologische visie*. Leuven: Garant, 1995.

Thomas Jr., R.R. *Beyond Race and Gender*. New York: Amacom, 1991.

TOPAZ. *Aanpak arbeidsdeelnamebeleid allochtonen in de zorgsector*. Wijk bij Duurstede: TOPAZ, 1996.

Trompenaars, F. *Zaken doen over de grens. Leren omgaan met andere culturen*. Amsterdam/Antwerpen: Contact, 1993.

Twuyver, M. van. *Een kansrijk perspectief. Culturele diversiteit in organisaties*. Schiedam: Scriptum Books, 1995.

Twuyver, M. van, N. Noorderhaven, and R. Derveld. *Intercultureel management. Lange termijn processen en mogelijke baten*. Tilburg: Tilburg University Press, 1997.

Veenman, J. "Langzaam voorwaarts; ontwikkelingen in de sociaal-economische positie van zes allochtone bevolkingscategorieën." *Migrantenstudies*, 11.4, (1994): 230-243.

Verhallen, S. "Interculturele communicatie en tweede-taalverwerving." In Vries, L. de (ed.). *Interculturele communicatie en Nederlands op de werkvloer*. Amsterdam: ITTA, 1995, 31-46.

Verkuyten, M. *Redelijk racisme. Gesprekken over allochtonen in oude stadswijken*. Amsterdam: Amsterdam University Press, 1997.

Vries, S. de. "Multi-ethnic Work Groups in the Dutch Police: Problems and Potential." *Policing and Society*, Vol. 3, (1993): 177-188.

Vugt, G.W.M. van (Red.) (1995). *Werken in multiculturele organisaties. Theorie en praktijk van intercultureel management*. Houten, Diegem: Bohn Stafleu Van Loghum.

Weiner, N. *Making Cultural Diversity Work*. Scarborough: Carswell, 1997.

Witte, F. "Leren en communiceren op het werk." In Vries, L. de (ed.). *Interculturele communicatie en Nederlands op de werkvloer*. Amsterdam: ITTA, 1995, 111-126.

WRR (Wetenschappelijke Raad voor het Regeringsbeleid). Allochtonenbeleid. 's Gravenhage: SDU, 1989.

CHAPTER 10

SHEILA ROGERS

NORTHERN IRELAND – GENDER, RACE AND THE NEW EQUALITY AGENDA

INTRODUCTION

The pace of change in Northern Ireland over the past three years has been unrelenting. It has seen the Belfast Agreement in April 1998, the setting up of new political institutions; devolution, its failure and a return to direct rule. This was followed by devolution for a second time early in 2000; the release of para-military prisoners on both sides of the divide; the debates around the decommissioning of para-military weaponry; and the establishment of new cross-border initiatives with the Republic of Ireland. The Patten Commission on the future of policing in Northern Ireland recommended a radical restructuring of the Royal Ulster Constabulary, including the application of a limited quota system for the recruitment of Catholics into the police. Further elements in this changing environment have been the establishment of a Northern Ireland Human Rights Commission, the adoption of the provisions of the European Convention on Human Rights and the setting up of a new Equality Commission for Northern Ireland.

Until recently the concepts of equality and inequality in Northern Ireland were tainted by the long-standing sectarian divide which meant that debate was stifled or coloured by lack of interest, misrepresentation and denial. The political imperative was equality of opportunity in employment between Catholics and Protestants and while there was anti-discrimination legislation in relation to sex discrimination, equality of opportunity between women and men was secondary to religious and political discrimination. For those from black and minority ethnic communities there was no legislative protection whatsoever until 1997. Unlike the rest of the United Kingdom members of black and minority ethnic communities in Northern Ireland could be subjected to racial discrimination without redress to the law. The importance attributed to the elimination of religious and political discrimination was reflected in fair employment legislation that contained provisions absent from any other anti-discrimination legislation in the United Kingdom, something that only served to reinforce the notion that religious and political discrimination was indeed the priority.

Employers subject to the provisions of the Fair Employment and Treatment Order 1998 are required to register with the body responsible for the enforcement of the legislation, the Equality Commission for Northern Ireland (EC for NI); they must monitor their workforces and applicant flows; review their employment practices and engage in affirmative action. There is also a limited form of contract compliance contained in the legislation. Together with the enforcement of individual rights all of these mechanisms have contributed to structural changes in the Northern Ireland labour market reflected in a shifting of the balance within the workforce as a whole in terms of

C. Agocs (ed.), Workplace Equality, 201–223.

Catholic and Protestant employment patterns. As the tenth monitoring report published by the Equality Commission demonstrates, over the ten year period between 1990 and 1999 the proportion of the Catholic population in the workforce increased from 35 percent to 40 percent. In addition, in both the private and public sectors there has been an increase in the number of male and female Catholic applicants over the same period (EC for NI, 2000: 7, 47, 58).

At the moment Northern Ireland has six separate pieces of equality legislation. Apart from the Northern Ireland Act 1998, which is discussed in more detail below, the Northern Ireland legislation applies to both the public and private sectors. The Equal Pay Act (NI) 1970 deals only with equal pay between men and women and no similar legislation exists in relation to any of the other grounds of discrimination. Appendix 1 (pages 220-222) summarises the main areas covered by the remaining four pieces of legislation. While there is similarity in the definitions of discrimination and the coverage of the legislation, when it comes to statutory obligations the table demonstrates that the fair employment provisions are much stronger.

It is hoped that the elements of fair employment legislation that have helped to bring such change about with respect to inequality on the basis of religion will in time be replicated in other areas of anti-discrimination law. For now, however, addressing systemic discrimination on grounds other than religion and politics will depend on the existing, somewhat weaker, sex and race discrimination legislation together with new statutory duties on public bodies in relation to the promotion of equality and good relations. What should also assist is the growing acknowledgement of the existence of institutional racism, defined as:

> The collective failure of an organisation to provide an appropriate and professional service to people because of their colour, culture or ethnic origin. It can be seen or detected in processes, attitudes and behaviour which amount to discrimination through unwitting prejudice, ignorance, thoughtlessness and racist stereotyping which disadvantage minority ethnic people (Macpherson, 1999:28).

Although this definition arose out of an investigation into the Metropolitan Police Service, in the wake of the murder of Stephen Lawrence in 1993, the concept has had a resonance for other sectors and has served to raise the level of debate around systemic or institutional discrimination in employment and the provision of goods and services, not only on grounds of race but also in relation to gender.

Finally, the Belfast Agreement, signed between the Irish and British Governments in April 1998 and endorsed by people throughout the island of Ireland, North and South, has the potential to bring about a sea change in the way in which the equality agenda in Northern Ireland is advanced. Along with other rights and safeguards the concept of equality of opportunity as a priority was set out in the Agreement that affirmed:

- the right to equal opportunity in all social and economic activity, regardless of class, creed, disability, gender or ethnicity;
- the right to freedom from sectarian harassment; and
- the right of women to full and equal political participation (Agreement, 1998: 16).

The equality dimension of the Agreement has been translated into legislation in the form of the Northern Ireland Act 1998.

This chapter aims to consider the position of women and members of black and minority ethnic communities in Northern Ireland in the context of anti-discrimination legislative provisions and their capacity to help eliminate unlawful discrimination and promote equality of opportunity. In recognition of the significant changes that have taken place recently in Northern Ireland in the field of equality the chapter concludes with an introduction to what has become known as the new equality agenda.

GENDER EQUALITY

The Position of Women in Northern Ireland

Gender segregation in employment, both vertical and horizontal, continues to be a feature of the working lives of men and women in Northern Ireland. Women make up 44 percent of the total number of those who are economically active in Northern Ireland but they are still over-represented in clerical, sales and personal services and under-represented in management and administration occupations (Equal Opportunities Commission for Northern Ireland, 1999). We have not moved far beyond the observation contained in the 1974 White Paper *Equality for Women* that "most women do low grade jobs in a narrow range of industries and services for much lower rates of pay than unskilled men" (Home Office, 1974). While both men and women in Northern Ireland earn less than their counterparts in the rest of the United Kingdom, overall it is women's work that attracts lower pay and lower status. In 1999 the Northern Ireland woman carrying out non-manual work earned only 72 percent of what a man doing non-manual work was earning. For manual work the comparable figure was 75 percent (Department of Enterprise, Trade and Industry, 1999). Part-time work is another important feature of women's working lives with over one third of women in employment working part-time (EOC for NI, 1999).

In childcare provision, Northern Ireland has traditionally lagged behind both within the United Kingdom and in comparison to most other European countries within the European Community. For example, in 1998 there were only 34.8 day nursery places for children in Northern Ireland compared to the United Kingdom average of 71.3 places per 1000 of the population of children aged 0 – 4 years of age (EOC for NI, 1999). Workplace provision has yet to become a viable option in Northern Ireland. Indeed, in a report on the provision of equality of opportunity in the private sector only one organisation included in the survey had a crèche facility. Even this was not viewed positively. As the report notes it was described as "a symbol of the long and acrimonious fight which women had waged for equality of opportunity in this organisation" (EOC for NI, 1998:49). An earlier report on the public sector had also identified the lack of childcare provision, including workplace facilities, as a major barrier to the achievement of equality (EOC for NI and Chief Executives' Forum, 1994: 89).

There has been some progress, however, particularly in relation to access to flexible working opportunities such as flexi-leave schemes, career breaks and, more recently term-time working which enables parents to be at home during school holidays. But issues around pregnancy and maternity provision continue to present considerable difficulties for working women. The statutory scheme applicable in Northern Ireland has only recently been improved to provide an entitlement to eighteen weeks leave regardless of length of service with additional leave available to those who have a minimum of one-year service. It also gives both parents the right to three months parental leave – regrettably, however, this is unpaid.

If training can provide a key to accessing and progressing within the labour market then Northern Ireland still has some way to go if it is to provide the skills and knowledge that will enhance opportunities. The former Equal Opportunities Commission for Northern Ireland reported that job related training is less available to workers in Northern Ireland than in the rest of the United Kingdom and access to training for women tends to depend on the sectors within they are employed. For example, women who work in associate professional and technical occupations[1] are twice as likely as men to access job related training. On the other hand, in professional occupations this picture is reversed (EOC for NI, 1997:16).

Another trend which is prevalent in Northern Ireland is that employers are less likely to pay for training and, in the case of women workers, over one quarter of them financed their training themselves or with the help of family compared to 13 percent of men (EOC for NI, 1997:17). Those participating in an assessment of the provision of equality in Northern Ireland's public sector pointed out that some large employers in the sector "were becoming exceptionally niggardly in this respect" and identified such cutbacks as having a significant impact on women's progress (EOC for NI, 1994:87). In the private sector employees held similar negative views of companies who were "perceived to resent the idea that people they trained might take their skills elsewhere…" (EOC for NI, 1998:46). In the area of government training schemes, in 1995 participation by women, while similar to men in adult schemes, was less than half that of men in youth training and similar schemes. In 1996, the government introduced its New Deal training program replacing existing training schemes. However, it has been noted that the changes have resulted in an adverse impact on women's training provision with a 15 percent decline in their participation rates (Training and Employment Agency, 1999).

This then is the current position of women at work in Northern Ireland. Clearly there is room for improvement. Unfortunately, sex discrimination is still a feature of life in Northern Ireland, and as long as the notion that women workers are marginal and secondary to the labour market persists, progress to bring about equality of opportunity will continue to be hampered. There is a need for mechanisms to enforce individual rights and protect men and women from unlawful discrimination on grounds of sex; but compliance with the law, in and of itself, will not bring about change. There needs to be a commitment by employers themselves to the concept of equality, a recognition of the business case for equality and a willingness to go beyond what is legislatively required of them in order to tackle stereotypes and confront prejudice and traditional views on the role of women in society today. There is still some way to go in terms of the development of initiatives that go beyond the legal imperative.

The next two sections provide an overview of the legislative framework for discrimination on grounds of gender and a discussion of how a comprehensive and structured approach to the provision of equality in the workplace can bring about change and tackle systemic barriers to progress.

The Legislative Framework

In 1970, with the passing of the Equal Pay Act (Northern Ireland), working women in Northern Ireland got their first protection from discrimination in the area of pay. This was followed in 1976 by the Sex Discrimination (Northern Ireland) Order which was modelled on the legislation in Great Britain.[2] The 1976 legislation followed the British Government's 1974 White Paper *Equality for Women* (Home Office, 1974), which had highlighted the loss for both the individual woman and for the economy generally when the talents of half of the population were not maximised and where equality of opportunity was not provided.

The 1976 Order provided for the establishment of the Equal Opportunities Commission for Northern Ireland, an independent statutory body with a mandate to eliminate sex discrimination, promote equality of opportunity between the sexes and keep the provisions of the Order and the equal pay legislation under review. In 1999 its functions were assumed by a new Equality Commission, discussed below.

The Equal Pay Act (NI) 1970 stated that women should be paid the same when they carried out the same or broadly similar work as men; a 1984 amendment brought the notion of equal pay for work of equal value into the legislation. This amendment has had little impact on the differential rates of pay of women and men, largely because the legislation is unwieldy and complex and the cost of pursuing a complaint through the legal process can be prohibitive. As a result, after sixteen years, only a few cases in Northern Ireland have been decided. Recommendations for changes to improve the legislation, both in terms of its coverage and the way in which it is administered, were proposed but, as yet, these have not yet been acted upon by Government (EOC for NI, 1990).

The Sex Discrimination (Northern Ireland) Order 1976 and its amendments have been used to bring about change and improve the lot of women in work in Northern Ireland. Its provisions make it unlawful to discriminate on the grounds of sex or married status, directly or indirectly:

- in the arrangements made for determining who is offered a job
- in the terms on which a job is offered
- by refusing or deliberately omitting to offer a person a job
- in any other benefits, facilities or services provided to employees
- in dismissals and any other unfavourable treatment to which employees may be subjected.

The legislation has been used, successfully, to clarify and extend the law in a number of areas including sexual harassment, vertical and horizontal employment patterns, pregnancy and maternity and family friendly policies and procedures.[3] In addition, women and men in Northern Ireland, as in the rest of the United Kingdom, can utilise the provisions of the Treaty of Rome and associated Community Directives on equal treatment such as those on parental leave, equal treatment in occupational social security schemes and the rights of pregnant workers.[4] These have helped to extend rights in areas such as maternity and pregnancy, parental leave and part-time workers' rights. Such provisions are accessed through the judicial process in tandem with an action under domestic anti-discrimination legislation.

The term positive action rather than affirmative action or positive discrimination is used in the sex discrimination legislation. The provisions of the Order aim to address the impact of past discrimination in the workplace. However, they extend only to the provision of special training or encouragement such as positive action advertising. The provisions are also qualified in a number of ways. For example, under-representation of one or other sex has to be established over the previous twelve months in relation to a certain type of work and it has to appear likely that the under-represented group will take up the work. Training bodies and others are also permitted to provide special training if there is a special need linked to having been engaged in domestic or family responsibilities. This extends not only to how such people are chosen for training but also to the provision of single sex training.

There is a limited form of contract compliance in fair employment legislation in Northern Ireland and a number of provisions at the European level contained in Directives deriving from the Treaty of Rome. The Equal Opportunities Commission for Northern Ireland has recommended that the sex discrimination legislation be amended to incorporate mechanisms to require contractors to engage in activities that would ensure the provision of equality of opportunity but these have gone unheeded to date (EOC for NI, 1997:27). Therefore, in the absence of legislative support, the body established to enforce the provisions of the sex discrimination legislation has had to consider other ways in which it might best encourage employers to implement equal opportunities programs throughout the workforce.

Equal Opportunities Programs

The mechanisms open to the Commission to eliminate unlawful discrimination and promote equality of opportunity and good relations include assisting individuals who consider that they have suffered unlawful discrimination by providing advice or representation by a solicitor or barrister to pursue a complaint; carrying out research to inform its work; raising awareness through education and promotional work; and formal investigations. In the absence of class actions it is up to the individual complainant to lodge his or her claim with the Industrial Tribunal within a three-month period of the cause of action arising. The Equality Commission may assist in this process. Remedies are limited to a declaration of the individual's rights and/or compensation for loss of earnings and injury to feelings. The Tribunal can also recommend that a Respondent take action to obviate or redress the effect of the discrimination on the complainant. It has been recommended that these remedies should be extended to include, among others, an order to re-instate an employee and an order that a Respondent should take action to negate the effect of discrimination in relation to any others persons in their employ and not just the individual complainant (EOC for NI, 1997:46,47).

Formal investigations allow for an investigation into a named organisation where the Commission has a belief that sex discrimination may be present, or into a sector or group of organisations in order to determine if equality of opportunity is featured. In the absence of class actions, formal investigations should have offered an effective tool in the fight against institutional discrimination since they did not depend upon the presence of individual complaints of discrimination. However, in practice it has proved to be a cumbersome, expensive and difficult mechanism to utilise, one described by Lords Denning and Griffiths as far back as 1982, in a race discrimination case in England, as being "...so elaborate and cumbersome that it is in danger of grinding to a halt" (CRE –v- Armari Plastics [1982] IRLR 252 CA). Formal Investigations were restricted even further in the 1984 decision in the Prestige Group case which held that, in this case, the Commission for Racial Equality in Britain had to have a reasonable belief that acts which were unlawful may have taken place (R –v- CRE ex parte Prestige Group [1984]IRLR 166). This was a particularly unfortunate turn of events given that in Northern Ireland, the fair employment legislation on religious and political discrimination in employment contained a different and less onerous formal investigation mechanism concerned with determining what an organisation should be doing to promote equality of opportunity. This did not require there to be a reasonable belief that there had been an unlawful act. The Equal Opportunities Commission for Northern Ireland's 1997 recommendations for changes to the sex discrimination legislation included those which would remove the distinction between the fair employment and sex discrimination legislation and which would enhance and improve how formal investigations would be conducted, including providing for effective remedies, such as legally binding undertakings, which could result from an investigation (EOC for NI, 1997:33). As noted above, the government has yet to act on these recommendations.

In the late 1980s the EOC for NI developed a strategy that included a framework for the implementation of comprehensive equal opportunities programs in the workplace. This it saw as an integral part of its promotional and educational role and one that complemented its enforcement powers on behalf of individual complainants or through formal investigations. Complementing the persuasive approach was the development of a negotiation and settlement strategy that was designed to address the problem of systemic discrimination where there was no legal imperative on an employer to implement change. Where a case involving an individual complaint of unlawful discrimination was to be settled rather than litigated, negotiations would be entered into in an effort to obtain terms of settlement which would not only provide a remedy for the individual complainant, but would also commit the respondent to engaging in a course of action which would bring about systemic change within the organisation. The ideal settlement to be achieved would, of course, be a commitment by the employer to introduce a comprehensive equal opportunities program containing all of the elements recommended by the Commission.

It was the view of the Commission that an integrated equal opportunities program, made up of a number of elements each of which has merit in its own right, will only result in real change when all appropriate measures are put in place in a strategic and planned way. To set the scene and the context for environmental change there must be commitment from the top that is reflected not only in a policy statement but also in the actions of the organisation that flow from it. This would provide the framework for future work and make it clear to employees and customers that the organisation is serious about working towards being an equal opportunities employer. However, fine words will achieve very little. What is needed is information and action.

In Northern Ireland there is widespread familiarity with the concept and purpose of monitoring. This is not the case in the rest of the United Kingdom because fair employment legislation that requires monitoring on grounds of religion and gender does not extend beyond the boundaries of Northern Ireland, and monitoring is not required under any other anti-discrimination laws. Northern Ireland's fair employment legislation imposes statutory obligations on many employers to monitor their workforces in order to determine, among other things, the labour force participation of Catholics and Protestants. They have also been required to include gender in their monitoring systems and, from 1999, part-time workers. This has meant that information is readily available to most employers which can be used to assess the participation rates of women overall as well as their position within the organisation. This facilitates the design and development of strategies and initiatives that will help to address under-representation and identify ways in which to tackle barriers to equality.

Comprehensive monitoring provides invaluable information on a range of issues. As has been noted (Kremer, 1991), the selection process can be problematic for equality of opportunity. Recruitment data shows who is and who is not applying for jobs and whether men or women are more likely to be short-listed or appointed. Any anomalies that are thrown up through analysis can be addressed through a review of practices and procedures. It is not so long ago that application forms could be found which contained questions about an applicant's age and personal circumstances, such as number and age of children or partner's occupation; some employers would question female applicants at interview about their intentions in relation to having children. While such actions may be less common today, nevertheless it is important to pay attention to all elements of selection to ensure that bias does not creep into the process -- from the design and use of an application form to inappropriate questioning at interviews or the use of selection tests which have not been equality proofed.

Managers must be trained in non-discriminatory practices and in avoiding stereotyping, for this can influence whether or not women or men are considered appropriate for promotion or training. Sensitivity to and the accommodation of particular employee needs associated with domestic and caring responsibilities should mean that employers will be flexible and show willingness to adjust and adapt their internal procedures so as to provide opportunities and encouragement to their employees. In both these areas monitoring can assist in identifying blockages and provide the rationale for the development of positive action measures.

As mentioned above there has been some progress in relation to the introduction of initiatives such as job-sharing, term-time working and flexible hours, which help women and men to combine work and domestic responsibilities and generally create the environment in which a better work/life balance can be achieved. Nevertheless, the whole area of positive action, however it is defined, continues to be problematic for some employers, particularly those in the private sector in Northern Ireland (EOC for NI, 1998:27). There is a need to counteract the perception that it is positive discrimination, and overcome the negativity associated with the concept.

As has been seen the Sex Discrimination (NI) Order 1976 contains legislative permissions in relation to positive action and employers need to be prepared to consider and, if appropriate, implement these actions if they are serious about the provision of equality of opportunity. As is known only too well in Northern Ireland, traditional recruitment practices can perpetuate inequality and lack of opportunity. Methods such as word of mouth recruitment, used in the past, impacted adversely on equality in relation to Catholics and Protestants as did accepting unsolicited applications for work or advertising employment opportunities in publications accessed mainly by those from only the Catholic or Protestant community. The use of the 'welcoming statement' has become very widespread now and derives from the provisions of the legislation that allow employers to encourage applications from the under-represented sex. Similarly, it is important for employers to be sensitive to where they advertise and ensure that this is done in a way that will be inclusive, so that all those who may wish to be considered for a job are aware of the vacancy.

Not enough has been done in the area of positive action training for women in Northern Ireland and employers need to think creatively about how they might use the provisions contained in the Order. Some initiatives have been undertaken in the public sector, for example women in management training courses, but provision is minimal and patchy (EOC for NI, 1994:37).

There has been progress in the area of gender equality but there is still much to be done before discriminatory behaviour and the impact of past discrimination is no longer a feature of Northern Ireland society. It will be one of the challenges for the new equality regime to ensure that work to enforce the legislation and promote good practice continues unabated.

RACIAL EQUALITY

Black and Minority Ethnic Communities in Northern Ireland

Northern Ireland's black and minority ethnic population is small, around 1.5 percent of the total population of 1.6 million. It is reflective of the notion that ethnic diversity is not a feature of the community that the Census in Northern Ireland, unlike the rest of the United Kingdom, has never included a question on ethnicity. This is to be remedied in the next Census, in 2001. The largest black and minority ethnic group is the Chinese with the Indian community, those from the African continent and Irish Travellers constituting the next largest groupings. There are also Pakistani, Filipino and Bangladeshi communities.

Irish Travellers are indigenous to the island of Ireland with around 1600 currently in Northern Ireland. Until the 1950s they lived a mainly rural and nomadic lifestyle that supported an economy based on horse trading, farm labour and tin-smithing. This economy, however, has now largely disappeared due to population movement to towns and cities, farm mechanisation and the development of plastics. The life experiences of Irish Travellers provide a recipe for severe marginalisation and alienation from mainstream society:

> Being a Traveller in Northern Ireland involves low life expectancy, high infant mortality and morbidity, low educational achievement, appalling living conditions and differential access to a range of state services. Clearly these outcomes cannot be viewed as a result of individual antipathies. The evidence of these obvious disparities is ipso facto evidence of discrimination, racism and institutional culpability (Noonan, 1994: 145).

Five years on from these observations an evaluation of the United Kingdom Government's implementation of the United Nations Convention on the Rights of the Child in Northern Ireland cited a UN official, who likened the environment within which Belfast Travellers were living as "conditions one expects to find only in third-world countries" (Children's Law Centre, 1999: 57). As will be seen, when legislation against racial discrimination was finally extended to Northern Ireland it paid particular attention to this racial group.

Attitudes and perceptions of those who are 'different' have been addressed recently in the report *Racial Attitudes and Prejudice in Northern Ireland* (Connolly and Keenan, 2000). On the one hand, the findings are encouraging in that many of those living in Northern Ireland have a positive view of equality of opportunity generally. However, the report's findings are alarming in relation to how people view particular groups of black or minority ethnic people. For example, in relation to Irish Travellers, the attitudes of people in Northern Ireland reflect prejudice and hostility with 40 percent stating that they would not accept Travellers as citizens of Northern Ireland, 66 percent as colleagues at work and 70 percent as close friends. Other minority communities fare somewhat better although more than one third of respondents would not accept an African Caribbean, Chinese or South Asian person as a colleague at work and over 40 percent would not accept such people as a close friend (Connolly et al, 2000:18). The stark fact is that people in Northern Ireland are almost twice as likely to exhibit racist attitudes, as they are to disclose sectarian attitudes. Ironic, then, that it is only recently that legislative protection has been extended to black and minority ethnic communities.

......An Issue Whose Time Has Come

Unlike sex discrimination and discrimination on grounds of religion and politics in Northern Ireland, racial discrimination and racism were considered by many to be non-issues until very recently. As one journalist observed in 1993:

> It is a strange anomaly: in Northern Ireland where successive governments have battled against bigotry and prejudice, racial discrimination remains quite legitimate. A quarter of a century of sectarian violence has spawned an elaborate framework of acts, quangos and tribunals designed to prevent discrimination on the grounds of religion. The Province even has its own Equal Opportunities Commission to ensure that women and men are fairly treated in the workplace. But when Belfast's landlords refuse to rent flats to ethnic Chinese students or employers select local white applicants with less experience than Asian graduates there is no redress (*The Guardian*, 1993).

The enactment of the Race Relations (Northern Ireland) Order 1997 was the culmination of a campaign which was not founded within the mainstream political sphere but rather gained its impetus from the non-governmental voluntary and community sectors, which considered it to be completely unacceptable that black and minority ethnic people could, routinely and quite lawfully, be subjected to racial discrimination and harassment. There was present in the Northern Ireland psyche the notion that legislation was not required because racism was not a problem and, anyway, there were no black people in Northern Ireland. It was a comfortable stance to take by the majority white and settled community, preoccupied as it was with its 'traditional' divisions along religious lines. It was, nevertheless, a myth. There were black and minority ethnic communities in Northern Ireland, some second and even third generation, and their members suffered racial discrimination and harassment. The campaign for legislation, therefore, had to address this added dimension of denial, something which McVeigh (1998:14) has argued is fundamentally dangerous in that linking the existence of racism with the presence of black and minority ethnic communities leads to the conclusion that the latter is the determinant of the former. Something of this ilk is currently happening in England and the Republic of Ireland in relation to newly arrived asylum seekers and refugees (The *Guardian*, March 10,2000; *Irish Times*, April 10, 2000). The campaign for the Race Relations Order wanted to see parity with the rest of the United Kingdom – legislation against racial discrimination and the establishment of a Commission for Racial Equality similar to the Commission for Racial Equality for England, Wales and Scotland. In addition, however, it wanted special protection to be extended to Irish Travellers. Government's response was less than auspicious and was characterised by inaction until the British Government was roundly criticised by the United Nations Committee on the Elimination of all Forms of Racial Discrimination in 1993. The observations of one Committee member, Mr Van Bouen, were reported as follows:

> Noting like other Committee Members, that legislation on racial equality was not extended to Northern Ireland, he said that the question of Northern Ireland was a serious one, with a long history and that the Committee expected stronger commitments on the elimination of racial discrimination there... (United Nations, 1993).

Even after the United Kingdom Government brought forward legislation, one Member of Parliament from Northern Ireland was heard to say in the House:

> "...I think it is a nonsense, like a great deal of the legislation relating to minorities that has passed through this house" (House of Commons, 1997:10).

It was against this type of backdrop that legislation was finally extended to Northern Ireland in 1997, some twenty-one years after the rest of the United Kingdom.

The Legislative Framework

The Race Relations (NI) Order 1997 provided for the setting up of an independent statutory body with a remit to eliminate racial discrimination, promote equality of opportunity and good relations and to keep the legislation under review. The Commission for Racial Equality for Northern Ireland (CRE for NI) opened its doors on 3rd August 1997 with a Board of seven individuals appointed by Government and seconded civil servants as its staff. It had a huge job to do with minimal resources. After so many years of campaigning for such a Commission, expectations within the communities were high for the new body. However, only eight months after the Commission was established Government had issued a White Paper entitled *Partnership for Equality* (House of Commons, 1998) in which it proposed a single Equality Commission for Northern Ireland, which would assume the functions of the Commission for Racial Equality. Two months after its second birthday the Commission was dissolved and responsibility for racial equality was taken over by the Equality Commission for Northern Ireland.

The Race Relations Order provides protection from discrimination on racial grounds, defined as colour, race, nationality or ethnic or national origins. Irish Travellers are specifically mentioned in the Order, which states that racial grounds

> Includes the grounds of belonging to the Irish Traveller community, that is to say the community of people commonly so called who are identified, both by themselves and others, as people with a shared history, culture and traditions including, historically, a nomadic way of life on the Island of Ireland (Article 5(2)(a)).

The legislation covers employment, the provision of goods, facilities and services, housing and education. It has the dual thrust of enforcement and the promotion of equality of opportunity and good relations. The Commission for Racial Equality for Northern Ireland and now the Equality Commission define the promotional and good relations function broadly and with a specific focus on capacity building within black and minority ethnic sectors. The definition of capacity building adopted by the Commission is that of the Community Development Foundation:

> Development work that strengthens the ability of community organisations and groups to build their structures, systems, people and skills so that they are better able to define and achieve their objectives and engage in consultation and planning, manage community projects and take part in partnerships and community enterprises (Skinner, 1977).

On the enforcement side, apart from assisting individual complaints of discrimination, discussed below, the Commission may also conduct formal investigations into sectors or organisations. This is, potentially, a powerful tool for tackling systemic discrimination. Indeed, when the 1976 Race Relations Act was being drawn up the formal investigation was considered to be the main way in which the Commission for Racial Equality in Britain (CREGB) would address discrimination (CREGB, 1998: 32). However, as outlined earlier in relation to gender discrimination, judicial decisions in Great Britain have rendered the mechanism somewhat sterile. Since it should provide an effective way in which to tackle systemic or institutional discrimination, the Commission for Racial Equality in Britain and the former Commission for Racial Equality in Northern Ireland have both recommended to Government that appropriate legislative amendments to race relations legislation must be made in order to make this happen (CREGB, 1998; CRE for NI, 1999).

Addressing Need

The challenge for any enforcement body is to be conscious of whose rights it is enforcing and whether it is meeting the needs of all of its potential users. The Commission for Racial Equality for Northern Ireland was concerned that it might not be addressing discrimination against black and minority ethnic communities when the profile of complainants showed that a large number of those using its services and complaining about racial discrimination were white, English, Irish or from Northern Ireland. Indeed the very first decision handed down in Northern Ireland was on behalf of a white Englishman (Robins –v- Norfil, 03343/97RR). Conversely, the numbers of complaints of unlawful discrimination from the Chinese community, the largest minority ethnic group in Northern Ireland, were very small, as they were from the black community. Certainly all complainants must have access to justice. In order to ensure that the Commission for Racial Equality for Northern Ireland itself, now the Equality Commission, was not acting, however unwittingly, in a way which constituted institutional racism, a study was undertaken to assess the need for community based advocacy services which might provide a link with the Commission so as to ensure that all people in Northern Ireland had appropriate access to its services. Perhaps not surprisingly, users reported that they found the legal processes to be complex and not user-friendly; a perceived conservative working culture within the Commission mitigated against accessibility; the distance between the Commission and the community needed to be addressed through outreach; and there was a need to produce guidance materials and information in appropriate formats (Leong, 2000:26). The study identified options including community-based services; services located within the Commission and provided by black and minority ethnic staff to raise credibility and provide a community link; and services designed to target the particular needs of different communities such as the Traveller or Muslim community. A feasibility study into how any such advocacy service might work is to begin in early 2001.

As noted above, the Commission is empowered to provide assistance to individuals who believe that they have been discriminated against on racial grounds. Such assistance can be limited to advice or can extend to the provision of the services of a solicitor or counsel. Legal aid is not available for proceedings in the Industrial Tribunals, the forum before which discrimination complaints in employment are heard. Hence the Commission's role is an important one in terms of access to justice, particularly for individuals who may not otherwise be able to fund their own case, although assistance is not limited to impecunious applicants. However, given that the race relations legislation has only a recent history in Northern Ireland, it is still too early to make any real assessment of how effective it will be in addressing racial discrimination here.

What we do know is that for many of Northern Ireland's black and minority ethnic citizens the issues of major concern to them revolve around access to appropriate services such as health care, education, social security and housing. Further, a large proportion of the cases that have been assisted to date are on behalf of Irish Travellers who have been denied access to everyday services such as bars, restaurants, hotels or shops.

On the employment front, the legislation covers the arrangements that are made for determining who should be offered employment, the terms on which employment is offered and the refusal or omission to offer employment on racial grounds. Thus the full range of employment relationships is covered and the cases assisted to date reflect this. Assistance has been granted to individuals who have been subjected to racial harassment at work, as well as those who consider that recruitment, selection, promotion or training policies and procedures have been applied in a racially discriminatory manner. Others allege dismissal or the refusal of access to benefits on grounds of race. The remedies available to individuals are a declaration of rights, compensation, which may include damages for injury to feelings as well as loss of earnings, and a recommendation that the respondent take action to obviate or reduce the adverse effect on the complainant of any act of discrimination to which the complaint relates.

The limited experience to date has reflected a similar trend as has become the practice in relation to gender discrimination cases; most do not proceed to hearing but are settled at an earlier stage. A negotiation and settlement strategy is being developed for racial discrimination complaints in an effort to persuade employers to undertake steps which will tackle discrimination in the workplace through actions such as reviewing and equality proofing recruitment and selection procedures; introducing anti-racist training programs for staff; undertaking positive action measures to encourage minority ethnic applicants; or adapting monitoring systems to include ethnic monitoring.

Such a strategy, if effectively implemented, should be instrumental in bringing about organisational change and tackling institutional racism. The importance of the impact of the Stephen Lawrence Inquiry Report (Macpherson, 1999) should not be under-stated for, as noted earlier, it has raised consciousness within many organisations and, as one recent report noted, "has become part of the conceptual vocabulary of substantial numbers of people" (Commission on the Future of Multi-Ethnic Britain, 2000: 71).

The use of positive action measures in the field of racial equality is still quite rare in Northern Ireland. The legislation contains fairly weak provisions in that actions to address the needs of racial groups are discretionary and limited. It enables action to be taken to afford members of a racial group access to facilities or services to meet their specific needs in regard to their education, training or welfare; and it provides for 'any person' to offer racial group-specific training and encouragement to take up particular work. However, the latter provisions are qualified by requirements in relation to under-representation in that particular work. It must be demonstrated that, during the previous twelve months, either no-one from the specific racial group was doing the work in Northern Ireland, or the proportion of those doing the work was small in comparison with the proportion of persons of that group among the population of Northern Ireland or an area within Northern Ireland. Of course, without ethnic monitoring it is difficult to state that no member of a particular group has been so employed; similarly with the proportionality test.

The particular problem in Northern Ireland is that, with no baseline data on the extent or range of black and minority ethnic participation in the labour market, it is difficult for training organisations or employers to exploit the positive action provisions of the legislation (CRE for NI, 1999: 6). However, information on employment patterns, training needs and personal aspirations among Northern Ireland's black and minority ethnic population is now beginning to emerge and it is likely that any concerted effort to tackle systemic or institutional racism in Northern Ireland will need to be approached in a variety of ways.

Anti-discrimination legislation such as the Race Relations (NI) Order can help, particularly if it is amended to address current defects and to include the strong provisions already found in fair employment legislation. Secondly, however, economic policy development at a macro level must take account of the reality of life within black and minority ethnic communities. A recent initiative, which is also part of the new equality agenda in Northern Ireland, aims to address the causes of social exclusion and promote the social inclusion of minority ethnic groups generally and Irish Travellers in particular. It will tackle the factors which lead to social exclusion by identifying unmet needs, considering the impact of existing programs and highlighting what needs to be done, and how, in a co-ordinated way across Government Departments (Central Community Relations Unit, 1999). It remains to be seen how the programs of action that are produced will be operationalised and whether they will be effective. Finally, while primarily anecdotal to date, there is a growing body of evidence that systemic racism is a fact of life in Northern Ireland (CRE for NI, 1999). It will not be addressed effectively without the full involvement of black and minority people and organisations in policy and program development. Such involvement is key if solutions are to be found but it will only be possible and meaningful if there is capacity within the communities themselves to respond, and it is particularly problematic when communities do not have resources or sufficient funding. This is an issue that is live in Northern Ireland at present in relation to the statutory duties under the Northern Ireland Act that are discussed below.

The Macpherson report has already led to improvements in legislative protection against racial discrimination in Britain and work is now underway to have similar amendments enacted to the Northern Ireland Order. The new statutory duty on public authorities in relation to racial groups and Government initiatives to tackle the social exclusion of Travellers and black and minority ethnic communities are important mechanisms for bringing about change. They, together with existing anti-discrimination legislation, represent a useful framework within which to move ahead. It is to be hoped that this framework will prove to be an effective tool in the fight against racism and racial discrimination in Northern Ireland.

THE NEW EQUALITY AGENDA

As noted earlier, the Government's White Paper *Partnership for Equality* was published in March 1998. It was framed around proposals for legislation and policies on employment equality in Northern Ireland and addressed issues around employment and unemployment, job skills, the role of Government and fair employment law in particular. Importantly it proposed two new initiatives that were to have a significant impact on the way in which equality issues would be advanced in Northern Ireland -- a single Equality Commission, and new statutory duties on public authorities in relation to promoting equality of opportunity and good relations. Both of these proposals were subsequently to become part of the Belfast Agreement signed the following month.

The Equality Commission for Northern Ireland

Reaction was swift in respect of the proposal contained in the White Paper to establish a single Equality Commission that would assume the functions of the Commission for Racial Equality for Northern Ireland, the Equal Opportunities Commission for Northern Ireland, the Fair Employment Commission and the Northern Ireland Disability Council. The proposal was subject to consultation and it was during this process that clear differences of opinion arose as to the efficacy of the intended way forward. Many held very definite views on one side or the other. Arguments around the benefits of a one stop shop for employers and the rationalisation and more effective use of resources were countered by impassioned pleas from others that the proposal would lead to a hierarchy of rights and a loss of focus for newer and developing areas of discrimination in Northern Ireland, such as race and disability. Both the Commission for Racial Equality for Northern Ireland and the Equal Opportunities Commission for Northern Ireland voiced concerns about the creation of a single equality body. The disability sector, too, was unhappy that there was to be no dedicated Commission to enforce disability discrimination legislation, as there would be in the rest of the United Kingdom. Less than one month later, on 10th April 1998, the determination to adopt this model was made clear in the Belfast Agreement, which committed the British Government to make rapid progress with "measures on employment equality included in the recent White Paper" (Agreement, 1998:19).

A Working Group (ECWG) was established in November 1998 with the remit to "...consider and make recommendations for the establishment of a new single Equality Commission....taking account of its duties in relation to public authorities and allowing for any new powers it will be given on disability" (ECWG, 1998:70). The Working Group was to address the following specific areas during its deliberations:

- a program of action to combine the four bodies and ensure continuity of work;
- proposals to ensure a single ethos, building upon the advances in the promotion of equality of opportunity that have already been made;
- options for the recruitment, composition and structure of the new Board of Commissioners;
- a scheme for transferring existing delegated...responsibilities to the new Commission;
- options for an interim and/or long-term staffing structure;
- identified strategic priorities for the new Commission;
- proposals for the apportionment of resources between functions previously exercised by the four bodies listed above; and
- a suggested list of priority activities to be undertaken and topics to be addressed by the Commission in the first few months of its existence.

The Working Group was also required to consult and all of this was to happen within a very tight time-frame. Originally a mere two months was allowed; this was subsequently extended by a further six weeks. The speed with which such fundamental changes were to be considered and recommendations proposed was adversely commented on by many of those who took part in the consultation process, and the Working Group itself makes reference to the imposition of such a tight deadline on a number of occasions in its final Report. Certainly had more time been allowed the Working Group would have been able to fully consider issues in relation to the most appropriate structure for a new single body and also consult on the most appropriate composition of the twenty person Board of Commissioners.

The Working Group proposed a Directorate structure for the new organisation at Day 1. This was in recognition of the realities of bringing together three pre-existing operations with differing strategic approaches and priorities and separate legal regimes. It also took account of the Commission's new responsibilities and legislation on disability and the new statutory duties on Northern Ireland public authorities. It recommended, however, that "in the longer term, common areas of work are brought together" (ECWG, 1998:2).

On 1 October 1999 the Commission for Racial Equality for Northern Ireland, the Equal Opportunities Commission for Northern Ireland, the Fair Employment Commission and the Northern Ireland Disability Council were dissolved and the Equality Commission for Northern Ireland came into being. However, the Commission is still required to operate under five different pieces of legislation – on gender and equal pay, race, religion and politics, and disability, as well as the new statutory duties on public authorities under the provisions of the Northern Ireland Act 1998. The Commission is on record as recommending that the legislative framework should be harmonised, and work to achieve this aim began early in 2001. It remains to be seen how effective the new structure will be in taking forward the various equality agendas on disability, gender, race and religion and political discrimination as well as the new statutory duties on public bodies. Certainly the Commission has committed itself in its first Corporate Plan to ensuring that it plays a leading role in bringing about an inclusive society and pushing the boundaries toward the provision of equality of opportunity and fair participation, the promotion of good relations, and the elimination of discrimination in Northern Ireland (EC for NI, 2000).

Duties on Public Authorities

Section 75 of the Northern Ireland Act 1998 and its associated Schedule 9 certainly have the potential for addressing systemic or institutional discrimination and for bringing about significant change within the public sector. New statutory duties now apply to most public authorities in Northern Ireland including Government departments, District Councils, the health and social services sector, education and library boards and a variety of other organisations that have a public function.

Over the past ten years efforts have been made in Northern Ireland to address the impact of public policy determination on equality of opportunity. The main instrument for so doing was the Policy Appraisal and Fair Treatment (PAFT) initiative that came into being in 1994 following the issuing of non-statutory guidelines in December 1993 (McCrudden, 1999:1712). Encouragingly, the guidelines covered more than the usual Protestant/Catholic nexus, including the grounds of age, disability, ethnic origin, gender, marital and family status and sexual orientation. The aim was to "ensure that issues of equality and equity inform policy making and action in all spheres and at all levels of Government activity, whether in regulatory and administrative functions or in the delivery of services to the public" (CCRU, 1995). Groups beyond the usual religious divide in Northern Ireland, rightly or wrongly, thought the guidelines finally offered an opportunity for their interests to achieve some sort of profile within Government. This did not turn out to be the case, something that was highlighted during the review of the fair employment legislation by the Standing Advisory Commission on Human Rights in 1996 (McCrudden, 1999:1716). This recognition of the ineffectiveness and deficiencies of PAFT was eventually built upon to create new statutorily based duties. These were outlined in the Belfast Agreement as part of the commitments on Rights, Safeguards and Equality of Opportunity which said that, subject to consultation, the British Government would "create a statutory obligation on public authorities in Northern Ireland to carry out all their functions with due regard to the need to promote equality of opportunity" on a range of grounds (Agreement, 1998:16). The principle behind the obligation is that equality ought to be a central consideration in public policy making, and implicit in the initiative are the notions of mainstreaming, transparency, user involvement and accountability.

The first of the duties, which are set out in Section 75 of the Act, is to "have due regard to the need to promote equality of opportunity":

- between persons of different religious belief, political opinion, racial group, age, marital status or sexual orientation;
- between men and women generally;
- between persons with a disability and persons without; and
- between persons with dependants and persons without.

In addition, the authority shall "have regard to the desirability of promoting good relations between persons of different religious belief, political opinion or racial group". It was important that racial groups were included in the good relations duty in order that public authorities would extend their thinking beyond the traditional 'community relations' which, for everyone in Northern Ireland, means relations between Catholics and Protestants. Equality of opportunity and good relations were also seen by Government as complementary and not competing goals, although the guidelines issued by the Equality Commission note that, should a tension between the two objectives arise, "the primary duty ...is (a public authority's) equality duty" (EC for NI, 1999:12).

The operationalisation of these duties is addressed in Schedule 9 to the Act, which requires the public authority to prepare an Equality Scheme that sets out its arrangements for:

- assessing how it is complying with the duties and for consulting on matters to which a duty is likely to be relevant;
- assessing and consulting on the likely impact of policies adopted or proposed on the promotion of equality of opportunity;
- monitoring any adverse impact on the promotion of equality of opportunity;
- publishing the results of such assessments;
- training its staff; and
- ensuring, and assessing, public access to information and services provided by the authority.

The Scheme must contain a timetable for the measures contained in it and there is also a requirement that the public authority consult with those persons who are likely to be affected by the Equality Scheme before submitting it to the Equality Commission for Northern Ireland.

This is the first phase of the new duties and, toward the end of 2000, the Equality Commission was engaged in assessing the Schemes that had been submitted to it. Public authorities are now required to determine the adverse impact of any policy, identify what steps might mitigate against this and suggest alternative policies. Implementation will then follow. It is the responsibility of the Equality Commission to approve a Scheme or refer it to the Secretary of State who, in turn, may approve the Scheme, request a revised Scheme or produce a Scheme for the authority. The Commission also has a role in relation to complaints that it may investigate and report on to the public authority complained about, to the Secretary of State and to the complainant. If the Commission has recommended that the authority take some action and this is not done then the matter may be referred to the Secretary of State, who may give directions to the authority.

Interestingly, in Britain the Race Relations (Amendment) Bill 1999 that received Royal Assent in late 2000 also contains a duty on public authorities in relation to racial equality. This parallels the Northern Ireland duty to some extent but differs in that it is not concerned with having due regard to the need to promote equality of opportunity or having regard to the desirability of promoting good relations but rather to have due regard to the need to eliminate unlawful racial discrimination and promote equality of opportunity and good relations (Commission for Racial Equality, 2000). Further, the Amendment Bill allows for the issuing of Codes of Practice that, while not a definitive statement of the law, may nevertheless be persuasive in a court of law. Finally, the duty will be enforceable in the courts by the Commission for Racial Equality in Britain. The Northern Ireland mechanism is just over one year old and the first stage is only now drawing to a close. So it remains to be seen which approach will be more effective for achieving change, eliminating discrimination and promoting equality of opportunity and good relations.

The public duties are important in a number of respects in Northern Ireland. First of all they impose obligations in respect of groups which, to date, have not been covered by any other aspect of equality law – those of different ages or sexual orientation; those with dependants and those without; those with a status other than married status. These groups will still not be afforded the protection of anti-discrimination provisions, but at least their interests should now be addressed within the very important arena of public policy and decision making. Secondly, the requirement for consultation as an element of the policy making process has the potential for ensuring very real user involvement and influence in the development of policies which affect the everyday life of Northern Ireland's black and minority ethnic communities, as well as children and older people, those who have a disability; and others. Finally, it is hoped that, as a consequence of having to address equality issues, the need for good relations and the needs of their users, Northern Ireland's public authorities as employers and as the providers of service will come to represent models of good practice, high quality and effectiveness.

CONCLUSION

These are interesting times in the field of equality of opportunity in Northern Ireland. As a result of the Belfast Agreement of 1998 equality is now high on the agenda and is included in the Northern Ireland Assembly's Draft Programme for Government released in late 2000 (Northern Ireland Executive, 2000). The commitment seems to be there – a single equality Bill, a review of the senior civil service, the new statutory duty on public authorities and initiatives to tackle social exclusion.

The proposal to harmonise the equality legislation offers an exciting opportunity to create a truly innovative and effective legal framework to address discrimination and encourage employers to take those much needed extra steps that will make a difference within the workplace. The review of the appointments and promotion procedures of the Northern Ireland senior Civil Service should help to address issues of under-representation of women, Catholics, those from black and minority ethnic communities and those with a disability. Undertaking this exercise will send out an important message to other employers in Northern Ireland and, hopefully, encourage them to engage in similar initiatives. The statutory duties on public authorities promise much in terms of bringing about change in the way in which the public sector generally engages with its users and employees across the broad spectrum of constituencies and interests. The concepts of user involvement and consultation, which are central to these new duties, should provide the citizenry of Northern Ireland with a real chance to influence public policy development and implementation. Encouraging too are the initiatives which are aimed at tackling social exclusion and promoting social inclusion. Acknowledging the reality of life for marginalised groups such as Irish Travellers is a step in the right direction; translating this into action is what is needed now.

This is not the time for complacency; great care must be taken to ensure that the interests and needs of all of the constituencies in Northern Ireland are addressed. Women played an important part in holding communities together throughout the 'troubles' and issues of concern to them must be tackled if they are to have the opportunity to play a full part in all aspects of life. The contribution of members of black and minority ethnic communities, so long ignored and marginalised, needs to be acknowledged and opportunities provided to facilitate full participation. Steps need to be taken to ensure that young and older people, those of different sexual orientations, those with dependants and those with a disability can become fully involved in the economic, social, political and civic life of Northern Ireland. The new equality agenda, its structures and legal framework are among the most far-reaching in Europe. As such it offers a real opportunity for progress to be made toward the elimination of unlawful discrimination and the promotion of equality of opportunity, fair participation and good relations in Northern Ireland in the years to come.

Appendix 1: Northern Ireland Anti-discrimination Legislation: Summary of Selected Provisions

The following is intended to be a general guide only. The Sections and Articles referred to are not identical in their wording or the extent of their coverage. The actual legislative provisions should be consulted.	Disability Discrimination Act 1995/Equality (Disability etc.)(Northern Ireland) Order 2000	Fair Employment & Treatment (Northern Ireland) Order 1998	Race Relations (Northern Ireland) Order 1997	Sex Discrimination (Northern Ireland) Order 1976
Definitions of Discrimination	Section	Article	Article	Article
• direct	5,14,20,24	3(2)(a)	3(1)(a)	3(1)(a)
• indirect	-	3(2)(b)	3(1)(b)	3(1)(b)
• victimisation	55	3	4	6
• aiding unlawful acts	57	-	33	43
• pressure to discriminate	-	-	31	41
• instructions to discriminate	-	-	30	40
Discrimination against Applicants for employment unlawful in respect of • the arrangements made for determining who should be offered employment • the terms on which employment is offered • refusing or deliberately omitting of offer employment	4(1)	19(1)(a)	6(1)	8(1)
Discrimination against Employees unlawful in respect of • the terms of employment • the way in which an employee is afforded access to opportunities for promotion, transfer, training or other benefits, facilities or services or by refusing or deliberately omitting to afford access to them • dismissal or subjecting employee to any other detriment	4(2)	19(1)(b) but 'promotion', 'facilities or services' not referred to	6(2)	8(2) but 'terms of employment' not referred to
Other unlawful acts include discrimination				
• against contract workers	12	20	9	12
• by employment agencies	19(3)(g)	22	16	18
• by those providing or making arrangements for provision of training services/vocational training	-	24	15	17
• by persons with statutory power to select employees for others	-	21	7	9
• by vocational organisations/trade unions/trade organisations	13	23	13	15
• by persons with power to confer qualifications	-	25	14	16
• by partnerships	-	26	12	14
• in occupational pension schemes	17	-	-	-
• in insurance services	18	-		-

Duties on Employers				
• Register with Equality Commission (10 employees or more)	-	48	-	-
• Registered employer to prepare and file monitoring returns	-	52	-	-
• Registered employer to review procedures every 3 years	-	55	-	-
• Commission can enquire/seek information re monitoring or review exercises	-	56	-	-
• Commission can seek undertaking pursuant to above enquiry	-	57(1)	-	-
• Commission can state employer 'not qualified' if in default of statutory obligations	-	62(2)	-	-
• Restriction on public authority entering into contract with 'unqualified' concern	-	64(1)	-	-
• General duty on district councils	-	-	67	-
Exemptions from the legislation include:				
• Small businesses with less than 15 employees	7(1)	-	-	-
• Employment in a private household	-	70(1)(b)	6(3)	10(2)(b)(b)
• School teachers	-	71	-	-
• Police (in relation to height, uniform, equipment and pregnancy)	-	-	- -	- 19(2)
• Prison officers	64(5)(b)	-		20 (in relation to height, equipment and uniforms)
• fire fighters	64(5)©	-	-	-
• military, naval or air force	64(7)		-	-
• ministers of religion	-	70(1)(a)	-	21(1)
Affirmative/Positive Action provisions include:				
• group specific training	-	76(1)	37(1)(a) 37(2)(a)	48(1)(a) 48(2)(a)
• group specific training for employees by employers			37(4)(a)	49(1)(a)
• measures to encourage applications from under-represented groups	-	74	37(1)(b) 37(2)(b) 37(4)(b)	48(1)(b) 48(2)(b) 49(1)(b)
• special needs of racial groups in regard to education, training or welfare	-	-	35	-

• provision of training for affirmative action purposes	-	72		
• training for those who have been discharging domestic or family responsibilities	-	-	-	48(3)

Sheila Rogers is Director -- Race Development, Equality Commission for Northern Ireland in Belfast, Northern Ireland.

NOTES

[1] This Standard Occupational Classification includes jobs such as Assistant Engineers, Retail Buyers and Financial Agents.
[2] Legislation extended to Northern Ireland by Order-in-Council of the British Government is referred to as an Order.
[3] M –v- Crescent Garage, 24/83SD; McClenaghan & Rice –v- British Shoe Corporation Ltd, 2688/91SD, 3207/91EP, 3206/91SD; Mulligan –v- Eastern Health and Social Services Board, 1258/93SD; Fryers –v- University of Ulster, 2736/93SD
[4] 97/75/EC; 96/97/ED; 92/85/EEC.

REFERENCES

Agreement reached in Multi-Party Negotiations. Belfast, April 10, 1998.
Central Community Relations Unit. New TSN – An Agenda for Targeting Social Need and Promoting Social Inclusion in Northern Ireland. Belfast, 1999.
Central Community Relations Unit. Policy Appraisal and Fair Treatment Annual Report. Belfast, 1994.
Children's Law Centre & Save the Children. Getting it right? An Evaluation of the United Kingdom Government's Implementation of the United Nations Convention on the Rights of the Child in Northern Ireland 1994 – 1999. Belfast, 1999.
Commission for Racial Equality. Reform of the Race Relations Act 1976. Belmont Press, 1998.
Commission for Racial Equality. The Race Relations (Amendment) Bill Questions and Answers. London, 2000.
Commission for Racial Equality for Northern Ireland. Into the Light Conference Report. Belfast, 1999.
Commission for Racial Equality for Northern Ireland. Recommendations for Changes to the Race Relations (NI) Order 1997 Consultation Document. Belfast, 1999.
Commission on the Future of Multi-Ethnic Britain. The Future of Multi-Ethnic Britain. The Runnymede Trust, 2000.
Connolly, P. and Keenan, M. Racial Attitudes and Prejudice in Northern Ireland . Northern Ireland Statistics and Research Agency, Belfast, 2000.
Department of Enterprise, Trade and Industry. New Earnings Survey. Belfast, 1999.
Disability Discrimination Act. 1995.
Equal Opportunities Commission for Northern Ireland. Gender and Equality of Opportunity in the Private Sector. Belfast, 1998.
Equal Opportunities Commission for Northern Ireland. Recommendations for Changes to the Equal Pay Legislation. Belfast, 1990.

Equal Opportunities Commission for Northern Ireland. The Sex Discrimination Legislation: Recommendations for Change. Belfast, 1997.
Equal Opportunities Commission for Northern Ireland. The Working Lives of Women and Men in Northern Ireland. Belfast, 1997.
Equal Opportunities Commission for Northern Ireland. Where do Women Figure? Belfast, 1999.
Equal Opportunities Commission for Northern Ireland and Chief Executives' Forum. Gender and Equality of Opportunity in the Public Sector. Belfast, 1994.
Equal Pay Act (Northern Ireland). 1970.
Equality Commission for Northern Ireland Corporate Plan 2000 – 2003 Consultative Draft. Belfast, 2000.
Equality Commission for Northern Ireland. Guide to the Statutory Duties. Belfast, 1999.
Equality Commission for Northern Ireland. Monitoring Report No.10 – A Profile of Northern Ireland Workforces Summary of Monitoring Returns 1999. Belfast, 2000.
Equality Commission Working Group. Report. Belfast, 1998.
Fair Employment and Treatment (Northern Ireland) Order, 1998.
House of Commons. Hansard. London, 1997.
House of Commons. Partnership for Equality. The Government's proposals for Future Legislation and Policies on Employment Equality in Northern Ireland. Cm3890: The Stationery Office, 1998.
Home Office. Equality for Women. London: HMSO, 1974.
Kremer, J. Recruiting and Selecting Fairly: A Summary Report. Fair Employment Agency, 1991.
Leong, F.C. Breaking Down Barriers –A Study to Assess the Need for Community-based Information Provision and Advocacy to Address Issues of Accessibility to Appropriate Advice and Assistance in relation to the legal process for racial groups in Northern Ireland. Equality Commission for Northern Ireland, 2000 (unpublished).
Macpherson, W. The Stephen Lawrence Inquiry. The Stationery Office, 1999.
McCrudden, C. "Mainstreaming Equality". *Fordham International Law Journal*. .22 (1999):1696.
McVeigh, R. "'There's No Racism Because There's No Black People Here': Racism and Anti-racism in Northern Ireland". *Divided Society: Ethnic Minorities and Racism in Northern Ireland.* In Hainsworth (ed.). Pluto Press, 1998.
Noonan, P. Travelling People in West Belfast. Save the Children, 1994.
Northern Ireland Executive. Draft Programme for Government. Belfast, 2000.
Race Relations (Northern Ireland) Order. 1997.
Sex Discrimination (Northern Ireland) Order. 1976.
Skinner, S. Building Community Strengths. Community Development Foundation. 1977.
The Guardian. Manchester, September 1993.
The Guardian. Manchester, March 2000.
The Irish Times Dublin, April 2000.
Training and Employment Agency. Analysis of Unpublished Statistics. Belfast, 1999.
United Nations Committee on the Elimination of all Forms of Racial Discrimination. Forty-third Session. Geneva, 1993.

CHAPTER 11

FRANK M. HORWITZ AND HARISH C. JAIN

EMPLOYMENT EQUITY IN SOUTH AFRICA: OVERCOMING THE APARTHEID LEGACY

South Africa's (SA) re-entry into competitive global markets in the 1990's created new managerial challenges. The legacy of workplace apartheid is systematically being eroded. By 1999 some 30 percent of SA managers are Black, with less than 8 percent prior to 1994. Employment discrimination is being replaced by policies and practices aimed at recruiting and developing Black managers. Management development, changes in corporate culture and Black advancement have become more prominent.

Chapter 2 of the new Employment Equity Act (1998) in SA prohibits unfair discrimination against designated employees. These include Black people, women and employees with disabilities. Legislative prohibitions against unfair discrimination are also intrinsic to South Africa's Constitution (1996). Chapter 2 (the Bill of Rights) contains an equality clause, and like the Employment Equity Act specifies a number of grounds which constitute unfair discrimination. Additionally, Schedule 7 of the Labour Relations Act (1995) considers unfair discrimination either directly or indirectly as a residual unfair labour practice. Grounds include race, gender, ethnic origin, sexual orientation, religion, disability, conscience, belief, language and culture. Labour laws have been at the forefront of the post-apartheid government's determination to remove unfair discrimination. A new act, The Promotion of Equality and Prevention of Unfair Discrimination Act (1999), seeks to prohibit discrimination in both civil society and in employment practices.

The legislative armoury against unfair discrimination is now quite formidable. However, the legacy of apartheid has resulted in structural inequalities in the acquisition of education, work skills and access to managerial, professional and occupational positions. Although changing, a "glass ceiling" remains for designated groups. Research shows that Black employees hold around 30 percent of managerial posts (Bowmaker-Falconer, 1999). Black employees comprise over 75 percent of the labour market, and women of all races around 50 percent. This disproportion is discussed below.

Historically, the labour market was a distorted one, with inequality in access to education, skills, managerial and professional work, based on race and ethnicity. Racial discrimination was created in labour legislation, for example in job reservation clauses that restricted access to skilled jobs, preserving them for white employees, in the Mines and Works Act (1904) and Industrial Conciliation Act (1956). These provisions have been abolished since 1980 and significant labour law reforms have occurred in the last five years. However, the apartheid labour market has left most employees inadequately trained and economically dies-empowered. SA's peaceful transition through its 1994 national election and constitutional measures has given hope that the constitutional democracy will provide equal protection and

C. Agocs (ed.), Workplace Equality, 225–242.

opportunity to all citizens regardless of colour, gender, religion, political opinion or sexual orientation. The draft Constitution adopted by the Constitutional Assembly on May 8, 1996 was approved by the Constitutional Court in November of 1996 (Corder, 1996). Section 9(2) states in part:

> To promote the achievement of equality, legislative and other measures designed to protect or advance persons, or categories of persons, disadvantaged by unfair discrimination may be taken.

Whenever unfair discrimination is alleged in terms of the Employment Equity Act, a reverse onus of proof is on the employer to establish that the practice is fair. As part of a required employment equity plan, all employers with 50 or more employees are required to review all their employment and human resources practices to remove any provisions or practices which may have a discriminatory effect. This includes recruitment and selection, and remuneration. It is in these two areas, as well as in the provision of substantive benefits and conditions of employment, where discrimination is most likely. The notions of disproportionate effect and adverse impact are considered in this regard, as will be illustrated later in this chapter.

Once an employee establishes discrimination, the onus of proof (or, more properly, the evidentiary burden) shifts to the employer to show that the discrimination is not unfair. It is nonetheless very difficult for an employee to conclusively prove discrimination, and especially pay discrimination. Whilst discrimination may occur, an employer may cogently submit that pay differences were not the result of unfair discrimination, but due to factors such as differences in performance, experience, competencies and service. Before the introduction of the Employment Equity Act, the onus of proof was a contentious issue. The SA courts have used different tests to establish what the employee needs to prove in order to establish "discrimination" before the onus shifts to the employer to show that such discrimination is not unfair. There needs to be prime facie evidence that discrimination has occurred. This onus is in the first place on the complainant. The mere allegation of discrimination is not sufficient.

SYSTEMIC DISCRIMINATION AND INEQUALITY: BASIC CAUSES

Earnings inequality has increased in developed economies such as the United States over the past fifteen years, due to a combination of skill-based technological change, globalisation and international trade, and an increase in relative demand for skilled workers (Freeman, 1997; Juhn, 1999). Freeman (1997:41) argues further that union density decline is a contributing factor. Similarly in SA, a developing economy, skilled jobs are growing and unskilled jobs are declining. Professional, managerial and transport occupations account for an increase of around two million jobs since 1970. More skilled employees have been absorbed into service industries, due to a structural shift from the primary sector to growth in services, accompanied by rising capital-to-labour ratios. Greatest demand is expected for skills in I.T. and finance (Bhorat, 1999). In SA most Black workers are manual or semi-skilled workers. The economy's ability to absorb Black labour into higher skill and managerial jobs is being nudged by supply-side measures such as employment equity legislation. Tables 1 and 2 show that employed Africans, both men and women, tend to be concentrated in lower income levels, according to the last census in 1996.

Table 2 (page 229) shows that three quarters of employed Africans had incomes of R1 500 or less a month, compared with 16 percent of whites, according to the 1996 census. Some 23 percent of coloured, Indian and white households had an income of R100 000 or more in 1998, while the equivalent proportion among African households was 1 percent (Jeffery, SA Institute of Race Relations, 1999/2000).

LABOUR MARKET AND STRUCTURAL FACTORS

A structural inequality in the skill profile exists: a shortage of occupationally and managerially skilled workers is contrasted with an excess of unskilled labour. Meanwhile fairly low economic growth and a lack of managerial skills have led to a comparatively low level of spending on training and development. The World Competitiveness Report (1999) has indicted, however, that organisational investment in training and development is a decisive competitive factor. In comparison to developed market economies, SA's per capita output is one-sixth of Switzerland's, one-fifth of that of the USA and one-quarter of Japan's. Ultimately, labour and capital productivity is a managerial function by ensuring investment in human resource development.

Apartheid created a distorted labour market with economic power concentrated in a few white hands. Until recent moves to disaggregate or unbundle large corporations such as Gencor and Barlow Rand, economic power was concentrated in eight conglomerates which controlled over 70 percent of the share capital on the Johannesburg Stock Exchange (Jubber, 1979: 42-44). There is also a concentration of managerial control through a system of interlocking directorates where the same person(s) serve on the boards of several corporations. This social closure has limited the upward mobility of Black managers and women. However, SA's re-entry into the international business community has forced an awareness about its relative competitiveness in the manufacturing and services sectors. Recently, statutory and governmental tender requirements have been towards employment equity and diversity at all levels. Several Black directors have been appointed to boards of directors. Although less than 15 percent of SA's company directors are Black or women, this is likely to change significantly by the year 2005.

Given the historical legacy of apartheid, South Africa has one of the highest Gini Coefficients, which reflects its particularly high earnings inequalities. Apartheid education and skills legislation created a relatively unique basis for skills and therefore earnings inequalities. Black access to trades and skilled work was legislatively prohibited by job reservation in favour of white employees, for example in Section 66 of the then Industrial Conciliation Act (1956) and the Mines and Works Act (1904). The latter barred Black employees from obtaining blasting certificates in the mining industry. These Acts were repealed in 1980 – some twenty years ago -- yet Black progress into skilled and managerial work has been slow. Research by the University of Cape Town's Breakwater Monitor Project shows that the percentage of Blacks moving into managerial positions increased 3 percent from 1997 through 1999. This research also found that 24 percent of managers promoted were women, though only 5 percent of these were Black women. Whilst legislative measures are now in place, the unequal and adverse impact of structural and remunerative inequalities arising from apartheid will not be eliminated or significantly reduced in the short term.

An earlier landmark case on pay discrimination in the then industrial court was that of the SA Chemical Workers' Union (SACWU) vs. Sentrachem (1988), where the court ordered that the company eliminate pay discrimination over a period. Sentrachem was found to have unfairly discriminated between its Black and white plant operators by paying Black employees less than white employees in the same job grade and doing the same work, and had so discriminated for a number of years. This case set the scene for subsequent jurisprudence, although this is evolving slowly.

Table 1: Proportional Distribution of Individual Monthly Income by Race, 1996[a]

	African	Coloured	Indian	White	Unspecified / Other	Total
None[b]	1.2%	0.8%	0.9%	1.2%	1.2%	**1.1%**
R1-R200	11.2%	5.0%	1.5%	1.5%	4.9%	**8.0%**
R201-R500	20.9%	17.3%	3.55%	2.3%	10.5%	**15.9%**
R501-R1 000	22.8%	19.2%	10.9%	4.1%	13.7%	**18.0%**
R1 001-R1 500	19.1%	20.5%	20.2%	7.1%	15.8%	**16.9%**
R1 501-R2 500	11.7%	16.0%	21.2%	13.7%	14.6%	**13.1%**
R2 501-R3 500	5.3%	7.8%	13.5%	14.1%	9.4%	**7.8%**
R3 501- R4 500	2.7%	4.3%	8.5%	12.3%	6.5%	**5.1%**
R4 501-R6 000	1.6%	3.0%	7.8%	13.1%	5.6%	**4.4%**
R6 001-R8 000	0.6%	1.1%	3.8%	8.7%	2.8%	**2.5%**
R8 001-R11 000	0.3%	0.5%	2.1%	6.4%	1.7%	**1.7%**
R11 001-R16 000	0.2%	0.2%	1.1%	4.0%	0.9%	**1.0%**
R16 001-R30 000	0.1%	0.1%	0.6%	2.4%	0.5%	**0.6%**
R30 000 or more	0.04%	0.04%	0.2%	1.0%	0.2%	**0.2%**
Unspecified	2.2%	4.1%	4.3%	8.2%	11.8%	**3.8%**
Total[c]	**100.0%**	**100.0%**	**100.0%**	**100.0%**	**100.0%**	**100.0%**

Source: Statistics South Africa

a Excluding institutions. Institutions are communal temporary, semi-permanent, or living arrangements for people in special circumstances, such as prisons, and homes for the disabled.

b Includes people working for family businesses and people receiving payment in kind.

c Figures should add up but may not, owing to rounding.

Table 2: Individual monthly income by race: 1996[a]

	African	Coloured	Indian	White	Unspecified / Other	Total
None[b]	67 867	9 154	3 299	22 015	1 018	**103 354**
R1-R200	636 718	56 697	5 762	28 561	3 991	**731 729**
R201-R500	1 186 478	195 228	12 587	42 558	8 590	**1 445 441**
R501-R1 000	1 293 717	216 618	39 445	76 298	11 248	**1 637 326**
R1 001-R1 500	1 088 001	231 507	73 339	131 265	12 913	**1 537 026**
R1 501-R2 500	667 021	180 879	76 952	253 713	11 944	**1 190 508**
R2 501-R3 500	303 914	88 647	49 189	261 581	7 683	**711 013**
R3 501- R4 500	154 853	48 656	30 908	228 432	5 309	**468 158**
R4 501-R6 000	90 060	33 424	28 238	242 336	4 609	**398 666**
R6 001-R8 000	34 873	12 595	13 771	160 617	2 256	**224 111**
R8 001-R11 000	19 464	5 596	7 631	118 943	1 387	**153 021**
R11 001-R16 000	9 406	2 335	3 857	74 709	719	**91 026**
R16 001-R30 000	4 817	1 253	2 078	45 169	395	**53 712**
R30 000 or more	2 070	465	858	17 677	151	**21 221**
Unspecified	123 216	46 463	15 573	152 579	9 703	**347 533**
Total[c]	5 682 476	**1 129 515**	**363 486**	**1 856 452**	**81 917**	**9 113 847**

Source: Statistics South Africa

a Excluding institutions. Institutions are communal temporary, semi-permanent, or living arrangements for people in special circumstances, such as prisons, and homes for the disabled.
b Includes people working for family businesses and people receiving payment in kind.
c Figures should add up but may not, owing to rounding.

EMPLOYMENT DISCRIMINATION: EVIDENCE FROM LEGAL CASES

Various key court decisions on employment equity and affirmative action reflect a range of perspectives, from hostility to lukewarm acceptance and full endorsement (Hodges-Aeberhard (1999: 249). They reflect on the usefulness of special measures to overcome discrimination. Recent cases in South Africa show that even in an environment where affirmative action to overcome past discrimination has been legislated as an appropriate method to achieve equity, there are differing interpretations by the business sector and government about its aims and effects.

The Constitution, as well as the prohibitions contained in the subsequent Acts mentioned here, distinguishes permissible discrimination from impermissible discrimination. (See Leonard Dingler Employee Representative Council v Leonard Dingler (Pty) Ltd (1998) 19 ILJ 285 (LC) at 294 F-H). In the employment context, the former type is based on the inherent requirements of the job test.

The reverse onus of proof in these statutes, whereby an employer is required to prove that discrimination is not unfair, has been criticised by employer organisations such as Business South Africa and NGOs such as the South African Institute of Race Relations (Jeffery, 2000). Organised business has however supported the intent of the equity legislation. Relevant in this regard is the requirement in Section 20 for all designated employers (those who employ 50 or more people) to prepare and submit to the Department of Labour an employment equity plan. The plan must set out goals, targets, timetables and measures to be taken to remove discriminatory employment practices and achieve greater representivity in the workforce, especially at managerial and skilled category levels. The Employment Equity Act does not set quotas, but rather enables individual employers to develop their own plans. Criteria regarding enhanced representivity include national and regional demographic information and special skills supply/availability. Section 27(1) of the Employment Equity Act requires designated employers to submit a statement of remuneration and benefits received in each occupational category and level to the Employment Conditions Commission established by section 59 of the Basic Conditions of Employment Act (1998). Section 27(2) requires that where disproportionate income differentials are reflected in the statement, a designated employer must take measures to progressively reduce such differentials. Section 27(3) indicates that these measures may include: (a) collective bargaining; (b) compliance with sectoral pay determinations made by the Minister of Labour in terms of Section 51 of the Basic Conditions of Employment Act; (c) applying norms and benchmarks set by the Employment Conditions Commission; and (d) relevant measures in the Skills Development Act (1998). The Employment Conditions Commission is required to research and investigate norms and benchmarks for proportionate income differentials and advise the Minister on appropriate measures for reducing disproportional differentials. The Commission is not allowed to disclose information pertaining to individual employees or employers.

There is likely to be considerable public and organisational policy debate around what constitutes an acceptable pay curve in respect of differentials within organisations, and indeed whether such pay structuring is possible in a market driven global economy. The Commission for Conciliation, Mediation and Arbitration (CCMA) established by the Labour Relations Act (1995) is hearing an increasing number of disputes dealing with unfair labour practices and discrimination claims. Several cases have been heard in the Labour Court and at the CCMA on discrimination claims dealing with promotion and fair procedures (George vs. Liberty Life Association of Africa Ltd (1996); Van Vuuren vs. Department of Correctional Services, Labour Appeal Court, 1988 Case No PA: G/980; Public Servants Association of SA vs. Minister of Justice (1997)(5) BCLR, 577; and Public Servants Association & Another vs. Provincial Administration, Western Cape (1999) 2, BALR 184 CCMA).

There is also growing awareness in SA of employees' and employers' rights regarding unfair discrimination in employment and pension fund benefits. In Leonard Dingler Employee Representative Council vs. Leonard Dingler (Pty) Ltd (1998) 19 ILJ 285 (LC), the Labour Court considered the effects of discrimination, regardless of intent. In fact, the Court held explicitly that intent was irrelevant for a finding of unfair discrimination to be proven against an employer. In this case, differentiation in access to a pension fund was made on the basis of a monthly/weekly paid staff distinction. Most of the latter were Black employees who were denied membership of a staff benefit fund. The Labour Court found that Black monthly-paid employees were not given membership of the fund. This was held to be direct discrimination. Weekly paid employees were discriminated against indirectly on the basis of race. The residual unfair labour practice provisions of item 2(1)(a) of Schedule 7 of the Labour Relations Act (1995) outlaw this form of unfair labour practice.

In the Leonard Dingler case, the judge argued that even if the monthly/weekly criterion for membership of a staff benefit fund was valid, it was applied inconsistently on racial grounds. Indirect discrimination also occurred where criteria, conditions or policies are applied which appear to be neutral but which adversely impact a disproportionate number of a certain racial group and where these criteria are not justifiable. Here, the reverse onus of proof becomes relevant, as the employer has to give a convincing response as to why the discrimination is not unfair in effect, particularly as an adverse and disparate impact occurred. The onus rests on the employer to show that the object of the discriminatory practice or policy is legitimate and the means used to achieve it are rational and proportional. South African labour law allows discrimination on the basis of inherent job requirements. But the object of an employer's conduct must be fair, and the means rational.

PROVING DISCRIMINATION: DEBATES IN THE CASE LAW

The principle of equal pay for equal work was also raised in regard to a transport allowance benefit in a CCMA arbitration: SACCAWU vs. Garden Route Chalets (Pty) Ltd, (1997). Employees at certain establishments of the company were provided with transport to and from work by the employer. At one, it paid an allowance instead, which was not enough to cover the transport cost. The commissioner granted employees a transport allowance equal to the cost of transport provided to employees in other centres. Cases of direct discrimination on pay leave have been more difficult to prove, even with the reverse onus of proof. In TGWU & another vs. Bayete Security Holdings (1999), the applicant's case was dismissed. He claimed that he and another person were promoted but the latter received a higher salary. The difference in salaries was claimed to be unfair discrimination. The labour court held that the applicant was obliged to prove that the employer's conduct amounted to discrimination. Only after the applicant proved that he was the victim of discrimination, did the onus shift to the employer to prove that the discrimination was fair. A mere averment that there was discrimination was not enough to shift the onus. The fact that an employer paid one employee more than another is not necessarily unfair discrimination. The applicant has to prove that the different salary levels were based on race or another arbitrary criterion.

This dissection of the burden of proof was particularly important in the Labour Court case of Louw vs. Golden Arrow (Pty) Ltd (2000) 21 ILJ 188 (LC). Michael Louw, a Black man, was employed as a buyer. He alleged that another employee (a Mr Beneke), who was doing work of equal value to that of Louw, was paid a higher salary because he was white. The employer conceded that the two employees were paid a different wage, but argued that the two did not perform work of equal value, and that the pay difference of 60 percent was also justified due to other factors such as experience, knowledge and skill, and performance. The judge held that Louw had failed to prove, on a balance of probabilities, that the difference between his salary and that of his white colleague was due to racial discrimination. This case raised the question of the "apartheid wage gap", as the two employees were both doing the same job as buyers in 1990, the year that the white person, Beneke, joined the company. The employer successfully argued, however, that Beneke had since been promoted to the position of warehouse supervisor and that the two jobs today were not of equal value. However, Louw argued that the pay disparity of about 60 percent originated in 1990 and continued at the same level to the time of the Labour Court hearing in 1999. (The case is currently on appeal to the Labour Appeal Court). The judge accepted the employer's argument, based on expert evidence, that the two jobs of buyer and warehouse supervisor were materially different and were not of equal worth, with the latter being evaluated at a higher job grade. The Court rejected Louw's argument that the jobs were subjectively of equal value to the employer, as the white employee (Beneke) never received a promotional increase when he was moved to the position of warehouse supervisor. The court also accepted the company's evidence that Black employees were in other senior positions, and that there was not a pattern of racially determined salaries.

Remunerative conditions of employment, including leave, may also form the basis of a discrimination claim. In FAWU & Others vs. Rainbow Chicken Farms [2000] 1 BLLR 70 (LC), Muslim butchers employed by a chicken abattoir claimed discrimination on grounds of religion, in that they were not given leave over the Muslim fast of Eid. The collective agreement entitled workers to statutory public holidays, but allowed Muslim workers unpaid leave to celebrate Eid, so long as arrangements with the appropriate manager were made. In 1998, the butchers refused to work on Eid and could not come to an acceptable leave arrangement with the employer. They failed to come to work and were dismissed. The labour court ruled that the requirement to work was not unfair discrimination because all employees were to work on Eid; no religion was preferred over another, although the court conceded that Christian holidays were statutory. The employer's refusal to grant leave was not held as unfair discrimination. It was not possible here for the parties to arrive at a reasonable accommodation.

A similar argument of justification to that used in Louw v Golden Arrow, has been raised by the employer in the Namibian Labour Court in the pending case of Mineworkers Union of Namibia v CSO Evaluations (Pty) Ltd (Case No LC 18/98). In short, the argument is that justifiable pay differences occurred within a job grade where individuals differed as to factors like educational qualifications, skills, training, age, previous earnings and work experience and performance. Whilst these factors appear neutral, it was argued in a supplementary expert affidavit on behalf of the applicants that without an active, coherent and objective set of policies governing all aspects of employment related decisions, the distortions of an apartheid labour market are more likely than not to have a discriminating effect on employment decisions. A remuneration policy involves two kinds of evaluation: the value of the job to the organisation and the value of the employee. The former, using job evaluation, aims at establishing a hierarchy of jobs of comparable worth / value, in order to set basic pay rates. Job evaluation per se does not determine the actual pay of an individual(s). This is determined by some of the above-mentioned factors, including market factors and collective bargaining, which may also determine the slope of a pay curve. Bias and subjectively may occur in both processes, however. Procedural irregularities and inconsistencies may have a distorting impact on the fair application of job evaluation, performance evaluation, and pay setting. Job evaluation is not a science. Other criteria for pay determination mentioned above are potentially more open to bias. In Golden Arrow the employer did not clearly rely on objective factors, an established grading and differential pay structure, and a coherent wage level stratification. The jobs in question were evaluated ex post facto only after Louw had declared a dispute, and only with regard to the two individual employees in question.

Once discrimination has been proved by the applicant, the employer has the onus of proving that it was not unfair discrimination. In Golden Arrow, as Louw did not establish that his work was sufficiently similar to Beneke's to determine unequal or unfair treatment, the court unfortunately did not enquire into the link, if any, between pay and job grade. Commenting on this case, Christie (2000:5) argues that the allegation of unfair discrimination ought not to have been met solely by whether the jobs were objectively different. Although the wage disparity was considerable, unequal treatment was not obviously disparate from a technical standpoint, and the employer had no case to answer. In contrast, in Whitehead v Woolworths (Pty) Ltd (1999) 20 ILJ 2133 (LC) at 2139, the Labour Court accepted that racial discrimination may involve a causal link on the facts, between race and other impermissible grounds, and pay disparity. The Labour Court was of the opinion that "fairness or unfairness of the discrimination cannot be measured against the profitability or efficiency of a business enterprise," and held that there was no objectively justifiable reason why the requirement of continuity of employment should be imposed on a pregnant job applicant. This was controversially overturned by the Labour Appeal Court in a widely debated judgement around whether the pregnant job applicant could provide continuity of service in a managerial position. Willis JA accepted that the operational requirements of a business or profitability could be taken into account in determining fairness.

Decisions based on race or gender, unless they related to a genuine occupational requirement, could be found to be arbitrary and unfair labour practices (Van Vuuren and Liberty Life cases). In Leonard Dingler the Labour Court was not willing to accept the employer's argument that the willingness to right past wrongs permits unfair discrimination. Affirmative action is not regarded as unfair discrimination in SA labour law and in the Constitution, as previously discussed. The policy context in which the dispute arises is pertinent. In Golden Arrow, the Court found that because it had not been determined in an objective valuation that the jobs were of equal value, racial discrimination in pay had not been established (Christie, 2000:72). The Court noted, however, that this "does not mean that the difference is not attributable to race discrimination, it does mean that racial discrimination has not been proven". Given the allegation of unfair discrimination, the Court did not consider whether there was a causal link on the facts, between race or other impermissible grounds, and the wage disparity (Christie, 2000:75).

Christie argues that an unsettling aspect of the Golden Arrow case is whether the real issue was that Louw and Beneke had been treated differently as employees; and that despite a 61 percent pay differential, the jobs were not sufficiently similar to necessitate an enquiry into the link, if any, of pay and job grade. Adding to this concern is the ex post facto job grading that occurred only because a dispute was declared. The applicants in this case argued in the alternative that the 61 percent difference in salaries was disproportionate to the difference in value of the two jobs. Yet the Court accepted the employer's expert testimony that there can be up to 105 percent difference between jobs that are two grades apart, and that large disparities are "normal". Yet here the pay system and criteria for pay setting were neither systematic nor transparent, and starting pay rates were not linked to an objective reference. The employer should have been required to point to some reliable factor(s) other than race. Customary disparities are not a justification for continuing discrimination (Christie, 2000:73).

A generalised reliance on labour demand, and subjective criteria such as attitude, may in a historically discriminatory labour market have the effect of entrenching imbalances that the law intended to remove. This is especially pertinent in the light of the expert evidence led by the Company in Golden Arrow that entry level "pegs" the employee's salary for years to come – in that case, both Louw and Beneke continued to earn the salaries they earned in 1990, coupled with similar incremental annual increases, despite Beneke's "promotion" in 1994. That must be seen against the background of a racially distorted market in 1990 – conceded by the expert witness – which would ensure a racially discriminatory entry level salary in the first place. It can therefore be argued that the current pay disparity is simply the perpetuation of past discrimination in respect of skills formation, promotion policy and diversity.

DIVERSITY AND HUMAN RESOURCE DEVELOPMENT

Human resource development (HRD) concerns the processes of acquiring the knowledge and skills necessary to perform both specific occupational tasks and other social, cultural, intellectual and political roles in a society. Organisationally, this requires an integrated approach (Figure 1) which considers HRD as:

- overcoming labour market discrimination through addressing past inequalities based on race, gender and class;
- linked to human resource objectives which are, in turn, a function of organisational strategy;
- an investment and not a cost.

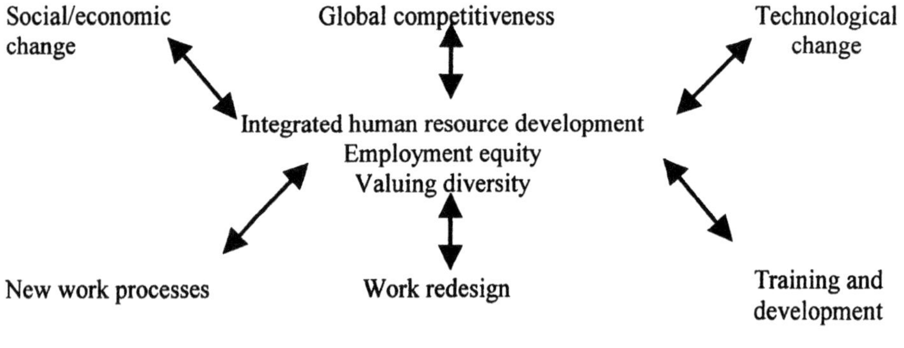

Figure 1: Integrated human resources development

The agenda associated with HR planning and development, as part of a strategic business process, represents an area of increasing co-operation between management and labour in SA. (Bowmaker-Falconer, Horwitz, Jain and Taggar, 1998). However, a mature corporate culture of people development does not yet exist in most SA organisations. It is estimated that around 2 percent of the corporate private sector's salary bill is invested in education and training each year compared with around 6 percent in leading industrial nations (Bowmaker-Falconer, 1996). The National Productivity Institute of SA estimates the national average, which would include large, medium and small organisations, to be around one percent.

The effective implementation of employment equality (EE) as part of human resource development in SA requires a robust strategy with a planned and holistic set of objectives to enhance skills capacity and provide real job responsibility. The term employment equity is subject to varying interpretations. It has been argued that EE is different from the concept of affirmative action (Thomas, 1990). Employment equity is based on the following premises: first, white men make up the business mainstream; second, a growing economy requires skilled, managerial and professional people; third, Blacks, women and other groups should be integrated into organisations as a matter of public and ethical policy; fourth, pervasive ethnic, racial and gender discrimination and prejudice are at the root of social and occupational exclusion; and finally, legal and social measures are necessary to bring about organisational change.

In practice, employment equity in SA has focused largely on the recruitment of Black managers. Managing diversity may in this context be understood to mean having an acute awareness of characteristics common to a culture, race, gender, age or sexual preference while at the same time managing employees as individuals (Overman, 1991). Calls by emergent Black managers for an Afrocentric rather than Eurocentric organisational culture are gaining support (Khoza, 1994; Mbigi, 1993; Motshabi, 1994). These arguments suggest that mono-cultural organisational values fail to consider diversity in organisations. This prevents the development of individual potential. The thrust of this debate does not view culture as a simple either/or choice, but as seeking synergy from diversity.

Managing or valuing diversity encompasses a range of activities aimed at making managers more aware or mindful that members of other cultures or subgroups, due to their upbringing, may espouse different values and assumptions which can affect the way they co-operate, compete, communicate, plan, organise and are motivated (Leonard, 1987). Thus the goal of valuing diversity is to capitalise on the strengths of each individual or subgroup to ensure that the whole is greater than the sum of its parts (Tung, 1995). South African society is diverse, and organisations have multicultural workforces. Managing such diversity requires skilful, informed and extensive managerial training in interpersonal skills, conflict resolution, appropriate systems and an understanding of both ethnic and corporate cultures.

Valuing diversity extends beyond understanding and co-operation and should, as an end goal, seek to improve organisational effectiveness. It should aim to build capacity. A failure to understand cultural and other differences can lead to misguided assumptions, poor working relations, under-performance and discrimination. Performance, level of contribution and personal growth are partly a function of how people fit into and are treated in the work environment. Many SA companies have instituted multicultural values sharing workshops (so called 'soft' approaches). Whether the management of diversity approach is something different from, or additional to, the real need to develop specific technical and managerial job competencies and advance Black people and women remains to be seen. It might be regarded as a deflection away from a systemic failure in most organisations to address successfully the issues of development and advancement. This could result in exactly the opposite of what is intended, by potentially reinforcing racial and gender stereotypes. Educational workshops, conferences and awareness training programmes are necessary, but not sufficient, for addressing systemic, structural, technical and skill inequalities and reward differentiation.

Individual level change without concomitant change in institutional and systematic practices to remove employment discrimination will not have an enduring effect. A review of cross-cultural training literature reveals that such training is in general effective, though contextual variables seem to operate differently in international versus domestic areas (Black and Mendenhall, 1990). Development is a dynamic process involving an individual's ability, motivation, and the way he or she is managed. Not unique to SA organisations is the problem of negative expectations which are associated with racial and gender stereotypes. Stereotypes reinforce an 'us and them' environment and can contribute towards under-performance. This has been shown to result in an internalisation of feelings of inferiority and marginalisation (Human, 1991). Management development programmes rarely address these issues. They tend to neglect the effects of institutional structures, organisational culture and entrenched management systems.

Research in SA suggests that certain methods of assessing managerial potential show a cultural bias. This bias may affect the design and context of training programmes. For example, in a sample survey of 22 organisations, 71 percent of respondents indicated that discrimination was found to constitute the greatest problem with regard to assessment, selection and development of Black managers (Shaw and Human, 1989). Racial bias was found to affect the validity and reliability of several development processes, including the interview, psychometric tests (particularly content validity bias) and superiors' evaluations. Too few organisations consciously assess potential via continuous assessment and development. The debate concerning the inappropriate use of psychometric tests is beginning to emerge, particularly as the Employment Equity Act prohibits testing not appropriate to job requirements.

Human and Bowmaker-Falconer (1992:25-26) question the human resource preoccupation with managing diversity as a "way of avoiding the real issues in empowerment, and risk entrenching existing stereotypes". Lakhani (1992:25-26) similarly argues that it is dangerous to consider diversity and multi-culturalism as largely a race issue, as it tends to address people as types. Ramphele (1993) asserts that changing institutional culture to reflect a more inclusive ethos should be central to equity programmes. She also stresses the need to address a skewed skills distribution in SA and a priority on HRD. Some SA organisations appear to confuse corporate culture with ethnic culture. This is a legacy of apartheid distortion of the multi-cultural concept to divide rather than unite people. Necessary attributes for HRD and advancement programmes include: training and attitude change for senior cadres; clarification of values and corporate philosophy; consultation in policy formulation and performance improvement; line management ownership and accountability to facilitate learning transfer; development targets; two-way communication; non-discriminatory practices; monitoring and follow-up.

REDRESSING SYSTEMIC DISCRIMINATION: BEYOND THE LAW

The successful implementation of employment equity at a national level requires systematic evaluation of change across regions and by economic sector as well as in the internal labour market of organisations. In this context, the Breakwater Monitor (BWM) national database and information service was established in 1991 as a partnership between employers and the University of Cape Town Graduate School of Business. This is a longitudinal research project, tracking the implementation of employment equality. Some 200 leading SA organisations submit internal labour market information electronically, using a generic survey questionnaire. Organisations voluntarily submit internal labour market information for comparative analysis, and the establishment of benchmarks. The longitudinal capacity enables the observation of the effects of organisational employment equity policies and evaluation of the rate of change in affirmative action implementation in particular. The research process involves participating organisations submitting stock and flow data bi-annually on: permanent staff strength by occupational level, race and gender; recruitment, promotion and exit patterns by occupational level, race and gender; training investment indicators; and educational donations to historically disadvantaged primary and secondary schools, and university and technikon bursaries/scholarships.

The effects of legislative pressures to remove systemic discrimination and redress past inequality are reflected in some organisational progress, albeit gradual. Between 1997 and 1999, changing patterns of representation show that advertising, banking and mining remain the most racially exclusive sectors, with 90 percent of managers being white. The percentage of Black people in managerial positions increased by 3 percent from 1997, to 16 percent in 1999. White males occupy 70 percent of managerial positions. Black people constitute 33 percent of new managerial appointments. Of white managerial promotions, 24 percent of these are women, but only 5 percent of managerial promotions were Black women. Although most managerial recruits were white, 80 percent of managerial terminations were also white. This suggests that white managers are increasingly leaving larger organisations for various reasons. These include restructuring, the push of affirmative action, voluntary severance with redundancy packages for employees close to retirement, and concern that their longer term advancement prospects are limited because of employment equity priorities. Sectors that have over 20 percent Black management representation include communications, financial services field staff, fast-moving consumable goods, oil and retail. The advertising and media industries have the highest level of female managers at 53 percent. Forty percent of media managers are Black.

In skilled jobs, nearly 40 percent of employees are Black, indicating some progress since 1994 when Black representation was less than 20 percent. The Skills Development Act will likely have a positive impact in this regard. Sectors with the highest rate of skilled Black employee recruitment were industrial (69 percent), financial services field staff (67 percent), media (56 percent) and research and professional organisations (48 percent). This suggests better progress in increasing representivity in these sectors.

In another research project Schlemmer (1999) found that 13 percent of large corporations had no formal affirmative action or equality programmes in place by late 1998. About 75 percent had set broad quotas or targets. This latter study shows a more positive picture than the Breakwater Monitor project but notes that many organisations have unwritten, non-codified policies. Schlemmer (1999:4) also found that corporations are not hostile to the concept of employment equity and consider its main advantage to be an economic one. However, particular policy implementation difficulties were around a shortage of qualified Black recruits in areas such as IT, lack of support from managers, unrealistic expectations of equity appointees, and failure to integrate equity and diversity objectives with business practices, training and performance management.

EMERGING PATTERNS OF CHANGE

Clear patterns of change are now emerging. In many cases these trends reflect a positive rate of change in SA organisations. These benchmarks will be difficult for less committed and less resourceful organisations to follow. The Top 15 organisations in the longitudinal Breakwater Monitor study are in sectors that are aggressively pursuing new markets. They can be divided into three categories: fast moving consumer goods, financial services, general retail and trade; commercialised public corporations that are subject to deregulation and political change; and multinationals that have been actively pursuing a form of affirmative action for the past few decades. Most of these firms appear to accept an economically beneficial basis for employment equity. They consider it to be in their business interests.

In interpreting the longitudinal findings it is important to keep in mind that the Breakwater Monitor sample is biased towards large employers. Furthermore, these organisations participate in the study on a voluntary basis and could by implication be considered more progressive in their practices. The difference in progress between the Top 15 and the national longitudinal sample is essentially threefold. First, the Top 15 had already made better progress at the start of the study period three years ago. This, together with a longer standing commitment to change, appears to have developed its own momentum. Second, the development focus is on both management and more highly skilled levels. Third, these organisations show high rates of change across the entire staffing process – specifically in combining recruitment and promotion activities. Projections based on the rate of change found in the longitudinal study show that by 2001, African, coloured and Asian managers could collectively represent over 35 percent of all managers in the Top 15. This could increase to 52 percent by the year 2003. The assumption made is that the management pool will continue to grow by 6 percent for every two-year period, and that the number of white managers will be substantially reduced. A similar pattern of increase in African, coloured and Asian representation in skilled occupational levels will be seen over the next five years, but off a much higher base than management.

Changing the overall skills capacity of the SA workforce remains, however, a major challenge, and will require most organisations to develop a more coherent strategy and a positive approach to education and training. A disturbing labour market trend, which has a direct bearing on the private sector's labour absorption ability, is the restructuring which has led to a net downsizing of just over 1.5 percent over the 1998-1999 period. Nonetheless, a positive finding is that African people make up over 20 percent of managers in leading companies, up 10 percent since 1997. All women in management have increased by an average of only one percent. In the Top 15 companies, African managers now make up to 71 percent of all new management recruits compared with 20 percent in 1994. Aggressive recruiting has also coincided with increased levels of promotion. At the top end, over 42 percent of all management promotions in the Top 15 companies are now African, compared with a national average of around 20 percent.

Certain organisations have taken up the challenge of transformation in a rigorous way, by changing organisational structures, and up-skilling the workforce. The approach taken in more successful organisations includes external recruitment coupled with internal development, advancement and involvement of employees in the process. This process is considered important to both improve productivity and create role models who are able to influence decisions and the institutional culture of the organisation at a senior level. A reliable system of information reporting is vital, especially for setting targets, executive reporting and evaluating employment equality performance. It is increasingly acknowledged that better human resource practices, and more attention to the structure and culture in which people work, can give organisations a competitive edge. Further research is needed on whether/how employment equity is integrated with broader human resource and business strategy and the extent to which it forms part of a policy to promote diversity and multi-culturalism in organisations.

CONCLUSION

Apartheid employment practices resulted in distortions in the labour market creating artificial, racially-based skills shortages. White employees were often paid premium salaries in order to attract and retain them. When employment discrimination was struck off the statutes, Black employees were taken on into trainee posts to qualify for skilled work. Once qualified and appointed to a substantive post, their pay was often lower than that of whites doing the same or similar work. Employers argue that they are now merely "correcting" a distorted labour market. In the CSO Evaluations case, it was argued that these distortions were organisationally internalised. The effect is that white employees occupied the more senior positions, and were paid more than Black employees doing work of equal value, or in the same grades. The cost of quick or once-off remedies for the "apartheid wage gap" is seen as prohibitive, especially in large organisations. A more appropriate remedy is to review relevant discriminatory practices, anomalies and distortions resulting from past discrimination, and develop a plan to systematically address the matter by a defined time. Even when employers explicitly espouse these policies, the consequences of years of systemic discrimination continue to skew both internal and external labour markets.

In the external labour market, skills shortages remain, requiring employers to continue to adjust remuneration policies to attract employees who have the skills, even though they may have been beneficiaries of discriminatory labour market policies. In the internal labour market, as previously discussed, an "apartheid premium" tends to persist. A pay premium, if based on an objective economic/business need to attract a specialised scarce skill, is not necessarily unfair discrimination. If the market were not subject to distortions of an unfair discriminatory nature, such as race, then the rulings in Rainey v Greater Glasgow Health Board (1987), ICR, 129 (HL) and Bilka-Kaufhaus GmbH v Weber von Hartz (1986) IRLR 317 (ECJ), would hold in the South African context. These judgements found that such a premium can be appropriate to meet a legitimate business need, and as such was not unfair discrimination (See Woolworths (Pty) Ltd v Beverley Whitehead (Case No. CA 06/99, L.A.C.), where the Labour Appeal Court, in a majority ruling, gave a commercial rationale of uninterrupted job continuity / availability primacy over fair labour practices in discarding a pregnancy claim for unfair discrimination in not appointing the applicant to the position of human resource manager). However, employment policies and practices are not used in a "neutral" or unbiased context. In the CSO case, the applicant union argued that the company relied on factors that depend on the external labour market: "market forces" and "previous earnings". This constitutes a reliance on market forces shaped by apartheid labour market policies. The case has been postponed for expert witness testimony for the applicants at the time of writing.

With Hodges-Aebehard (1999:249), we conclude that major court decisions on discrimination variously reflect a range of interpretations rather than a coherent jurisprudence; this is especially true for pay discrimination. Despite the constitutional and legislative assault on unfair discrimination and a reverse onus of proof, it remains very difficult to prove that discrimination, especially in pay, is due to race or gender. Courts faced with similar fact, arrive at different results. Hodges-Aeberhard (1999:269) rightly asks: "Why should affirmative action be struck down in a country like SA, where the conditions for such measures exist par excellence." She proposes that through the ILO, an international standard of a normative character be set with tighter tests and norms, and that the composition of courts, with greater race and gender sensitivity on the bench, be considered. Mao Tse Tung was once asked his opinion on the value of the French revolution. His response was, "it is too early to tell." This may well be so in SA. Post-apartheid employment equity legislation is barely two years old. Its jurisprudence on pay discrimination is scant, often inconsistent and baffling. Designated employers were required to submit employment equity plans to the Department of Labour in 2000 for the first time. These plans require evidence of a review of any discriminatory employment practices and measures to address them.

There is a need to improve race relations, erode a tradition of adversarialism and nurture a sense of common purpose. The latter requires the visible advancement and economic empowerment of Black people in order to create employment equity and the stability necessary for economic growth. The diversity of SA organisations creates an insistent need to find common goals and shared values and to foster reconciliation after the divisiveness of apartheid. Raising managerial competence in strategic management, resource utilisation, negotiation and operations is vital for organisational effectiveness. Performance improvement, greater accountability, and active measures to address racial and gender mixes in the occupational structure are necessary. While management development emphasises formalised planned interventions, informal experiences often provide meaningful learning.

Whilst a significant and valid attack on employment discrimination is enabled by labour law in SA, the law may at best achieve compliance to its objectives. It cannot guarantee internal commitment and managerial support for broader transformation of organisations, or indeed institutional capacity building. The law therefore has its clear limits. Where it ends, employers can make strategic choices about employment equity, affirmative action and skills development. Organisational prerequisites for moving from compliance to a commitment model in respect of employment equity and capacity building are vital.

Frank Horwitz is Professor of Human Resource Management and Industrial Relations at the Graduate School of Business, University of Cape Town, South Africa. Harish Jain is Professor of Human Resource Management and Industrial Relations at the Michael de Groote School of Business, McMaster University, Canada.

ACKNOWLEDGEMENT

The assistance of the Division for Social Sciences and Humanities of the National Research Foundation for participation in the 12th World Congress of the International Industrial Relations Association, Tokyo, Japan, 29 May-2 June 2000; and this associated research, is gratefully acknowledged.

REFERENCES

Bhorat, H. Quoted in Quarterly Trends – National Business Initiative December (1999): 3.

Bilka-Kaufhaus Gmbh v Weber von Harz. IRLR (1986): 317 (ECJ).

Black, J and Medenhall, M. "Cross Cultural Training Effectiveness." *Academy of Management Review* 15.1 (1990): 113-134.

Bowmaker–Falconer, A (Ed). Breakwater Monitor Report on Employment Equity. University of Cape Town , 1999, 1-80.

Bowmaker-Falconer, A, Horwitz, F, Jain, H and Taggar, S. "Employment Equality Programmes in South Africa." *Industrial Relations Journal* 29.3 (September 1998): 228-233.

Christie, S. "Litigating the Apartheid Wage Gap." *Contemporary Labour Law* 9.8 (2000): 71-75

Corder, H. "The Draft South African Constitution." Manuscript, Faculty of Law, University of Cape Town, 1996

Central Selling Organisation (CSO) Evaluations v Namibian Mineworkers' Union . Namibian Labour Court November 1998.

FAWU & Others vs. Rainbow Chicken Farms [2000] 1 BLLR 70 (LC).

Fogey, H. et al. South African Survey 1999/2000 – South African Institute of Race Relations. Johannesburg. Census Statistics, 1996, 295-296.

Freeman, R. "When Earnings Diverge". National Policy Association, Washington, 1997, 39-42.

"George vs. Liberty Life Association of Africa Ltd." *Industrial Labour Journal* 17.3 (1996): 571-601.

Hodges-Aeberhard, J. "Affirmative Action in Employment: Recent Court Approaches." *International Labour Review* 138.3 (1999): 247-272.

Human, L. "Black Advancement, Affirmative Action and Managing Diversity." *IPM Journal* 3.2 (1991): 10-12.

Human, L and Bowmaker-Falconer, A. "Managing Diversity: Avoiding the Issue." People Dynamics, 10.12 (1991) : 25-30.

Jeffery, A. "The Equality Bill". Fast Facts: South African Institute of Race Relations, No 1 (2000): 2-3.

Jubber, K. *South Africa Industrial Relations and Industrial Sociology*. Kenwyn: Juta & Co, 1979, 36-44.

Juhn, C. "Wage Inequality and Demand for Skill." *Industrial and Labour Relations Review* 52.3 (1999): 424-425.

Khoza, R. "The Need for an Afrocentric Approach to Management." *Business Alert*. University of the Witwatersrand, 151 (1994): 1-7.

Lakani, K. "Myths of Multi-cultural Communication." *People Dynamics* 12.7 (1994): 25-27.

Leonard, D. "The Political Realities of Africa in Management." *World Development* 15-7 (1987): 899-907.

Leonard Dingler Employee Representative Council & Others vs. Leonard Dingler (Pty) Ltd. (1997) BLLR 1438 (LC).

Le Roux, P. "The Woolworths Case: Facts and the Law." *Contemporary Labour Law* 9.9 (April 2000): 2-6.

Motshabi, K. "Cultural Differences in South African Business." *Breakwater Monitor Update*, 1 (1994): 8-10.

Louw v Golden Arrow Bus Services (Pty) Ltd (2000) 21 ILJ 188 (LC).

Mbigi, L. "The Spirit of African Empowerment". *People Dynamics* 11.3 (1993): 13-15.

Mineworkers Union of Namibia vs. CSO Evaluations (Pty) Ltd. Case No: LC18/98, Labour Court of Namibia. Supplementary Affidavit (12 October 1999): 1-10.

Overman, S. "Managing the Diverse Workforce." *HR Magazine* (April 1991): 32-36.

Public Servants Association of SA & Another vs. Provincial Administration, Western Cape. (1999): BALR 184 (2), CCMA.

Public Servants Association of SA vs. Minister of Justice. BCLR, 5, (1997): 577-656.

Ramphele, M. "Employment Equity: Its Implications for South Africa." Seminar address Graduate School of Business, University of Cape Town. 21 September 1993: 2-8

Shaw, D. and Human, L. "Assessment of Managerial Potential." *South African Journal of Labour Relations* 13.2 (1989): 4-17.

Rainey v Greater Glasgow Health Board. 1987. ICR: 129 (HL).

Schlemmer, L. "Corporate Business in a Wider Role." *Centre for Development and Enterprise (CDE) Focus* 4 (June 1999): 2-8

South African Chemical Workers' Union v Setrachem Ltd, Industrial Court, May 1988.

TGWU & Another vs. Bayette Security Holdings. Labour Court. BLLR. 4 (1990): 401-420.

The Employment Equity Act 1998. Kenwyn:Juta & Co Publishers.

The South African Constitution 1996. Kenwyn: Juta & Co Publishers 1998: Chapter 2.

Thomas, R. "From Affirmative Action to Affirming Diversity." *Harvard Business Review* (April 1990): 107-116.

Tung, R. "The Global Human Resource Challenge; Managing Diversity". Proceedings of 10th World Congress, International Industrial Relations Association, Washington DC, (June 1995): 16-24

Van Vuuren vs. Department of Correctional Services. Case No: PA 6/98, Labour Appeal Court, 1998.

"Whitehead v Woolworths (Pty) Ltd." *Industrial Law Journal*. 20, 2133 (LC) (1999): 2139.

Woolworths (Pty) Ltd v Whitehead, CA 06/99, Labour Appeal Court.

World Competitiveness Report. University of Lausanne: World Economic Forum and the Institute for Management Development 1999: 1-12.

CHAPTER 12

MARY F. RADFORD

AFFIRMATIVE ACTION IN AMERICAN EMPLOYMENT LAW: PAST, PRESENT, AND FUTURE

Affirmative action in American employment law has evolved through a series of governmental proclamations, court decrees, and voluntary programs instigated by employers in the private sector. Affirmative action programs and plans typically are designed to remedy the effects of the systemic discrimination that has imbued the American workplace. However, although the motives behind these programs may be admirable, their implementation is highly controversial. This chapter examines the development of the concept of affirmative action in American employment law and explores its future viability in light of recent occurrences in the judicial, legislative, and political arenas.

FROM THE EMPLOYMENT-AT-WILL DOCTRINE TO AFFIRMATIVE ACTION

Affirmative action in American employment law must be viewed in the larger context of government regulation of public and private employers. In the United States, government regulation of the employment relationship takes a variety of forms. Since the beginning of the twentieth century, the federal government has played a dominant role in policing worker safety and in directly controlling employees' wages and hours. In the areas of hiring and firing, however, the principle that prevailed until the middle of the century mandated against government involvement. This principle is known as the "employment-at-will" doctrine.

The employment-at-will doctrine allows an employer or employee to commence or terminate the employment relationship at any time and for any reason whatsoever. From the standpoint of business owners, this meant that employers were free to hire whomever they chose and to fire whenever they felt like it, free from any government regulation or oversight. Prior to the 1960s, the employment-at-will doctrine thus allowed employers to make employment decisions that reflected markedly discriminatory treatment of members of minority groups and women. The social and cultural stereotypes and biases of employers pervaded these decisions, resulting in substantial disadvantages to women and minorities based simply on their membership in an "inferior" class. By 1964, unemployment rates were twice as high among Blacks as among whites and those Black men and women who were employed were clustered almost exclusively in lower level blue-collar positions. Unemployment rates for women were also higher than those for men. Furthermore, employers were allowed to segregate jobs and to require, for example, that

C. Agocs (ed.), Workplace Equality, 243–264.

certain management-level positions be occupied only by white men. In an attempt to remedy injustices of this type, the United States Congress began in the early 1960s to enact a series of civil rights laws that severely restricted the employment-at-will doctrine. With the emergence of these laws, government's previous stance of non-involvement in the hiring and firing processes changed dramatically. As originally designed, the anti-discrimination laws did not dictate whom an employer must hire or whom an employer could not fire. Rather, the laws prohibited an employer from imposing different hiring or firing standards on an individual because of the individual's race, colour, sex, religion, national origin, age, or disability. However, either out of respect for the social origins of the law or fear of being sued under it, many employers went a step further and began affirmatively to hire members of certain historically disadvantaged groups. Many of these actions withstood judicial challenge. Additionally, in attempts to remedy past discrimination by employers, courts themselves imposed affirmative action requirements on defendants in employment discrimination suits. At the same time, federal and state governments intervened directly in the employment relationship by adopting affirmative action plans whose sole purpose was to ensure that the governments and those who contracted with them would hire and retain members of the historically disadvantaged groups. The historically disadvantaged groups who have been the targets of affirmative action have traditionally included Blacks, individuals of Hispanic origin, and women (all of whom fall under the Title VII categories of race, national origin, and sex) and individuals who are disabled (whose protected status stems both from the Rehabilitation Act of 1973 and the Americans with Disabilities Act of 1990).

The term "affirmative action" became both a buzzword and a battle cry. Proponents of affirmative action speak glowingly of its potential to wipe out the effects of prior discrimination and to raise women and minority groups to their deserved status in society. Opponents speak disparagingly of how "the quota system" not only penalises individuals who played no part in perpetrating the prior discrimination but also stigmatises those who are theoretically benefiting from it. The tension that characterises the affirmative action debate is centred on the question of whether affirmative action is in fact an appropriate mechanism for achieving equality for women and minorities in the workplace, or instead, a subtle but definite form of the type of discrimination that the United States Constitution and the civil rights acts were designed to prohibit.

The dualistic nature of affirmative action affords ample opportunity for government participation on either side of the issue. On the one hand, the legislative and executive branches of states and the federal government regulate the hiring of millions of workers through grants, contracts, and other incentive programs that require employers to engage in affirmative action. Also, Title VII of the Civil Rights Act of 1964 allows courts and the Equal Employment Opportunity Commission (EEOC) to order affirmative action as a resolution for discrimination suits filed against employers. On the other hand, the federal courts and the EEOC are empowered to handle (and, in the case of the EEOC, to initiate) a variety of employment discrimination cases, including cases of "reverse discrimination" which arise when a member of a majority group complains that preferential treatment of a minority group or individual has denied him his right to be treated equally regardless of his race or gender.

The affirmative action debate is played out in many arenas. Sociologists and psychologists dispute whether affirmative action will break down racial and gender barriers or in fact make them more apparent. Politicians argue as to whether the government should have any role in promoting social change, or at best should just ensure that the non-discrimination laws are enforced. Legal scholars argue on the one hand that affirmative action is against the law and on the other hand that it is the law.

Implicit in most debates is that the two sides are arguing about the same concept. Yet there is a basic incongruity in the affirmative action debate in that, although many people have an opinion about affirmative action, few can accurately or adequately describe what the term means. The purpose of this chapter is, first, to explore the various meanings of affirmative action by examining its sources in the law, its manifestations in the employment context, and its treatment by the courts. The fundamental contours of the affirmative action debate will then be fleshed out through a review of the major jurisprudential theories on affirmative action. Next, the chapter examines whether affirmative action truly results in effecting a change in the social and economic status of women and minorities. At the conclusion, some predictions will be offered as to the prospects for affirmative action in the United States over the ensuing years of this decade.

LEGAL DEFINITIONS OF AFFIRMATIVE ACTION

The inability of most people to define the term affirmative action is understandable in light of the fact that there exist in the current statutes, Executive Orders, and government regulations only a very few clearly delineated or comprehensive definitions of the concept. The Constitution of the United States contains no reference to affirmative action. Of relevance in the affirmative action debate is the Equal Protection Clause of the Fourteenth Amendment which provides that no state shall "deny to any person within its jurisdiction the equal protection of the laws." The following is a brief historical sketch of the development of the affirmative action concept in the executive and congressional arenas and through state legislatures:

* Kennedy Executive Order 10925: The term "affirmative action" first appeared in Executive Order 10925, which was signed by President John F. Kennedy on March 6, 1961. The Kennedy Executive Order followed a series of orders issued by every President since Franklin D. Roosevelt that required government contractors to agree not to discriminate against employees or job applicants because of race, creed, colour or national origin. The Kennedy Executive Order additionally mandated that these contractors agree to "take affirmative action to ensure that applicants are employed, and employees are treated during employment, without regard to their race, creed, colour or national origin."

* The Civil Rights Act of 1964: This anti-discrimination act did not contain any mandate that an employer engage in "affirmative action." Title VII of the Act makes it an "unlawful employment practice" for an employer to make employment decisions about an individual "because of such individual's race, colour, religion, sex, or national origin." Under very limited circumstances, an employer may base hiring decisions on religion, sex, or national origin if that factor is a "bona fide occupational qualification (BFOQ) reasonably necessary to the normal operation of that particular business or enterprise." The Act does not include race as a BFOQ and thus, arguably, does not contemplate that race will ever be an appropriate hiring determinant. (One 1994 study indicates that about 80 percent of American private sector employees work for employers that are subject to the mandates of Title VII [Bloch, 1994: 100].).

* Johnson Executive Order 11246: This 1965 order, issued by President Lyndon Baines Johnson, reiterated almost verbatim the words of the Kennedy Executive Order. Two years later, sex was added to the categories listed in the Executive Order. As of 2000, the Regulations

promulgated under Executive Order 11246 apply to companies in the United States that employ some 26 million workers who comprise 22 percent of the civilian workforce (U.S. Department of Labor, 2000). The Regulations require the implementation by contractors of an affirmative action plan to which the contractors commit to apply a "good faith" effort.

* Nixon Executive Order 11478: At the beginning of the administration of President Richard M. Nixon, the Office of Federal Contract Compliance established a number of area-wide compliance programs designed to implement the Johnson Executive Order. Of these programs, the "Philadelphia Plan" is the best known. The Philadelphia Plan contained specific hiring quotas designed to increase the proportion of Black workers in the construction labour force in Philadelphia. The Comptroller General refused to honour the Philadelphia Plan on the ground that it imposed quotas in violation of Title VII. The Comptroller General took his disagreement to Congress, where he convinced the Senate to attach a rider onto its supplemental appropriations bill that would essentially defeat any application of the Philadelphia Plan or similarly-designed plans. The Senate passed the rider but President Nixon convinced the House to defeat it and promised to veto any appropriations bill that contained the rider. Despite this Presidential endorsement, subsequent revisions to plans such as the Philadelphia Plan replaced the blatant quota system contained in the original Plan with a system of goals and timetables.

* Congressional ratification of affirmative action became more explicit in 1971-72, when Senator Sam Ervin introduced a series of proposed amendments to Title VII that would explicitly prohibit all affirmative action programs promulgated under the Johnson Executive Order. The sound defeat of these amendments was seen as formal Congressional sanction of the system of affirmative action goals and timetables that constituted the revised Philadelphia Plan.

* Rehabilitation Act of 1973: This 1973 Act protects employees of federal government agencies from discrimination on the basis of disability and requires each agency to formulate an affirmative action plan to increase its employment of individuals with disabilities. The Americans with Disabilities Act of 1990 expanded the prohibition against discrimination on the basis of disability to include private employers as well as the federal government.

* Civil Rights Act of 1991: The main purpose of this amendment to the Civil Rights Act of 1964 was to "strengthen and improve Federal Civil Rights laws," particularly in light of a 1989 Supreme Court decision that had "weakened the scope and effectiveness of Federal civil rights protections" (CRA 1991, preamble, Sec. 1). Although both Houses of Congress had carried on extensive discussions of affirmative action during the debates, the only reference to it in the new Act appears in Sec. 116: "Nothing in the amendments made by this title shall be construed to affect court-ordered remedies, affirmative action, or conciliation agreements that are in accordance with the law."

* Proposed Equal Employment Act of 1995: Congress again addressed affirmative action in 1995, when it considered, but did not pass, the "Equal Employment Act of 1995." This Act, whose principal Senatorial sponsor was Robert Dole, would have clearly prohibited any agency of the federal government from intentionally discriminating against or granting "a preference" to any individual or group based on race, colour, national origin, or sex.

* Clinton Executive Order 13005: President Bill Clinton added his contribution to the series of Executive Orders on affirmative action in government contracting with Executive Order 13005 (5/16/96). For the first time, however, the presidential focus of affirmative action shifted from members of the traditional minority groups (classified by race, national origin, and gender) to

individuals who lived in areas of "general economic distress". "General economic distress" is defined in this Order with reference to the poverty and unemployment rate rather than to any racial or ethnic group.

* State Initiatives: Two states, California (Proposition 209, 1996) and Washington (Initiative 200, 1998), passed initiatives designed to prohibit the use of affirmative action in state matters. Significantly, these initiatives were directly voted on by the populations of each state (as opposed to being enacted by the states' legislatures) and in each state the vote easily exceeded the 50+% majority required for passage. California's Proposition 209 prohibits the government from "giving preferential treatment to any individual or group in public employment, public education, or public contracting on the basis of race, sex, colour, ethnicity or national origin." The wording of Initiative 200 is modelled after Proposition 209.

A quick glance at the dates of the executive and legislative actions described above shows a gap between the mid-1970s and 1990. During this period the affirmative action debate shifted from the executive and congressional arenas to the courtroom.

JUDICIAL DECISIONS ON AFFIRMATIVE ACTION: FROM BAKKE TO ADARAND

The Supreme Court of the United States has on several occasions examined whether affirmative action plans are valid under both Title VII of the Civil Rights Act and the United States Constitution. While the theories behind the anti-discrimination mandate of Title VII and the equal protection mandate of the Constitution are substantially similar, the Court obviously has a longer history of decision-making under the Constitution. One challenge to observers of developments in the affirmative action arena has been that the Court has at times applied different logic in the constitutional cases (which deal primarily with government employers) than in the Title VII cases (which deal primarily, although not exclusively, with private employers). The Court's decisions have not been confined to affirmative action in employment but cover also affirmative action as it relates to education, minority set-asides for government contracts, and minority set-asides in the transportation and communications industries. No overview of the Court's employment law cases would be complete without at least a summary of their holdings in these related cases.

* Bakke: The first and perhaps best known Supreme Court decision on affirmative action is Regents of the University of California v. Bakke, 438 U.S. 265 (1978). Mr. Bakke sued the University system when he was denied a place in the entering class of the Medical School of the University of California at Davis. The Medical School had a special admissions program whereby it reserved 16 of the 100 places in its entering class for minorities. Mr. Bakke claimed that this program violated Title VI of the Civil Rights Act as well as the Fourteenth Amendment of the Constitution. The Court agreed. However, the Court refused to close completely the question of affirmative action plans in that it would not go so far as to prohibit the University from any consideration of race in the course of its admissions process.

* Weber: One year after Bakke, the Court decided the seminal employment discrimination case of United Steelworkers of America v. Weber, 443 U.S. 193 (1979). The case involved a challenge to an affirmative action plan that constituted part of the United Steelworkers and Kaiser Aluminium master collective bargaining agreement. The agreement established an in-house training program in which 50 percent of the spaces were reserved for Blacks. Writing for the

majority, Justice Brennan stated the Court's position quite clearly: "We hold that Title VII does not prohibit such race-conscious affirmative action plans." Justice Brennan also explained that a "permissible" affirmative action plan must: 1) mirror the purposes of Title VII ("to break down old patterns of racial segregation and hierarchy"); 2) "not unnecessarily trammel the interests of the white employees;" 3) not "create an absolute bar to the advancement of white employees;" and 4) be a "temporary measure" that "is not intended to maintain racial balance, but simply to eliminate a manifest racial imbalance" (Weber, 443 U.S. at 208-09).

* Stotts: Five years later, in Firefighters Local Union No. 1784 v. Stotts, 467 U.S. 561 (1984), the Supreme Court again visited the issue of affirmative action plans in the employment context and held that Title VII prohibited affirmative action plans that interfered with bona fide seniority systems. In this case, Justice Byron White made the sweeping statement that the policy behind the section of Title VII that authorises court-ordered affirmative action was "to provide 'make-whole' relief only to those who have been actual victims of illegal discrimination" (Stotts, 467 U.S. at 580). This statement raised two related questions which the Court was forced to address in later cases. The first question was whether a court could order or approve affirmative action relief only if there had been a finding of actual discrimination by the employer. If so, the second question was whether the relief ordered had to be limited to those individuals who had actually suffered from the discrimination.

* Post-Stotts Decisions: Decisions in the subsequent three years more clearly delineated the contours of the affirmative action debate among the then-sitting members of the Court while attempting to answer the two questions raised in Stotts. In Wygant v. Jackson Board of Education, 476 U.S. 267 (1986), a public school system's collective bargaining agreement geared the hiring of minority teachers to the percentage of minority students and limited layoffs of these teachers at the expense of more senior white teachers. Because the plan involved a state employer, the Court's analysis was based on its previous constitutional jurisprudence. The Court rejected the layoff plan as a violation of the Equal Protection Clause of the Constitution because it unnecessarily burdened the senior white employees who had lost their jobs. The Court also did not find the purpose of providing role models for minority teachers to be "compelling" enough to justify the blatant race-based preference.

In Local 28, Sheet Metal Workers Intern. Ass'n. v. EEOC, 478 U.S. 421 (1986), the Court upheld fines for contempt that were levied on a union that had violated judicially mandated goals for hiring minorities. The plan in question in this case was a hiring goal rather than a plan that resulted in the layoff of majority-group workers. Also, the defendant was a union rather than a public employer. Four members of the Court stated that court-ordered, race-conscious affirmative action relief need not be limited to those individuals who were the actual victims of prior discrimination. The deciding fifth vote, cast by Justice Lewis Powell, seemed limited to the egregious nature of the union's non-compliance as well as the fact that no innocent third parties were injured by the plan.

One year later, in U.S. v. Paradise, 480 U.S. 149 (1980), the majority of the Court echoed Justice Powell's opinion when it stated that race-based affirmative action by the government is appropriate when there has been a finding of past government action that was "long-term, open, and pervasive" discriminatory conduct.

* Voluntary Plans: In Local 93, Firefighters v. Cleveland, 478 U.S. 501 (1986), the Court distinguished a plan that was adopted under a consent decree as a "voluntary" plan that was thus

subject to fewer restrictions than the court-ordered plan involved in the Weber case. In this case, a strong majority (six Justices) agreed that a voluntary affirmative action plan could be adopted even if it benefited persons other than those who had actually suffered from the employer's past discrimination.

In 1987, in Johnson v. Santa Clara Transportation Agency, 480 U.S. 616 (1987), the Court faced a more individualised form of voluntary affirmative action than that of its previous cases. The Transportation Agency, a public employer, had concluded that women were significantly underrepresented in certain job categories. The Agency thus promoted a woman who had scored slightly lower on a pre-promotion test than her male counterparts because it considered her gender as a "plus" factor in the decision. The Court upheld this approach.

* Minority Set-Aside Cases: In City of Richmond v. J.A. Croson Co., 488 U.S. 469 (1989), the Court struck down the city's minority set-aside plan because Richmond had not made a preliminary finding of past discriminatory action by anyone in the Richmond construction industry. The Court refused to accept the effects of past societal discrimination as a compelling enough reason to justify race-conscious action by the municipal government.

The Court did not reach the same conclusion one year later in Metro Broadcasting, Inc. v. FCC, 497 U.S. 547 (1990), a case that involved an FCC program to increase the licensure of minority radio and television broadcasters. In his final year on the Court, Justice Brennan wrote for the majority in Metro Broadcasting that "benign" race-conscious affirmative action mandated by Congress need not be limited to remedial measures designed to compensate past victims of government discrimination.

* Adarand: The holding in Metro Broadcasting that accepted "benign" affirmative action was effectively reversed in 1995 after Justice Brennan and Justice Thurgood Marshall had retired from the Court. Adarand Constructors, Inc. v. Pena, 515 U.S. 2097 (1995), involved another Congressional affirmative action program that provided a financial incentive to government contractors who hired minority subcontractors. The Court applied strict scrutiny to this race-based program and found that it violated the Fifth Amendment to the Constitution. The Court confirmed that a finding of systemic and egregious discrimination by the government would justify a race-based remedial program so long as the program was a narrowly tailored remedy.

The series of Supreme Court cases that culminated with the Adarand case cast some doubt on the continued viability of a variety of affirmative action programs. First, Adarand confirms that any race-based program sponsored by a public employer, whether federal or local, must meet the demands of strict scrutiny. The Adarand holding would seem to indicate that such a program would be upheld only if an initial finding of past governmental discrimination was made, combined with an assurance that the program itself was not too broad to survive strict scrutiny. The cases preceding Adarand that dealt with court-ordered affirmative action dictate that a court must find some "egregious" prior discrimination in order to justify any order requiring affirmative action. Additionally, such an order is more likely to be upheld if it does not result in unnecessary intrusion on the rights of majority-group workers. Private employers' discretion to engage in voluntary affirmative action under Title VII is much broader than the discretion of the courts to order such action.

Following the Supreme Court's Adarand decision, President Bill Clinton ordered a comprehensive review of federal programs that made distinctions on the basis of race or ethnicity. The Department of Justice concluded after the review that affirmative action based on race or ethnicity was still appropriate in those cases in which the federal government had a factual basis on which to assume that past discrimination had taken place, and that some limited consideration of race as a factor may be appropriate if no other reasonable means of including minority participation was available (U.S. Department of Justice, 1996).

The Supreme Court has declined two important opportunities to review cases involving affirmative action in light of its Adarand decision. The first of these, Hopwood v. Texas, 78 F.3d 932 (5th Cir. 1996), involved an affirmative action plan by the University of Texas law school that was designed to increase the number of minorities in its entering class. The Supreme Court refused to review the decision of the Fifth Circuit Court of Appeals, which had struck down the program as unconstitutional. In the employment arena, the Court also has refused to review the Third Circuit's decision in Piscataway Township Board of Education v. Taxman, 91 F.3d 1547 (3d Cir. 1997), in which the court invalidated a school board's lay-off plan that gave preference to a Black teacher over a white teacher who had been hired at the same time. (The Piscataway case is discussed in detail later in this chapter.) Thus, the contours of the Adarand decision have as yet to be clarified through further pronouncements of the Supreme Court. For example, it remains to be seen whether the Adarand decision will have any effect on affirmative action plans engaged in by private employers under Title VII of the Civil Rights Act.

Another open question is the effect of the Adarand decision, which applied only to classifications on the basis of race or ethnicity, on government affirmative action programs that are designed to address gender discrimination. A decision handed down by the Court in the year following Adarand may shed light on how the Court would deal with gender-based affirmative action. The decision in United States v. Virginia, 518 U.S. 515 (1996), involved the exclusion of women from the state-run Virginia Military Institute (VMI). The Court struck down the exclusion as unconstitutional. In so doing, the Court announced the standard of review that it would apply to government actions that are gender-based. The Court stated that the justification for such action must be "exceedingly persuasive" and not hypothesised. Although the Court's announced level of scrutiny of gender-based action did not rise to the level of "strict scrutiny" that was applied to the race-based action in Adarand, the heightened scrutiny applied by the Court to the exclusionary policy in the VMI case will probably also be applied by the Court when it examines government affirmative action plans that are designed to work in women's favour.

FORMS OF AFFIRMATIVE ACTION IN THE WORKPLACE

As noted above, while many people have opinions about affirmative action, few can articulate a precise definition of the term. Instead, taking the "I know it when I see it" approach, employers and employees alike generally define affirmative action by offering examples. Most of the examples revolve around classifications made on the basis of race (often favouring the Black race), sex (usually favouring women), or national origin (often favouring those of Hispanic origin), although there is also a growing tendency to use examples of affirmative action that favours individuals with disabilities. For the purpose of efficiency, and with full realisation that women constitute a numerical majority rather than a minority in many countries, these classifications will be referred to as classifications made on the basis of minority status. For the sake of simplicity, the following discussion will also speak of "merit" and "qualifications" as if such terms refer to objective, easily identifiable criteria, while in fact such criteria are not always neutral and may be consciously or unconsciously used to manipulate the outcome of employment decisions.

Some employers and employees equate the term affirmative action with quotas. Quotas involve statistical comparisons of the proportion of minorities in the employer's workforce with the proportion of minorities in a designated pool. Affirmative action in this context is defined as the hiring or promoting of members of minority groups for the sole purpose of achieving a specified proportion of those groups in the workforce or in certain ranks within the workforce. The employer's action in these circumstances may or may not be tied to merit. For example, an employer may strive to employ a proportion of the minority group that mirrors the proportion of qualified minority applicants in the applicant pool. Presumably, then, no individual who is not qualified will be hired but some qualified members of the majority group may be passed up in favour of similarly qualified minorities. On the other end of the spectrum, an employer may wish to employ a proportion of minorities that represents the proportion of that minority group in the general population. Particularly in the more highly skilled positions, such an approach may well result in the hiring of minimally or even unqualified minorities instead of qualified members of the majority group. Quotas are generally frowned upon by the courts. However, lower courts have been known to order affirmative action relief in the form of hiring "goals" which have later been recharacterized by some Supreme Court Justices as "quotas" (Local 28, Sheet Metal Workers, 478 U.S. at 489, 499).

In a more individually oriented context, some describe affirmative action as the choice by an employer to hire a member of a minority group over a member of the majority group for a specified position. Once again, the employment decision may or may not also be tied to merit. If the goal of hiring a minority is the sole determining factor in the employment decision, the employer may hire a minority who is not qualified while passing up a qualified member of the majority group or may simply refuse to consider the applications of individuals who are not members of the targeted minority group. On the other hand, the minority status of the applicant may be simply a tie-breaker -- that is, the employer who is faced with two similarly qualified applicants may choose to hire the minority group member. Between these two extremes, minority status may be a motivating or "plus" factor in that the employer may hire a minority group member who is somewhat less qualified (lower test score, fewer years of experience) than the majority applicant under the theory that the goal of hiring a minority overrides the relative inequality of the applicants' credentials.

Affirmative action need not always take the form of a determinant in a hiring or promotion decision. An employer who wishes to hire more members of a minority group may choose instead to recruit aggressively at historically Black colleges or to instigate a new training program that targets women who have exhibited management potential (Holzer and Neumark 2000: 241). This type of affirmative action, which is sometimes referred to as "outreach," is generally more palatable in that majority group applicants do not see themselves as blatantly denied a job or promotion which is granted to a minority group applicant. One commentator refers to this approach as "good affirmative action," as opposed to "bad affirmative action," which is the use of preferences as job determinants (Eastland, 1996). Critics of this "outreach" form of affirmative action may view an extensive investment of resources into the hiring or promoting of members of minority groups as an investment that must eventually result in a denial of benefits or positions to members of the majority group. On the other hand, proponents would argue that an outreach program does not deny the majority group members benefits to which they are entitled but rather only removes from them the unearned advantages they have traditionally enjoyed by being members of a group that advanced its own interests to the detriment of the interests of minorities.

WHY EMPLOYERS ENGAGE IN AFFIRMATIVE ACTION

Basically, an employer engages in affirmative action for one (or any combination) of four reasons: 1) the employer is required to do so by law or otherwise ordered by a court to do so; 2) the employer has no independent desire to engage in an affirmative action program but perceives that the program will be instrumental in accomplishing another goal of the employer; 3) the employer perceives that an affirmative action program will have a direct beneficial effect on the employer's business; or 4) the employer desires to engage in affirmative action to remedy perceived injustices in society. Commentators and some courts refer to plans that are established for the first reason as "involuntary" affirmative action and all other plans as "voluntary" affirmative action (Zimmer et al., 2000: 316; Player, 1988: 313).

Involuntary Affirmative Action

Executive Order 11246 requires the government as an employer to engage in affirmative action. Involuntary court-ordered affirmative action is also authorised by Title VII of the Civil Rights Act. Section 706(g)(1) allows a court that has found that an employer has intentionally engaged in prohibited discrimination to "order such affirmative action as may be appropriate," including reinstatement or hiring or "any other equitable relief as the court deems appropriate." This section would seem to give the court broad powers to force an employer to engage in a program that is designed to achieve and maintain a higher proportion of minorities in its workforce. However, this section takes on a much more narrow cast when read in light of other relevant sections of Title VII. For example, section 703(j) cannot be ignored when considering the validity of court-ordered affirmative action. This section states clearly that Title VII shall not be interpreted to require an employer to grant preferential treatment to any individual for the sole purpose of remedying an imbalance in the employer's workforce. Another section of Title VII that is relevant to court-ordered affirmative action is subsection (2) of section 706(g). This subsection provides that a court may not order the reinstatement or hiring of an individual who was fired or not hired for any reason other than the minority classification (e.g., poor credentials, poor job performance, dishonesty).

Voluntary Affirmative Action

Many employers have "voluntarily" initiated affirmative action plans for the three other reasons described above. Some employers institute such plans even when they prefer not to because they have discovered that an affirmative action program is a prerequisite for another goal the employer wishes to achieve. The goal may be a simple one, such as the avoidance or settlement of a lawsuit. For example, the EEOC, which is authorised to negotiate with employers to settle pending discrimination claims, may include an affirmative action program as part of the conciliation agreement (29 C.F.R. Ch. 14, Sec. 1608.6). Alternatively, the employer may choose to implement an affirmative action program in order to be eligible for federal funding (Civil Rights Act, T. VI) or for work under a government contract (Exec. Order 11246).

It is arguable that the type of "voluntary" affirmative action described above is more coerced than voluntary. However, the second and third reasons for establishing "voluntary" plans truly reflect an uncoerced decision by an employer. An employer might engage in an affirmative action program if the employer perceives that the affirmative action program will have a direct beneficial effect on the employer's business. In this case, the employer views affirmative action as a strategy for ameliorating its productivity or the marketability of its products rather than as an indirect means of acquiring government funding or immunity from a lawsuit. For example, a bank that operates offices in a major metropolitan area may determine that an increased visibility of Black branch managers will boost its business prospects. A television station may choose to hire a female rather than a male anchorperson in order to attract a wider array of viewers. A law firm that represents management in employment discrimination cases might choose to hire a Black woman litigator whose presence in the courtroom will help dissipate a jury's suspicion of its clients. In the Weber case, Justice Brennan noted how ironic it would be if Title VII were to be interpreted to prohibit private voluntary affirmative action plans. After pointing out that Section 703(j) (which provides that employers would not be forced to grant racial preferences in order to achieve a balanced workforce) was designed to "avoid undue regulation of private business," Justice Brennan observed that a statutory prohibition against private affirmative action plans would "augment the power of the Federal government and diminish traditional management perspectives" (Weber, 443 U.S. at 206-07). However, as noted above, the Supreme Court of the United States would seem to frown on even private plans unless their purpose is to ameliorate the effects of prior discrimination.

The final reason why an employer might choose to engage in affirmative action is simply that the employer wishes to play a role that it perceives will better our traditionally discriminatory society. For example, an architectural firm that has never intentionally discriminated in the past may decide that it would like to sponsor a promising young Black architect. The firm then turns down other "better qualified" architects in order to achieve its socially oriented goal. Some would argue that such an altruistic employer would be a rare find in that business owners rarely make decisions that are not motivated at some level by their own economic interests. Such an approach, however, is not unusual with public employers. In 1989, the township of Piscataway, New Jersey made such a decision. The school system in the township had not discriminated in hiring faculty; in fact, the percentage of Black teachers in the system exceeded the percentage of available Black employees in the work force. The township faced the prospect of extensive cutbacks and found itself forced to lay off teachers in order of seniority. Two teachers of equal qualifications, a Black teacher and a white teacher, had begun working for the school system on exactly the same day. The system decided to lay off the white teacher because the Black teacher was the only Black teacher in the Business Education department and the system was committed to maintaining a culturally diverse faculty. The Court of Appeals for the Third Circuit examined the school board's motivation in light of the earlier Weber and Johnson cases and determined that the affirmative action plan did not pass muster under Title VII (Piscataway Township Board of Education v. Taxman, 91 F.3d 1547 [3d Cir. 1997]). The court pointed out that the purpose articulated by the school board -- that is, the achievement of diversity in the school system's faculty -- was not one of the purposes of Title VII. In fact, the court went so far as to say that the only time a voluntary affirmative action plan would be valid would be when its purpose was to remedy the effect of past discrimination by the employer school system. While the Weber and Johnson plans had focused on eliminating the effects of past discrimination, the school board's plan seemed motivated more by the social goal of maintaining a diverse environment. The Court of Appeals found that that type of goal did not outweigh Title VII's basic prohibition against considering an individual's race when making an employment decision. (As noted above, the Supreme Court of the United States declined the opportunity to review the Piscataway decision.)

JURISPRUDENTIAL THEORIES OF AFFIRMATIVE ACTION

Jurisprudential discussions of affirmative action are beset with a series of dichotomies: neutrality vs. reverse discrimination; victims vs. sinners (or, more precisely, nonvictims vs. nonsinners); compensatory justice vs. distributive justice; benign discrimination vs. invidious discrimination; and individual rights vs. group rights. An interesting irony of these discussions is that theorists on either side envision the same goal: a society in which an individual's race or sex or national origin or other status is not viewed or treated as a negative factor. The arguments for the most part revolve around the ways and means of reaching that goal. The arguments purport to cover all of the types of affirmative action described above, but in reality revolve primarily around the use of racial or other preferences as the determinant in a hiring or promotion decision.

For some theorists, affirmative action is simply the reverse of the type of discrimination that is prohibited by the laws of the United States. These purists (referred to also as "neutralists" [Tribe, 1986: 202] or "fair shakers" [Abram, 1986: 1313]) label as invalid any circumstance in which an employer considers an individual's race, colour, religion, national origin, sex, age, or disability in the course of making an employment decision. Proponents of this theory argue as follows: The Constitution of the United States mandates that states and the federal government shall not deny equal protection of the laws to individuals (U.S. Constitution, Amends. V, XIV). As stated by William Bradford Reynolds, former assistant U.S. Attorney General, "[I]t is clear beyond doubt that the intent of the [fourteenth] amendment was to command that all government decisions be made on a race-neutral basis; that the amendment was meant to guarantee equal opportunity, not equal results; and that it would not permit preferences by reason of race" (Daly, 1985: 2-3). Additionally, the federal anti-discrimination laws prohibit public and private employers from making employment decisions that are based on an individual's status. Title VII of the Civil Rights Act specifically states that the Act is not designed to require an employer to grant preferential treatment to employees of any minority group merely because there is an imbalance of members of that group in the employer's workforce (Civil Rights Act, T. VII, '703(j)). Recent revisions to the Civil Rights Act indicate that the anti-discrimination laws are violated whenever an individual's race, colour, religion, national origin, or sex was a "motivating factor" in an employment decision (Civil Rights Act, T. VII, '703). Therefore, except in the narrow case where sex, religion, or national origin is a BFOQ, prohibited discrimination occurs in any circumstance in which the individual's race or other characteristic plays a role, regardless of whether the employer is hiring a Black individual or a white individual, a man or a woman, a Baptist or a Jew, and regardless of why the employer chose to consider the characteristic.

The purist stance was perhaps best articulated in Justice John Marshall Harlan's famous dissenting statement in the 1896 case of Plessy v. Ferguson: "Our constitution is colour-blind."

From this viewpoint, there is virtually no difference between discrimination and affirmative action -- and both are definitely and in all circumstances illegal.

Opponents of this theory counter the purists' reliance on the Constitution by arguing that the Fourteenth Amendment in its historical context was passed primarily to protect Blacks from hostile state action (Fiss, 1976: 85-86). Drew S. Days III, former Solicitor General of the United States, points out that "[t]he Congress that ratified the Civil War amendments itself engaged in affirmative action. The Freedman's Bureaus were explicitly designed to benefit Blacks, and they used racial classification" (Daly, 1986: 4). Legal philosopher Ronald Dworkin criticises the purist stance even more strongly: "There is no language in the Constitution whose plain meaning prohibits affirmative action. Only the most naive theories of statutory construction could argue that such a result is required by the language of . . . the Civil Rights Act of 1964 or any other congressional enactment" (Dworkin, 1985: 298). These proponents of affirmative action argue that a society that has historically discriminated against certain classes of individuals owes that group some remedial action. (For this reason, these theorists are sometimes referred to as "social engineers" [Abram, 1986: 1313].)

Opponents and proponents of affirmative action often clash on the notions of victimisation and "sin." As noted above, early affirmative action cases questioned whether affirmative action should be available only to those who actually had been victimised by the prior discrimination of the employer, rather than to more recent job applicants who had not suffered from the employer's actions. Stephen Carter (1988: 421) describes this concept of victimhood as "bilateral individualism, because it invents a reality in which the only victims are those who have suffered at the hands of transgressors." Dr. Benjamin Hooks, former Executive Director of the NAACP, responds to the "victims-only" argument by stating that "all Black folks are victims of discrimination. Therefore, we were all intended to be helped by these laws" (Daly, 1986: 10). On the other hand, Ronald Fiscus (1992: 10) views this notion "that all Blacks are the equivalent of members of a single family" as "in a word, racist." He explains that this notion "equates, legally and morally, individual Black men and women with their racial identity".

The label of victim is not restricted to those who have suffered from or continue to suffer from past discrimination. Purists point out that innocent members of the majority group (non-sinners) may easily be victimised by an affirmative action program that denies them benefits while favouring members of the minority group. Such an approach is manifestly unjust, observes Judge Richard Posner (1974: 16), because "the nonminority people excluded because of the preference are unlikely to have perpetrated, or to have in any demonstrable sense, benefited from, the discrimination". On the other hand, Derrick Bell is very suspicious of this claim: "I wonder whether the claim that whites are victimised by affirmative action is sincere, or whether it is nothing more than a self-aware appropriation of victim status for self-gain....The myth that racial remediation programs are responsible for whites' economic woes persists despite the fact that whites continue to be employed at rates vastly outpacing African-Americans" (Bell and Singer, 1993: 276).

Kathleen Sullivan (1986: 80) characterises the overall themes of victims/non-victims and sinners/non-sinners as unduly focussed on the past rather than "justifying affirmative action as the architecture of a racially integrated future". Fiscus criticises the approach because it is based on a model of compensatory rather than distributive justice. He explains that compensatory justice is the "claim to compensation for discrete and 'finished' harm done to minority group members or their actions," while distributive justice is "the claim an individual or group has to the positions or advantages or benefits that would have been awarded under fair conditions" (Fiscus, 1992: 8). Fiscus justifies affirmative action in the form of proportional quotas under the distributive justice model but is quick to point out that under this model "individuals or groups may not claim positions, advantages, or benefits that they would not have been awarded under fair conditions" (Fiscus, 1992: 13). Kent Greenawalt, on the other hand, feels that the distinction between the Aristotelian models of compensatory and distributive justice "largely collapses" in the affirmative action context because both rest "on assertions of past injustice" (Greenawalt, 1975: 579).

The affirmative action debate at times revolves around a perceived distinction between "benign" as opposed to "malign" or invidious discrimination. Some theorists argue that affirmative action is not illegal because illegal discrimination occurs only when an employer intentionally makes a negative employment decision based on an individual's minority status. For example, a white man who refuses to hire Blacks or women is engaging in the type of action that the anti-discrimination laws were designed to prevent. On the other hand, an employer who engages in affirmative action is not performing an illegal act because the discrimination involved is "benign" discrimination in favour of individuals who traditionally have suffered due to their minority status. These theorists contend that true equality in society will not be achieved unless individuals in these groups are placed on an equal footing with those who have always enjoyed this society's benefits. Proponents of benign discrimination are not opposed to preferential treatment of individuals in certain groups because they see the preference as a way of society paying its debt to these groups and of eventually achieving an environment in which race, sex, and all the other characteristics will no longer play a role. Opponents of affirmative action argue that even "benign" discrimination may have malign effects. These theorists attack the notion that all Blacks or members of other minority groups are in fact benefited by affirmative action. Led by such visible spokespersons as Justice Clarence Thomas, these theorists argue that many minority group members are opposed to affirmative action because it stigmatises them and confirms stereotyped notions about their inferiority (Smith, 1996: 9). In *Confessions of an Affirmative Action Baby*, Stephen Carter describes his feeling upon realising that he had been accepted to Harvard Law School because of his race: "The insult I felt came from the pain of being reminded so forcefully that in the judgement of those with the power to dispose, I was good enough for a top law school only because I happened to be Black" (Carter, 1991: 16).

Proponents of affirmative action as "benign" action are comfortable with an analysis of rights that focuses on groups rather than on individuals. Owen Fiss justifies affirmative action if its purpose is to advantage groups that have been historically disadvantaged. He refers to his theory as "an ethical view against caste, one that would make it undesirable for any social group to occupy a position of subordination for an extended period of time" (Fiss, 1976: 128). He rationalises a "special judicial solicitude on their behalf" without which certain segments of our society would continue as a "perpetual underclass" (Fiss, 1976: 133). Former U.N. Ambassador Morris B. Abram, on the other hand, highlights the danger of this group-oriented action:

> The social engineers' approach also fails to confront the problem of who decides what groups are sufficiently disadvantaged to deserve special treatment. They offer no mechanism for neutral decision-making on this issue. . . . In the absence of any neutral decisionmaking mechanisms, the attempt to end discrimination through colour-conscious remedies must inevitably degenerate into a crude political struggle between groups seeking favored status (Abram, 1986: 1321).

The focus on individual as opposed to group rights was emphasised by the Supreme Court in the Adarand case. In that case, Justice Sandra Day O'Connor harkened back to Justice Powell's statement in Bakke that constitutional standards can be applied consistently only if "it is the individual who is entitled to judicial protection against classifications based upon his racial or ethnic background because such distinctions impinge upon personal rights, rather than the individual only because of his membership in a particular group" (515 U.S. at 2111, citing 438 U.S. at 299).

AFFIRMATIVE ACTION: DO WE NEED IT? DOES IT WORK?

The debate of politicians, judges, and scholars revolves around whether affirmative action is constitutional and fair. Perhaps the more pragmatic questions are these: Do we need affirmative action at all? If we do, does it work to accomplish our goal? Proponents of affirmative action explain that it is designed to address the inferior economic position held by women and minorities in the American workplace. Because this inferior position results from past discrimination, affirmative action is a necessary component of an equal opportunity system (Clayton and Crosby, 1992: 4). The proponents remind us that before the Civil Rights Act of 1964 became effective, blatant and overt discrimination by employers against women and minorities was not only legal but also well accepted. One probable effect of this discrimination was that female and minority workers were underrepresented in the workplace, particularly in positions of high compensation and power. For example:

* In 1964, unemployment rates for Black men and Black women were roughly double those for whites and unemployment rates for women of both races were higher than the rates for males of the same races (3.4 percent for white males age 20 or over, 7.7 percent for Black males, 4.6 percent for white women, and 9.0 percent for Black women) (Bloch, 1994: 42).

* In 1966, 85 percent of Black men who worked for private employers and 69 percent of Black women held blue-collar positions, as compared to 39 percent of white men and 37 percent of white women (Feagin and Feagin, 1986: 44).

* In 1966, the average white male who had graduated from high school earned 40 percent more than his non-white male counterpart. This gap became progressively wider as the education level of each group increased (Bell, 1992: 809).

* In 1965, women earned $.60 for every dollar earned by men (Feagin and Feagin, 1986: 45).

* In 1967, 33.9 percent of Black families lived at or below the poverty level while only 9.1 percent of white families lived at or below the poverty level (U.S. Census Bureau, 2000: Historical Poverty Tables-Table 4).

* A study of federal employees in 1962 indicated that Blacks comprised 18.1 percent of employees in the lower grades (GS 1-4) and only .8 percent of employees in the highest grades (GS 12-18). Women also were grossly underrepresented in the higher grades, comprising only .10 percent of employees in grade 13-18 in 1971 (Kellough, 1989: 31-37).

Have the relative economic positions of women and minorities improved since the dawn of affirmative action programs? Statistics are available that support both affirmative and negative responses to that question. These are examples of the evidence that is cited to show that the plight of women and minorities has improved:

* By 1994, unemployment rates for both white woman and Black women were lower than those for white and Black men (Bloch, 1994: 42; U.S. Dept. of Labor, 1996). However, in the first six months of 2000, the unemployment rate for white women was slightly higher than that for white men (Employment Standards Administration, 2000).

* In 1999, for every dollar earned by white men, Black men earned almost $.79, white women earned $.78, and Black women earned $.64 (Bureau of Labor Statistics, 2000: Table 1).

* In 1999, the percent of female hourly workers who were paid at or below the prevailing federal minimum wage was 5.9 percent, as opposed to 3.4 percent for men. The gap in these figures has decreased substantially since 1979, when 20.2 percent of female hourly workers earned wages at or below the minimum wage, while the comparable figure for male hourly workers was 7.7 percent (Bureau of Labor Statistics, 2000: Table 18). Also, college-educated women by 1999 were earning 75.7 percent of what their male counterparts earned, as opposed to 66.6 percent in 1979 (Bureau of Labor Statistics, 2000: Table 15).

* In the two decades following enactment of the first civil rights laws, Blacks and women increased their proportional representation in the highest grades of federal government employment (Blacks to 6.4 percent in GS 12-18 by 1984 and women to .27 percent in GS 13-18 by 1984) (Kellough, 1989: 31-37).

* The proportion of managers who are women grew substantially between 1980 and 1990 (from 27 percent to 35 percent for white women and from 3 percent to 7 percent for women of colour) (National Council for Research on Women, 1995: 6) and the percentage of women and Black workers who hold managerial or professional positions increased between 1983 and 1998 (40.9 percent of women workers in 1983 up to 49 percent in 1999; 5.6 percent of Black workers in 1983 up to 7.6 percent in 1999) (U.S. Dept. of Commerce, 2000).

* The pace at which Fortune 500 companies were adding women to their boards of directors slowed steadily in the mid-1990s (with a 9 percent increase between 1993 and 1994 slowing to only a 3 percent increase between 1995 and 1996 [Catalyst, 1996]) but then showed a dramatic increase (24 percent) between 1993 and 2000 (Catalyst, 2000).

On the other hand, equally compelling evidence indicates that women and minorities not only have a long way to go but, in some cases, may be worse off now than they were thirty years ago. For example:

*By 1992, the gap between the unemployment rates for Blacks and whites had increased from that of 1964: 13.4 percent for Black males as opposed to 6.3 percent of white males and 11.7 percent for Black females as opposed to 5.4 percent for white females (Bloch, 1994: 42). While national unemployment rates had decreased by 1995, the substantial gap still remained: 10.7 percent for Black men as opposed to 4.8 percent for white men and 8.2 percent for Black women as opposed to 4.4 percent for white women (U.S. Dept. of Labor, 1996). The first six months of 2000 showed a similar gap in the rates: 8.1 percent for Black men as opposed to 2.9 percent for white men and 7.4 percent for Black women as opposed to 3.1 percent for white women (Employment Standards Administration, 2000).

* In 1998, 8 percent of white families lived at or below the poverty level, while 23.4 percent of Black families lived at or below the poverty level (U.S. Census Bureau, 2000: Table 4).

* The average income of Black families in the late 1980s was lower than the average income for Black families in the 1970s (Bell, 1992: 808). The median income for Black families (in constant 1993 dollars) was $21,969 in 1970 and $21,542 in 1993 (U.S. Dept. of Commerce, 1995).

* In 1970, median Black income was 61.3 percent of median white income; by 1989, median Black income had decreased to only 56.2 percent of median white income (Bell, 1992: 812).
* In 1990, only 6.3 percent of women managers and 3.6 percent of minority managers earned incomes in the top 20 percent (National Council for Research on Women, 1995: 4).
* In 1994-95, women of colour represented only 15 percent of the women in managerial and administrative positions and earned less on average than their white female counterparts (Catalyst, 1999).
* As of 1995, white men comprised only 33 percent of the American population but still comprised 85 percent of partners in law firms, 85 percent of tenured professors, 80 percent of the House of Representatives, 90 percent of the U.S. Senate, and 95 percent of Fortune 500 CEOs (National Council for Research on Women, 1995: 6).

It is obvious that a variety of factors have contributed to the statistical situation outlined above. Educational opportunities for women and minorities have increased, but relative rates of achievement in many public schools have gone down. The drug culture has dominated the lives of certain segments of our society, particularly low-income Black families. The number of single mothers raising children has increased substantially. The number of women who enter the workforce on career-oriented paths has also increased. Finally, there is no compelling evidence to show that affirmative action was actually implemented during these years on any standardised or consistent basis. Thus it is difficult to use these statistics to make any definitive evaluation of whether affirmative action has worked.

Perhaps more telling are those studies that concentrate particularly on the implementation of Executive Order 11246, which requires the federal government and all federal contractors to engage in affirmative action. Unfortunately, these studies are also inconclusive.

In 1984-85, Jonathon S. Leonard conducted studies of the enforcement mechanisms employed under the Executive Order and of the impact of the Executive Order on the employment of women and Blacks. He concluded that the enforcement mechanisms were targeted more at large white-collar-intensive establishments than at those establishments that had a relatively small proportion of women and minorities (Leonard (1) 1985: 383). Despite this poorly targeted enforcement, he found several positive effects of affirmative action. He concluded as follows:

> In the contract sector affirmative action has increased the demand relative to white males for Black males by 6.5 percent, for nonBlack minority males by 11.9 percent, and for white females by 3.5 percent. For a program lacking public consensus and vigorous enforcement, this is a strong showing (Leonard, 1984: 459).

A 1989 study by J. Edward Kellough examined the effect of the goals and timetables instituted by the federal government in 1971 as part of its equal employment opportunity program. The study found no significant gains by Blacks in the higher grades of government employment, where Blacks had been traditionally underrepresented. There were slight increases in the proportion of women employed in these higher grades, but women still remained substantially underrepresented in these grades. On the other hand, examination of the rates of employment in particular government agencies indicated that the agencies that experienced the most substantial increase in employment of women and Blacks in the higher grades were those that had had the lowest proportion of women and Blacks in these grades prior to the instigation of the affirmative action program. The author of this study made three general observations. First, he concluded that the problem at hand (the under-representation of women and Blacks in high-level government positions) was complicated dramatically by broader social inequities. Second, he found that the goals and timetables had not altered substantially the trends for hiring women and Blacks. Third, he concluded that the goals and timetables had had some impact and definitely had a symbolic value that would be important for minorities and women who were considering jobs in the public sector (Kellough, 1989: 108-115). This study reaffirmed Leonard's 1985 conclusion that goals and timetables "have a measurable and significant correlation with improvements in the employment of minorities and females" at businesses that are subject to review under Executive Order 11246 (Leonard (2), 1985: 18).

A 1994 study took a somewhat different approach to determining whether government regulation of the employment process justified the problems inherent in giving preferred treatment to certain members of the society. This study focused in part on the differences in hiring practices between those firms that contract with the federal government (and thus are covered by the Executive Order 11246 affirmative action requirement) and those firms that are non-contractors. The results confirmed an earlier 1990 study that showed that "contractors have fostered significantly higher growth in the employment rates of protected class members [women and minorities] than non-contractors" (Bloch, 1994: 96). However, when attempting to reconcile this conclusion with the increasing gap in the unemployment rate among Blacks and whites, the author of the study observed that "the contractor-noncontractor differences primarily represent demographic shifts across these two employer categories rather than net economy-wide gains for minorities" (Bloch, 1994: 103).

More precise and positive findings about affirmative action were reported in 2000 by Harry J. Holzer and David Neumark. Their study included both government contractors and employers who were not covered by Executive Order 11246 and also made a distinction between affirmative action in recruiting and affirmative action in hiring. Holzer and Neumark (2000: 269) found that establishments that use affirmative action in recruiting "generate greater flows of minority applicants, and more recent hires (or employees) who are minority or female" without sacrificing standards related to qualification or performance. These firms "recruit applicants much more extensively and screen them more intensively; rely more heavily on formal rather than informal means of evaluation (both before and after a worker is hired); are more likely to ignore stigmatising personal characteristics and histories when they hire; and are more likely to provide training to candidates they do hire" (p. 269). Establishments that use affirmative action in hiring (a smaller number of the pool of establishments surveyed) were found to be more likely to hire candidates with lower qualifications. However, these establishments also tended to provide more training with the result that "[f]or most groups of minorities and women, job performance is not relatively lower in these establishments than in establishments that do not use Affirmative Action" (p. 269).

FUTURE OF AFFIRMATIVE ACTION IN AMERICAN EMPLOYMENT LAW

As the affirmative action debate rages into the twenty-first century, a variety of issues remain to be resolved. As with most decisions in the United States, the final fate of affirmative action will be dictated less by direct governmental or judicial intervention than by the tide of public opinion. Both opponents and proponents of affirmative action are speculating as to the effect of the 2000

Presidential election on affirmative action in American employment. Both Al Gore and George W. Bush are on record as opposing quotas. A Gore administration would most likely continue the "mend it, don't end it" strategy adopted by the Clinton administration after the 1995 review of governmental affirmative action programs. The Republicans have taken a firm stance against any preferential treatment based solely on minority status, but have committed to closing the gap between the economic statuses of the races. Thus, regardless of which political party takes power after the 2000 elections, it is likely that affirmative action for federal employers and government contractors will not be abolished completely. Attention will be given to these plans in two arenas: the courts and the executive branch.

Assuming that governmental affirmative action plans are continued, within the next five years the Supreme Court will probably be called upon often to decide what type of programs meet that standard of scrutiny. Adarand made it clear that an affirmative action plan based on race will be subjected to strict scrutiny. Consequently, the government will need to show both a compelling governmental purpose for the plan and that the plan is narrowly tailored to fit that purpose. The Court's decision in Adarand indicated that actual past discrimination by the employer that was of a "pervasive, systematic, and obstinate" nature will justify race-based affirmative action by a government. In the near future, the Court will be called upon to decide whether other justifications are significantly compelling so as to justify race-conscious treatment.

In the executive branch, a shift of focus may well occur, with less emphasis on hiring minority group members and more emphasis on aggressive recruiting and training. Also, government programs will focus far less on race and gender categories and more on the category of "economically disadvantaged groups." While this latter change may have only a marginal effect on most minority groups, it remains to be seen whether women will be deemed to have been traditionally economically disadvantaged and thus continue to be included in these programs.

The true influence of either choice of President will be measured, however, not by the man who is elected but by the individuals whom that President appoints when vacancies occur on the United States Supreme Court. As the foregoing discussion indicates, the Court holds the power to promote or eradicate almost any affirmative action approach that is taken by the President, the Congress, or the states. As of the writing of this article, the voting records of the current Justices indicate that affirmative action plans that are not narrowly tailored to remedy proven past discrimination may well be invalidated. The current Justices were all sitting on the Court when Adarand was decided. Five of the current Justices - Chief Justice Rehnquist, Justice Kennedy, Justice O'Connor, Justice Scalia, and Justice Thomas - comprised the majority in the 5-4 Adarand decision. (All five of these Justices were appointed by Republican Presidents.) The replacement of any of these Justices by an individual whose views on affirmative action are less restrictive could well change the shape of affirmative action in the United States. This will happen in the context of the review of voluntary affirmative action by private employers, which will garner the long-term focus of the courts and state and federal laws.

The fate of voluntary affirmative action by private employers is in some ways dependent upon the fate of government-sponsored plans, but private plans have traditionally been given greater leeway by the courts. The next few years will see a proliferation in the number of "reverse discrimination" lawsuits brought by whites or males who feel disadvantaged by an employer's affirmative action plan. Such lawsuits will offer the courts the opportunity to decide the degree to which private businesses will or will not be subject to extensive governmental oversight. The threat of such suits, combined with general public disapproval, will surely result in the demise of "quota"-type affirmative action plans. On the other hand, Epstein (1995: 180) predicts that "the forces for diversity and affirmative action are simply too powerful to be denied" and thus that private employers will become more and more inclined to make employment decisions based on race or gender for compelling business reasons. Recent studies indicate that the American public tend to favour some forms of affirmative action (e.g., recruiting and training efforts that are designed to help women and minorities) but are opposed to other forms (e.g., actual "preferential treatment" or quota-oriented hiring or promotion) (Holzer and Neumark, 2000: 243). As the demographic predictions for American society show increasing diversity among members of the consuming public, businesses may well strive to increase minority participation in their workforces in order to make themselves more attractive to those with whom they do business. In other words, the concept of "affirmative action," which carries tremendous emotional and political baggage, may well be integrated into the American employment culture simply as another form of rational decision-making.

The irony in the projected increase in voluntary affirmative action is that, in all of the cases in which the Supreme Court examined private plans, it has made clear that the purpose behind the plan should mirror the spirit of Title VII -- that is, the correction of the lingering effects of past discrimination. If the Court holds private employers to this rule, then employers would not be authorised to take race-conscious or gender-conscious affirmative action simply because it makes good business sense. Consider, for example, a company that builds hardware and software for "virtual reality" communications. Such a company and industry have no history of past discrimination if for no other reason than that neither existed even a few years ago. If this company decides to hire a Black saleswoman to market its product to Black-owned businesses, Title VII would seem to offer the company no protection from a lawsuit.

If a court or legislature takes this approach, the various camps involved today in the affirmative action debate will splinter and new alliances will be formed. For example, some current opponents of affirmative action argue that the government should not be in the habit of "social engineering" and thus should be involved only minimally, if at all, in business decisions. These opponents would probably favour an approach that allows business-oriented decision-making even if it is race-conscious or gender-conscious. However, other current opponents of affirmative action take the purist stance that any type of discrimination for whatever reason is wrong. These opponents, who would not accept the notion of "benign" discrimination in government-oriented affirmative action programs, could not logically accept an approval of such action even on a private scale. In fact, this group may be the most vocal harbingers of the danger for abuse with such an approach. Some current proponents of affirmative action favour affirmative action because it raises certain societal groups to an equal level in our society. These proponents also would focus quickly on the danger that a "business decision" may easily result in a majority-group member getting a job selling products in majority-group communities. These proponents of affirmative action would then find themselves arguing that race or gender should not be allowed to be a consideration in hiring or promotion decisions. The current proponents of affirmative action who justify such action as remedial would have difficulty arguing that race or gender can be considered as a corrective feature if the business or industry has no history of past discrimination. Thus, perhaps the only prediction that may be made safely about the future of affirmative action in America is that the shifting contours of the surrounding debate will have the kaleidoscopic effect of separating and regrouping politicians, judges, theorists, and voters whose current stance seems -- to them, at least -- so solidly rooted as to be both unquestionable and enduring.

Mary F. Radford is Professor of Law, Georgia State University College of Law, Atlanta, Georgia, U.S.A.

ACKNOWLEDGEMENT

An earlier version of this article appears in Kaufman, Bruce E., (ed.) *Government Regulation of the Employment Relationship.* Industrial Relations Research Association , 50th Anniversary Volume, 1997, pp. 343-67.

REFERENCES

Abram, Morris B. "Affirmative Action: Fair Shakers and Social Engineers." *Harvard Law Review* 99. 6 (April 1986): 1312-26.

Bell, Derrick. *Race, Racism, and the Law.* 3d ed. Boston: Little, Brown, & Co., 1992.

Bell, Derrick, and Linda Singer. "Making a Record." *Connecticut Law Review* 26. 1 (Fall 1993) : 265-84.

Bloch, Farrell. *Antidiscrimination Law and Minority Employment.* Chicago: University of Chicago Press, 1994.

Bureau of Labor Statistics, U.S. Department of Labor. *Highlights of Women's Earnings in 1999*, 2000.

Carter, Stephen L. "When Victims Happen to be Black." *Yale Law Journal* 97. 3 (Feb. 1988) : 420-47.

Carter, Stephen L. *Confessions of an Affirmative Action Baby.* New York: Basic Books, 1991.

Catalyst. "Boards Add Women at Slower Pace," reported in *The Atlanta Journal-Constitution* (Dec. 6, 1996): F-1.

Catalyst. *Women of Colour in Corporate Management: A Statistical Picture*, 1998.

Catalyst. *INFOBRIEF: Women on Corporate Boards*, 2000.

Clayton, Susan D. and Faye J. Crosby. *Justice, Gender, and Affirmative Action.* Ann Arbor: University of Michigan Press, 1992.

Daly, John Charles. "Affirmative Action and the Constitution." *Proceedings of Public Policy Forum* 64 . Washington, D.C.,(May 21, 1985). Washington, D.C.: American Enterprise Institute for Public Policy Research, 1985: 1-29.

Dworkin, Ronald. *A Matter of Principle.* Cambridge: Harvard University Press, 1985.

Eastland, Terry. "Special to Insight: Should Washington Halt Race-Based Policies for Hiring and Contracting? Yes: Restore the Standard of the Civil Rights Act of 1964." *Insight Magazine.* (May 6, 1996).

Employment Standards Administration Office of Federal Contract Compliance Programs, U.S. Department of Labor. *Affirmative Action Fact Sheet.* Washington, D.C.: GPO, 2000.

Epstein, Richard A. *Simple Rules for a Complex World.* Cambridge: Harvard University Press, 1995.

Feagin, Joe R. and Clairece Booher Feagin. *Discrimination American Style: Institutional Racism and Sexism.* Malabar: Robert E. Krieger Publishing Co., 1986.

Fiscus, Ronald J. *The Constitutional Logic of Affirmative Action.* Durham: Duke University Press, 1992..

Fiss, Owen M. "Groups and the Equal Protection Clause." in Cohen, Marshall, Nagel, Thomas, & Scanlon, Thomas (eds) *Equality and Preferential Treatment: A Philosophy & Public Affairs Reader*, Princeton: University of Princeton Press, 1976, 87-154.

Greenawalt, Kent. "Judicial Scrutiny of 'Benign' Racial Preference in Law School Admissions." *Columbia Law Review* 75. 3 (April 1975): 559-602.

Holzer, Harry J. and David Neumark."What Does Affirmative Action Do?" *Industrial and Labor Relations Review* 53 (January 2000): 240-66.
Kellough, J. Edward. *Federal Equal Employment Opportunity Policy and Numerical Goals and Timetables.* New York: Praeger, 1989.
Leonard, Jonathon S. "The Impact of Affirmative Action on Employment." *Journal of Labor Economics* 2. 4 (1984): 439-63.
Leonard, Jonathon S. "Affirmative Action as Earnings Distribution: The Targeting of Compliance Reviews." *Journal of Labor Economics* 3. 3 (1985): 363-384.
Leonard, Jonathon S., "What Promises are Worth: The Impact of Affirmative Action Goals." *Journal of Human Resources* 20.1 (1985): 3-20.
National Council for Research on Women. "Affirmative Action: Beyond the Glass Ceiling and the Sticky Floor." *Issues Quarterly* I. 4 (1995).
Posner, Richard A. "The DeFunis Case and the Constitutionality of Preferential Treatment of Racial Minorities." *Supreme Court Review* 15 (1974): 1-25.
Player, Mack A. *Employment Discrimination Law.* St. Paul: West Publishing Co., 1988.
Smith, Steven. "Justice Thomas: The Record Speaks." *The Defender* 11. 6 (May/June 1996): 1, 8-9.
Sullivan, Kathleen M. "Sins of Discrimination: Last Term's Affirmative Action Cases." *Harvard Law Review* 100. 1 (Nov. 1986): 78-98.
Tribe, Laurence H. "In What Vision of the Constitution Must the Law Be Colour-Blind?" *John Marshall Law Review* 20. 2 (Winter 1986): 201-07.
U.S. Census Bureau. *Historical Poverty Levels.* Washington, D.C.: GPO, 2000.
U.S. Department of Commerce. *Statistical Abstract of the United States.* Washington, D.C.: GPO, 1995.
U.S. Department of Commerce. *Statistical Abstract of the United States.* Washington, D.C.: GPO, 2000.
U.S. Department of Labor. *Employment and Earnings, January - April.* Washington, D.C.: GPO, 1996.
Zimmer, Michael J., Charles A. Sullivan, Richard F. Richards, and Deborah A. Calloway, *Cases and Materials on Employment Discrimination Law.* New York: Aspen Publications, Inc., 2000.

CASES

Adarand Constructors, Inc. v. Pena, 515 U.S. 2097 (1995).
City of Richmond v. J.A. Croson Co., 488 U.S. 469 (1989).
Firefighters Local Union No. 1784 v. Stotts, 467 U.S. 561 (1984).
Griggs v. Duke Power Company, 401 U.S. 424 (1971).
Hopwood v. Texas, 78 F.3d 932 (5th Cir. 1996).
Johnson v. Santa Clara Transportation Agency, 480 U.S. 616 (1987).
Local 28 of Sheet Metal Workers Intern. Ass'n. v. EEOC, 478 U.S. 421 (1986).
Local 93, Firefighters v. Cleveland, 478 U.S. 501 (1986).
Metro Broadcasting, Inc. v. FCC, 497 U.S. 547 (1990).
Plessy v. Ferguson, 163 U.S. 537 (1896).
Piscataway Township Board of Education v. Taxman, 91 F.3d 1547 (3d Cir. 1997).
Regents of the University of California v. Bakke, 438 U.S. 265 (1978).
U.S. v. Paradise, 480 U.S. 149 (1980).
U.S. v. Virginia, 518 U.S. 515 (1996).
United Steelworkers of America v. Weber, 443 U.S. 193 (1979).
Wygant v. Jackson Board of Education, 476 U.S. 267 (1986).

CHAPTER 13

MORLEY GUNDERSON

PAY AND EMPLOYMENT EQUITY: THE ROLE OF MARKETS, COLLECTIVE BARGAINING AND LEGISLATION

Legislative or regulatory initiatives are a key mechanism for attaining social goals at the workplace, such as pay equity and employment equity. This is the mechanism emphasised by policy makers, politicians and the general public. Yet there are other mechanisms for dealing with social issues such as discrimination at the workplace. These mechanisms are the private, unregulated market, as emphasised by economists, and collective bargaining, as emphasised by the industrial relations community.

These other mechanisms are often thought of as "part of the problem" rather than part of the "solution." This can be true. Yet they also can be an important complement to legislative initiatives, and, they may even be a viable substitute[1]. As well, they may often undo the legislative initiatives, and they may lead to unintended and often undesirable side effects in response to the legislative initiatives. They may also be spurred on by the legislative initiatives in more positive ways. As such, it is important to understand the role of these three mechanisms (markets, collective bargaining, and legislation) for regulating the employment relationship in general, and pay and employment equity in particular. That is the purpose of this chapter.

The chapter begins by outlining the generic role of each of these mechanisms in regulating the employment relationship. It then applies that template to each of pay and employment equity, dealing with both the conceptual rationales for the policies, as well as the practical issues of design and implementation.

The concepts of pay and employment equity are used here as they have been applied in the Canadian context. Pay equity refers to equal pay for work of equal value where female-dominated jobs are to be the paid the same as male-dominated jobs of equal value where the value of a job is determined by gender neutral job evaluation schemes. It generally involves four steps: (1) determining the gender dominance of a job; (2) evaluating the value of the jobs according to gender neutral job evaluation schemes that value the generic components of skill, effort, responsibility and working conditions; (3) relating pay to job value, for example, through pay lines relating pay to job evaluation points; and (4) adjusting the pay in undervalued female-dominated jobs to the pay of male-dominated jobs of comparable value.

Employment equity is designed to enhance the employment and promotion opportunities of the target groups to ensure that they are represented in the particular workplace in the same proportion, at least, as they are represented in the externally available workforce. It too involves four generic steps:

C. Agocs (ed.), Workplace Equality, 265–278.

(1) an internal audit within the firm to establish the number of target group members and their position, (2) a comparison of this internal representation with their representation in the externally available labour market of the firm, (3) establishing goals or targets to ensure that the internal representation matches the external availability, and (4) establishing a plan and timetable to achieve the targets.

MARKET MECHANISMS

As indicated, markets are generally regarded as part of the problem and not part of the solution in dealing with labour market discrimination. This is so because discrimination in both wages and employment opportunities tends to persist in markets, as documented by the vast majority of empirical studies[2].

Markets as a Force to Dissipate Discrimination

Yet market forces can be a potentially important mechanism to dissipate discrimination. Quite simply, discrimination on the part of employers is an inefficient work practice in that employers are paying excessive wages, for example to males, when they could hire equally productive females at lower wages. This should reduce the demand for male workers and increase the demand for female workers, with those two forces dissipating the discriminatory wage gap. Firms that do not discriminate should expand relative to firms that discriminate, since the latter firms are paying excessively high wages to favoured groups. There is no "survival value" -- to use the Darwinian phrase -- in such practices, just as there would be no survival value in paying 40 percent more for a blue machine compared to an otherwise identical red machine that produced the same output.

Factors Sustaining Discrimination in Competitive Markets

While markets can be a powerful force in dissipating discrimination, there are also forces at work that can sustain the outcomes of discriminatory actions even in competitive markets.

Market mechanisms take the constraints, including discrimination, arising from outside the market as given. Such constraints can have important implications for labour market behaviour and hence wage and employment determination, but they need not reflect discrimination *in the labour market.* For example, since women tend to bear a disproportionate burden of household tasks even when both parties work in the labour market[3], this is likely to affect such factors as absenteeism and even productivity in the labour market. It should not be surprising that holding two full-time jobs, one in the labour market and one in the household, can lead to adverse productivity effects in the labour market, as well as pressures on the domestic front. Similarly, if women are reluctant to take a promotion because it may threaten their husband, or if they are reluctant to make a geographic move because it may threaten family stability, or if they have to take a job that is near a day-care centre, such Hobson's "choices" will obviously affect their labour market wages and employment opportunities even if employers themselves are not the source of the discrimination. Such discriminatory pressures arising from within the household (marriage is generally not an "equal opportunity employer") will not be directly dissipated by market forces, albeit there may be some indirect pressure on the household if there is recognition of the cost, in terms of foregone family income, of the bypassed opportunities.

The same applies to discriminatory pressures arising from educational institutions, where there can be gender stereotyping and streaming. This in turn can influence the wages and employment opportunities of women even if employers themselves do not discriminate. Again market forces would not directly serve to dissipate such stereotyping and streaming outside of the market, albeit there may be an indirect effect if the costs of such practices in terms of squandered opportunities and wasted talents become apparent and place pressures on the educational institutions.

Markets may engage in "statistical discrimination" whereby individuals are judged according to the average characteristics of their group. Such practices can "survive" -- indeed thrive -- in competitive markets if they are inexpensive screening devices. This is so even if "mistakes" are occasionally made in the sense that some individuals are bypassed; the costs of reducing all such mistakes to zero may simply not be worth the benefits. The outcome may be efficient, but it certainly need not be "fair" to each individual.

Markets can also reflect the preferences of customers who may have discriminatory tastes and are willing to pay the price to indulge those tastes. For example, if customers prefer to be waited upon by male waiters and are willing to pay a premium for such service that could be provided equally well by female waitresses, then employers may well hire only males and pay a male premium. Such customer discrimination can be sustained in competitive markets, just as price premiums can be sustained for certain types of bottled water that may be no "better" than the local tap water. "Better" is in the eye of the beholder.

Even if profit maximising firms have an incentive to hire women who have lower wages relative to equally productive men, the lower "cost" of women may be offset somewhat by other costs. If male co-workers discriminate, then hiring women can adversely affect the performance of men, and they may devote time and effort into non-cooperative behaviour against females. This can obviously also affect the performance of women. Employers can seldom "instantly replace" higher priced male labour with equally productive but lower priced female labour given the transaction costs involved, including termination costs and possibly legal costs. Doing so through attrition and turnover may simply take a long time. In essence, markets can dissipate discrimination in the long run – but the long run may take a very long time.

Clearly, there is a wide range of forces that can sustain discrimination in competitive markets even though market forces should dissipate discrimination. In *non-competitive* markets, the likelihood of discrimination being sustained is even greater since there is less pressure to "arbitrage" a wage difference for equally productive workers. In such markets, inefficient workplace and pay practices can be sustained without jeopardising the survival of the firm.

The belief that "markets are a woman's best friend" is likely confined mainly to neo-classical economists. Nevertheless, it is hard to dismiss the proposition that promoting the best person, or hiring the lower wage but equally productive person, enhances the "bottom-line" – it is simply "good business." In that vein, market pressures can be an important force in dissipating discrimination. In essence, market forces can be part of the "solution."

Value in Exchange vs. Administrative Concepts of Value

In markets, the concept of value (including the value of a job) is "value in exchange" as determined by the interactions of the forces of supply and demand. This can yield a low wage if demand is low (perhaps reflecting the discriminatory tastes of customers) or if supply is abundant (perhaps because of a readily available pool of women in households willing to do certain work). The economic concept of market "worth" is based on what people are willing and able to pay relative to what people are willing and able to sell, not by some subjective concept of worth.

This is in marked contrast to the pay equity concept of equal pay for work of equal value where the value of a job is determined by a gender neutral job evaluation scheme. To most economists, this is an administrative and not an economic concept of value. It is akin to the concept of "value in use" that gives rise to the diamond-water paradox: diamonds have a high value in exchange simply because they are in scarce supply; water has a high value in use but a low value in exchange, simply because it is generally in abundant supply.

While pay equity does involve an administrative concept of value, it is not bereft of economic principles. Pay equity procedures involving the estimation of pay lines relating pay to job evaluation points effectively estimate the "shadow price" of a job evaluation score in male dominated jobs, and apply that shadow price to the same points in female-dominated jobs. The procedure of estimating shadow or hedonic prices for attributes is well established in economics. It is used, for example, to provide estimates of compensating wage premiums for risk, which in turn are used to provide estimates of the (statistical) value of a life, which are used, for example, in compensation for personal injury awards. The shadow price procedure is also used to provide estimates of the shadow or hedonic price of certain attributes of goods, which in turn are used to correct the consumer price index for quality changes.

Principles of economics are also considered, for example, in many of the exemptions which are allowed in pay equity legislation[4]. Although they vary across the different jurisdictions in Canada, such exclusions include pay differences that reflect shortages, merit, temporary training assignments or geographic location.

Impacts of Pay and Employment Equity

To the extent that market forces are in operation, basic economic theory has straightforward predictions about the impact of pay and employment equity legislation. By raising the wages and hence costs of employing women[5], pay equity legislation should reduce the employment of women as firms substitute other inputs for more expensive female labour (substitution effect) and as some firms reduce their scale of operations, perhaps even closing an operation (output effect), in response to the cost increase. The adjustments would not occur instantaneously, especially because complementary equal employment opportunity or employment equity legislation may make it difficult to substitute male labour for female labour. The adjustment would be more long run and subtle, occurring at the margin of employment changes, such as through the slower growth of the higher priced jobs.

Other subtle adjustments would also occur. For example, the requirements of the job may become more onerous, although under pay equity this could lead to higher job evaluation scores and hence subsequent pay increases. Some of the displaced labour from the female-dominated jobs would also go to the non-covered sector, and this supply influx could also depress wages in those sectors. Pay equity could also foster occupational segregation by reducing the monetary incentive to leave female-dominate jobs, although Robb (1987) and others have argued that females, especially older females, should not have to leave their job to get the same pay as a man doing work of the same value.

There are factors that may offset at least some of the adverse employment effects that economics emphasises will result from pay equity. While we tend to think of pay as reflecting productivity, it may also work the other way, with higher pay inducing higher productivity. This is a variant of the "efficiency wage" argument where higher wages can "pay for themselves" by inducing loyalty and commitment and reducing turnover. There may also be shock effects that induce employers to save elsewhere in the system, for example, by rationalising their whole pay structure[6]. (Economists emphasise, however, that if these were "profitable" in the first place, employers would have done them without the legislative prodding).

By increasing the demand for female labour (or whatever the target group) employment equity (as defined in the introduction) can increase both the wages and employment of female labour. It is in that sense that employment equity could be somewhat of a *substitute* for pay equity since, by increasing the demand for female labour, employment equity may induce the wage increases without the adverse employment effect. In fact, both wages and employment should increase. The wage increases come about to the extent that employers have to raise wages to attract females to meet their employment equity targets. Such wage increases resulting from this increased "competition" for women also likely enhance the perceptions of self-worth of women since employers are competing more for their services.

Employment equity legislation is designed in large part to compensate for the legacy of the cumulative effects of the past history of discrimination. It is the equivalent of "competitive handicapping" in tournaments designed to provide a "level playing field" and facilitate a "fair race". It is easier for society to accept unequal outcomes in markets when they are the results of decisions of persons who had equal opportunities to make those choices. Such outcomes are more unacceptable when they are based on "choices" that are limited by the impact of discrimination, present as well as past. Much of our aversion to following market mechanisms stems from the fact that people do not start out with equal "endowments" of wealth, skills or intelligence such that we could simply accept their "choices" as their exercising their "consumer sovereignty." Most people are not offended by the fact that Evil Kneival makes a good living by risking his life doing stunts in cars. But they are understandably offended by the fact that some poor people have to earn a living by risking their life in unsafe and unhealthy jobs even if that is their so-called "choice". Employment equity legislation can be regarded as an intervention designed to provide similar "choice sets" for men and women to offset the legacy of the history of cumulative discrimination. In that vein, it can facilitate the acceptance of the market outcomes that result from this fairer race.

Interdependent Preferences

As indicated, the social acceptability of market outcomes depends in large part on the extent to which the market participants have choices to make. There is the adage that "economics is about how we make choices; sociology is about why we have no choices to make." Discrimination can affect the well-being not only of the person discriminated against, but also of other "third-party" members of society if they feel that discrimination unfairly reduces the options of those who are discriminated against. Many may be offended by the discriminatory actions of others even if those others "pay" for that discrimination by not hiring the lower cost person or by bypassing the best person. The negative effect of that discrimination on members of society who are offended by the discrimination must also be considered in any social welfare calculus.

Of course, this can work both ways and hence be a dangerous principle to follow. For example, "third parties" to the actions may also be offended if particular groups have equal opportunities to be successful. This was likely the case in the US South under the emancipation of Blacks, and in South Africa under Apartheid. In these circumstances, the instruments of the State and social sanctions were used to repress minorities, and to inhibit market forces from dissipating discrimination. Such third-party views can also come from those who believe that a "women's place is in the home" and that women take the jobs of men. In such circumstances caution should obviously be exercised in arguing for intervention in market mechanisms on the grounds that the preferences of "third-parties" should be considered in any social welfare calculus. What the State gives, the State can take away.

COLLECTIVE BARGAINING MECHANISM

Collective bargaining is another mechanism for regulating the terms and conditions of employment at the workplace. It is especially significant in countries like Canada, given the importance of unionisation, especially in the public sector.

Prominence of Unionisation

In Canada, slightly under one-third of the workforce is unionised[7]. Specifically, in 1999, 30.1 percent of the non-agricultural paid workforce was unionised and 32.6 percent were covered by a collective agreement. The importance of unions goes much beyond their role in representing their membership. Even in organisations that are not unionised, the *threat* of union organising can play an important role in gaining terms and conditions of employment for non-union workers that are similar to those of union workers. At the least, such threats can be a viable discipline device inhibiting management from arbitrary and capricious treatment of their employees.

Importantly for purposes of pay and employment equity, union density is much higher in the public sector (70.9 percent) compared to the private sector (18.2 percent), and women constitute a large portion of the public sector workforce where pay equity is more prominent. The two largest unions in Canada are public sector unions – the Canadian Union of Public Employees (CUPE) and the National Union of Public and General Employees (NUPGE). As well, the growth of unionisation has been much greater for females than males (Mainville and Olineck, 1999) so that by 1999, union density and collective agreement coverage were almost identical between females and males. Furthermore, given the higher growth in the employment of women relative to men, women now constitute almost half of the union membership in Canada. Union militancy has also increased substantially among female union members (Briskin and McDermott, 1993). As well, while union density and union influence has declined in most other industrialised countries, it has been sustained in Canada, largely because of the earlier growth of unions in the public sector (Mumme, 2000: 534-535).

In such an environment it is not surprising that issues pertaining to pay and employment equity have taken on increased importance especially in the public sector in Canada. This reflects the interactive effect of the range of forces discussed: greater union density in the public sector; prominence of women in the public sector; prominence of large public sector unions; propensity of women to joint unions that is the same as that of men; growth of the female workforce (and hence of female union membership); the increased militancy of female union members; and the sustained influence of unions in Canada.

Influence of Women within Unions

While the market mechanism responds to the preferences of persons at the margin of decision (e.g., to the threat of exit or to the need to attract new personnel), the collective bargaining mechanism responds to the median union voter who is likely to influence the decisions of the union. That is, "voice" in the union sector is the dominant force for ensuring change in the employment relationship, compared to "exit" or the threat of exit under the market mechanism.

In the "old world of work" dominated by male, blue-collar workers in heavy manufacturing, that voter was likely to be an older male with preferences for such factors as seniority, wages and pensions. In the "new world of work", however, characterised by a more diverse workforce in white-collar and service jobs, females are more likely to have an influence in union decision making.

In such circumstances, it is not surprising that issues of pay and employment equity have taken on increased importance especially in the public sector in Canada. Women are prominent in that sector, as are unions, and women within those unions. In essence, the median union voter is likely to be a woman in those sectors, and hence the union is likely to be responsive to the preferences of the female union membership.

Role of Unions in Pay and Employment Equity

At the workplace, unions can play a variety of important roles -- roles that are particularly important for initiatives such as pay and employment equity. Unions can *determine and articulate* the preferences of their membership, especially with respect to the difficult internal membership trade-offs that are typically involved amongst various issues. They can serve an important *information role*, providing information "upstream" to management and "downstream" to the rank-and-file.

Unions can provide *expertise* in areas that are complicated such as with pensions and pay and employment equity. This is especially important in the area of pay equity given the complicated technical issues that are involved at almost every stage of the process. Expertise is required with respect to such dimensions as:

- job evaluation systems
- determining the gender composition of jobs
- finding appropriate comparator groups
- determining the appropriate definition of the establishment and the job
- determining the appropriate definition of pay, to also include non-wage compensation
- estimating paylines (e.g., linear or non-linear; extrapolation where there are no comparators; appropriate regression procedures if used)

- adjusting pay (e.g., job-to-job; job-to-payline; payline-to-payline)
- determining exemptions and exclusions, and
- determining appropriate phasing periods

Each of these areas is complicated and can require often-expensive expertise. The totality of *all* areas being complicated obviously compounds the issue.

In complaints-based systems, unions can play a crucial role in *initiating complaints* – an important factor given that the legal and other costs of initiating a complaint are likely beyond the means of most individual employees. Unions can also *protect employees against reprisals* on the part of management if complaints are laid or the process is carried out in an adversarial manner. Given their presence on the "shop-floor," unions can play an important role in *monitoring and enforcing* pay and employment equity. They can utilise the *grievance procedure* as a formal mechanism to deal with complaints in the administration of the process. Unions can play an important role in the *joint labour-management committees* that are often established at the workplace to deal with many of the technical issues that are involved in pay equity. Unions can also use their "ultimate weapon" – the strike – to achieve pay equity. They can also play an important role, often through their central organisation, in *lobbying the political process* to establish and sustain laws and social programs, such as pay and employment equity.

While legislative initiatives like pay and employment equity automatically take precedence over collective agreements, unions can incorporate the principle requirements of the legislation into the collective agreement. This serves as a signal of union commitment both to the rank-and-file and to management, and it enables the procedure to be subject to the grievance procedure. Furthermore, it gives a degree of permanence to the initiatives since they still would apply through the collective agreement if the legislation is rescinded or not effectively enforced.

Especially in the public sector, unions may also use pay equity to garner wage gains that they otherwise could not achieve through the collective bargaining process. In effect, this legislative route provides another avenue for augmenting the wages of their membership.

Barriers Created by Unions

While unions can play a variety of positive roles for their membership, especially in the difficult technical issues involved in implementing pay and employment equity, they can also create barriers to the effective implementation of the policies. Historically, and reflecting the pressures of the times, craft unions especially fostered and institutionalised discrimination through such means as separate promotion and pay lines for discriminated groups. While such practices no longer prevail, some unions may not properly represent the interests of particular target groups who are subject to discrimination[8]. This is especially true when women or other target groups are a minority of the membership and the union executive. While labour relations legislation allows such groups to bring an "unfair representation" case against the union, such actions are difficult especially since they are being brought against the very organisation – the union – that workers typically rely on to bring their case to higher authorities.

Seniority – the "sacred cow" of unions – can also be a barrier to the promotion *and retention* of target groups under employment equity especially since such target groups are often new to the workforce (e.g., visible minority immigrants and women who return to the labour market from a period of child raising or household work) and hence have little accumulated seniority (Singh and Reid, 1998). Under pay equity, higher pay is often an "allowable exception" if it is based on seniority even if it adds nothing to the "worth" or "value" of a job as determined by gender neutral job evaluation schemes. Since males are often able to accumulate more seniority than are females, who often break their seniority in periods of child raising, then this effectively is a systemic bias in the pay equity process itself. In the Ontario Pay Equity legislation "bargaining strength" is also an "allowable exemption." That is, after pay equity has been achieved, pay differences between male and female jobs are allowed if they are due to differences in bargaining strength.

When pay equity awards have been made, unions may try to downplay the source of the award as coming from the legislative requirement. This is so because they may get more "credit" for the wage increases if it looks like they came from the collective bargaining process as opposed to the legislative requirement. This is allegedly one of the reasons for the low-level of worker knowledge about the source of their wage increase in the case of pay equity awards[9]. In that vein, both unions and employers have an incentive to downplay the importance of the legislative requirements in accounting for wage increases. Both unions and employers have an incentive to make it appear that they were the source of the increase, rather than it being legislatively mandated.

While unions can foster such barriers to the implementation of pay and employment equity, these effects seem minor relative to the positive initiatives unions bring to the establishment and implementation of pay and employment equity. In fact, these initiatives are largely undertaken by unions, especially in the public sector.

LEGISLATIVE MECHANISM

In addition to the mechanisms of the market and collective bargaining, the legislative mechanism is a third mechanism for regulating the employment relationship. As indicated in the introduction, however, this mechanism is often regarded as *the* mechanism for dealing with social problems arising out of the employment relationship, with little recognition of the importance of the market and collective bargaining. This is understandable since, if a problem occurs, it seems natural to pass laws or regulations. And if loopholes emerge, or implementation problems arise, it seems natural to pass additional layers of regulation to try to close those loopholes.

Pressures for Legislative Responses

While the market response to workplace issues is driven by the threat of "exit" of employees at the margin of decision, and the collective bargaining response is driven by the "voice" of the median union voter, the legislative response is driven by the median political voter and influenced by pressure groups[10]. In the "new world of work" characterised by workforce diversity and the increased participation of women, it is not surprising, therefore, that pay and employment equity issues have taken on increased importance. Once policies are established they can also take on a "life of their own" as bureaucracies and vested interests get established around the policies.

While legislation is ostensibly established to regulate the behaviour of parties subject to the regulations, it can be *"captured" by those who are regulated* and used for their own ends. For example, incumbent firms that are already functioning under the regulations may support them because they may deter new entrants to the industry because of the costs of complying with the regulation. This may explain, in part, why firms generally oppose new legislation, often arguing that the existing law (under which they are now functioning) works well and is sufficient. They may even oppose eliminating the legislation (that they previously fought against) because they are now functioning under that legislation, and if it is eliminated, new competitors may enter the industry because of the lower costs.

Pressures for Deregulation

In the world of global competition and trade liberalisation, the legislative mechanism may be on the defensive. This is so because employers are now under more global competitive pressures, and they have a more credible threat of relocating their plants and investments in countries or jurisdictions within countries that impose fewer costly regulatory constraints on their operations. With freer trade, firms can now locate their operations in countries with fewer regulatory costs, and export back into countries that have higher regulatory costs. This is enhanced by the increased mobility of capital as well as the mobility of executive and professional/ technical labour to assist in the re-establishment of such operations. Flexible factories linked by advanced communication and transportation systems further enhance the ability to relocate production.

In such circumstances, political jurisdictions are under pressure to compete for "footloose" business investment and the jobs associated with that investment. In effect, the market mechanism is expanding to the political market place with political jurisdictions under more pressure to compete against each other for investment and jobs. One way to compete is to be more "open for business" by reducing legislative and regulatory costs, including those associated with governing the employment relationship. It is likely for these reasons that many countries (especially the US and the UK) have deregulated extensively, with similar pressures prevailing on other countries as well as jurisdictions within countries.

In such circumstances, there will be pressure for a "race to the bottom" or "harmonisation to the lowest common denominator" – that is, to the jurisdictions with the least regulatory costs. This need not occur, however, if the regulations serve an efficiency rationale and have positive feedback effects on the productivity of the workforce and the competitiveness of organisations (Gunderson, 1998).

Effect on Competitiveness

Whether this is the case with pay and employment equity initiatives is an interesting and open question. Proponents of the policies argue that they are merely doing what markets should be doing in the first place – hiring and promoting the best people, and paying them in accordance with what people in the male dominated jobs are paid for their skill, effort, responsibility and working conditions. Positive effects should also ensue in such areas as morale and reduced turnover, as well as in rationalising the whole pay and human resource management structures.

Opponents argue that if these are simply "good business practices" all that is necessary is to inform the parties and they will obviously voluntarily follow them. They argue that the sources of the unequal outcomes in the labour market likely come from outside of the labour market (e.g., the household and educational institutions) and it is unfair and inefficient to penalise employers for such consequences. It treats the symptoms rather than the causes, and thereby reduces the incentive to ameliorate the more fundamental causes, many of which emanate from outside of the labour market. Opponents of the legislative initiatives also argue that the requirements under employment equity for an internal representation of the target groups that is equal to their representation in the external labour force assumes that such persons are "suitable and available" for the jobs, and this is often not the case. In the pay equity area, substantial administrative costs are incurred for the job evaluation procedures and for implementing the complex system. This is especially the case if legal proceedings ensue given the costs of lawyers and expert witnesses. Moreover, while the morale of recipients of awards may improve, the morale of others can fall if they feel that they have been subject to reverse discrimination or missed opportunities, for example, because they are in occupations that narrowly miss being categorised as female dominated.

Clearly, this is a debate that is not likely to be readily resolved, albeit empirical evidence on these issues would narrow the range of the debate.

CONCLUDING OBSERVATIONS

At the risk of heresy, the "uneasy case" for more attention to market mechanisms to deal with outcomes to be corrected by pay and employment equity initiatives will be made in these concluding observations. It is an "uneasy case" because discriminatory outcomes prevail in markets and it is by no means obvious that advocating "more markets" will reduce the discriminatory outcomes. It is "heretical" because markets are generally regarded as the source of the problem and not part of the solution.

As a pragmatic matter, there is the reality that market forces are on the ascendancy given global competition as well as inter-jurisdictional political competition for investment and the jobs associated with that investment. At the minimum this places a premium on streamlining the legislative initiatives and reducing their administrative costs and complexities. Pay equity initiatives can be particularly impenetrable given the complexities that are involved in each and every step[11]. As stated by Pat McDermott (1991: 22), "When it comes to implementing pay equity schemes, numerous technical issues usually emerge. Indeed the very complexity of pay equity is an issue about which pay equity advocates should become concerned." Streamlining administrative and legal costs is particularly important because they use up real resources, while for transfer costs (e.g., the pay equity awards themselves), what is a cost to one party is at least a benefit to recipients. As colourfully stated by Debra Lewis (in Fudge and McDermott, 1991: 225): "that is the final beauty of pay equity: it consumes so many resources there is little left for anything else."

Ensuring that the policies are applied in a fair and even fashion may reduce employer resistance to such policies and facilitate competition on the basis of a "level playing field." This is especially the case if market power enabled employers, and their few competitors, to pay a premium to discriminate, or to pass the cost of discrimination on to customers. Employers are more willing to accept interventions that apply equally to all, including their competitors. Assistance provided in a non-adversarial fashion may also help, especially for small employers where the technical expertise and knowledge may be absent.

Active labour market policies that facilitate the efficient allocation of labour will obviously help ensure that the most qualified are hired and promoted and that pay reflects the productivity of workers and not discrimination. Such policies include labour market information, mobility and training. Quite simply, replacing higher priced labour with equally productive lower priced labour (a process that will reduce their wage gap) is facilitated if there is better labour market information and mobility.

Full employment policies and tight labour markets will also facilitate the operation of market mechanisms in dissipating discrimination. Replacing higher priced labour with equally productive lower priced labour, and hiring and promoting target groups, are both facilitated if there is turnover and new job creation. Moving from labour surplus to labour shortage can create incentives for employers to fill those shortages by hiring target groups – a process that increases both their wages and employment opportunities. This can be mitigated, however, by the possibility that employers lower their costs by restructuring through the contracting out of "good" jobs, and the creation of contingent jobs in which women are over-represented.

As discussed previously, equal employment opportunity and employment equity initiatives creates incentives for employers to increase both the wages and employment opportunities of target groups, in contrast to pay equity which will likely reduce employment opportunities due to the higher wages. In that vein, adherence to market mechanisms favours employment equity over pay equity, albeit that is obviously only one aspect of the equation.

To the extent that the sources of discrimination and unequal labour market outcomes arise from outside the labour market, more attention should also be paid to policies that affect discrimination outside of the labour market. This can include education and training institutions. Given the growing importance of self-employment, it may also include micro financing to assist the self-employed.

Given the unequal division of labour within the household, childcare policies may reduce the dual burden faced by many women. More controversial, policies that facilitate divorce and child support may enhance the bargaining power of women in otherwise oppressive households, reducing restrictions that are otherwise placed on their labour market decisions.

Harnessing such market mechanisms can facilitate markets being part of the solution rather than the problem. At the very least, more attention should be paid to market mechanisms as complements to the mechanisms of collective bargaining and legislation in regulating the employment relationship in this and other areas. To ignore the market mechanism is like "throwing out baby with bathwater" – a temptation that has crossed most of our minds at one time or the other, but that should be resisted.

Morley Gunderson is the CIBC Professor of Youth Employment at the University of Toronto, and a Professor at the Centre for Industrial Relations and in the Department of Economics. He is also a Research Associate of the Institute for Policy Analysis, the Centre for International Studies, and the Institute for Human Development, Life Course and Ageing, and an Adjunct Scientist at the Institute for Work and Health.

NOTES

[1] The extent to which the alternative mechanisms can be substitutes for each other may be limited, however, by the fact that they often operate in different spheres. Market mechanisms may have limited application to the public sector, where unions are very prominent and where legislation and regulation are important.

[2] For reviews of the evidence, including the Canadian evidence, see Gunderson (1989, 1994a: 23).

[3] Based on a survey of middle-managers in a large Canadian organization, Cannings (1991) found the following: female managers spend about four times as much time on housework as did male managers; 69 percent of the male managers compared to only 15 percent of the female managers thought that their own careers were more important to the family than were the careers of their spouses; and 28 percent of the males but only 19 percent of the females had professional/ managerial spouses who would be willing to move for the sake of their spouse's career.

[4] Weiner and Gunderson (1990: 112) list these exclusions as they exist across the different jurisdictions in Canada.

[5] Formally, it is all persons in female-dominated jobs that are eligible for pay equity.

[6] Discussions and examples of these positive effects are given, for example, in McDonald and Thornton (1991), Read (1996) and Rhoades (1993).

[7] Information for this section is from Murray (2000)

[8] In a pay equity award in Iowa, for example, Orazem and Mattila (1990) found that unions and professional groups lobbied for modifications of the initial award, with those modifications improving their position at the expense of women in general.

[9] In a pay equity award in Minnesota, for example, Evans and Nelson (1989) found that almost half of the recipients of the pay equity award did not know that their wage increase came from pay equity.

[10] In the United States, Evans and Nelson (1989: 72) indicate that three preconditions were common for the successful implementation of pay equity: "public sector collective bargaining; Democratic control of the state; and energetic pressure groups such as Commissions on the Status of Women." Similar generic preconditions seem to prevail in Canada (Gunderson, 1995: 233).

[11] For discussions of these complexities in the Canadian context, see, for example Gunderson (1994b) and McDermott (1991).

REFERENCES

Briskin, L. and P. McDermott (eds.). *Women Challenging Unions: Feminism, Democracy and Militancy.* Toronto: University of Toronto Press, 1993.

Cannings, Kathleen. "Family Commitments and Career Success: Earnings of Male and Female Managers." *Relations industrielles/ Industrial Relations* 46.1 (1991): 131-158.

Evans, Linda. And Julie Nelson. *Wage Justice: Comparable Worth and the Paradox of Technocratic Reform.* Chicago, University of Chicago Press, 1989.

Fudge, Judy. "Limiting Equity: The Definition of 'Employer' Under the Ontario Pay Equity Act." *Canadian Journal of Women and the Law* 4.2 (1991): 556-563.

Fudge, Judy and Pat McDermott,(eds.). *Just Wages: A Feminist Assessment of Pay Equity.* Toronto, University of Toronto Press, 1991.

Gunderson, Morley. "Male-Female Wage Differentials and Policy Responses." 27.1 (March 1989): 46-72.

Gunderson, Morley. *Comparable Worth and Gender Discrimination: International Aspects.* Geneva, Switzerland: International Labour Office, 1994a.

Gunderson, Morley. "Pay and Employment Equity in the United States and Canada." *International Journal of Manpower* 15.7 (1994b): 26-43.

Gunderson, Morley. "Gender Discrimination and Pay Equity." In Aspects of Labour Market Behaviour: Essays in Honour of John Vanderkamp Edited by Louis Christofides, Ken Grant and Robert Swidinsky. Toronto: University of Toronto Press, 1995, 225-247.

Gunderson, Morley. "Harmonization of Labour Policies Under Trade Liberalization." Relations industrielles/ industrial relations 53.1 (1998) : 11-41.

Mainville, D. and C. Olineck. "Unionization: A Retrospective." Perspectives on Labour and Income, Supplement. No. 75-001. Ottawa: Statistics Canada, 1999.

McDermott, Patricia. "Pay Equity in Canada." In Just Wages: A Feminist Assessment of Pay Equity. Edited by Judy Fudge and Patricia McDermott. Toronto, University of Toronto Press, 1991.

McDonald, Judith and Robert J.Thornton. "Private Sector Experience with Pay Equity in Ontario." Canadian Public Policy 24.2 (1998): 185-208.

Mummé, Carla Lipsig. "Trade Unions and Labour Relations Systems in Comparative Perspective." In Union-Management Relations in Canada. 4th ed. Edited by Morley Gunderson, Allen Ponak and Daphne Gottlieb Taras. Toronto: Pearson Education, 2000: 521-538.

Murray, Gregor. "Unions: Membership, Structures, Actions and Challenges." In Union-Management Relations in Canada. 4th ed. Edited by Morley Gunderson, Allen Ponak and Daphne Gottlieb Taras. Toronto: Pearson Education, 2000: 79-116.

Orazem, Peter and J. Peter Mattila. "The Implementation Process of Comparable Worth: Winners and Losers." Journal of Political Economy 91 (Feb. 1990): 134-152.

Read, Jean. Review of the Pay Equity Act. Toronto: Pay Equity Review Office, 1996.

Rhoads, S. Incomparable-Worth: Pay Equity Meets the Market, Cambridge: Cambridge University Press, 1993.

Robb, Roberta Edgecombe. "Equal Pay for Work of Equal Value: Issues and Policies." Canadian Public Policy 13 (December 1987): 445-461.

Singh, Gangaram and Frank Reid. "Are Seniority-Based Layoffs Discriminatory? The Adverse Impact of Layoffs on Designated Groups." Relations industrielles/ Industrial Relations 53 (Fall 1998): 730-749.

Weiner, Nan and Morley Gunderson. Pay Equity: Issues, Options and Experiences. Toronto: Butterworths, 1990.

SUBJECT INDEX

Library of Public Policy and Public Administration

1. D. Rahm, J. Kirkland and B. Bozeman: *University-Industry R&D Collaboration in the United States, the United Kingdom, and Japan*. 2000 ISBN 0-7923-6073-7
2. R. Torenvlied: *Political Decisions and Agency Performance*. 2000 ISBN 0-7923-6092-3
3. O. Elgström: *Images and Strategies for Autonomy.* Explaining Swedish Security Policy Strategies in the 19th Century. 2000 ISBN 0-7923-6571-2
4. O. van Heffen, W.J.M. Kickert and J.J.A. Thomassen (eds.): *Governance in Modern Society*. Effects, Change and Formation of Government Institutions. 2000 ISBN 0-7923-6653-0
5. H. Wagenaar (ed.): *Government Institutions: Effects, Changes and Normative Foundations*. 2000 ISBN 0-7923-6720-0
6. M.W. Bauer: *A Creeping Transformation? The European Commission and the Management of EU Structural Funds in Germany*. 2001 ISBN 1-4020-0006-5

Volumes 1–6 were published by Kluwer Academic Publishers.

7. C. Agocs (ed.): *Workplace Equality*. International Perspectives on Legislation, Policy and Practice. 2002 ISBN 90-411-1843-8

KLUWER LAW INTERNATIONAL – THE HAGUE / LONDON / NEW YORK